ODYSSEY

The definitive examination of

MUSIC FROM
THE ELDER

KISS' cult-classic concept album

**By Tim McPhate
& Julian Gill**

"The elder is an ideal... They are the wisdom of the ages and the power of goodness and knowledge... Since the dawn of time, they have watched silently over a virgin world and all its creatures... Now they have assumed the form of man that they might walk amongst him and guide him" — ("Elder" script treatment, 1981)

Editor's note: The editing of the interviews comprising this work has been approached with a desire to leave the original intent and "voice" of the interviewee as intact as possible — even at the cost of correct grammar. Except in the most egregious cases, a minimum of correction has been done, and in some cases the ubiquitous [sic] has been inserted, out of respect to what are simply transcriptions of conversations converted into a more readable form. Hopefully, the unique character and tone of each interviewee's "voice" is preserved and won't cause too much reader discomfort!

CONTENTS

Introduction

Nineteen hundred and eighty-one.

It has to be one of the most intriguing, fascinating, yet misunderstood years in KISStory.

KISS was fresh from their hugely successful 1980 tour of Australia and New Zealand — the zenith of the Super KISS era. Building off this high, the band — Paul Stanley, Gene Simmons, Ace Frehley, and new drummer Eric Carr — went back to work with the focus of recording a traditional hard-rocking KISS album.

By the time the calendar turned to November, KISS and producer Bob Ezrin had completed work on "Music From The Elder," a sophisticated concept album, ripe with elaborate musical arrangements, choirs, orchestras, falsetto vocals, chanting, and peculiar pieces featuring instruments such as the crumhorn (a Renaissance-period woodwind instrument).

What exactly happened?

The book you hold in your hands is your opportunity to find out. "Odyssey" is the most expansive examination of this cult-classic KISS album to date.

But, in the spirit of full disclosure, this book started as something more modest.

What merely began as the latest interview for KissFAQ's Interview Series spiralled into another interview, and then another. Suddenly an idea materialized: Let's conduct a series of "Elder" specific interviews and mix in some new feature content and document this obscure KISS album like never before.

More than 30 interviews were conducted, all with the intent of putting this album and era of KISStory back into the spotlight. Through the accounts of various individuals who either worked on the project or have some sort of tie to it — many of whom have never gone on record about their "Elder experience" before — this book presents credible insight into the creative and recording processes and the challenges unique to this chapter in the band's history, as well as some candid viewpoints, fun stories and maybe even a surprise or two.

The book's special features examine cool topics such as the bloodline of rock concept albums, KISS' activity from late 1980 to early 1982, cover versions of "Elder" songs, biographical information on the album's participants, details about "The Elder" companion film script, and much more.

Why bother with "The Elder," KISS fans might ask? It's a fair question, and one that is perhaps best answered with another question: Why not?

In truth, KISS fans would be hard-pressed to find an album shrouded in more mystery than "The Elder." And it's arguably the most polarizing album in KISS' catalogue — some love it, others (including some band members themselves) probably would just as well erase it from KISStory.

No matter where you stand, if you're reading this, chances are you're a diehard member of the KISS Army. I hope this book proves to be an entertaining read and a valuable addition to your KISS library — as you read through it, I invite you to dig out the album and give it a fresh spin.

The odyssey continues.

— Tim McPhate

The Album

Music From "The Elder" Detailed

"The Elder" Album Overview

U.S. Release Details:

Casablanca NBL5/8/P-7261 (U.S., 11/16/1981)
Casablanca/PolyGram 824-153-2/4 (U.S. reissue, 1985)
Casablanca/PolyGram 824-153-1/2 (U.S. reissue, 1989)
Mercury 532-390-2/4 (International remaster, 10/7/1997)
Casablanca/UMe 06025377856-9 (LP/digital reissue, 6/29/2014)

Tracks*:

A1. *fanfare*
(1:22) – Bob Ezrin / Paul Stanley

A2. Just A Boy
(2:30) – Paul Stanley / Bob Ezrin

A3. Odyssey
(5:36) – Tony Powers

A4. Only You
(4:19) – Gene Simmons

A5. Under The Rose
(4:49) – Eric Carr / Gene Simmons

B1. Dark Light
(4:12) – Ace Frehley / Anton Fig / Lou Reed / Gene Simmons

B2. A World Without Heroes
(2:40) – Paul Stanley / Bob Ezrin / Lou Reed / Gene Simmons
[● USA #56; UK #55]

B3. The Oath
(4:32) – Paul Stanley / Bob Ezrin / Tony Powers
[● JPN, *did not chart*]

B4. Mr. Blackwell
(4:53) – Gene Simmons / Lou Reed

B5. Escape From The Island
(2:50) – Ace Frehley / Bob Ezrin / Eric Carr

B6. I
(3:52) – Gene Simmons / Bob Ezrin
[● AUZ #24; GER #62; HOL #48; JPN, *did not chart*]

Album Details:
Produced by Bob Ezrin. Associate Producer Brian Christian. Recorded at Ace In The Hole Studio, Wilton, CT, January – August 1981; A & R Studios, New York City, NY, May 1981; Record Plant, New York City, New York City, May, July – September 1981, Ezrin Farm Studio & Sounds Interchange, Toronto, ON, Canada, Phase One Studios, Scarborough, ON, Canada, March – September 1981; by Brian Christian, Rick Hart, Robert Hrycyna and David Brown. Additional engineering by Rob Freeman, Corky Stasiak, and Kevin Doyle. Mixed at Manta Sound Studios, Toronto, ON, Canada. Spoken-word dialogue, between Morpheus and one of the Elder, follows the final track on the album and is known as "The Summoning" or "Dialogue."

* The 1997 remaster sequence is referenced rather than the various other versions that have been available over the years.

Players:
Paul Stanley ⋯ Rhythm guitar/lead guitar on B2/bass/lead vocals on A2, A3, B3 & B6.
Eric Carr ⋯ Drums on all tracks except A1, A3 & B6/guitar on A5/backing vocals.
Gene Simmons ⋯ Bass/rhythm guitar on A4/lead vocals on A4, A5, B2, B4, & B6.
Ace Frehley ⋯ Lead guitar/rhythm guitar/bass on B1/lead vocals on B1.
Bob Ezrin ⋯ Bass on B5/keyboards/percussion.
Tony Powers ⋯ Piano on A3.
Allan Schwartzberg ⋯ Drums on A3 & B6.
Robert Christie ⋯ Voice on "The Summoning."
Anthony Parr ⋯ Voice on "The Summoning."

Chart Action:
Chart Peak (USA): #75 (1/23/82) with 11 weeks on the Billboard Top-200 chart.

12/5/81	12/12/81	12/19/81	12/26/81	1/2/82	1/9/82	1/16/82	**1/23/82**
175	108	95	86	86	78	76	**75**
1/30/82	2/6/82	2/13/82	2/20/82				
89	112	149	X				

Other countries: AUS #12; AUZ #11†; GER #10; HOL #39; ITA #23; JPN #21; NOR #7; SWE #19; UK #51.

174	176	3	**SWITCH** Switch Gordy G8-1007M1 (Motown)		8.98	SLP 48
⭐175	NEW ENTRY ➡		**KISS** Music From The Elder Casablanca NBLP 7261 (Polygram)		8.98	
176	177	20	**JOURNEY** Infinity			

† Australian Kent Music Report (12/19/81). The album generally performed poorly internationally. One standout charting performance (see below) occurred in Norway (released 11/9) where the album charted for 10 weeks maintaining a top-10 position for three of those weeks. The dates below correspond with debut charting of W47/1981.

11/17/81	**11/24/81**	12/1/81	12/8/81	12/15/81	12/22/81	12/29/81	1/5/82
19	****7****	13	9	8	12	12	12
1/12/82	1/19/82	1/26/82					
17	23	X					

RIAA/Sales:

By early 1982 the album had sold in excess of 200,000 copies in international markets. "The Elder" remains uncertified in the U.S. by the RIAA. It has sold more than 110,000 copies since the Nielsen SoundScan® era commenced in 1991 and has been rumored to have passed the level needed for gold certification. However, recertification of the album seems unlikely.

Supporting Singles:

(USA) - Casablanca NB-2343: "A World Without Heroes" / "Dark Light" Chart Peak (USA): #56 (1/23/82) with 9 weeks on the Billboard Hot 100 chart. Other countries: UK #55

12/5/81	12/12/81	12/19/81	12/26/81	1/2/82	1/9/82	1/16/82	**1/23/82**
103	92	88	78	78	74	66	****56****
1/30/82	2/6/82	2/13/82					
56	96	X					

(Rufus), R. Murphy, MCA 51203

92 NEW ENTRY → A WORLD WITHOUT HEROES—Kiss
(Bob Ezrin), P. Stanley, B. Ezrin, L. Reed, G. Simmons,
Casablanca 2343 (Polygram)   CLM

One mainstream review noted: "Sure doesn't sound like KISS. The group's collaboration with Bob Ezrin yields a sober, sophisticated tune which recalls the poetry of the Moody Blues" ("Billboard," 11/14/81).

Chart Peak (USA): #57 (1/30/82) with 9 weeks on the Cashbox chart.

12/12/81	12/19/81	12/26/81	1/2/82	1/9/82	1/16/82	1/23/82	1/30/82
86	79	71	X	X	65	59	**57**
2/6/82	2/13/82	2/20/82	2/27/82				
62	69	92	X				

(INT) - Casablanca 6000-717: "I" / "The Oath"
Other countries: AUZ #24; GER #62; HOL #48.
"I" was released as the first single in most markets, with an edit version that replaced the lyric "balls to stand alone" with a more radio friendly "guts to stand alone" (the edit was also used on both versions of the promotional video for the song). Performance of the single was generally poor with the standout market being Australia where it reached #24. A highly prized "San Remo" special edition picture sleeve was issued in Italy.

Performed Live:
With the exception of "A World Without Heroes," which was performed regularly during the Unplugged era (along with brief bits of other songs off the album), material from this album has generally been ignored by the band. The only contemporary live performance took place on Jan. 15, 1982, during the filming of the band's appearance on ABC's "Fridays" television show (a weekly late-night live comedy show). The band performed "The Oath," "A World Without Heroes," and "I." KISS stunned fans on their third annual KISS Kruise in 2013 when they performed "The Oath" in full, Oct. 29 – 30. More recently, the band has performed "A World Without Heroes" at a special unplugged concert in Southern California in April 2014. "I" became the set closing song for the KISS Kruise VII electric shows in 2017.

Quick Tour Notes:
The band/management investigated touring Mexico and South America in support of the album but plans never made it to fruition. There was also a

feeling that Japan was a possibility, on the strength of the previous album's performance there, though likely economics also put paid to that idea. A U.S. tour, that would have seen the band performing in their home market for the first time in two years, was ultimately scrapped due to the album's lack of success and other economic factors. However, the process of staging conceptualization had at least reached a starting point.

U.S. singles (L - Europakdisk, New York City; R - PRC West, Compton, CA)

Geek alert! What are all those numbers that show up on various parts of record releases? It's really not much more exciting than identifying where a particular part was printed or pressed. Gauging rarity is difficult, particularly dependent upon region. For album covers, common indicators are "501" or "0704" which denote Shorewood Packaging Corp. (New York, NY) or Album

Graphics, Inc (Chicago, IL) as the manufacturers respectively. A third variety has no identifier in either of the locations illustrated above. With a lack of printer registration markings, other than U.S. Patent No. 3,301,467 (only visible when one unglues a cover), this version is identified as a Shorewood Packaging "Shorepak." The one-piece record jacket was originally invented by Weyerhaeuser in 1965 (they introduced the "Unipak" single-sheet gatefold in 1968). While Shorewood had plants in various locations they had partnered with Bert-Co in Los Angeles for exclusive West Coast printing services.

For the common album center-rings, a similar situation is the case: The "72" marking denotes vinyl pressed at PRC in Richmond, IN with labels printed by Moore Langen of Terre Haute; "53" denotes Hauppauge Record Manufacturing (HRM) in Hauppauge, NY. An immediately noticeable difference between these two main varieties is the weight of the vinyl with the HRM pressing being on lighter vinyl than PRC's. Looking at the etchings in the run-out area of the vinyl should show an etching identifying the pressing plant. A third variety has no pressing plant identifier printed on the label stock. An examination of the run-out etching clearly sources this version from PRC-C, in other words Compton, CA (plant "26").

The "Elder Album Focus" Refocused!
Revisiting "Music From 'The Elder'"

The official KISS Army Newsletter reported in late 1980, "A new album is already in the works. It will be hard and heavy from start to finish — straight-on rock and roll that will knock your socks off. This will be the first chance you'll have to hear Eric on record. You'll freak out when you do" (KAN, Fall 1980). One can suppose that plenty of fans indeed did "freak out" when they heard the new album...

Before the beginning, an ending...

(Music From) "The Elder" has long been considered to be one of the most divisive albums in KISS' extensive studio catalog. There is very little middle ground when considering the merits of the album subjectively. The album and accompanying era are, in essence, nearly guaranteed to cause heated debate during discussions between fans — who generally seem to either love it or hate it; either for what it represented artistically or as a representation of that particular period of the band's history. "The Elder" can be debated on many levels: Musically, artistically, comparatively or even visually. The band members, particularly Paul Stanley, seem to tend towards a generally negative sentiment towards the album; at least in terms of measuring "The Elder" as a KISS recording rather than looking at it individually as the unique project that it was; or considering the circumstances under which it was conceived and constructed. Paul has certainly not shied away from objectively appraising the album in hindsight: "'The Elder' is probably the biggest misstep of our whole musical career. It was everything that was wrong with us. It was pompous, contrived, self-important and fat. It was mediocre. We were living in fancy houses. I think the band was losing sight of what made us what we are and how good and special that was" ("Behind the Mask"). And it is difficult to either fault or counter such a point of view.

In his 2014 autobiography, Paul was particularly brutal towards the album: "The problem was that the stuff we were writing was no better than the songs on 'Unmasked.' In fact, it was probably worse. We'd lost the plot. My songs were nothing to write home about; Gene's were no better. But then Bob entered the picture, and he floated the idea of a concept album — which really came out of left field. Gene quickly bought into it and came up with a generic, vague, typical concept: It was about a kid who was the chosen one. Bill got behind the idea, too. It would be our attempt to woo the critics... Trying to show people how talented and bright you are is the best way to make an idiot of yourself, and we ended up doing that with flying colors" ("Face the Music"). During a 2014 Indianapolis KISS Expo appearance, Paul was directly asked about the album. He continued the aforementioned theme in his response, "We were clueless. We had become so full of ourselves, and so enamored with success and fame and money, that we really forgot why we started making music. We forgot about the love of rock 'n' roll. We forgot that we did this without any regard for whether other people liked it. And, all of a sudden, we're trying to make music and it had no teeth."

And yet, searching through the somewhat revisionist appraisals, and delving behind the mask, perhaps "The Elder" might best be described as *the* album that the band didn't want to make; an album they were ultimately forced to make for the label rather than themselves — by any means necessary. Pandering to the critics was a secondary consideration and one really only worthy of contemplation had the project actually have been successful. In the context of the genesis of the recordings it also really has no place and is little more than another excuse for the project's failure. Gene has generally been somewhat more restrained regarding the album but has echoed that suggestion that the band were perhaps pandering to the critics. He recalled, "This was the first KISS project where someone — in this case, Bob Ezrin — talked the band members into the notion that credibility and respect from the critics are as important as the love of the fans. As a result, it was a very serious record for us... All the work that went into *The Elder* seemed to be for nothing. We had a record that, for the first time, bombed so badly it didn't even go gold" ("KISS & Make-Up").

It would be unfair to deflect and place the "blame," should any really need to be apportioned, solely on the shoulders of Bob Ezrin or "critics." There is plenty to go around if "blame" is even required, rather than simply suggesting that the band tried something different and simply failed. Bob Ezrin is far too convenient a target within the larger context of the band's parlous state in 1981. There are too many other issues that need to be factored into the equation. The convergence of a multitude of factors had been a long time coming for the band. In terms of any band's lifecycle, KISS was perhaps by 1981 overdue for a "correction" of their place in the market. However, it is more than the band simply "getting their comeuppance." There were financial pressures, within and without. The band had to live up to the new 1980 Phonogram record contract, building on the mild success "Unmasked" had enjoyed internationally. Starting out strongly within the new corporate reality was critically important with the sums of money involved, and as one of the few marquee acts to survive the transition as a semi-independent Casablanca was rolled into an international corporate behemoth. Equally, the band's organization had become a money hungry operation whose appetite was insatiable; in addition to being encumbered by out of control spending habits. Internally, the dynamics within the band were changing and approaching a nadir. Peter Criss had been replaced by a non-voting salaryman. Ace Frehley no longer had a partner in crime and was teetering on the brink of personal annihilation. Gene and Paul were both looking outside of the band for new creative outlets, be it music or visual. The band's relationship with their manager, Bill Aucoin, was also in decline well before "The Elder" ever hit the stores. Combine all of those factors and there is simply more than a band that doesn't really want to make an album and doesn't feel inspired. Having no choice but to deliver an album results in a recipe for disaster and acts of desperation that only really become apparent in hindsight. The positive remains that at least they tried.

For many years the party line has been that "The Elder" was a good album, just not a good KISS album. That sentiment sounds like a nice neutral albeit slightly revisionist appraisal. However, it is also weak and utterly disingenuous, and as the evidence will soon determine does not do justice to the reality that the band was entrenched in during the period in which the album was conceived and recorded. Within the context of the band's 1979–81 studio efforts, the album is understandably a bit of a head-scratcher for the direction it saw the band taking; yet once one digs much deeper into that evidence the album starts to make a lot more sense... On multiple levels! Where "Unmasked" had been vilified in many quarters, due to its overly polished production and overt pop sensibilities, "The Elder" is generally reviled. "Dynasty" too is misunderstood as a "disco" album, even though only one song had any traits that could place it on the periphery of that genre. The rest of the songs on "Dynasty" were more what would have been expected from KISS as a continuation on from the "Alive II" studio side (with the possible exception of Peter's contribution, though it is stylistically similar to his previous contributions on both "Rock and Roll Over" and "Love

Gun" put through the KISS sonic blender). It is clear that the band's output and image had lost any sense of danger, or artistic fire for that matter — even with the benefit from Frehley's increased contributions to the songwriting (for some Ace's songs are the only saving graces for those albums).

What was clear was that the Vini Poncia-produced albums had seen the band moving further away from their hard rock roots into more radio, child and parent-friendly AOR territory; regardless of any improvement in song craft. "Pop-crossover" had become a popular catchphrase in 1980, predominately from R&B acts attempting to make the jump to the mainstream, but the same was the case from the opposite side of the spectrum. Crossover could result in the jump from respectable 600,000 sales into the millions. That was appealing not only to artists, but to the bean-counters at the labels. In other words, even when attempting to avoid becoming mired in revisionism: The band had simply become safe as they aimed for success in the broader and more homogenized AOR market in the knowledge that they had already reached a zenith and commenced a descent. They were simply too safe and diametrically opposed to the black-leather clad rebels they had been at their inception. Decaffeinated and diluted, almost "KISS-lite," the band had become boring and mainstream. They had been downgraded from R to G-rated as they attempted to broaden their appeal to a wider audience, the sort of market, perhaps, that had lapped up "Beth" in 1976. At home at least...

At the end of the "Unmasked" album cycle KISS stood upon a precipice. They knew, from the sales of "Unmasked" that their popularity in the U.S. had waned to the extent that they had been unable to even tour their home market; with the exception of a single smaller-scale show that served to introduce new drummer Eric Carr. That performance had seen the band return to the same venue in New York City where they had made their professional industry debut back on New Year's 1973 – 74 (the Academy of Music, renamed the Palladium). Album sales had tanked, with "Unmasked" having barely scrapped to what would have been considered paltry RIAA Gold certification (July 30, 1980). The album had also topped out at #35 on the Billboard 200 album charts. The 14 weeks it charted indicates little staying power and only one of the two singles, released to support the album, charted with "Shandi" stalling at #47 and dropping like a brick afterwards. The follow-up, "Tomorrow," didn't chart or even "bubble under." However, internationally the band and management possibly saw a savior in the stronger performance of the album internationally. It hit #1 in Norway and New Zealand, #3 in Austria and Australia, #4 in Germany, #5 in Holland, #11 in Italy; #12 in Canada, #15 in Japan, #17 in Sweden, and #48 in the United Kingdom. Those chart positions translated into European album sales of just over 250,000 by early August 1980 and provided a glimmer of hope for the band on the continent they'd not visited since 1976.

In Australia the band sold 110,000 copies of "Unmasked" on the first day of release (Sydney Morning Herald, 6/22/80) while in Germany it took until September 30 to reach that same level! Likewise, "Shandi" was a top-10 hit in several markets: Norway (#4), Australia (#5, with sales of 75,000 copies), New Zealand (#6) and Austria (#10). Elsewhere it struggled to gain any traction, even though being perceived as the best single option by Phonogram for the European markets. In Germany the single has sold a respectable 52,000 copies helping it reach #28. The follow-up, "Talk to Me," failed to make it higher than #32 in any market other than Switzerland (#10). From those illustrative album and single positions, it was clear that certain markets were worthy of exploration, particularly as Phonogram Baarn consolidated distribution across the disparate markets and settled into their role as the overlords of Casablanca Records. KISS too was motivated to tour Europe, according to C.K. Lendt, because "Phonogram was especially anxious to see KISS on the continent since they were about to commit to another six KISS albums to the tune of $15 million." Additionally, the fact that an earlier tour, scheduled to start in May 1980, had been cancelled aggravating promoters and the band's booking agency. Japan had also tentatively been scheduled for a run of seven concerts during the last 10 days of October, but those were ultimately abandoned.

Paul reduced the band's plight to a purely clinical appraisal: "'Unmasked' tanked in the States and we spent most of 1980 inactive... The single 'Shandi' was a hit abroad, however, and we booked a tour of Europe and Australia for the fall" ("Face the Music"). As a result, the band took their show on the road internationally and even the U.K., with its general rejection of all things KISS to that point, was included in the itinerary and used as a base of operations. The prospects of the European tour were not economically optimistic from the onset. Tour budgets projected a loss of some $675,000. When revised, with dates in Lisbon being cut and staffing being reduced, the loss was still expected to be somewhere near $474,000. Playing to half-filled venues across Europe, in many cases much smaller than their American counterparts, must have been depressing following years of excess in their homeland and reminiscent of the less than spectacular debut on the continent in 1976. Economically, the band also failed to sell merchandise, and in the case of Italy no merchandise was even on-hand for sale. The band also threw themselves off a cliff into financial oblivion with uncontrolled spending during the tour continuing to live the rock 'n' roll lifestyle to which they'd become accustomed. C.K. Lendt has recounted the band's $70,000 hotel bill for one week in London, and him running around the city trying to cash the American Express letters of credit he carried with him.

The reception and KISS-mania that the band experienced in Australia was not indicative of some wildly successful "Unmasked" touring cycle. The band were highly aware of that fact and hoped to use it to their advantage: "Let the press know what went on in Australia during the tour, and to make them aware of the continuing super-star status the band enjoys in places outside of the United States. It reinforces that, despite current feelings in the press in America about KISS, the band is still creating mob scenes and hysteria around the world, and maybe the press should take a second look" (KISS publicity campaign proposal). Australia had been more about hype than substance, and while the tour did take on epic proportions when compared with the previous two U.S. outings, there was enough evidence that a house of cards was being constructed. Regardless of the reality, it certainly was a time of excitement for the Australian fans.

Initially scheduled to arrive on November 8 and play their first show three days later, the band arrived in Australia early on the morning of November 1, 1980. At the Town Hall appearance with the Lord Mayor in Sydney the following day, of the "100,000 expected by the KISS public relations machine, [only] about 4,000 turned out" (Sydney Morning Herald, 11/3/80). So brief was the band's appearance, to throw out some trinkets to the natives and pose for some photos that minutes later they departed for their press conference at the Sebel Town House Function Centre. Reality was severely skewed from the months of press coverage the prospective "cosmetic disco-rock group" (The Age, 6/20/80) touring had received following the initial rumors in June until the actual announcement. That announcement finally came on Tuesday, July 15, the anniversary of the release of "Dynasty," at the Pavilion on the Park Restaurant in Sydney. For comparison, a crowd of more than 300,000 greeted the Beatles on their arrival in Adelaide in 1964...

The likes of Neil Bogart or Malcolm McClaren would have been proud of the manufactured hype, affectionately referred to as "KISSteria." It was most certainly a matter of selling to the Australian public something that wasn't reflected in reality. Perhaps it was a need from the consumer side to embrace something perceived as exciting, a "Beatles" experience for a new generation. According to Glenn A. Baker, "the Australian editor of America's 'Billboard' magazine, a misleading image of KISS as 'the biggest band in the world' has been thrust down our throats by the media. Mr. Baker, himself a KISS fan who wouldn't miss the concert, describes KISS as a second level act which has had one big album... 'The average kid probably thinks KISS are number one in America. They're a great band but somebody should tell the media moguls that KISS have a few notches to get on their belts yet,' Mr. Baker said" (The Age, Melbourne, 11/13/80). It wouldn't be fair to suggest that the hype was all the band's own making. The Australian press hopped on the bandwagon with aplomb, and with promoter Kevin Jacobsen having rolled the dice to the tune of $2 million, all the hype possible was needed — expecting the tour to service 150,000 patrons at $13 a ticket was going to take some doing in a country with a population of less than 15 million, even one that pre-tour economic analysis indicated had a per capita entertainment expenditure of $14.28, the second highest globally.

By early August sales of "Unmasked" had reached 139,146 in Australia, particularly impressive compared with Europe and the U.S. (Japan had only reached 40,000 at the same time). By the end of 1980 the album had reached 206,475 copies (4X platinum) buoyed by a combination of the band's exposure and a hefty dose of merchant discounting. However, even before the tour had ended the hype had commenced its inevitable dissipation. That there were 8,000 tickets remaining unsold two days prior to the second Sydney show is only partially illustrative of that fact. An article in the Sydney Morning Herald pointed to the over-merchandising and lack of consumer demand. One manufacturer, Plough Australia, had produced 200,000 KISS make-up bags, but had only sold half. One licensee for KISS coins had manufactured 20,000 units, selling only 419 pieces. Even the "Unmasked" sales figures were becoming tarnished by heavy discounting of the album (Sydney Morning Herald, 11/20/80). C.K. Lendt, in his excellent "KISS & Sell," suggested that the band played to over 250,000 fans and grossed in excess of $3 million, yet the tour still apparently lost $250,000. The band may have had the time of their lives during the tour, but the excesses approached legendary levels. According to one article, "Backstage at venues he [promoter Kevin Jacobsen] built them a swimming pool, a games tent with mini-golf and pinball machines and the obligatory hospitality tent. Each plane they flew on was stocked with enough Dom Perignon to serve everyone in it. 'It was insane, there was a party every night,' he recalls. 'We would go out to dinner and take over a restaurant.' Jacobsen says he lost a lot of money (about $200,000) on the KISS Tour. He refers to it as a milestone in history: The last example of outrageous rock star extravagance in Australia" (The Age, Melbourne, 11/6/87). Departing Australia, there might well have been the mystical aroma of burning bridges wafting through the subconscious of the participants...

Much of the excess was rooted in the need to maintain the mystique of the masked band, therefore preventing them from being able to play "normal" tourists during their periods of downtime. The band had become prisoners of their fame, more so in an unfamiliar environment than they were at home. Having to pay for 4 charter planes to New Zealand and increasing security at shows following the press reports of injuries at one of the Adelaide shows also contributed to the costs of the tour borne by the promoter. Bomb threats also added to the siege mentality while keeping the band in the press. While KISS received around $800,000 for the tour Jacobsen suggested, "We cut even, and the band didn't make any money either" (The Sydney Morning Herald, 3/22/81), taking into account its large personal touring entourage and "Super-KISS" expenses. The touring entourage, outside of the staging staff, included Bill Aucoin, George Sewitt, John Harte, Ken Anderson, Jack Tessler, Chris Lendt, Doug Hull, Ernie Bostock, Warren Linney, Wally Andrews, Mick Chiodo, Ron Blackmore, Pixie Esmonde, Robert Franco, Robbie Robertson, Patti Mostyn and often Kevin Jacobsen. Outside of hotels were the massive costs involving staging, sound, lighting, and transport, 15 trucks worth according to some press reports. However, the hype and hysteria had also worked against the promoter. The promoter "Had to spend an extra $28,000 on security after an exaggerated newspaper story claimed that 200 people were injured at the Adelaide concert. And he was forced to charter four flights across the Tasman at $27,000 a tip" (The Sydney Morning Herald, 3/22/81). Sydney rock journalist Glenn Baker perhaps sums up the tour best, "It was the result of a remarkably adept and stunningly successful marketing campaign. Kevin [Jacobsen] did something in the best traditions of showbiz — he gave people a lot of fun and was successful."

Post-Antipode Situation

Little would KISS have known that Ace Frehley had performed his last full concert with the band at the final 1980 tour date in Auckland, New Zealand, on December 3 (until the 1996 reunion) — though there may well have been signs that were either missed or were willfully ignored. While there may have been interpersonal challenges within the band, matters had yet to come to a head. Fortunately, a soundboard of that show was captured for posterity and circulates for collectors to enjoy. For the band, catalog sales throughout the markets they had toured were reasonable. In Germany, the clearance of Bellaphon product was strong as was demand for the new Phonogram distributed releases. The same was the case in Australia where Astor had been supplanted by PolyGram distribution. While not a financial windfall, the visibility and intensity of the tour would have left the band at least hopeful for the new decade having survived their first outing with a replacement member.

The period in which "The Elder" was born was one in which the recording industry was facing a new series of challenges. Irwin Steinberg, "Chairman and chief executive officer of the recently formed PolyGram Record Operations, U.S., admitted the U.S. marketplace is both in a crisis and an evolutionary period" (Billboard, 5/3/80). The crisis was not wholly the result of the then existing economic uncertainty, though there would continue to be a marked decline in the U.S. economy throughout 1980 into the following year. Similarly, the same factors were present in the international marketplace where the contraction of PolyGram was illustrative of the manner by which many businesses were dealing with the challenges of the new decade. But what were the challenges? Pricing increases, where the base single-LP SRP increased from $7.98 to $8.98 was matched with increases of wholesale prices (on certain product lines) and SRP in other markets at a time when the entertainment market was considered "soft." Pricing increases were designed to offset decreases in volume while matching the increase in raw materials. Home tape-recording had become the new battlefield for labels who felt they were losing sales on the home recording of radio station broadcasts of top 40 singles or even whole albums. As with any technology, the increase in the popularity and adoption of the cassette format would see it become the preeminent format for the 1980s, even as the next populist format, the compact disc, stood waiting in the wings (the first commercial compact disc was released in Japan in 1982).

Collectors may note the decrease in varieties of KISS vinyl product post-1980 as the company reduced the number of plants they were using to press product from 20 to 4.

There were also many moving pieces that started to fall into place with major ramifications for KISS. Having invested $15 million in Casablanca, as a minority stake in 1977, the February 1980 buyout of Neil Bogart removed from Casablanca the primary issue afflicting the label: Neil Bogart. But the culture that Neil had engendered, and at some points prospered at the label, remained (for a time). Neil blamed the buyout on a fundamental difference of opinion with PolyGram, "The philosophical gap between myself and a multinational corporation like PolyGram was simply too wide" (Eugene Register-Guard, 2/14/80). According to Cecil Holmes, "It just got to a point where Neil felt uncomfortable being with PolyGram. He wasn't able to do the things he wanted to do. Casablanca was his company, but PolyGram owned it" (Pop Matters). For PolyGram Neil had been "the ringleader of what they perceived to be a long line of terrible business decisions" ("Going Platinum"). The buyout would also have larger ramifications: The partnerships of foreign licensing had to be brought in line with PolyGram distribution as contracts expired, spelling the death-knell for independent distribution in international markets (Billboard, 12/22/79). And that started the process of the aforementioned distributor contraction.

In May 1980 PolyGram appointed Harvey Schein as President of U.S. operations. Schein's credentials were never in doubt — he had brought Clive Davis to CBS in 1962 — but there was an inherent dysfunction to the American operation as PolyGram continued their plan to become a major player on a similar scale to the WEA and CBS operations. More than 100 acts remained on the roster, few with a reasonable chance of succeeding to the economic levels required by the label. Successes had to fund the plethora of failures. Some acts, such as Captain & Tennille were simply allowed to disappear. Toni Tennille recalled, "PolyGram was busy ripping the remnants of Casablanca apart and have very little interest in us" ("Toni Tennille: A Memoir"). The acts that were successful were also problematic once the leadership of the label changed. Neil's departure invoked "key-man" clauses in some of the major act contracts, which, in the case of Donna Summer, ultimately allowed her to depart Casablanca and become the first signing for Geffen Records. In June 1980 she also sued Casablanca for $42 million, having been managed by Neil's wife and former KISS manager, Joyce. She recalled, "I was one of the people that were selling mega-records at the time, but I wasn't being compensated for them. Let's put it like this, my original contract was not up to par and so there was a deficiency in what I should have been making. I was making the money for them, millions of dollars, which I wasn't seeing. At some point, I got a lawyer and started to investigate what was going on and it wasn't pretty" (Pop Matters). Perhaps KISS was following things a little too closely...

While Summer was ultimately successful in leaving the label, the court determined that she still owed her label an album and "She Works Hard for The Money" was released on one of Casablanca's successor labels (Mercury) in 1983; becoming her biggest hit of the decade. Casablanca also started transitioning its roster away from a heavy disco orientation into other genres, even as Lipps, Inc. topped many international charts with "Funkytown." Like KISS, disco act the Village People had lost a critical member, with lead singer and writer Victor Willis having departed in late-1979 — he was replaced by Ray Simpson (who had sung backing vocals on KISS' "Love Gun"). Their 1980 release "Can't Stop the Music" missed the U.S. Top-40 and was their last album for Casablanca (in the U.S.). The band executed a similarly ill conceived "new wave" reinvention in 1981 with their "Renaissance" album which flopped. The label, dating back to Neil Bogart's tenure at the head of the ship, had also flirted with the Casablanca-Nashville concept which saw acts such as Mac Davis (He'd have a #3 country hit with "It's Hard to Be Humble" followed up later in the year with the #12 "Texas in My Rearview Mirror") and Pure Prairie League being brought onto the roster. Other more mainstream acts including Stephanie Mills (perhaps as a rather too transparent attempt at replacing Donna Summer) were also added in order to broaden the roster.

If things weren't pretty for Donna Summer, then PolyGram knew that KISS also had a "key-man" clause in their 1977 contract with Casablanca: "Company may assign this agreement to any person, firm or corporation acquiring all or substantially all of its assets provided however that should Neil Bogart cease to be an executive officer of Company charged with the responsibility of running Company's business on a day-to-day basis Artist may terminate this agreement upon 60 days' notice in writing." KISS was of the few acts on the label that was actually selling albums, and 1979 had been a particularly successful year for the band both domestically and internationally (at least in relation to albums sales versus bloated touring). That success, coupled with Summer's departure, gave the band unprecedented leverage in renegotiating their contract with PolyGram, particularly as the roster dropped from 100 to 48 acts. Even had they wanted to follow Bogart they were restricted from doing so by Bogart's severance agreement with PolyGram where he had agreed not to poach any of Casablanca's acts for his new label. As had been the case in 1975 there likely wouldn't have been any shortage of new options had they wanted to leave, other than surrendering the special treatment they'd become accustomed to.

In April 1980 the band signed a new worldwide six-album contract with PolyGram. It was the start of a new era — with the band shown in a Billboard Magazine (May 17, 1980) piece with Casablanca president Bruce Bird and Irwin Steinberg, chairman of PolyGram Record Operations (PRO). Yet it also marked the beginning of a period of flux at the label and for the band. For the label change continued unabated. By December a trade press reported, "Another 25 employees were terminated at the four-building Casablanca Records complex on Sunset Blvd. in the past 10 days. Approximately the same number remains from a total work force of 110 a year ago. President Bruce Bird, among those pared, is looking for office space for a new label" (Billboard, 12/13/1980). Other victims of the cull included promo exec Bobby Applegate and VP of artistic development, Don Wasley. As employees departed, the remaining acts lost those whose support and efforts had buttressed them in so many different ways.

PolyGram, by necessity had started the process of blood-letting that was going to provide a change to the corporate operation that would result in a culture-shock for many of those who survived the culls and the artists who remained. Things were changing, but the perception of whether it was for the best was uncertain. Perhaps it is telling of the situation that Neil Bogart took his Boardwalk Records to CBS for distribution in mid-1980. For collectors the process is one where 1979–80 was marked by many distribution companies that had been in place since 1975 in some cases, disappeared to be replaced with PolyGram affiliates. In many new product lines were immediately issued and the older release versions started disappearing. This centralization was more than just an exercise in cost-cutting, removing duplicate functions from markets, or restricting complexity of processes. It was more a reaction to the emergence of global markets as the industry attempted to realign itself for the future.

One major change was PolyGram Distribution taking control of the "dispatch of product samples, parts, jacket artwork and merchandising material from the U.S. PolyGram companies — Polydor, Phonogram /Mercury and Casablanca — to affiliates abroad" (Billboard, 6/14/80) rather than continue the prior practice of allowing the affiliates to handle those functions independently. Other functions that were centralized included promotion and marketing. It was expected that the centralization would allow the "labels [to] concentrate on creative (product) thrust" (Billboard, 6/21/80) while no doubt unifying product and release schedules. Advertising and promotion would be handled in the same manner regardless of the market. In the U.S. Bruce Bird took the opportunity to restructure Casablanca. "All in all, the consolidation of support personnel in New York has taken that unnecessary responsibility from me and provided me with more time to ponder pertinent problems" (Billboard, 8/23/80). And that ultimately was the key, buying time for Casablanca and realigning its roster.

For Casablanca, it was convenient time for pan-European consolidation under the Phonogram umbrella, with many distribution agreement periods coming to a close. Not all the transitions went smoothly. In France, Vogue put up a fight and took their displeasure to court, "for arbitration. The Villetaneuse, France label claims it has been damaged $7 million worth when the local label failed to provide it with a second KISS album for the one-year, period ending March 31, 1980. The plaintiff accuses KISS of conspiring to induce the breach" (Billboard, 5/10/80). Durium, in Italy, was one exception, maintaining its distribution deal "with agreement with PolyGram Italiana" (Billboard, 5/31/80) perhaps due to it having completed major extensions to its local pressing plant and this being seen as beneficial to the relationship. In other countries new companies took over from distribution companies such as Pye/PRT (U.K.), Bellaphon (Germany), Victor (Japan), etc. As the worldwide marketplace contracted and sales stagnated the RIAA also reversed its 120-day certification delay, to 60 days, leading to a skewed increase of certifications as a backlog of albums was processed. Ironically, in 1980 there was a drop in the number of platinum certified albums with only those at the lower gold level increasing.

Even before the band had returned from the Australian tour there had been communications concerning prospective producers for the KISS 17 album project. One such candidate was Chris Kimsey (Peter Frampton, Rolling Stones), though his involvement was considered tentative at best. How serious his consideration was is unclear with Kimsey having been engaged to construct the Stone's "Tattoo You" album, a process that took place between October 1980 and June 1981 (interestingly, much of the material on the album would be sourced from band's vaults, some dating back to 1972). By early December consideration of then "hot" producer Robert John "Mutt" Lange had also been discarded. Lange is of particular interest, as a prospective producer who had then just recently started his emergence as a major force in rock album production. Who knows what might have come from that union considering his successes during the period, including AC/DC's "Highway To Hell" and "Back In Black," Foreigner's "4," and Def Leppard's "High 'N' Dry" (which while not being a commercial runaway success was a quantum leap for the Sheffield band setting the stage for their next album's success — it was recorded at the same time KISS started recording "The Elder"). Regardless, Lange purportedly didn't want to record outside of England at the time and KISS apparently weren't willing to relocate there for the duration of the project (one can imagine the costs at a time when Casablanca artists were almost considered unwanted nuisances on PolyGram's roster in the post-Neil Bogart era when the true situation at the label was rapidly becoming apparent to the new owners). Lange's schedule was also fluid, and he was unable to provide a firm commitment to a KISS project until mid-February 1981, after the band hoped to have already started working. Unexpected delays (working with the Cars) would keep Def Leppard from commencing their recording for several months.

By early 1981 some foreign distributors were clamoring for new KISS product. Contacts from Japan requested the band's plans for recording. Australia enquired politely, "we are eagerly awaiting the new KISS album and still want to do a 2LP 'Best of KISS' at mid-price in October/November" (BA-WMA letter, 1/15/81). From both the European and Australian perspectives, "Unmasked" had been a decent starting point, but the band needed to follow it up quickly in a more structured manner. And strongly. Lessons had been learned from "Unmasked" album cycle and the complaints from international partners. The main concern echoed across the globe had been that there had not enough lead-time for releases for proper planning of promotional efforts. Partners wanted 45–60 days' advance notice for KISS #17 in order to get their marketing plans finalized and in place. AMI also didn't want last minute completions and wanted all aspects of the release planned and scheduled. The problem simply was that the band weren't in a creative frame of mind. They even considered the prospect of touring without an album with Japan again a primary consideration.

Cometh the Hour, Cometh the Man

By early 1981 KISS had convened at Ace Frehley's newly built Ace in The Hole home studio in Wilton, Conn., for pre-production demo sessions with engineer Rob Freeman. This location was convenient, particularly for Ace Frehley, not only for being out of the public eye but due to the care with which it had been designed, built, and equipped by John Storyk. One of the first songs recorded was "Deadly Weapons," which is particularly notable more for it being one of the first performances by Eric Carr on tape. While the band had told the media that the new album would be a return to a heavier-edged sound, the song definitely comes across as being something of an "Unmasked" cut-off or transition piece. In some ways it would have been right at home on that album with similar production values. Unfortunately, song never surfaced on any album and was eventually recycled by Gene Simmons becoming "Love's A Deadly Weapon" on "Asylum" in 1985. Other material recorded during this early phase included "Feel Like Heaven," "Nowhere to Run," and yet another attempt at Gene's long-suffering "Reputation" (Bonutto, Dante — "Kerrang" #155). These four disparate tracks make it somewhat difficult to determine exactly what direction the band were really taking, since the styles seem disjointed and lacking any uniformity. This is hardly surprising considering the band were simply in the early stages of preparing for their next album and trying to get some new ideas down on tape.

Defining the recording of what ultimately became "The Elder," it is important to include those first sessions, even though they predate Bob Ezrin's involvement in the project. According to Eric, "The album was recorded in three different passes over the course of the last year. We first went into the studio last January and recorded tracks that were powerful but that sounded too like the same old KISS. We then went in last May with Ezrin in Toronto and came up with more good material. But it still seemed like an extension of the same image, and we wanted something radically different" (Montreal Gazette, 1/9/82). Gene echoed the sentiment: "In fact, we had five tracks for another album already recorded and it was very adept, very hard stuff. It was as good as if not better than anything we've done or is out now. But we weren't excited by it. We've always gone against the grain" (Toronto Star, 11/28/81). It seems likely that material such as "Don't Run" and the instrumental "Heaven" was probably worked on at this time, the latter by Ace and Eric independently. The former was certainly alluded to in early PR while the band started recording and one such early instrumental was later recycled by Gene as Black 'N' Blue's "Promise the Moon."

Paul Stanley has previously confirmed the connection with the latter of these songs with the pre-"Elder" project: "It's from the sessions that preceded 'The Elder.' We started an album and we aborted ... but before that, we had cut about five songs, of which one of them was a song that Eric Carr had written that never got a melody or lyrics put to it" ("Sound Attitude," 1992). Left incomplete at the time, "Heaven" later surfaced as "Breakout" on Ace's "Frehley's Comet" album (when lyrically completed by Ace's then-guitarist Richie Scarlet); and as "Carr Jam 1981" on KISS' "Revenge" album (in a highly edited and butchered form). At the time "Heaven" remained an instrumental that included a drum solo section that was used as the central feature of "Carr Jam." This song was the only studio recording of an Eric Carr drum solo. According to Eric, "It was supposed to be my 'Moby Dick' with the drum solo on it ... you know there was like a three-minute drum solo in the middle of the song then came back in the way Ace did and end it. We tried, all during the recording of 'The Elder,' to write lyrics for this thing and nobody could figure out what the hell to sing to it" (KISS Neon Glow #1, 1992)! What is clear from the pre "Elder" material is that the band was clearly on the right track for breaking away from the softer material.

Other songs committed to tape around this time included "Every Little Bit of Your Heart," which had found a reasonable form musically, but would require quite a bit of work on its arrangement and lyrics. The song often appears on bootlegs labeled as "I Want You Only" in what appears to be an instrumental version. However, the song may have become an "instrumental" through the degradation caused by multigenerational tape reproduction of a poor original source. Varying quality versions of "Every Little Piece of Your Heart" do circulate, but Paul's vocals are so low in the mix that they can easily be missed. The phrase "I Want You Only" does form part of the lyrics to Paul's original song, which may explain why some of the instrumental takes of the song having been given this unofficial title. However, those lyrics may simply have been scat vocals, partially at least, since there is a very slight similarity between them and Linda Ronstadt's "Hurt So Bad" (originally written by Teddy Randazzo and Bobby Hart for Little Anthony & The Imperials). In the case of some of those instrumental versions, it may simply have been a matter of the tape generation in trading circles resulting in the decline of the sound quality of the song, since the vocals are so low in the mix in the first place. The similarities between this piece and "A World Without Heroes" are most noticeable on the bass line and the initial minute of the song before the piece changes tempo and style. Paul ultimately abandoned the song to work on other material for the album. Gene, however, liked the melody of the piece, rather than the lyrics and, along with Bob Ezrin and Lou Reed's input, later revamped the piece in the form of the album's sole U.S. single, "A World Without Heroes."

Reed, another performer Ezrin had worked with in the 1970s, assisted with the songwriting the same way he'd worked with Nils Lofgren in 1979 — Lou took ideas and generated lyrics, rather than being a traditional co-writer. His input into the song seems to have resulted from scrawling the song's title on a piece of paper. According to Paul, "Lou was so into our 'Elder' project, that when we called and explained it over the phone to him, he said, 'I'll get back to you in an hour.' And he called back an hour later with good basic lyrics to 'Mr. Blackwell,' 'World Without Heroes,' and a lot of other stuff that hasn't been used yet." Gene knew a good song title when he saw one and utilized it. According to Paul, they "changed the title once Bob Ezrin thought we should do a concept album. The music worked but lyrically it didn't fall in. It became kind of a group project. By group, I mean, Lou Reed, Ezrin, Gene." This seems to indicate that Paul, for whatever reason, wanted to distance himself from the song and its creation or simple retain credit for the melody.

Other efforts at Ace's studio were not completely abandoned and Reed also played a role in the transformation of "Don't Run" into "Dark Light," likely in a manner similar to the previously mentioned song. The song was a striking departure for Ace — while it has a standard rock underlying nature, many of the lyrics are vocally spoken or mumbled — providing a stylistic contrast to his earlier compositions. The song was initially based on a riff idea that Anton Fig had come up with. Anton recalled, "I had a riff which Ace really liked and so he took my guitar riff and then he wrote some more stuff and the song kind of came out" (KISS Online). Clearly Ace was invested enough in the harder sonic direction at the time, though the level of his participation in the sessions, even at his own studio, has also been questioned. As far as the album's direction, the KISS Army spring 1981 newsletter also went so far as to provoke, "A voice I've never heard before is doing the lead vocal — could it be Eric?" And while only a teaser, without any serious credence, it was an interesting suggestion that first asked the question of when and if Eric would be allowed to sing a lead-vocal on a KISS album. Ace recalled, "Lou Reed rewrote some of the lyrics" ("No Regrets"), likely with Gene's input considering the song's transformation.

With a roughly 100-mile round trip Ace's studio was not particularly convenient for the other band members commuting in from New York City. As a result, they also utilized Penny Lane Studios in the city for some late-night sessions for overdubs and vocals. "Deadly Weapons" would be completed at that studio, and both "Nowhere to Run," and "Feel Like Heaven" reached nearly complete forms, though without guitar solos. According to engineer Rob Freeman, "all that was left to do at Penny Lane was a final round of overdubs, including lead and background vocals, and then mix." Whatever the case, the band didn't think the recordings were working, nor was working on their own. And perhaps the disparate material is particularly illustrative of the fact. They needed a producer to help drive things forward and there was really only one choice considering the situation. For Aucoin, the selection of a producer was more a matter of pragmatism: "No one was in the mood to either write and/or record one. As the pressure came down on us to come up with a new album and I realize that they guys weren't writing; nor did they feel like recording a new album. And I thought that the only person I knew, that knew them well enough and could get us through this, was Bob Ezrin — an incredibly bright producer who was capable of helping them write as well as producing the album" (Bill Aucoin - "13 Classic KISS Stories").

In KISS Alive Forever, Ric Aliberte recounted a meeting where a suggestion was raised, "Let's get Bob Ezrin back to do Destroyer II." Those final two words, "Destroyer II," are probably the most accurate description for "The Elder" as an album possible. Under the guise of a "concept album," it is a facsimile of the band's most successful studio recording utilizing Bob Ezrin's playbook in totality. It makes the album a carbon copy constructed using the exact same blueprint, under a similar atmosphere of desperation, as the iconic album had been in 1976. Yet five years was a lifetime in the music business — a period more than the lifespan of many a critically successful act — and many of the ingredients had changed during the interim (not necessarily for the better by that point). Yet, one question was only really considered at the time: Who else could get the band to record an album at a time when they didn't want to? It was hoped that Bob would be that person.

Ultimately, Bob became the "candidate" and both the band and label saw him as being the genius producer who could help get KISS the exposure they desperately needed at that time. This made his selection a good choice, according to internal Aucoin memos, since the band would be able to coattail the exposure his name would bring at a time when the band badly needed it. For Gene it was a straight-forward matter, "one reason we got involved with Bob Ezrin is that he's not just another producer you get to record another album. You look for something different" (Toronto Star, 11/28/81). Another reason for his selection was that he had been responsible for "Destroyer," an album and success story that KISS was desperate to repeat. During the recording of that album both the band and resulting album seemed to really benefit from his artistic and creative input. That was also the album that had forced a certain amount of unplanned artistic development on the band, pushing them to new artistic and musical limits. KISS had certainly settled on the idea of recruiting Bob for the project by the time he met with the band and management at Aucoin's offices on Feb. 26, 1981 — in fact, the band's management had written to Phonogram and PolyGram requesting their advance for the album on Feb. 19. Soon afterward he showed up at Ace's studio and collected the material the band had been working on and departed for Canada. If nothing else, this date provides a useful start for the "Elder" period proper, even if the album's concept had not yet crystallized.

The selection of Bob as the producer of the KISS 17 studio effort was a highly calculated measure by the band and their management. It was also a decision favored by PolyGram, and was pushed particularly by then corporate president David Braun following the suggestion by A&R. While Braun only lasted a year in the position, following his appointment in November 1980, his legal and artist representation background gave him a basis of understanding more from the artistic side of the business than the corporate side he was operating in. One major issue Braun hoped to address was the dumping-ground status that the Casablanca label had fallen into following the departure of Bogart and the first wave of PolyGram culling of staff and executives that followed the departure of the remaining Casablanca founder, Cecil Holmes, in late-1980. Braun felt there had been a "critical misjudgment to go for the fast sale, not artist development. For the long pull, a company requires artistic elements that can maintain success for at least a five-year period." His plan focused on "signing heavyweights early on [to] energize a company" ("Billboard," Dec. 27, 1980). These signings were in turn expected to attract other artists onto the roster and grow sales. It was in direct contrast to the quantity over quality ethos of the late disco period. Bob Ezrin was a particularly powerful case study for this new ethos.

According to internal management memos, he was "newsworthy — no one in the industry expects Ezrin to produce another KISS album." Tying Ezrin's name to KISS, and more importantly to Casablanca, from his then recent highly successful work with Pink Floyd was an irresistible attempt to coat-tail that success. Most importantly, from the band's perspective, was the perception that there would be "more support from label to KISS because PolyGram sees Ezrin as insurance for successful LP." Bricks in the wall, indeed...

It seems probable that Ezrin's selection was ultimately in the hands of Gene and Paul, but there was certainly pressure from other quarters for the band to do something substantial. Ace was already considering quitting KISS and was simply going with the flow. For Ace matters were simple, "Peter's departure allowed them to exercise that control to an extent I hadn't anticipated" ("No Regrets"). Following years of the band wallowing on the periphery of AOR-oriented "safe" music, which perhaps represented a fundamental paradigm shift away from the "dangerous," or in the very least, mainstream rock of the pre-1978 era — chock full of sexual innuendo and allusions to adult carnal activities — "Dynasty" and "Unmasked" had been safe for the band's changed demographics' parents to purchase; and more theoretically more appealing to the broadened listener base the band were hoping to court. Eric recalled, "KISS had pretty much done everything it wanted to do and was ready for a change. The band was disappointed with the public reaction to 'Unmasked' [KISS' last LP of 'pop' music released in 1980] and the guys had just gone through the hardship of a personal change. So, we decided that as long as everything else was up in the air we'd do something really different" ("The Montreal Gazette," Jan. 9, 1982). With the band knowing that they had to turn around from the pre-puberty kids with short attention spans and attempt to recapture some of the dynamic teen market — a market that was lapping up albums and tours by bands such as AC/DC, Van Halen, and Judas Priest.

It was recognized early during project strategy meetings that there was a need to bring in outside songwriters to assist the band. Ostensibly, this would bring in an objectivity and new perspectives to the songwriting process, because "the band has been writing their own material for such a long time, they know their own style as well as each other's [and as a result] cannot be as objective as an outside source, or introduce fresh ideas to the material" (PolyGram). What had worked was obviously no longer working — illustrated by metrics based on commercial success — and then recent albums had demonstrated that the writing could benefit from new external input ("I Was Made for Lovin' You"). It might seem obvious, but if the band members were uninspired then perhaps new co-writers would provide that spark of inspiration. The internal discussion used "Destroyer" as the gold standard. It had been a "classic heavy metal LP" with Ezrin rightfully seen as the key factor in its creation and success. It had received heavy airplay, something that the band needed again — even if the majority of that 1976 success had been a result of the sonic and stylistically contradicting "Beth." While the band had, in 1976, nearly panicked following the release "Destroyer," fearing that they had taken too great a stride in their artistic endeavors, by 1981 they knew they had to do something equally drastic. Taking into account all of these factors, the label, band, and their management seem to have at least had some semblance of a plan on how to take the project forward. The problem would ultimately be in the execution of that plan. The road to Hell is paved with ~~good intentions~~ great expectations!

Towards the late '70s, concept albums were enjoying increasing popularity, culminating with the massive success of Pink Floyd's "The Wall" in 1979; so there had to be a factor of some emulation, or at least hopping on that particular bandwagon. Not only was the Bob produced "The Wall" a cult film and smash record, but other artists including artists such as Yes and Rush had built solid reputations making concept albums based upon obscure premises. In the former case Pink Floyd were tying music, film, and eventually stage together — this must have been highly appealing to the cash hungry KISS machine which was slowly being starved to death. Members of KISS were also highly familiar with the Who and their "Tommy" and "Quadrophenia" rock operas, which while not being concept albums illustrate a great band making a grander artistic statement than an album as a simple collection of songs. The main difference between KISS and these acts was that they seldom made dramatic jumps into other styles of music, more organically moving from one album "sound" to the next. For KISS, who had built a solid career on meat-and-potatoes rock married with "the show," a band who had nearly been scared to death by the initial response to their first truly artistic experiment in the form of "Destroyer," it was perhaps a step too far to be accepted for musical and creative prowess — regardless of the quality of the final product. Soon Bob and the band were discussing concepts and the "concept" became the theme for the album. Or albums, since there was a larger idea for a series of albums: "This album is part of bigger designs, although nothing is planned yet... And we're thinking of it perhaps as the first of a two-or-three-album series" (Toronto Star, 11/28/81). This perhaps begs the question, why was "The Elder" not a double-LP? Whatever the case, it was a grand plan, mired in myth and grandiose ideas, requiring an artistic proficiency boost in the band's musical execution to present something so they considered bold and demanding of respect and attention.

The first proper studio rehearsals were scheduled for April 23 – 25 at SIR's Studio D, at their 310 West 52nd Street facility in New York City. These rehearsals were planned to allow the band to rehearse material before Bob joined them at SIR's Studio B, at 250 West 54th Street, on April 28 through May 1. Studio A, at the same facility, but without Bob, was booked for Gene and Eric, May 4 – 6, and the whole band, May 7 & 8. The album sessions were scheduled to commence on May 11 at Phase One Studios in Toronto, with the plan being to record material in small batches and then return to rehearsals to refine further songs. Simply put it seems that the band didn't have enough material to record the whole album in one go. How or why the studio album evolved into a concept project is not entirely clear, and time may have affected some of the stories and memories of those involved. Some sources have suggested that Bob was the main force behind the idea, insisting that the band ignore the work that they had already done. Paul has been quoted as saying in 1982, "The direction of the album was very much Bob's ... We felt almost dependent on him" ("Kerrang" #32). That comment rings of deflection in the face of the obvious failure of the album and making Ezrin the scapegoat.

Other sources suggest that Gene was the catalyst, mainly due to his comments about a proposed film or story idea that he had been working on. Gene recalled, "The basic idea is a short story I wrote, a kind of fable about the elder and about good and bad. I don't think it is the kind of album we could have done before this, but now we are in a position to take a chance, so we did. I think there may be a film or a musical in the material" (Kurt Lassen, syndicated news article). It is certainly known that Ace revealed in his biography that he felt Bob had jumped on a small Gene idea and blown it up into a "sort of big multimedia, cross-platform vehicle" ("No Regrets"). Gene had moved to Hollywood and was involved with Diana Ross (amusingly some blamed Gene for Diana's harder-edged "Mirror, Mirror" song released on her "Why Do Fools Fall in Love" album in Sept. 1981), following his relationship with Cher. It's known that Gene had started looking for something bigger than his career with the band. He had screen tested for, and been offered the lead, in a television show, "Grotus," but had rejected part as he felt he wouldn't be paid well enough to quit KISS. He had also been rumored (in the press) as being considered, along with Dustin Hoffman and George Segal, for the title role in the movie "Schultz."

However, for Aucoin, in retrospect the concept was something of a crutch: "When we started to think about doing another KISS album, no one was very much into it. And we came up with an idea, hopefully that would help us and would get us through this problem. And the idea was to do a concept album. That concept album turned out to be 'The Elder'" (Bill Aucoin - "13 Classic KISS Stories"). Whatever the case, the "Elder" concept was very much incomplete and disjointed. A 130-page script from the project (written by Russell and Jeffrey Marks) was sold at the 2001 KISS/Butterfields auction for approximately $500. Initially, Gene only had a short script/treatment that was built around the "when the earth was young, they were already old" premise, a tried and tested mythological starting point for any good-ole fight between good and evil. The general consensus is that Gene showed his ideas to Bob, who immediately grabbed at the idea of the script being perfect for a KISS concept album. The result was the band — Gene, Paul and Bill — bought into plan. Part of the reason for liking the concept of the album came not only from it being a challenge to center all of the songs on an album around a common theme, with something of a storyline to hold them together in some cognitive fashion, but the obvious ego factor. Ego dictated that KISS, a band often written off by critics, would do something musically challenging and impress everyone who heard it. They would become serious artists and gain the respect of peers who had hitherto found them laughable. "On a mountain high somewhere / Where only heroes dare / Stand the stallion and the mare." Oh, so very precious. However, using a concept as the methodology for the album may also have been a way to inspire the songwriting since it provided various themes based on the story.

Perhaps Gene and Paul saw the idea as feasible and liked the idea of making the definitive "heavy metal" concept album. As a challenge to the band perhaps, it was also a sort of project that they had never done before. One thing is clear — Ace was not happy with the idea (he suggests in "No Regrets" that he found the whole idea ridiculous), and he also certainly had misgivings about Bob's involvement in the project; remembering how he had been treated in 1975/6. Eric too, while only being an employee of the band, thought it was a mistake, believing that the band needed to get back to its roots. Eric went as far as to vehemently complain about his misgivings about the project, but he was told in no uncertain terms that the band (Gene and Paul) knew what they were doing. Thus, his first appearance on KISS vinyl was to be a strange and rather odd experience, and one that would in some respects serve to be a disappointment and rude awakening to the harsh realities of the music business (of which he should already have been well aware). However, there were also issues within the KISS infrastructure.

Quite simply, the whole period around the recording of "The Elder" was about change and Casablanca Records, with their new PolyGram masters, were ill-equipped to deal with the band. KISS was also unable to cope with their own changing situation having changed from four partners to "three + employee" model. In numerous ways the band were unsure of themselves. Paul had even suggested getting rid of the makeup, but it was decided that it would remain for the time being, though "not necessarily hiding from cameras off stage when not wearing it" (PolyGram). The band also wanted to develop the member's personalities by adding "dimensions to themselves and characters like actors on and off stage by not always hiding their faces" (PolyGram). Both of these points, presented in internal PolyGram documents, suggested that the makeup was starting to be seen a liability, or in the least a hindrance to the development of Gene and Paul as credible artists. It was perhaps time to slowly transition the band out of the makeup.

In the middle of recording the album, Gene and Eric travelled to Austria for what would be their final appearance wearing the "Unmasked" costumes. Having already cut their hair, they had to wear wigs in order to appear somewhat as expected costumes and not give away any of the planned changes. They received the Golden Otto award for "Best Rock Band in the World" award from Rennbahn-Express and conducted an onstage interview at the Town Hall in Vienna at a multi-artist event for 13,000 music fans. Gene was reticent to discuss the new album other than commenting that fans would be in for all new surprises when the project was completed later that year. The visit was brief with the party (Gene, Eric, Bill, George Sewitt, John Harte and Laurie Greenan) arriving in Vienna on May 30th. With the promotion being held on the afternoon of the following day there was little time available to schedule other events though there was a meeting with Phonogram. Upon their return to the U.S., the band was scheduled to continue working with Ezrin on the second batch of songs at SIR Studio B, on June 2, before moving up to Canada for recording sessions from June 15 through early July. As a result of the intermittent sessions "The Elder" took longer than any previous KISS album to record — some seven months, start to finish. It also resulted in the use of the greatest number of studio facilities for any KISS record to date. The project was challenging enough that, by September, Bob had cancelled scheduled work with Heart, citing exhaustion and the need to take an indefinite break ("Billboard," 10/3/81). It should be noted that while recording "The Elder," Bob had been pulling double-duty in finishing up work on the Kings' sophomore album "Amazon Beach" at the same time as working with KISS leading to some intervals where the band worked or rehearsed on their own without him. And this is in addition to working with Scots-Canadian Murray McLauchlan on his "Storm Warning" album released in June.

(Screen capture of Gene & Eric in Vienna, 1981)

In examining "The Elder" from a song perspective, Paul and Bob came up with the odd "fanfare," a medieval sounding horn-based piece, which is particularly illustrative of the experimentation that led to the studio work taking so long. In the original sequencing of the album, this piece was used as the first track, but it was eventually shortened and repositioned to become an interlude between "The Oath" and "Just A Boy" following the PolyGram re-sequencing of the album (it was restored in 1997 with the release of the remastered catalog). Bob played around with the mixing of tracks, notably "Just A Boy" (the first song he and Paul worked on together for the album), as it grew from conception to completion with Paul becoming more comfortable with the vocal. Bob recalled, "He and I went into a little four-track studio in Aurora, Ontario, where we messed around for an afternoon and came up with an idea for a song called 'Just A Boy.' I think 'Just A Boy' is a phenomenal song. It belongs on Broadway, but certainly not on a KISS record. We made a demo of it with Paul on guitar and bass and me thrashing away on drums and playing organ" ("Behind the Mask"). The organ was a Farfisa organ and the circulating tapes document an arduous process of trying to arrange the concept into a realized work. According to Bob, this piece pre-dates the "Elder" concept actively being worked on, which, while the possibility of him misremembering its placement within the timeline, makes the concept project even more confusing.

Numerous takes exist for this particular track demonstrating that they threw just about everything at the track during their efforts, be it acoustic guitars and piano, organ, or simply playing with different mixes. The concept behind this piece would be shoe-horned into the story to be representative of the trials of the protagonist of the plot, who feels "exempt from the responsibility of leadership because of his age" (KISS PR). In other notes, concerning the storyline, the premise of the song is that the young hero needs to look inside himself and take control of his destiny — this in turn applying to the listener. Or as the analogy goes, "steer their own ships" without looking for excuses not to do so. Several different experimental mixes of this song circulate, including an odd version featuring a Bach "Toccata & Fuge"-styled organ that provide a gothic feel perhaps more suitable for a cathedral. The rehearsal takes illustrate the challenges Paul faced with the falsetto vocal performance and make more impressive his efforts. According to Bob, in hindsight, they really should have stopped the whole project when they heard this resulting piece!

Lou Reed was also appropriately involved in the darker songs on the album including "Mr. Blackwell." Oddly, in one plot synopsis for "The Elder," the Mr. Blackwell character is a Washington, D.C., power broker "who turns out to be the story's villain, and the worldly representative of the Powers of Darkness" (KISS PR) who is holding hostage a world leader. This seems quite different than the character Gene and Lou Reed eventually wrote into the song, a character who seems almost Dr. Jekyll-ish. The character may well have simply been a Demon-esque device used to provide an almost "God of Thunder" analogue for atmospheric purposes. Reed also wrote other pieces of lyrics/dialog for the project that went unused, including the interesting "Morpheus Descending": "Give us a verdict now; now is the hour of decision / Don't be slow when you go / Unless you can quickly show to us / A boy prepared to be our hero // Morpheus descending from the spirit / Morpheus descending to our court / Morpheus do send to us a hero // And, Morpheus we thank you very much." Given the details about the character with Morpheus as the "caretaker" there seems to be a bit of a disconnect present.

Eric also made his first significant contribution to the band, co-writing "Under the Rose." Eric recalled his role in the writing of the song: "I had all the music exactly the way it is on the album. I then brought it to Gene, and he worked on the lyrics. I think Ezrin was involved in that too" (Dark Light, spring '90). While working on the album the band had come up with a list of possible song titles, phrases or keywords that in some way connected with the embryonic plot. Eric had simply selected one of these to work with, but it is impressive that he had the confidence, at that early stage of his career with the band, to attempt to make a positive contribution on the creative side. According to the plot, the challenge the boy hero faces, the first step was for him to accept his destiny as he appeared before the Order of the Rose (PR). According to Eric, "It was supposed to be about the chant meetings, the oath that these people take in this ancient 'order.' So, I just decided that might be something to work on. A lot of the stuff that I would play on my own when I play guitar kind of had an eerie kind of thing to it. I figured maybe I could handle that. I just went in and I fooled around with stuff" (KISS Neon Glow #1, 1992). Eric hadn't written any lyrics, so he simply recorded a scat of the melody on his demo before turning it over.

Eric also earned a credit on the "Escape from the Island" instrumental. According to Eric, the 2:50 instrumental, "was a jam that me, Ace and Bob Ezrin did. We got together at Bob's house jamming in his little studio room in his basement. They started pulling things together, and that's how that song came about" (Dark Light, spring '90). This in turn is contrary to the general allegation that Ace had refused to travel to Canada when he was most certainly present there at times. Bob also played bass on the album version of the recording, which is not in itself of particular significance. However, this does put the track in a class of its own for not including either Gene or Paul on it. The song also harkens back to "Firehouse" with the use of sirens (in this case air-raid versus fire sirens) on a KISS song. The instrumental wasn't present on U.S. test pressings of the album made in early October which included the mix ultimately used in Japan. However, the song had been included in the earliest known track sequence dating from Sept. 16. Why the instrumental was excluded from the remix is unknown, but it may have been added back in to heighten Ace's profile or guitar-oriented material on the album. It may also simply have been considered an extra track more suited for B-side utilization as per the Japanese model. Interestingly, a studio reel exists with eight takes of Eric, Ace and Bob on bass working on the track as it developed from Ace's original riff idea into its final form. Enticingly, one additional Ace and Eric jam is included on that reel which does not circulate in fan circles — it could be described as a primitive bed track that would have needed much work, but it is at least additional guitar-oriented Ace Frehley from the period. Sadly, these were some of the few songs featuring Eric's input to ever make it onto a KISS album.

Whatever the case, for most of "The Elder" sessions Ace was simply not enthusiastic about the direction the band had taken and declined to actively participate — even when the band were recording at his home studio! It has been suggested that Ace had the band send him the 24-track masters for him to add his guitar work to, but otherwise he generally avoided working on what he considered a doomed project. Bob then selected the parts, by all of the players, which would be used on the actual tracks. This was a freedom that Gene and Paul felt they had to give Bob in his role as producer and conceptual guru. This argument, that all players had material left on the cutting room floor, seems an ineffectual sop to "fit the narrative to the dialogue." Ace has suggested that there is additional material he contributed, and that one version of the album includes uncut solos that were later arbitrarily edited out by Bob. Paul and Gene naturally defend this, suggesting that additional overplaying by all members was edited out of the final mix. There is also the question of how much Ace can actually remember from the time, though his anger was palpable: "I remember getting a cassette copy of it and listening to it and smashing it against the wall because a lot of my solos had been edited out and I wasn't really happy overall with the album. I mean, I don't think it's a bad album musically, I just don't think it's a good KISS album" (Creative Loafing). Interestingly, in 2011, Ace announced that he uncovered some of his lost "Elder" work: "I have over 100 reels of two-inch tape from my studio in Connecticut that I had in the late '70s and early '80s. ... There's unreleased solos that I did on ... what was my least-favorite album...'The Elder.' A lot of my stuff was edited out of that record, but I have a lot of the original solos. So that may be something interesting to KISS fans" (Talking Metal).

It should be noted that Ace's opposition to the project was not a vehement as he would suggest in later years. He commented in late 1982: "He [Bob] hypnotized us ... We lost sight of what we really are ... I don't hate the album but I'm not crazy about it either. Basically, I'm just a heavy metal guitarist, that's my forte, and I don't think it's indicative of KISS" ("Kerrang" #32). This sort of comment provides a stark contrast to the tape-smashing stories Ace would later tell. Ace has also commented that the band was essentially coasting at the time, yet the creativity attempting to be displayed by "The Elder" seems to contradict that sentiment. There is little doubt that the band were not in touch with reality, or more aptly were suffering a confusion about their identity; and to a certain extent they were clutching at straws for new ideas hoping that some drastic action would result in commercial resurrection. By 1981 even established acts such as AC/DC, Journey, Styx, and Rush saw stagnant sales, but most of those acts were coming off a string of successes. Competition, within the genre, meant that fans were buying albums from other artists as more and more new groups broke onto the ever-expanding metal scene. Many other hard rock acts had eaten into KISS' fan base as they enjoyed their own rises in popularity and exposure. More importantly, perhaps, after nearly eight years on the touring circuit, and in the public eye, KISS had simply become routine.

In an effort to freshen their songwriting, the band also elected to record Brill Building-alumnus Tony Powers' "Odyssey," a powerful ballad-styled piece that fit in nicely with the storyline due to its subject matter. Paul had heard writer Powers' version of the song and had asked him to use it for the album. (Powers later released the song himself, including it on his 26-minute video "Don't Nobody Move [This Is A Heist]," which featured two other songs and actors Lois Chiles and John Goodman). He also asked Powers to assist with some of the writing on other songs. "Odyssey" was a song that may have led to some debate with Gene admitting that he had wanted to do the lead vocals on the song. Ultimately, it seems that Paul wasn't happy with the resulting performance. Years later he described his vocal effort to author Ken Sharp as "just tragic" ("Behind the Mask") because he couldn't take his performance where he felt the original vocal had gone; and therefore, he couldn't really make the song his own. Powers contributions were also musical, and he played the piano on the KISS recording, keeping a connection with his original piece.

Another Gene song, "Only You," was a recycling of one of his earliest recordings, one that had even been performed live by Wicked Lester. "Eskimo Sun" had been transformed into "Only You" several years before being used for "The Elder." Gene's original demo was modified for use within the context of the story (by adding part of another of Gene's demos), though the original version was later recorded by Doro Pesch on her Gene Simmons-produced "Doro" album in 1991. Following the storyline, the song was about the boy hero believing in himself and accepting his destiny that he is the only one who can fight the powers of darkness (KISS PR). "Eskimo Sun," which had appeared on Gene's publishing tape around 1970, was certainly developed enough in its original form to have been demoed and performed live — some sources have suggested that it was more conceptual prior to being fully realized in 1981.

The heavy metal-styled "The Oath" and anthemic "I" finished off the album with a much harder edge and more straight-forward metallic approach. "The Oath" was a song that Paul had requested Powers' help with finishing. Powers took what lyrics had already been written, and keeping in mind the concept of the song, forged it into its completed form rather than working directly with Paul and bouncing ideas off each other. Recording the song provided additional challenges. According to Paul, "For whatever reason, I didn't seem able to hit the high notes full voice at that point and wound up singing some passages in falsetto, which is hardly to my liking at this point" (2001 Box Set notes). Comparing the guitar solo on the album version of "The Oath" with the one Ace performed on "Fridays" live in early 1982, it would seem to indicate that another guitarist played lead on the track and Ace's work, if any was provided, wasn't used. Gene's "I" certainly seems to reflect an annoyance with Ace given the inclusion of what could be interpreted as being lyrical digs at Ace's lifestyle — or it was simply another opportunity to pontificate while keeping with the overall message of the album proclaiming Gene's known puritanical views on alcohol and drugs. But ultimately, the lyrics were more of a message for the purity of the concept of the leading character in the story. Interestingly, this would be the last album track, until "Revenge," on which Gene and Paul traded lead vocals. Following the end of the song, the lone surviving spoken-word dialog sequence closes the album. "Elder: Morpheus, you have been summoned here to offer your judgment of the boy. ..." It is listed on some versions of the album as "The Summoning" or "Dialogue."

Session drummer Allan Schwartzberg was brought in to complete the drum tracks on "I" and "Odyssey." Eric allegedly "couldn't get the feel for the song," though it seems odd that a drummer who had performed all sorts of material during his struggling club days would be unable to perform in a manner that the producer demanded. While disappointed, Eric dealt with the situation in a professional manner and Bob is adamant that Eric simply could not pull off the shuffle to his standard, regardless of his skills. He does not denigrate Eric in any way with the decision being business rather than personal. According to Paul, "Allan was a well-known session player in NYC and Bob Ezrin our producer at the time felt Eric was not playing the sound with the feel that Bob felt it needed. One of the rules we have always tried to adhere to when we work with Bob is to give him final say. It avoids ongoing, endless and sometimes unresolved issues" (KISS Online - "Paul Speaks"). It should be noted that Eric seemed to play the song live on "Fridays" without any problems, though the difference in character is obvious.

It has long been postulated that Schwartzberg was not the only musical "ghost present on the album, performing a more primary instrument than the exotic crumhorn. A persistent suggestion exists in that at least Anton Fig provided some drum services, the obvious choice being on "Dark Light," which he had had a hand in writing. In fact, Bob has recalled Anton being present at one session, but can unfortunately recall enough detail to determine whether he was performing. The original demo, "Don't Run," is generally thought to have been recorded prior to Bob's involvement and certainly makes the most sense for having Anton wielding the drumsticks on. That means that there may well be the possibility of another demo session with Bob working directly with Ace and Anton. In other areas it is clear that there are other uncredited performers, notably on guitar, or possibly members of the band Ars Nova for the medieval instrumentation — Bob Ezrin had used the services of instrumentalist Jon Pierson on Lou Reed and Alice Cooper projects previously. While Paul should never be underestimated, there are solos, particularly on "Just A Boy," that fall quite outside the normal sonic signature of both he and Ace. It is more than a matter of simple feel or execution, that it suggests Ezrin dipping into his playbook and quick-dialing available players appropriate for a particular part. It is unfortunate that it is too late to ask Dick Wagner about some of the songs with audio samples in hand. The obscure "St. Robert's Choir" was not simply an amusing name for the band members, Bob, and other's gang-vocals for backgrounds. Bob had sought permission to use the name from a local school and members of its dramatic society, for whom he'd produced their production of "Jesus Christ Superstar," performed backing vocals. By September the basic recording of the album's tracks had been completed. What was left was for Bob to piece the album together into a cognitive story, a task easier said than done.

According to Robert Conte, in his liner notes for the 1997 remaster version of the album, the track sequence for release was also changed to "emphasize 'The Oath' and 'A World Without Heroes' as potential singles." These songs ultimately became the lead tracks on each side of the album, and "Escape from The Island," which hadn't been listed on some copies of the album's packaging was added. The re-sequencing of the track order also made the planned inter-song dialogue pointless, so that was either removed or simply abandoned (that "The Summoning" survives seems to suggest the former). Few of those questioned recall with absolute certainty hearing a version of the album with the dialogue. All that is currently beyond doubt is that a dialogue recording session did take place at Sound Interchange Studios on Sept. 16. Canadian actors Christopher Makepeace, Robert Christie and Antony Parr were contracted and participated with a script that varies from film treatment. Makepeace, who starred in films such as "Meatballs" (1979) and "My Bodyguard" (1980), read the role of the boy. Unfortunately, listeners have never had an opportunity to hear him on the album with "The Summoning" being restricted to an Elder speaking with Morpheus. That brief exchange is pruned down from a larger Elder question on the 9-page script: "And we do so convene this gathering of the Elder in the shade of the rose. Morpheus, you have been summoned here to offer your judgment of the boy. You have had him in your care for his first cycle of years... He approaches manhood now. Do you still deem him worthy of the fellowship and of the task we must set him?" It should be noted that spoken word dialogue might actually have helped illuminate the album's concept and make less confusing. Multiple sources have explained that the dialogue was to serve as a bridge between the songs, similar to the function served by brief "aural vignettes" on "The Wall." It is not clear who made the final determination to remove it. The restored sequence that appeared on the Japanese release and the remastered CD certainly works better as a storyline as opposed to the rather disjointed version that appeared on the originally released album.

When initial copies of the album were distributed to affiliates the response was slightly more concerned. Australian label executives immediately contacted Phonogram in Holland, commenting, "This is not what Australian KISS fans are looking for and release will possibly damage their standing. We were advised we would be getting a back to basics rock 'n' roll album in concept form. Side B is OK" (Telex, 10/16/81). It's not clear what B-side they had heard since there had been at least two sequences prior to the remix that followed the concerns being voiced by so many label parties. Holland telexed Bill Aucoin: "KISS is in a different stage of their career in comparison with the USA. For many kids the band is a new experience after the last successful tour and a sudden change in direction would not be understood and therefore a big risk to say the least" (Telex, 10/16/81). It is clear that there was a palpable panic towards the project...

While changing the sequence may have made sense to change the focus to seemingly more accessible songs, it made the concept pointless since the product (with the juggled track order) was confusing and didn't flow, much like the project itself. According to Aucoin, "Now 'The Elder' was done helter-skelter. It was really a rough one to do. It was not easy in any respect. The songs were hard to write, no one was in the mood to do it, Bob was frustrated by it, both Gene and Paul were, Ace really didn't want to do it and he didn't want to work with Bob... We started off with the album and dragged ourselves through it and we finally finished it... We delivered it to the record label and the record label hated it. In fact, when we first played it for them, they just said, 'why don't we just can this album and do another album.' Well, the thought of that was definitely not going to happen. It was hard enough just to get this album done. And that was really kind of the beginning of the end, both with me and KISS and for a number of things" (Bill Aucoin - "13 Classic KISS Stories").

PolyGram also demanded that the album be remixed to bring the guitars more into the foreground. This appears to have been rather more complex than originally considered with KISS catalog consultant Robert Conte commenting that the number of varying master mixes for "The Elder" far exceed those available for other albums. This suggests that there are several versions of "The Elder," or in the very least songs, in the vaults somewhere — which probably means in Universal's hands, even though it was from Bob that the supposed masters for "Heaven" were magically discovered in 1991–92. Eric pointed to other problems during the recording of the album that didn't help matters: "The producer wouldn't show. He would just leave notes telling us what he wanted us to do." This sort of interaction was far from helpful, and Eric didn't remember the recording sessions as being particularly enjoyable for his first experience in the studio with the band.

The music on "The Elder" was generally straightforward, but as a concept the story was confusing to most listeners and difficult to reconcile the songs. Additionally, little of the concept was communicated on the packaging making the album a guessing game. Even Bob commented on the challenges the album presented in national media: "They're scratching their heads over this record at PolyGram ... They're not sure why we didn't just do another 'Dynasty ...' And I can't say I blame them. I don't know if I'd be able to sit back and be objective about one of my biggest acts when there's a divergence from a tried and true formula. But the formula is no longer true. It's tried — and it's trying — but it's not working anymore. If we'd just made a typical KISS album with a typical KISS cover, it wouldn't even have sustained a slumping level of interest" ("Billboard").

Perhaps it should be suggested that regardless of the concept, "The Elder" simply tried too hard to replicate "Destroyer" and shoehorn all of the usual Ezrin sorts of elements into a project. Where that latter album was organically created, the product of an initial creative coupling at a challenging time in the band's history, the former was rather too calculated, overwrought and over thought. The band also at least had a deeper well of material from which to draw the songs that were recorded in 1975 – 76. The parallels between the two albums are almost too obvious to notice. Should one step away from "the concept" the album simply appears to be an analogue, almost "Destroyer II" — albeit affected by the baggage the various participants were carrying in 1981. Certainly, it would be fair to suggest that Bob who was perhaps by 1981 no longer the same Bob Ezrin of 1975 – 76. The same can be said of Gene, Paul, Ace and Bill Aucoin.

While debatable (or delusional), "The Elder" represents a similar modus operandi as 1976, instead of dipping into Fowley's catalogue, the external songwriters are employed. Right down to the selection of "A World Without Heroes," almost a transparently obvious parallel to the surprising success of "Beth" in 1976; forgetting in their delusional haze the reasons, both how and why, that song had become surprise hit. "Oh, let's try that again," to the point where it was so calculated it was utterly doomed. Demon tears indeed... "Mr. Blackwell," in some ways is a poor analogue of "God of Thunder," simply the "atmospheric" song for the "Demon" to sing even if it alludes to a composite character in the story. "The Oath," the first-person declaratory song, could easily be a "Detroit Rock City;" and similarly for the anthemic call-out song "I" versus "Shout It Out Loud" (right down to the traded vocals). There certainly had been other atmospheric "Demon" songs, such as "Almost Human," or anthemic callouts like "Tomorrow and Tonight," but never so transparently repeating the 1975/6 model (the lack of ballad being the obvious, at least on "Love Gun").

In October 1981, "press kits and advance copies of 'The Elder' were made available to PolyGram Records ... and radio stations. Reactions were, 'mostly negative and unsupportive' (Conte). One such nationally syndicated review suggested, "A song like the anthemic 'I' is as close enough to being important that it shows how very pretentious the rest of the material is" ("TV Compulog Services"). However, "Billboard" bucked that trend in their Nov. 28, 1981, review of the album: "On this LP, KISS finally makes the transition from a one-dimensional gimmick attraction to a multifaceted not-to-be-taken-for-granted group. Maybe it was Ezrin's production or the group's realization that all those adolescent fans are growing up, but KISS has delivered a mature concept LP which will surprise skeptics. 'A World Without Heroes,' the first single, just might be the softest sounding KISS yet. Well balanced between rockers and slower material, with even some dreamy Pink Floyd-like aural textures mixed in, this album turns a new page for the group. Best cuts: 'A World Without Heroes,' 'Under the Rose,' 'Odyssey,' 'Dark Light'" ("Billboard"). Even the dreaded "Rolling Stone" magazine managed an almost unbiased review, "For all its Marvel Comics predictability, however, Music From 'The Elder' comes off quite well, thanks mostly to producer Bob Ezrin. By scaling down the band's bluster and adding orchestral sweetening, Ezrin makes KISS sound strangely like Jethro Tull. Throw in some honest-to-goodness melodies and you've got a KISS LP you can listen to without embarrassment. Well, almost" ("Rolling Stone," Feb. 1, 1982).

Along with a new musical direction came a new KISS image. Gone was the long hair, replaced with cropped cuts and hair-bands — a definite continuation of the identity crisis from the preceding few years. While most, when asked about KISS' appearance in 1981, will either comment on their shorter hair styles or Paul's purple headband, there was a certain logic behind the jettisoning of the bulky Vegas-esque designs that had essentially been in use since 1979. Streamlined is one word that seems at least somewhat comfortable to describe the new look. Lighter, too. The comfortable colors of black and silver remained core in the new costume designs, but simplicity was a key with Gene's in particular being lightened. Also gone were the platform boots, perhaps a prophetic metaphor for coming back down to earth. Cost, too, certainly played a part in the design process since there was an effort made to scour older costumes and recycle elements. Frantic searches of various storage locations were undertaken to try and locate the requisite material.

It is probably reasonable to start the investigation into KISS' 1981 "look" with the promo photos that they included in their press kit. Gene is drastically redesigned. Chainmail leggings are complimented with knee-high black boots. In some variants the chain mail extends down the shin, just leaving the top of the black boot exposed. His forearms are protected by black leather gauntlets supplemented by 1" diameter rings. His customary codpiece appears more a black-leather-covered jockstrap with a minimalist sword design in studs (pointing upwards). An open-chest black leather open-chest upper is supplemented by thick black belt and studded diagonal strap. Sides are large gauge chain mail to the back, with padded black leather shoulder pads (usually chained to the upper armbands). Shortened hair is slicked back and tied into a ponytail with boar tusks attached, though a top knot remains. Silver upper armbands provide more of a metal contrast. If there is an American football game in the land of "The Elder," then Gene would be ready to play a medieval kabuki quarterback. Neither the chainmail leggings nor boots would survive, being replaced with a more standard black Lycra legging and higher leather boot. His "Love Gun/Alive II" gauntlets eventually also make a return.

The simplification of Paul was more fashionable with him adopting a baggy-black-satin jacket top, thick black pearl (round-things) necklace, and silver forearm sweatbands. His baggy satin bottoms were augmented with a fancy black leather belt with dangling silver chains. Initially he wore knee-high pirate boots, with double side-buckles, which later became near thigh high shiny leather, and were later supplemented with additional decorative chains. The "New Romantic" look was completed, when jacket was removed, with Paul wearing a pair of suspenders. Ace's bulky "Unmasked" era costume was stripped back to a minimalist black body suit with padded silver lamé (a type of material that has metallic threads incorporated to provide a realistic metal appearance) lightning bolt from shoulder to knee (and at the elbows). With silver boots and a lightning choker and wrist bands all he was missing was a helmet as KISS' "Spaceman." Depending on the event Ace's choker and wrist bands were optional. Eric, apparently, had developed a zipper fetish. Multi-zipper pants and jacket were supplemented with zipper choker, belt, and bracelets.

By the time of the Halloween video shoots Gene would be wearing black Lycra sleeves, black leather armbands, and a lighter forearm gauntlet. He supplemented the addition of black with a silver skull necklace, while his hair wasn't as restricted or pulled back. Instruments for the "I" performance were interesting with both Paul and Ace using Steve Carr built models, Paul a white flying-V and Ace a mini-Explorer. Gene used his Axe bass. In other appearances (Mexico TV) and photo shoots Gene would forgo the Lycra under sleeve on his arms.

One of the most interesting promotional activities in support of "The Elder" occurred before the release of the album. On Sep. 24, 1981, the band undertook a promotional visit to Mexico, irreverently known internally as the "Don't Drink the Water Tour." While south of the border the band appeared on TV channel 13 and were interviewed by Jimmy Forson on "Show Aplausos." Oddly, for their performance, the band was incongruously dressed in their "Elder" outfits, and lip-synched "Charisma" (which the band chose over the recommended "Talk to Me") and "I Was Made For Lovin' You," rather than perform anything from the then-forthcoming album. While those tracks had been popular in Mexico — the "I Was Made For Lovin' You" 7" single had sold 252,803 copies in that country by September 1981, plus an additional 121,354 copies of the 12" backed with "Charisma" — it doesn't really explain why the band ignored "The Elder," even if it certainly helps explain the song selection.

Planning for this excursion had been underway since July, and it had originally been intended to promote both the album and announce a Jan. 1982 Latin American tour. The promoter had, at least, gone as far as to retain the services of Gerry Stickells, president of GLS Productions, based in Los Angeles, as an advisor for the tour. Gerry had "previously coordinated a 1981 Latin American tour by Queen" ("Billboard, Jan. 5, 1985) and would later coordinate for the 1985 "Rock in Rio" festival. Queen's Feb. / Mar. 1981 tour had included many of the same venues that were being suggested for KISS. The president of The Twenty Eighth Company (which references the longitudinal line that separates the U.S. from every territory south of the Texas border), José Rota, was also not an unknown quantity within the South American touring industry and was a proponent for bringing international acts to Latin America. He used the economic argument that the Latin American market was not being properly exploited by many acts. In relation to the Queen tour he suggested, "Before the tour, Queen's sales in Argentina, Brazil, Venezuela and Mexico were only 100,000 units. Three months after the tour they had reached 700,000. What are the record companies waiting for"; however, he did admit: "You have to know that it takes half a day just to have cup of coffee" (Billboard, Aug. 7, 1982). From this perspective, it was clear that there was a different way of doing business in the market and that acts needed to be particularly flexible and understand the differences in the market.

The proposed tour was not particularly onerous from a scheduling perspective. The band would fly into Buenos Aires on January 5, 1982 and conduct a press party two days later. They would then perform concerts in that city on Jan. 9–10. While not detailed the band would likely fly via charter to Porto Alegre for a concert there on Jan. 13 followed by two concerts in São Paulo on Jan. 16–17. The South American leg would culminate with a single show in Rio de Janeiro on Jan. 20, following which the band would fly to Monterrey, Mexico for a show on Jan. 24. The Mexican leg would include a show in Guadalajara on Jan. 27, and end with two shows in Puebla, sixty miles from Mexico City, on Jan.30–31. Even with a mix of air and ground transportation the proposed schedule was not particularly arduous, though the logistics of touring equipment movement are naturally far more complex. Even more complex and crucial are the financial and organization aspects of touring: Concerts needed permits. Concerts needed contracts. Concerts needed a finely tuned and properly executed plan by people who knew exactly what to do or knew the people who did. And facilities. While it would be highly insular to suggest that expected venues mirror what the band had become accustomed to in the U.S., Europe (for which there was more than enough criticism), and Japan. However, according to Chris Lendt, the band had already had a highly negative encounter with Mexican promoters who had tried to bring the band to that country in 1980: "What they call stadiums in most Latin American countries are simply enormous concrete shells with tiers of concrete slabs for people to sit on. There aren't any seats, and the facilities backstage, if there are any, are more suited to the cattle than people. The stink of manure from the animal stalls was nauseating. I doubt there was enough electrical power in any of those places to run a toaster let alone 400,000 watts of sound and lights. They're built to house huge crowds of 100,000 and 200,000 to watch soccer matches or bullfights, not high-tech stage productions" ("Kiss & Sell"). Of more concern was the manner in which business was conducted, primarily late-night meetings in police station basements...

The 1980 experience goes some way towards explaining any perception of wariness the band had for touring Latin America. From a business perspective it was clear that they lacked the experience to deal with the promoters from those markets, or at least that the people and systems they encountered when doing so were totally alien. They also clearly lacked understanding of the cultures of those markets, but rapidly learned to protect themselves financially against the endless "no problem" responses to any concerns. The approach in 1981 for the early 1982 tour was conducted in a far more professional manner. In fact, there were two approaches, the first of which, through promoter Carlos Espadone, made it as far as a $100,000 deposit being paid and contracts signed at AMI's offices in New York. According to Lendt, "the proposed deal was worth over $1 million — to come to South America... These would be big events, broadcast live on local TV. Half a million or more people would be at the shows" ("KISS & Sell"). Lendt dates the meetings surrounding the 1982 tour as occurring in October 1981; however other documents seem to contradict that timeline, with the separate promoter, Rota, having been in contact earlier in the year. In fact, a photograph of Aucoin, Jeff Franklin, Rota, and Espadone was published in Cashbox Magazine in July 1981 noting a 10-date tour. Whatever the case, soon after the contracts were signed the tour fell apart and AMI never heard from Espadone again. Rota stepped in and attempted to pick up the pieces using his more suitable connections. Ultimately, his efforts met the same fate and he disappeared along with the prospect of a $1 million payday for a band that was in dire need of financial injections. Within AMI the party line was as general as non-descript as possible when dealing with the press. Ric Aliberte stressed, "When referring to touring in South America and Mexico, please be very general. I would suggest that you say we will be touring sometime in early 1982 in Latin America" (memo, 9/22/81). This, in turn, suggests that touring plans outside of the U.S. were not completed dead in late-September while the Mexican promotional tour was being organized.

Gene expanded on the possible touring configuration in October: "One idea is to have two segments in the show, do all the standards and then do 'The Elder'. We have some interesting ideas and we won't be using tapes; anything you hear, you'll see in front of you, I don't think there's anything wrong with having extra people onstage. Tapes don't give you the freedom to let the music breathe, but [there are] lots of plans on how we're going to do it and if we tell you now, we're going to put our boots in our mouths" (Sounds, 2/13/82). However, with the release of the album slipping from the intended Oct. 1982 date and the touring plans remaining in limbo, other than debuting the new costumes other current affairs were ignored during the Mexican visit. A scheduled appearance on "Hoy Mismo," originally scheduled for the morning of Sept. 27, was cancelled due to the early start time needed and the audience demographic being deemed unnecessary to the band's PR efforts. While in Mexico the band visited an orphanage at Chimalhuacan to distribute toys and candy. The orphanage visit was a concerted PR effort to "dispel any negative rumors about KISS being socially unacceptable. It will help our image greatly" (Memo, 9/15/81) and assist in the plans for concert dates in the country. The entourage returned to the States on Sep. 28.

(Screen captures from the unreleased "I" video)

On Nov. 16 "The Elder" was released, supported by the "A World Without Heroes" single in the U.S. and "I" internationally. Videos, directed by Bruce Gowers, were filmed for both songs over the Halloween weekend, but only the former was released. Amusingly, one fan present at the 5-hour filming of "I" (Vinnie) was introduced by Gene as the band's "worst critic," and was tasked with holding Paul's guitar during a break. Ace would call out for a six-pack of beer. Two versions of a video for "I" song exist. One professional, with the band performing on a "Fortress of Solitude" styled stage edited in early November, and another that was piecemeal collection of clips from just about every pre-1981 video source (that appears so low-budget that it could have been pieced together by a fan). The second version (dated 12/6) is known as the "The Story of 'I'" (Curt Gooch), though that date is obviously confused with the "Solid Gold" footage it contains having not yet been filmed by that date!

It should be noted that broadcast of the "A World Without Heroes" video was very limited at the time. David Braun also affected PolyGram artists in other ways during his brief tenure as the head of the label. With the launch of the fledgling MTV Music Television channel on Aug. 1, 1981, PolyGram held firm in the belief that they should be paid for MTV broadcasting their artist's videos, rather than seeing the prospective free advertising and exposure for their artists. As a result, PolyGram artists were initially excluded from MTV's rotation, though the label soon realized their error and jumped on board that particular bandwagon in early 1982. According to then PolyGram VP Len Epand, "I felt MTV should pay some sort of licensing fee. This was Warner Communications and American Express, after all. This wasn't some impoverished start-up. PolyGram's president, David Braun, wouldn't budge [and] MTV launched without any PolyGram videos. Meanwhile, our competitors' acts were getting all this exposure. Eventually we acceded to their demands" (Tannenbaum, Rob & Marks, Craig — "I Want My MTV: The Uncensored Story of the Music Video Revolution," Plume Publishing, 2012). At the time, there would have been limited other forums for the display of either video.

On release, both album and single failed to make any commercial inroads in any market of note. The album stalled at No. 75 on the Billboard 200 while the "A World Without Heroes" single only reached No. 56, in early 1982, with a mediocre nine weeks on the chart. It was the worst performance of a KISS album on the U.S. charts in seven years. Interestingly, the band and Bob had tossed around ideas to transition "The Elder" into a film project, complete with additional music: "We're going to make a life's work out of it ... If a film is made there might be a soundtrack, which would take it as far as three albums. But any further than that I think is too much" ("Billboard"). Ultimately, the album's poor commercial performance resulted in the cancellation of any plans for future "Elder" projects. The band also abandoned any tour plans to support the album. Paul had initially been positive about the prospect of touring, "I think we can do a big and extravagant show, but the way we do it has to be different than it's been in the past. It's impossible to go out at this point with the type of show that we went out with before. If we were trying to compete with what we've done before, we'd have to bring the National Guard on stage with us" ("Hit Parader"). In early October Glickman/Marks were provided with a financial summary regarding an U.S. tour starting in December and running through some 25 dates into early February. The tone was perhaps necessarily ominous from a financial perspective with an introduction that started with, "shows what we can expect to lose on the kind of tour now being contemplated" (Memo, 10/7/81). Even at this date touring of Latin America was being considered and could have been used to offset some of the expenses of getting the band on the road (costumes, rehearsals and equipment). At this time the band envisaged an overall guarantee of $40,000 per show (split $30,000 for band and the remainder for production). Three weeks of musical rehearsals would be followed by two-and-a-half weeks of production rehearsals prior to the tour, budgeted for $120,000. Major expenses would be over $200,000 in commissions paid to ICM, AMI, and Glickman/Marks. The tour was calculated to lose $200,000. Touring expenses were nearly $1 million, including more than $125,000 for lighting and $100,000 for keyboards/synthesizers. To tour "The Elder" it seems apparent in October 1981 that the band still had "Cadillac Dreams." The salary budget included 2 additional keyboard players, a travelling crew of at least 11 specialists (wardrobe, electronic techs, riggers, etc). What is clear that there was a massive amount of risk included in the plan and the overall tone of the prospectus seemed to question the viability for touring activities to be worthwhile.

By December, when it was clear that the album was not performing, nor was the band's visibility increasing U.S. tour plans were placed on hold and Latin American touring was abandoned, "The logistics did not work out, so now they are going to play in the U.S." ("Billboard," 12/12/81). Without doubt, the whole KISS business must have been extremely disappointed to see the culmination of their year's work come to nothing; and by this time the response to the album and the problems in the studio had pretty much helped Ace make up his mind to quit the band. Ace simply no longer felt any affinity with the band or its direction. Not only was his personal life out of control, but within the band his views were seemingly ignored. With Peter gone he knew that had no chance of winning any of the democratic votes against Paul and Gene.

On the promotional trail for the album the band agreed to appear on "Solid Gold," a lip-synched appearance taped on Dec. 7, 1981. Hosted by Andy Gibb and Marilyn McCoo, the show was taped on Stage 6 at KTLA Studios, the former Warner Bros. Studios, in Hollywood, Calif. The show was broadcast the following month. The band also appeared on ABC's syndicated television program "Fridays" (Season 3, Episode 13) performing "The Oath," "A World Without Heroes" (augmented musical director Fred Thaler on keyboards) and "I" live. The episode was filmed during an effort on Friday, Jan. 15, 1982, at ABC Studios in Hollywood. The special guest host for the episode was Tab Hunter. "Fridays" was a West Coast alternative to "Saturday Night Live," which by the time KISS performed was midway through its final season of a short three-year run. As the singular contemporary live performance of "Elder" material, this broadcast has become very popular in collector circles. The footage was finally officially released as part of the "KISSology Vol. 2" DVD released in 2007. As an interesting side note, in the audience for that performance was one Blackie Lawless, of the early '80s metal band W.A.S.P. fame. Lawless was a childhood friend of Ace's and was readying his own musical assault in Los Angeles.

In a final promotional appearance, on Jan. 28, 1982, KISS appeared live, lip-synching "I" from the Soundworks stage at the then-infamous Studio 54 via satellite to the San Remo Music Festival in Italy where they were due to receive the "Golden Cat" award for the "Most Important International Artist Of The Year." The band had been invited to attend in person, but were unable to do so, resulting in the first ever live satellite performance for that event — reaching a purported audience of 32 million on the Eurovision Network ("Record World," Feb. 13, 1982). In that country, at least, the album continued to perform well into mid-1982. For the latter performance, KISS surprisingly appeared as a trio. Ace had gone AWOL and couldn't be bothered to show up, though at the time Paul used the standard excuse that Ace was sick. In reality, Ace had simply lost all interest in the band and was preparing to transition out. Other outlets, on which KISS had historically appeared, either no longer existed (the "Midnight Special" had ended in May 1981; the "Mike Douglas Show" in November 1981) or were on their last legs ("Tomorrow Coast to Coast" which ended in December 1981 with "Late Night with David Letterman" taking the time-slot). This leaves the appearance to some that promotion was lackluster, or in plain terms simply lacking, though coupled with the MTV issue the avenues of promotion had contracted.

By the time it was apparent that the album was a failure, several countries were still planning on issuing second singles for the album. Japan released

"The Oath" on Jan. 25, 1982 backed with "Escape from The Island," a non-album B-side for that country since the instrumental had not been included on the domestic version of the album. Most importantly, the Japanese album featured a mix of the album that was different from other markets, complete with sound effects and the linear track sequence that was partially based in part on the general plot of the story. This structure was somewhat restored to the international versions with the release of the 1997 remaster. Attempting to bolster performance of the album, in markets where it had been expected to do well, "A World Without Heroes" was released in Holland and England (which issued 7,500 copies of the single and 10,000 copies of the 7" picture disc) in early February 1982. Phonogram in Australia and Germany planned to follow suit once any residual value had been wrung from the performance of the "I" single. That single had charted as high as No. 24 in Australia but was limited to a highly disappointing No. 62 in Germany (where it had been expected to be a top-5 hit) and No. 48 in Holland. The few promotional appearances did little to help sales either — not only did they fail to get widespread attention in the States, but overseas sales also suffered with "The Elder" shifting less than 100,000 copies in Japan and Australia in its first three months of release. The release of Australia was delayed by a week after the record label there received a bad master from the U.S. and needed a replacement. Few countries ever issued a second single from the album and simply allowed the album to die as the band abandoned it as well.

(Holland single picture sleeve)

In the middle of 1981, there had been an optimism regarding touring options. Japan was seen as a possibility, due to the performance of the "Unmasked" album there (and aborted October 1980 tour there). Visits to Hong Kong and Bangkok were also seen as possibilities, though for the distances involved both markets would have had to have been coupled with other countries in the region to make any sort of economic sense. Transportation of the staging would likely had required the band to reconsider their normal model in place of one that was more locally sourced, even at the cost of production values — that might in some way explain why the band never toured the regions, outside of Australia and Japan individually. In early 1982 Glickman/Marks again revisited the viability of a touring cycle. By that time, it would have been clear that "The Elder" was dead and buried, however they considered a 70-date tour July through October. Even with reduced KISS guarantees and the elimination of the per show production fee, the tour was still only forecast to result in a net profit of $100,000 to the band. Production rehearsals being reduced to one week also indicate that the complexity of the tour had been scaled back even if three weeks of musical rehearsals were still required. Most noticeable amongst the expenses were $2,000 per week allocated for a lead guitarist and the lack of commission for AMI. Also gone were the multiple keyboard players and synthesizers indicting that the tour was not going to be based on the original concept of that album. The band were contemplating various set list ideas around this time which indicate that while not completely abandoned that the album was certainly no longer see as a way forward.

The original staging concept provides yet another parallel with that used back in 1976 for the previous Ezrin produced album. Where that stage had been recreation of a desolate cityscape frankensteined with towers and multiple other elements, similar structures provided the basis for "The Elder" stage concept. Perhaps it is less than original to consider replacing on type of tower with another, but the scope for such touring sets is somewhat limited in scope and the reality of execution. Where the "Elder" stage attempted to take the band in different directions were more with the effects envisaged. It was almost going to be KISS meets David Copperfield with band members disappearing and reappearing elsewhere, perhaps Spinal Tap on steroids. Stage towers would represent the band member's characters: A lover's castle, a demon's dungeon, a spaceship, and the fox's lair. The performance would transcend a concert and become theatre with dialogue being used to embellish the performance and involving the audience with the show to leave the sense that they were "being let in on a secret." Scenarios from the "Elder" concept would be acted out with effects to provide a sense of melodrama.

Of the staging only the "battle wagon" drum riser gained any traction – it would be used on both the "Creatures of the Night" and "Lick It Up" tours. A lighting rig over the riser would be powered by faux-jet thrusters. Other effects seem to lack cohesive connection with the overall (known) story of "The Elder." A swarm of killer bees were envisaged to be destroyed by a laser canon – which merely seems to be a new interpretation of Ace's rocket shooting gimmick. Perhaps more amusing was "the use of explosions and pyrotechnics for a reason in conjunction with a scenario" — since when does KISS need a reason to blow shit up — they were obviously unhinged. Other concepts considered simply boggle the mind. An inflatable serpent or beheading a "monster" and "holding the dripping head" seem simply ludicrous. A "Well of The Unknown" was essentially a wishing well containing a trap door effect below. Amplifiers would be mounted on wooded carriages like medieval artillery. Perhaps most useful in a pre-Miley Cyrus world was a prop wrecking ball which could be used to destroy elements on stage.

The nightly work of the stagehands/roadies would not be complete with setting up the stage. It was suggested that they could be used "as actors; i.e. Monks in robes, alien creatures, in character/antagonist costumes." Anyone considering these concepts might immediately be reminded of the theatrical use of robed stage "Jawa" characters, and other devices, on Neil Young's 1978 "Rust Never Sleeps" tour, or the "Stonehenge" sequence in "This is Spinal Tap" or reminiscent of the little-person on Ozzy's "Diary of a Madman" tour. KISS' concepts went further than the dramatic into the melodramatic, suggesting that someone from the audience, a local heroine (or two), could be saved. Saved from what, within the context of the story, is not clear. The dramatic would be embellished with Eric's drum riser, as a battle wagon with smoking cannons and lasers.

While "Unmasked" and "Dynasty" harmed KISS' image with the fans and public, "The Elder" very nearly destroyed the band. Not only did it cause some of the final problems that resulted in the departure of Ace from the band — Aucoin was also soon to leave as the band's manager, replaced by Howard Marks of Glickman/Marks Management Corp. in a more business manager role for the band than in the traditional sense of the role — but public reaction in the U.S., their home market, showed that people were willing to ignore KISS as other bands filled in the space in popular culture they had once occupied. But neither was "The Elder" necessarily a bad album, simply it was the wrong album by the wrong band at the wrong time — had Paul and Gene listened to Eric and Ace's opinions then the result might have been somewhat different, or not, considering the band's decline in their home market. Aucoin summarized the album: "It was not a pleasant time" (classicbands.com — Gary James). Nor would it be a pleasant time when Gene and Paul fired Aucoin in April 1982. Bill recalled, "We'd had a couple of meetings about whether we were going to stay together or not, and finally one day Gene and Paul walked into my office and said, 'Well Bill, I think the time has come...' We decided to part. That it was the time. They needed to go on and do what they wanted to do, and I needed to do what I had to do" (Bill Aucoin - "13 Classic KISS Stories").

The fact that the members of KISS have generally ignored the album — almost to the point of seeming to deny its existence — has not seen the album disappear but has given it veritable cult status within sectors of the KISS Army. The blame game went somewhat further with Paul trying to distance the band from the album by late 1982: "I think with the last album or two, people thought we had gone off in a new direction. Our last was a 'concept' album [Music from the Elder]. Some people around us though that it was a good idea. A lot of those people aren't around anymore" ("Rockford Register Star," Dec. 26, 1982). Ironically, when KISS embarked on the KISS Convention tour in 1995, playing an assortment of unusual songs specially rehearsed to fit in with fan requests, some of the most vocally demanded material was from "The Elder." The band finally had to give in and though they failed to make much of their attempts at performing parts of "Just A Boy" or "The Oath," they did manage to incorporate "A World Without Heroes" into the set list. This was a song that was later featured on the "MTV Unplugged" performance and album. To this day, whenever the band tease a crowd with a few bars of material from "The Elder" the response is usually the same: The more schooled members of the audience go nuts, after a moment of complete shock, while everyone else looks on blankly.

In the grand scheme of KISStory, "The Elder" is an album seemingly built on a confused and incomplete concept, recorded with great skill and attention to the most seemingly insignificant detail. There is a certain amount of artistic meandering on the album, exquisite artistic touches and flourishes that immediately grab the attention of a fan for not being expected on a KISS recording (or long forgotten since the experimentation of the

"Destroyer" sessions). While it may only make for a mediocre "KISS" album, there is little doubt that the music and concept form a masterpiece of execution. The definition of "masterpiece" should be contextualized within the realms of what KISS had done prior (and following) the creation of the album. Gene was pragmatic about the band's situation, even before the futility of their recording effort was apparent: "I don't care if you're Zeppelin or The Stones or whoever. There are peaks and there are valleys. Some albums do better, and some don't do so well. Superman wasn't always popular, but you don't change your basic premise to suit the whims of the public. The last two years have been a readjustment for the band. All bands go through that, and it's just one of those things" ("Lisa Robinson on Rock," Jan. 1982). Perhaps the band already had a good idea that they had a flop on their hands, but Gene's words do foreshadow the way the band would essentially operate for the rest of the decade chasing both sound and style that were accepted by the public. It is probably only fitting to let Ace have the final word: "Ezrin has willingly taken considerable heat for that album over the years and admitted he was doing a lot of drugs at the time, which clouded his judgment. I was doing a lot of drugs, too, but I could still see that the project was going to be a flop" (Frehley, Ace — "No Regrets").

"The Elder" Track-By-Track

Revisiting what's been written or said about the tracks comprising "The Elder," and in some cases the demos that were created first

"fanfare"
(Bob Ezrin / Paul Stanley)

Were any track to be singled out to illustrate the pomposity of "The Elder" concept, then "fanfare" — the original opening track for the album, with its medieval instrumentation and feel — would be it. Listen closely for the foghorn, bells and chanting monks. There were not things you'd expect in conjunction with KISS. For many listeners these elements were most obvious on the Japanese pressings that utilized the original track order. The version on the altered track-listing was shortened with elements buried in the mix. Perhaps Bob has summed the album, as represented by this track, best, in one word: Contrived. Paul once said: "We've done a lot of fuck-me-suck-me songs and we thought we might like to go a slightly different route" ("Hit Parader," February 82). And this track is indicative of how far down that different route the band went! As the lead-off track on the album it is hardly surprising that the suits at PolyGram freaked out and demanded changes to the album!

"Just A Boy"
(Bob Ezrin / Paul Stanley)

This piece was written by Bob and Paul while working together in a small studio north of Toronto with Bob playing drums. The concept of the song focuses on the protagonist of the plot and his "feeling exempt from the responsibility of leadership because of his age" (KISS PR). In other notes concerning the storyline, the premise of the song is that the young hero, and indeed individuals, need to look inside themselves and take control of their destinies to, as the analogy goes, "steer their own ships" without looking for excuses not to do so. According to Bob, they really should have stopped the whole project when they heard this resulting piece!

Collectors can also obtain assorted work mixes of the song that demonstrate the attempts to find a final form for the piece. On a version that we'll call the "Strong Keyboards Mix," the song has an almost "Phantom of The Opera" feel to it with the very prominent organ that permeates the track.

It's very Bach, a la Toccata & Fuge in D Minor. Structurally, the song differs from the album version in that it is simply the first verse and chorus repeated twice with no breaks or guitar solos. Paul also sings the whole piece in falsetto and the piece eventually fades out over the keyboards. On another version, a so-called "Heavy Guitars Mix," the song still has keyboards that are noticeably lower in the mix, with the primary focus being the guitars. Lyrically, like the other alternate mix, the song structure is simply the verse and chorus repeated with no solo. Over the second repetition of the verse a rougher electric guitar is present versus the acoustic guitars in the first. With all that Ace has said about having his solos cut out of "The Elder," one could assume that this mix of the song is one of the prime examples where this could have been the case — or something was being roughed out for him to try. In the event, this sort of material would be perfect for an "Elder: Resurrected" release.

It should be noted that in collectors circles a so-called "Just A Boy" / "Nowhere to Run" (Segue Mix) circulates that marries one of the versions of "Just A Boy" with the early 1981 demo of "Nowhere to Run." The source of this oddity is not clear, but it is most definitely a fake, simply combining the two demos. That a version circulates in which "Just A Boy" segues directly into "Nowhere to Run" is something of an interesting enigma, which would initially seem to make a certain amount of sense in the context of the storyline of "The Elder." The whole piece runs 7:14. Interestingly, the 4:58 version of "Nowhere to Run" is slightly different in that it lacks any lead guitar work. This version is some 20 seconds longer than the other circulating demo version of "Nowhere to Run" though much can often be explained away with fan-adjusted running times.

"Odyssey"
(Tony Powers)

Initially, KISS recorded the song before its writer Powers released his version. Powers was formerly a songwriter in the employ of hit songwriters Jerry Leiber and Mike Stoller. He later wrote and performed a comedy video piece, "Don't Nobody Move (This Is a Heist)," which included "Odyssey" and two other songs, the title track and "Midnight Trampoline." This was also released as an EP on Sony in 1984. In the storyline this song represents the hero's knowledge, "that there is something greater than one's self involved" (KISS PR). This KISS recording includes Allan Schwartzberg on drums and Powers on piano. Gene had originally wanted to sing the piece with Paul only taking the lead vocal at the last moment in a performance that he has since described as being "tragic."

"Only You"
(Gene Simmons)

While this song was written by Gene, the concept seems more likely at home with the sort of things Paul would rap about in concert. The message is about believing in yourself, in the context of the boy hero, and accepting the destiny that he is the only one who can fight the powers of darkness. According to Gene, the song was the result of recycling an ancient demo titled "Eskimo Sun" (Sharp, Ken - Goldmine) that had originally been demoed around 1970 and included on his rejected publishing tape. That version, timed at 3:55, was written solely by Gene. In that form the song had also been performed live by Rainbow/Wicked Lester (Sharp, Ken - BtM). On an interesting musical note, the song's bridge quotes the main melodic motif in "Just A Boy," helping to thread the album's concept further. "Only You" later reverted back to its pre-"Elder" form when German singer Doro Pesch recorded it in 1990, with Gene producing, for her self-titled debut album (which included Tommy Thayer on guitars and as associate producer).

"Under The Rose"
(Eric Carr / Gene Simmons)

During the early part of his career with KISS, Eric made an immediate impact and added to the creativity within the band. He had plenty of ideas, but perhaps most importantly brought a fresh perspective to bring the band, particularly with his enthusiasm. This song combined Eric's musical idea with lyrics by Gene. Eric had chosen the song from a list of song titles that dealt with the plot of Gene's embryonic idea. With the challenge the boy hero faced, the first step was for him to accept his destiny as he appeared before the Order of the Rose. The song attempted to embody the atmosphere imagined at one of the solemn meetings of the order. The song closed side one of the album.

"Dark Light"
(Ace Frehley / Anton Fig / Lou Reed / Gene Simmons)

This song was based on an Ace demo idea originally titled "Don't Run." The song was essentially one of Ace's final musical contributions to the band and constitutes his only major — and obvious — appearance on the album. Based on a riff that Anton Fig had come up with, the song that resulted was unusual from the sort of style that KISS and Ace had previously presented, with its more spoken word lyrics that seem influenced by the style of material that Ace was working on with friend "Crazy" Joe Renda ("Eugene"). Rather disjointed, the initial song lacked fundamental direction, even if Ace was embracing his sense of humor: "What's wrong?" / "You're not happy girl (Well what can I do about it?)" / "Now, be strong" / "And get confidence (You know you can't stick your head in the ground forever)" / "You got problems" / "So does everyone, so does everyone (You don't want me to give you charity)" / "So use your mind" / "'Cause it's all you've got (Well your body's not too bad… humph!)."

Fortunately (or not) the song was co-opted by Gene and Lou Reed to be representative of the fear being caused by the powers of chaos and destruction who revel in disorder. Contrary to popular belief, Anton Fig didn't drum on the studio track in place of Eric but may well have been on the demo. In recent years Ace toyed with the idea of performing this song live, but it has yet to make it into one of his set lists.

"A World Without Heroes"
(Paul Stanley / Bob Ezrin / Lou Reed / Gene Simmons)

This song evolved out of a piece that Paul had abandoned. While Paul had a clear idea for the melodic structure of the ballad, it was equally apparent that he was still fleshing out the lyrics and hadn't yet found a perspective. The original sappy lyrics included: "I know you / Don't know what you want to do / I want you only // 'Cause there's nothing better / We went through it all before / I was so lonely / I want you only // Every little bit of your heart / They're not the only tears you've got / Our lips are lonely" (or something similar since the lyrics are extremely difficult to decipher). The quality of the circulating recording also explains why some of the early instrumental takes of "A World Without Heroes" are often referred by the title "I Want You Only." However, those lyrics may simply have been scat vocals, partially at least, since there is a very slight similarity between them and Linda Ronstadt's "Hurt So Bad" (originally written by Teddy Randazzo, Bobby Weinstein and Bobby Hart for Little Anthony & The Imperials). In the case of some of the instrumental versions, it may simply have been a matter of the tape generation in trading circles resulting in the decline of the sound quality of the song, since the vocals are so low in the mix in the first place. The similarities between this piece and "A World Without Heroes" are most noticeable with respect to the bass line and the initial minute of the song before the piece changes tempo and style.

Gene, however, liked the melody Paul had created, though not the lyrics and took parts of it and with Bob revamped it into what became the album's sole single in the United States. The title came from Lou Reed simply writing down idea phrases and possible song titles on a piece of scrap paper that caught Gene's attention. And as a result, this song might be most representative of a band like KISS working with someone like Reed and trying to create something far greater than the original sum of the parts. The song appears chock full of the sort of sarcasm that dated back to Reed's earliest songs (such as 1964's "The Ostrich," with its "put your head on the floor and have somebody step on it" lyric mocking the popular dance songs of the time). If nothing else the song mocks Reed's suggested literacy with clichéd or overly simplistic metaphors such as "never-ending races," a "bird without wings," or the "bell that never rings." In some ways it might be a weak Simmons facsimile of what he thought Reed would say.

According to sample artwork for the abandoned "KISS Exposed II" video cassette (1992) a version of the song exists with Lou Reed on lead vocals. The song was KISS' first full concept video, due to it being an artistically shot performance piece ending with a tear from the Demon's eye ("Demons don't cry," as noted by Gene in "KISS: The Early Years"). This is in contrast to the pseudo-live performance videos that the band had first used for promotional purposes in 1975 ("Shandi" is partially concept mixed with performance). It should be noted that the guitar solo is performed by Paul in a form inspired by what he thought Bob Kulick would have created for the track. This song was one of four KISS titles announced in May 1997 as being recorded in an instrumental for Muzak's Environmental Music channel customers following the approach of Gene.

"The Oath"
(Paul Stanley / Bob Ezrin / Tony Powers)

Powers had come to Toronto to help the band and finishing off this Paul Stanley/Bob Ezrin composition that needed some work, primarily with regard to the lyrics. While the song was ultimately changed to be the album's lead track (to emphasize it as a possible single), it was originally sequenced towards the end of the story, appearing in the middle of side 2 of the album. As had been the case with other songs Paul had challenges hitting the high notes resulting in his falsetto vocal performance. Comparing the album version with the one performed with Ace on "Fridays" live in early 1982, it seems probable that Paul played lead on the track and Ace's work wasn't used. "The Oath" was released as a single in Japan, backed with

"Escape from The Island," which hadn't been included on the Japanese version of the album.

(Japan single picture sleeve)

"Mr. Blackwell"
(Gene Simmons / Lou Reed)

In one odd plot synopsis for "The Elder," the Mr. Blackwell character is a Washington, D.C., power broker "who turns out to be the story's villain, and the worldly representative of the Powers of Darkness" (KISS PR). It is this character who is holding hostage a world leader for some nefarious purpose. This seems quite different than the character Gene and Lou Reed wrote into the song, a character who seems almost Dr. Jekyll/Quasimodo-ish in an almost "God Of Thunder" nature, though the name itself is indicative of the character: "Black" = Dark + "Well," as in a dark well or depths of evil/malice. The character represents the antithesis of the "wishing well" concept that was included in early plans for a possible tour stage.

"Escape From The Island"
(Ace Frehley / Bob Ezrin / Eric Carr)

This was KISS' first instrumental since "Love Theme From KISS" on the band's debut album in 1974. Initially the song was not included on the Japanese version of "The Elder," and it was instead the B-side to "The Oath" released in that country as a single. The song was also included on the Japanese release of "Killers" the following year. Ace and Eric certainly collaborated during the sessions also creating several other instrumentals, "Heaven," a song that ultimately became Frehley's Comet's "Breakout," and another untitled idea. While "Heaven" was not lyrically completed at the time, the masters remained in Bob's vault until 1992. Several different takes of the recording exist in collector's circles for those who want to compare the exquisite original with the later KISS hatchet job released on "Revenge." With no count off, one version of the track simply starts with the main riff and runs 6:18. This features the full 2:46 drum solo rather than the shortened 46-second version. "Escape from The Island" was originally titled "The Chase," reflecting its purpose in the storyline. Numerous takes of the track exist illustrating its development from conception to completion.

"I"
(Gene Simmons / Bob Ezrin)

The album's closing track (on both versions) sums up the change in the boy as he learns to believe in himself. The 3:52 song includes one verse that has long been seen to be both a dig at Ace's lifestyle and a statement of Gene's personal philosophy: "Don't need to get wasted" / "It only holds me down" / "I just need a will of my own" / "and the balls to stand alone." Interestingly, this was the last studio track, until "Revenge," on which Gene and Paul shared lead vocals and took a form that could loosely be considered the sort of anthem that would be expected from KISS. Unfortunately, reviewers noted the almost welcoming target such a song provided on the album: "A song like the anthemic 'I' is close enough to being important that it shows how very pretentious the rest of the material is" ("Newburgh Evening News," Jan. 24, 1982).

A single edit was released in several countries and used as the backing track to lip-synch performances. It simply replaced the "the balls to stand alone" lyric with "the guts to stand alone." Certainly, that minor change was nothing particularly earth-shattering, and completely understandable in the attempt to gain airplay. The single managed to reach No. 24 in Australia, while stalling at No. 62 and No. 48 in Germany and Holland respectively. According to Gene it was also a hit in Italy, where it was issued with two sleeves, the second commemorating the San Remo event, where KISS performed a lip-synched version of the song from Studio 54 in New York as a trio. Ace, by that time, had simply stopped returning the band's calls. In late October 1981 the band and management flirted with the idea, suggested by a Mexican label representative, of re-recording the song with a Spanish language vocal.

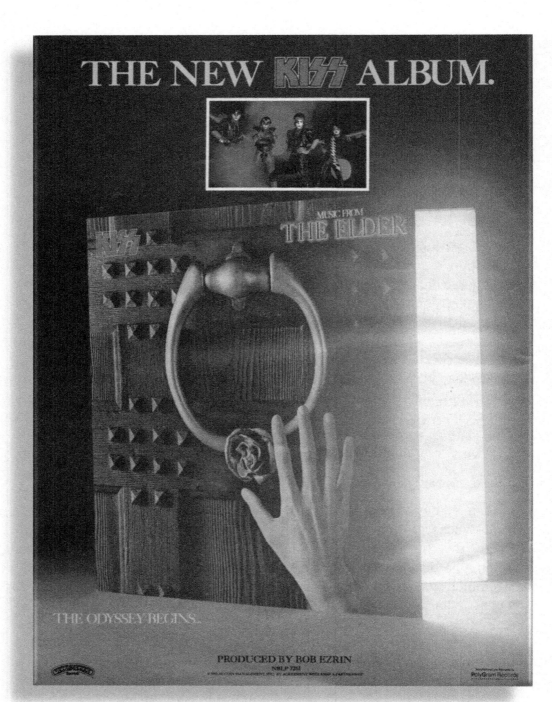

"The Elder" Timeline

Between completing the huge 1980 Antipodean tour, planning and recording a concept album with Bob Ezrin, press and publicity, and a death in the family, KISS had a full plate from October 1980 through mid-1982. Take a closer look at the band's busy "Elder"-era

October 1980

X - David Braun appointed President of PolyGram essentially replacing Irwin Steinberg (who would remain in the Chairman role through the expiration of his contract in 1981). His mission, he felt, "pride in PolyGram must be one of my first priorities and it's been frankly lacking... Talent just doesn't come into a company, it must be a place it feels comfortable to live in" (Billboard, 10/11/80). He moves into offices at Casablanca's Sunset Strip building signaling possible intent...

9 - Aucoin Management file for a trademark for "KISSVision" for use on goods and services related to prerecorded Videocassettes. While not granted until Oct. 19, 1982, the logo first appears on the unreleased "I" video.

10 – 11 - PolyGram, including new President David Braun, host an internal conference in Tarrytown, NY to discuss the label's profitability...

November 1980

X - Final founding partner and vice president, Cecil Holmes, departs Casablanca. He forms Gold Coast Records (with Marv Stuart), distributed via Capitol Records. According to Larry Harris a full-scale purge of Casablanca staff occurred soon afterwards.

29 - KISS fly from Sydney, Australia, to Auckland, New Zealand, via Qantas flight #51 arriving at 2:50 p.m.

29 - KISS fly from Auckland, to Wellington, via ANZ flight #427 arriving 5:05 p.m.

30 - KISS performs at Athletic Park Stadium in Wellington on a wet and windy Sunday evening.

December

1 - KISS fly from Wellington to Auckland, via ANZ flight #434 arriving at 7:45 p.m.

3 - KISS performs at Western Springs Arena in Auckland. This performance marks the band's last full concert appearance with Ace Frehley until the "reunion" in 1996.

4 - KISS departs New Zealand for Los Angeles via ANZ flight #6, bookending the "Unmasked" era.

13 - Bruce Bird, President of Casablanca, at the time KISS signed their 1980 contract with Phonogram, is culled from the workforce during wholesale layoffs.

January 1981

X - PolyGram Australia starts planning a "Best Of" album in case KISS fails to deliver a new studio album on time.

5 - Late night rebroadcast of "KISS Meets the Phantom of The Park" on certain NBC affiliates.

23 - Aucoin Management files for a registered trademark for the "KISS ARMY" logo with the United States Patent & Trademark Office (Registration 1398939 would be granted on June 24, 1986).

February

7 - Recording sessions commence at Ace in The Hole studios with engineer Rob Freeman behind the console.

13 - Tabloid reports of an impending marriage between Gene Simmons and Diana Ross are denied in national press articles.

14 - In Australia, "The Inner Sanctum" TV special filmed during the band's 1980 tour airs on channel 10. It primarily features footage from KISS' Nov. 22 concert in Sydney.

19 - Glickman/Marks Management requests the contractually defined advance for the next KISS record officially marking the beginning of the KISS 17 product cycle.

26 - Bob Ezrin, Bill Aucoin and the band meet to discuss a new album project.

March

1 - Ace Frehley and family depart for a vacation in Key Biscayne, Fla.

3 - Paul Stanley interviewed by Dutch Radio TROS. Bill Aucoin reports an agreement with Rob Freeman, to Howard Marks, to pay him off for the 200 hours of work he has completed engineering the band's recordings the previous month. AMI notifies leadership at Phonogram Baarn of Ezrin's recruitment to the KISS 17 project.

5 - Gene Simmons and Eric Carr interviewed at AMI Offices by "Popcorn Magazine" (Germany).

6 - Ace Frehley returns from his Key Biscayne vacation.

14 - KISS reported in the studio with Bob Ezrin in Lisa Robinson's syndicated music column.

17 - Eric participates in an interview with "Bravo" magazine at AMI.

April

7 - Peter Criss' daughter, Jenilee, is born. Gene films a screen-test for "Grotus" for ABC television. Ultimately offered the show, Gene felt he wouldn't earn enough from the project versus what he'd lose from band related revenue.

8 – 11 - Second Year production of Andrew Lloyd Webber and Tim Rice's "Jesus Christ Superstar" by St. Robert's Catholic High School's Loyal Orange Players recorded at Manta Sound Studios. Bob Ezrin serves as executive producer... Students from this school would be used as backing vocalists on "The Elder."

14 - Rehearsals scheduled at Matrix Sound Studio A in New York City.

23 – 25 - Rehearsals scheduled at SIR Studio D in New York City, without Bob Ezrin.

25 - Still promoting the "Unmasked" album, which has sold some 80,000 copies domestically, "Talk to Me" is released as a single in Japan. The band's popularity had remained high in that country.

28 – 29 - Pre-production sessions scheduled at SIR Studio B in New York City with Bob Ezrin.

29 - AMI staff and artists invited to the opening of Interferon Club on 30 West 21st Street in New York City.

30 - Pre-production sessions scheduled at SIR Studio B in New York City with Bob Ezrin.

May

X - Paul reported in tabloids as dating "Evita" star Patti Lupone.

1 - Pre-production session scheduled at SIR Studio B in New York City with Bob Ezrin.

4 – 6 - Pre-production session scheduled at SIR Studio A in New York City for Gene Simmons and Eric Carr without Bob Ezrin.

5 - KISS receives United States Patent & Trademark Office registration (#1153088) for the KISS logo ending a process that had commenced March 14, 1978 with the initial filing for the trademark!

7 – 8 - Pre-production session scheduled at SIR Studio A in New York City without Bob Ezrin.

11 – 12 - Album recording sessions scheduled at Phase One Studios in Toronto, Ontario.

12 - Gene Simmons interviewed by "Illinois Entertainer Magazine" while in Toronto.

13 – 22 - Album recording sessions scheduled at Phase One Studios in Toronto, Ontario.

25 – 28 - Rehearsals scheduled in New York City.

29 - Gene Simmons, Eric Carr, Bill Aucoin, Laurie Greenan (wardrobe supervisor) and George Sewitt fly to Frankfurt, Germany, via Lufthansa flight #401, arriving at 8:10 a.m.

30 - Gene Simmons, Eric Carr, Bill Aucoin, and George Sewitt fly to Vienna, Austria, via Lufthansa flight #250, arriving at 10:30 a.m. They stay at the President Hotel.

31 - Vienna promotional event for Rennbahn-Express takes place at the Town Hall with Gene Simmons and Eric Carr receiving an award (No. 1 rock band in Austria) from soccer star Hans Kronki, in front of 13,000 music fans. In a brief Q&A they are asked about recording and touring plans, while a film clip from the 1980 Australian tour is played.

(Music from the "Elder." This show didn't take place.)

June

X - The KISS catalog finally receives an official release in South Korea via Sung Eum Limited. Unfortunately, some material contained is considered "immoral" and tracks are removed from "Dressed to Kill," "Destroyer," "Rock and Roll Over," and "Love Gun" by Ministry of Culture censors. The band members are congratulated in a June 17 internal AMI memo for being "immoral and subversive songwriters." All songs from "The Elder" would pass muster when released in that market later in the year.

1 - Gene Simmons, Eric Carr, Bill Aucoin, Laurie Greenan and George Sewitt fly to Frankfurt via Austrian Air flight #401, arriving at 8:40 a.m. They fly on to New York via Lufthansa flight #400, arriving at 12:45 a.m. the following day.

2 – 6 - Rehearsals scheduled in New York City.

8 – 12 - Rehearsals scheduled at SIR Studio B in New York City with Bob Ezrin.

13 - Scheduled date for a Peter Criss Benefit concert at Westhill High School in Stamford, CT. This date was to raise funds to aid Gateway Communities of Stamford and serve as Peter's first public appearance since leaving the band. He had certainly been rehearsing (at Electric Lady) in the period with guitarist Larry Federman. Country singer Mary Joie and French rock group Export were also noted as performing on the bill. The show was cancelled.

15 - Aucoin Management are receives a prospective touring itinerary from The Twenty Eighth Company for a 10-concert tour of South America and Mexico in January 1982. The planned tour encompassed concerts in Buenos Aires, Porto Alegre, São Paulo, Rio de Janeiro, Monterrey, Guadalajara and Puebla.

15 – 23 - Album recording sessions scheduled in Toronto, Ontario.

16 - Expiration of the KISS inter-album contract period. Following this date markets, such as Australia, were considering releasing a territorial "Best Of" album with the release of the KISS 17 album not being solidified.

23 – 26 - Bill Aucoin travels to Los Angeles for a meeting with Twentieth-Century Fox Licensing regarding U.S. and foreign KISS merchandise and license agreements.

24 – 26 - Album recording sessions scheduled in Toronto, Ontario.

27 - Band members interviewed by Mexican press. Press members also attend a band photo session with Barry Levine.

28 – 30 - Album recording sessions scheduled in Toronto, Ontario. These don't take place.

29 - Paul, Eric, and Bob working on material at Paul's.

30 - Eric attends a meeting with Bob at Paul's.

July

X - The search for the voice actors for the album commences. Many notable Hollywood figures are suggested for consideration.

1 – 3 - Album recording sessions scheduled in Toronto, Ontario.

7 - A soundtrack album for the Brooke Shields film, "Endless Love" (Mercury SRM-1-2001), released. It includes KISS' "I Was Made for Lovin' You."

10 - Aucoin Management files for the trademark of Eric Carr's makeup design. It would be granted on Dec. 14, 1982.

15 - Gene scheduled to fly to Toronto and stay with Bob at his home.

19 - KISS' road manager, Ric Aliberte, gets married.

22 - Continued planning for the packaging includes the idea for a parchment paper inner dust sleeve.

August

4 - PolyGram Mexico agrees to the conditions for the planned Sept. 24–28 promotional tour.

13 - Bob Ezrin advises AMI that he and the band have named the new album "Music from The Elder."

28 - The Children's Museum in Indianapolis opens their "Making Faces" exhibit, which includes an in-store "Elder" poster. The exhibit explores the use of masks in entertainment and runs through Nov. 8, 1982.

September

X - Bob Ezrin pulls out of producing Heart, who were ready for a change from co-producer Mike Flicker, citing the need to take an indefinite break ("Billboard," 10/3/81).

2 – 4 - Vocal recording sessions scheduled at Record Plant Studio C, with hold dates for Sept. 5 – 6.

5 – 27 - Record Plant Studios' "White" remote truck is rented for use at Ezrin Farm in King City, Ontario.

8 - Studio time at Sounds Interchange studio #2 in Toronto booked by Bob Ezrin.

9 - Recording session scheduled at Sounds Interchange studio #2, 6 P.M. – 2 A.M.

9 - AMI rent an MCI JH-114 24 track tape machine for use in Canada, Sept. 9 – 23.

10 - George Sewitt and Ric Aliberte fly to Mexico for two days of discussions concerning KISS' planned promotional visit and possible South American touring activities. A recording session at Sounds Interchange Studios studio #1 is scheduled, 4 P.M. – 4 A.M.

11 - Recording session scheduled at Sounds Interchange studio #2.

12 - George Sewitt and Ric Aliberte return to the U.S.

12 - Paul Stanley and Eric Carr are interviewed at the AMI offices by various publications, including "Hit Parader," "Music Life" (Japan), and "Pop/Rocky" (Switzerland).

14 - Brian Christian flies into New York from Toronto to prepare for the ASO session.

15 - Orchestral recording session at A&R Studios in New York City for sweetening of "Fanfare," "Closing Theme," "Odyssey," and "A World Without Heroes." Gene and Bob fly into New York in the morning from Toronto. Gene goes to Suga for a haircut. Ace arrives in the afternoon. Bob and Brian Christian return to Toronto in the late evening. By this time Bob had provided a rough sketch of the album rear cover with the earliest known track sequence.

16 - Glickman/Marks/KISS meeting with Twentieth Century-Fox Licensing regarding album and tour merchandising. Character dialogue recording session at Sounds Interchange Studios, 2 – 10 P.M.

18 - Recording session at Sounds Interchange Studios, 2 P.M. – 3 A.M. A gong and wind chimes were rented for the session. Also purchased were sound effects from R.S.S.

21 - Band members are invited to attend the christening party for Jenilee Criss in Darien, Conn.

22 - New York City Mayor Ed Koch's Office of Motion Picture and Television use Ace's "New York Groove" as the theme song for their Motion Picture Industry party.

23 - Ric Aliberte flies to Mexico City as the advance man for the touring party.

23 – 30 - Mixing of "The Elder" at Manta Sound in Toronto.

24 - KISS fly to Mexico City from JFK via Eastern flight #901, arriving at 1 p.m. They are guests of PolyGram Mexico, with whom they dine that evening.

25 - Press conference at the hotel's Cero Cero disco and gold and platinum record presentation by PolyGram followed by radio appearances in make-up/costumes for Radio 590 "La Pantera" and Radio Exitos.

26 - Autograph session at Phonogram offices and interviews with Mexican press. Afternoon visit to Mexican orphanage followed by an evening photo-shoot at pyramids.

27 - TV appearance lip-syncing "Charisma" and "I Was Made for Lovin' You" for channel 13 with interview by Jimmy Forson.

28 - Time booked at Sterling Sound in New York City for the mastering of "The Elder." This date would be cancelled.

28 - The band returns to the U.S. via Eastern flight #900, arriving at JFK at 11:30 p.m.

30 - "The Elder" mastered at Sterling Sound with George Marino.

October

1 - Deadline day. The delivery of "The Elder" to the record label on this day was critical due to contractual obligations. Aucoin had been warning the band and Ezrin of the deadline since June since missing it could have resulted in an unfavorable re-negotiation of their contract with PolyGram.

2 - Listening party for "The Elder" at Glickman/Marks' Madison Ave. offices.

7 - First plans for touring in support of the album discussed. A 25-show U.S. tour, over seven weeks starting in December 1981, is envisaged.

8 - Test pressing of the album, with original track sequence, by PRC vinyl plant. AMI have already received test pressings from Hauppauge Record Manufacturing, Ltd. (HRM).

16 - PolyGram strategy meeting scheduled with Aucoin Management and Glickman/Marks to discuss "The Elder."

19 - Dante Bonutto interviews Gene and Paul at the AMI offices for Record Mirror (U.K.).

20 - Rescheduled from the prior day, Pete Makowski interviews Gene, Eric and Paul at the AMI offices for Sounds Magazine (U.K.). Photographer Ross Halfin attends, not to take photographs just to say "hello."

25 - Scheduled release date of "The Elder" in Japan. Press for the release campaign was designed to stress that the release there was before any other country in an attempt to prevent the sale of cheaper import versions of the album. The version of the album released was also unique.

26 - Gene Simmons, Paul Stanley and Eric Carr travel to Los Angeles for press/publicity interviews.

26 - A release date for the album. This date slips due to the re-ordering of the track sequence.

27 - The "A World Without Heroes" single officially released in the U.S.

27 – 29 - Press/media publicity interviews.

29 - Gene Simmons, Paul Stanley and Eric Carr return to New York.

29 - AMI respond to a PolyGram Mexico request for a Spanish language version of "I" for a single positively, if the incurred costs of doing so can be spilt.

30 - Staging preparations at Boken Studios in New York City for the "Elder" video shoots.

31 - Video for "A World Without Heroes" filmed, directed by Bruce Gowers for Gowers, Fields & Flattery.

November

X - The Frehley Estate is listed for sale by Sotheby's International Realty for $1,500,000. "This secluded 4-acre retreat — the country estate of dynamic rock star Ace Frehley of KISS — boasts a dramatic brick and cedar Contemporary residence. The fully customized 14-room interior is complete with a 24-track 'state-of-the-art' recording studio. Convenient commute to Manhattan" ("Billboard," 11/28/81). Ace continued to own the property until late-1986 and was named in a lien against the property by Connecticut Light & Power in January of that year.

1 - A "You Asked for It" TV segment and the video for "I" filmed in New York City (same details as Oct. 30 – 31). 100 extras, including AMI employees, are used in as the audience.

3 - The band receives news of album pre-sales in Germany, Norway, Holland and the U.K. reaching a combined 111,000 units.

5 - "The Elder" released in Japan. The initial 50,000 copies include the following premiums: A large color poster, color sticker, KISS logo pin badge, and a special yellow vinyl "Elder" bag in which to carry all the goodies. Also issued is the "I" single backed with "Just A Boy." The liner notes suggest the song was recorded at Ace's studio...

5 - Edit of the soundstage performance version of the "I" video completed. According to Bill Aucoin, "The video didn't turn out how we wanted it. It wasn't KISS enough in the presentation. It was all wrong and never used."

9 - "The Elder" album is released in Austria, Belgium, the U.K., France, Germany, Holland and Norway

12 - Eric Carr interviewed by "Adelaide News," Australia.

16 - Gene Simmons and Eric Carr interviewed by "Pop Foto" and "Hitkrant," both Dutch magazines.

16 - "The Elder" released in the U.S. The album is also released in Australia following a one-week delay due to faulty master tapes.

17 - German "Elder" sales reported at 77,000 units. The "I" single is reported at 20,000 units and expected to enter the "Pop Singles" charts the following week.

20 - Gene Simmons interviewed by "Toronto Star" (first Canadian "Elder" interview for the album).

21 - Bob Ezrin discusses "The Elder" in a "Billboard" magazine profile.

23 - Gene Simmons and Paul Stanley conduct press interviews with "Rock USA," "Billboard," and "Rolling Stone" magazine Radio Report. The "Billboard" article runs in the Dec. 12 issue.

24 - Gene Simmons and Eric Carr conduct Australian press interviews (Juke Magazine, 3XY, 5AD, 2SM, 6PM, 6IX, and Sydney Sun).

30 - "The Elder" reaches its high point of No. 10 during 17 weeks on the German charts.

December

X - A second video clip for "I" is constructed using assorted live and archival video clips of KISS in concert dating back to 1974's "In Concert," but also including shots from other promo videos and the band's appearance on "Solid Gold." (The date on the video lead-in is 12/6, but "Solid Gold was 12/7 leaving room for confusion of the actual edit date).

1 - Gene Simmons and Paul Stanley interviewed by Swiss, German and Swedish press outlets and "Circus" magazine.

2 - Gene Simmons interviewed by "Popcorn Magazine" (Germany), "Edmonton Journal," and News Script Service. That evening he attends the premier of the film "On Golden Pond" (starring Katharine Hepburn and Henry Fonda) with Miss Diana Ross, being caught unmasked by photographers.

3 - Paul Stanley attends the Party for American Dance Theater Performance at the 55th Street Theater to aid the Alvin Ailey Dance Theater.

5 - "The Elder" debuts on the Billboard 200 album chart at No. 175. The "A World Without Heroes" single misses the Billboard Hot 100 chart at No. 103.

7 - Scheduled date for the "Solid Gold" TV taping at the Golden West Broadcasters in Los Angeles. The band lip-syncs "I." During the day the band also tapes a "Where Are They Now?" segment for Entertainment Tonight at the same studio. "The Elder" charts at No. 13 on the Australian album chart.

8 - KISS interviews/press in Los Angeles.

9 - KISS interviews/press in Los Angeles.

12 - "The Elder" charts at No. 108 on the Billboard 200. The single, "A World Without Heroes," debuts on the Billboard Hot 100 singles chart at No. 92 and No. 86 on Cashbox.

14 - "The Elder" debuts at No. 10 on the West German (Musikmarkt) album chart. The album drops out of the top-20 within two weeks.

17 - Pre-recorded interview segment and "A World Without Heroes" clip broadcast on "Entertainment Tonight."

19 - "The Elder" charts at No. 95 on the Billboard 200. "A World Without Heroes," moves up to No. 88 on the Hot 100 singles chart and No. 79 on Cashbox. The album reaches its high point on Australia's Kent Music Report charts at No. 11.

26 - "The Elder" charts at No. 86 on the Billboard 200. "A World Without Heroes" moves up to No. 78 on the Hot 100 and No. 71 on Cashbox. The video for "A World Without Heroes" is broadcast on "America's Top-10" along with a pre-recorded interview.

January 1982

X - Gene is rumored in the press as being considered, along with Dustin Hoffman and George Segal, for the title role in the movie "Schultz."

2 - "The Elder" charts at No. 86 on the Billboard 200.

5 - Gene Simmons and Paul Stanley film their "Flo & Eddie" television appearance in New York City. During the day the band also attend a party at the United Cerebral Palsy Center, on E. 23rd Street, to film a segment for their telethon and give out gifts to youngsters.

9 - "The Elder" charts at No. 78 on the Billboard 200. "A World Without Heroes" moves up to No. 74 on the Billboard Hot 100.

9 – 12 - Rehearsals scheduled at SIR Studio C in New York City for the "Fridays" television appearance.

14 - Rehearsal scheduled at Studio 55 in Los Angeles for the "Fridays" television taping. An interview with WABC-TV's Storm Hunter is also aired on that channel's "Eyewitness News."

15 - Run-throughs (2), dress-rehearsal, and filming of "Fridays" ABC television appearance broadcast live at 9 – 10:30 p.m.

16 - "The Elder" charts at No. 76 on the Billboard 200. "A World Without Heroes" moves up to No. 66 on the Hot 100 singles charts and No. 65 on Cashbox. The United Cerebral Palsy telethon on WOR-TV airs.

20 - "Bosom Buddies" actress Donna Dixon surprises Paul Stanley with a 30th birthday party at L'Ermitage restaurant in Los Angeles.

23 - "The Elder" charts at No. 75 on the Billboard 200, its highest point. "A World Without Heroes" moves up the Hot 100 singles chart to its high position of No. 56. The single also charts at No. 59 on Cashbox.

25 - "The Oath" is released as a single in Japan backed with the non-album track "Escape from The Island."

28 - KISS lip-sync "I" as a trio, without Ace Frehley, at Studio 54 for a satellite broadcast to the Italian San Remo festival where the band are awarded the Best International Band award. Additionally, an interview with Billboard's Gary Hamilton is scheduled during the event.

29 - This week sees the broadcast of KISS' television performance of "I" on "Solid Gold" along with part of the "A World Without Heroes" video.

30 - "The Elder" charts at No. 89 on the Billboard 200. "A World Without Heroes" drops off the Billboard Hot 100 after seven weeks. The single hits its high position of No. 57 on Cashbox. KISS' "Solid Gold" appearance is broadcast. The show is hosted by Andy Gibb.

February

X - The band files a lawsuit their record label claiming, "failure to pay $1,772,655 in royalties on the part of Phonogram on album product released between June 1977 and March 1979." The suit claimed that Phonogram's predecessor, Casablanca Records & Filmworks, had harmed the band by "engaging in massive and unwarranted over shipments" of the band's albums "at distress or 'schlock' prices" ("Billboard," Dec. 25, 1982). The band also asked for $5 million in punitive and at least $10 million in exemplary damages. A jury would award the band just $520,000 in U.S. District Court on Dec. 13, 1982.

5 - "A World Without Heroes" is released as a single in the UK in two versions: 7,500 copies of a picture sleeve and 10,000 copies of a 7-inch picture disc.

6 - "The Elder" charts at No. 112 on the Billboard 200. "A World Without Heroes" charts at No. 62 on Cashbox. Sales figures for the album in Australia and Japan are reported internally at 47,000 and 46,000 copies, respectively.

10 - Plans for an "Elder" tour are again discussed. Expanded to 70 dates, starting July 1, with four weeks of musical and production rehearsals, the costs are scaled back, though a $2,000 per week for "lead guitarist" is one budgeted line-item.

13 - "The Elder" charts at No. 149 on the Billboard 200. "A World Without Heroes" charts at No. 69 on Cashbox.

20 - "The Elder" album drops off the Billboard 200 after eleven weeks. "A World Without Heroes" charts at No. 92 on Cashbox.

25 - Paul flies to Hanover, New Hampshire, from Teterboro, planning to return two days later. Hanover was where plastic surgeon Dr. Frederic Rueckert was based. He'd perform work on Paul's ear.

27 - The "A World Without Heroes" single drops off the Cashbox chart after nine weeks.

March

2 - KISS are offered a song to perform in "The Pirate Movie" movie (which stars Christopher Atkins and Kristy McNichol) soundtrack. The band are already working with producer Michael James Jackson at The Record Plant in

Los Angeles and he is provided a copy of the prospective song. PolyGram had taken "operational and managerial" control of 20th Century Fox Records earlier in 1982 and became owner of the label's catalog later in the year. It is likely that the collaboration was sought as part of the integration of the businesses.

24 - Meeting scheduled with Mark Ravitz to discuss the design of the stage for the proposed "Elder" tour. It's not clear whether this meeting took place.

26 - Paul Stanley and Gene Simmons attend Diana Ross' 38th birthday party in Beverly Hills, Calif. Paul is photographed with Adam Mitchell, with whom he would co-write songs for "Killers" and "Creatures of The Night."

27 - WCBS-TV New York premieres the "Flo & Eddie" television show with an episode that features Gene Simmons and Paul Stanley at 1 a.m. A clip from the "A World Without Heroes" music video is also aired.

27 – 28 - The "A World Without Heroes" video shown during the national Easter Seals Telethon.

April

3 - Peter Criss reported in "Billboard" as completing his third solo album with producer Vini Poncia at Conway Recording Studios. The album includes "Feel Like Heaven," a song written by Gene Simmons before the transformation of the 1981 recording sessions into "The Elder."

12 - A CARAS music industry conference with Bob Ezrin and author Alvin Toffler, scheduled to take place prior to the 1982 Juno awards at Harbour Castle Hotel in Toronto, was cancelled due to lack of advance registrations.

22 - Peter's "Let Me Rock You" album mastered at Soundmixers Studio in New York City by Bob Schaper.

24 - Appearance of an Aucoin Management ad in "Village Voice" prompts "Billboard Magazine" to raise the question on whether Ace Frehley is leaving the band...

X - KISS fire Aucoin Management.

May

1 - George Sewitt marries Linda Ferguson. A reception at J.P's on 1st Avenue follows. George and Linda would later manage a solo Ace Frehley.

8 - Neil Bogart dies at Cedars-Sinai Medical Center in Los Angeles.

11- Memorial held for Neil Bogart at Hillside Chapel in Los Angeles. Neil Diamond, Donna Summer, Gladys Knight, and many others sing the spiritual ballad "Gonna Keep His Eye on Us." Nearly 1,000 attend the service, including the then California Governor Jerry Brown.

19 - Italian compilation album "Tutto San Remo '82" (EMI 3C-1647808081) charts at No. 3 in Italy, selling more than 200,000 copies. The album, commemorating that year's festival, includes KISS on the cover and the track "I" (side 4, track 1).

June

29 - David Roberts' "All Dressed Up" (Elektra E1-60127) album is released. While working with KISS during 1981, Bob Ezrin had heard the material Roberts was recording and passed a tape to Gene Simmons. Gene, in turn, passed the tape onto Diana Ross who recorded one of the songs, "Anywhere You Run To," on her "Silk Electric" album released later that year.

July

X - The band place ads in national press seeking lead guitarist: "American Supergroup looking for heavy metal lead guitarist. Next major U.S. arena tour to begin this summer. Must be outstanding onstage performer, tall (6 ft. range), long hair, and must sing and write. Professionals only to respond."

AMERICAN
SUPERGROUP
looking for heavy metal
lead guitarist. Next major
U.S. arena tour to begin this summer.
Must be outstanding on-stage performer,
tall (6 ft. range), long hair, and must
sing and write. Professionals only to respond.
Please send tape, photo, and resume to:

Supergroup
321 S. Beverly Dr., Suite B
Beverly Hills, CA 90212

The Oath Interview Series

"The Oath" interview series reveals the complicated story of "Music from The Elder" through the lens of recollections of individuals who were involved with the project. Through exclusive interviews with those who participated in various creative capacities on "Music from The Elder," including some who have not shared their story before, and additional conversations with other personalities, you'll gain unique insight and perspective into arguably the most fascinating period in KISStory.

Marty Cohen

Early bandmate of Gene Simmons recalls a possible early influence on KISS' decision to challenge their critics

There are few people who can say that they played with both Gene Simmons and Paul Stanley prior to KISS. Steve Coronel is one. Marty Cohen is the other. In this exclusive interview excerpt, Cohen was kind enough to discuss his history with Gene and Paul and correct a few things that have appeared on the KissFAQ website over the years. One thing of note that came to light was an "Elder" connection of sorts, which provides a basis for the band being receptive to a concept album and musical challenge in 1981.

Let's talk about your and Gene's disagreement.
Marty Cohen: That was also, back in the old days, [and] part of my problem with playing with Gene and Stan. I felt a little bit different and isolated from them with my level of musicianship. I still do. When I was at that club that night [late in 1980], with Gene and Stan, and we were at Copperfields. Afterwards, [Gene] was supposed to drive me home and I accidentally insulted him, and he didn't drive me home anymore. He dropped me off at Penn Station to take the train. Gene can be very very condescending, especially to musicians that were not touring on a world level and they were people who'd played with him and he says to me, "You gotta shake your ass up there. You gotta do the stuff you used to do. Why aren't you doing it like me?"

I just said, "Gene, look there's a big difference between us. You're like the circus act of music and I'm the musician end. And that's the way it is." I said, "I don't look at music as that performance end. You're great at what you do and it's you, but it's not me." And he was really insulted by that because I was in a way saying, "You're not a musician, you're just a circus performer." He's proven himself time and time again, so whatever he is, he is.

No one's going to deny that the gimmick took them places that the music didn't or wouldn't.
I think Gene was always frustrated on a level. That's why he came out with the album "The Elder." This is not something I've talked to Gene about, but an outside/kind of inside perspective. I felt he was always looking to do

something bigger and grander, involving an orchestra — something that the Beatles used to incorporate into their music with real production. You could tell the difference from the other stuff they did. But that was Gene's influence totally.

So, could it be your fault that after Copperfields he felt insulted and decided to record something musically valid, resulting in them unleashing "The Elder" on the world? (Laughs)
I don't think I could interpret that way. You're welcome to interpret it that way. I don't really think that anything I would have done would have affected Gene Simmons in any particular way except for at that moment, since we were old friends and all musicians together and we did play together, and he knew who I was. You know, he also interpreted me as an Ace Frehley kind of guy. Ace was more of an alcohol/drunk kind of guy. Gene was as straight as an arrow. He didn't understand what people do when they get high, he just didn't understand it. And Stan was really the same way...

Dennis Woloch

Longtime KISS art director details the creative process for the unusual album artwork for "Music from The Elder"

Dennis, the Beatles have "The White Album"; Metallica have "The Black Album"; and with KISS' "Music from The Elder" we have "The Brown Album."
Dennis Woloch: Is that what we're calling it? (Laughs)

(Laughs) So, it's 1981 and KISS are finishing up "Music from The Elder." As art director, when did you first become aware of this particular project?
I don't remember. They were there all the time in the office. When they weren't touring, they were basically in our office. [Bill] Aucoin shared space with my boss, Howard Marks. We were the advertising agency. Of course, I was doing their albums at that point, and all their advertising, and all of their marketing — everything you can name, we did it for them. In '81 Aucoin was still sharing space with us.

The Madison Avenue building?
It was 655 Madison, yep. That's been taken over now by Donna Karan or somebody, DKNY. The front entrance that used to be on Madison is now closed off and it's a store front. And you have to enter that address on 60th Street now, but it's a smaller entrance. The building looks different now. I don't know what happened to our floor.

I think Aucoin was still with us at that point. So, the band was always up there, walking around. When new projects came along, I heard about them right away. They would say, "Dennis, we're going to be doing this and start thinking about it." Exactly when I heard about it, I don't know. But I was in on the stuff right away.

When did you learn that this particular album was a "concept album"? Did the band or Bill pull you aside and give you the lowdown?
Yeah, it was explained to me, probably by Bill, that it was not going to be the usual KISS album. You know, it had all these stories and mysteries, and sorcerers and wizards and it was that sort of deal. And I said, "Fine." Other

bands had done that too. I figured it was time for KISS and sure enough they were doing it.

Once you learned about the album's details, what was the process for developing the creative direction for "The Elder" album art?
Well, I got as much information of what the album was about as I could stand. A lot of it seemed to me to be (pauses) ... you know, it was ground that was gone over before by others. I mean to me, it would be like somebody coming out and saying, "I'm thinking of writing a book series or a movie about a little boy and a sorcerer that becomes his mentor." And I say, "Well, wait a minute. Didn't we just see that some place?" That's kind of how "The Elder" felt to me, even though it was '81. They weren't breaking any new ground. Maybe in their minds this was all very [new] ... if you want to make something sound important, you shroud it in mystery, even though it isn't important. That's kind of how "The Elder" felt to me.

I know some fans would agree with you. But there is a group of fans who absolutely love the album.
Yeah, I mean, this is before I heard a note of music or anything else. When the concept was being explained to me, I'm thinking, it's like your eyes roll back in your head and you say, "Oh crap." Not because KISS is not doing KISS music, I couldn't care less. Let them stretch their creative wings but could you be a little bit more ... unique. It just sounded like old stuff to me when I first heard about it. I got into it after a while.

So how did you actually start in terms of a concept?
I guess I looked at some of the titles. I didn't hear any of the music. I had no idea ... they just kind of tried to explain [it]. You know that paragraph ... "In the beginning, The Elder ..."

The text in the gatefold.
Yes, that thing. I may have had some of that verbiage. I'm not sure. But I guess I had some rough outline of what it was about and the feeling I was supposed to be evoking, a little bit of the story: the young boy, he goes to where "The Elder" resides and all of that stuff.

Early on, I got the image of a little boy in front of a big dungeon-type door, or a castle door. And I looked through some of my illustrator's annuals, samples of illustrator's work and photographers work and stuff like that — just trying to get something going in my mind. I saw a picture of a little boy, about the right age — 10, 11, 12 — and he had his back to the viewer, but he turned around like if you said (whispers), "Hey, kid." And he turned around looking over his shoulder, like a little cautiously. I don't even know what the background was; I don't know where the kid was standing or what situation he was in or anything. But the kid was the perfect age. He was a perfect-looking little boy. I loved the expression that the illustrator had on his face.

I said, "I'm going to use this image. I'm just going to rip it off for the layout." Not that we would use it for the final or anything, you can't do that. [It was] just for my layout, you know it saved me four hours of sitting there trying to draw a little boy when I could just do this. I did that, I cut him out and I guess I got a dungeon door someplace and I put him in front of this scary wooden door, like he was just standing there just about to go in. But then he turned around, it's like he was thinking, "Should I be doing this? I'm in a dangerous situation. This is spooky." It looked great; it had a nice mood. And I showed that to the guys. I think that was the only layout I did, and I don't remember what they said really and I don't want to invent things. Apparently, they shot that down. I guess they just said, "Maybe just a hand and a knocker," somebody must have suggested that to me.

(Inspiration for the cover? From the opening sequence of the 1932 movie "The Most Dangerous Game")

Who would have suggested that, Gene, Paul or Bill?
Gene and Paul were the guys who mostly had input on that stuff. And of course, at that time, the other two guys were kind of on the outs anyway, weren't they?

Eric Carr was new at that point. And Ace was nearing the end of his first tenure in the band.
Eric didn't have any ... he had no power. He was just a hired drummer really.

The "boy" treatment, is the rough layout lying around somewhere?
No, all that crap is gone. It's not gone; it's probably sitting there somewhere.

Gene probably has it?
Yeah, probably. They sued my boss in 1990 and that's when they parted ways. I guess they accused him of ripping them off or something like that. They had a big lawsuit [and] at the end of the lawsuit, we just packed up all the KISS stuff that was ever done for KISS. And it was taken away. Every last sketch and doodle...

So, you don't have anything?
I don't have any of the original layouts and stuff like that. No. I have nothing. I got a couple of posters here and there, laying around, but that's it.

Outside of the initial layout and what became the final art, was there another treatment considered?
I think that the only layout I did was the little boy thing. And it's not that they didn't like it, but I think possibly they just didn't want any other human beings on the album cover. If it wasn't going to be them, then it shouldn't be anybody. I kind of get that. Somebody said, "OK, I know. Let's have a hand reaching for a knocker so it's not an identifiable person but you can see it's a little boy ..." They liked that concept, the hand reaching for the knocker.

Where did you get the door?
I had it made by a place called Manhattan Prop Works, I think.

Was it a full-scale door?
No, it was about half of a door. Full scale, but it was only about a half.

[Manhattan Prop Works] was on Great Jones Street, downtown. I don't think it's there anymore. The guy's name was Bill Finneran. I don't know how I remember that. I walked around Manhattan looking at churches because I figured old churches would have the closest kind of a door that I was looking for. Don't forget: no computers, no Google, no Internet, no nothing.

Indeed.
We had to do everything, you know, the old-fashioned way. I guess I could have gone to the library and looked up pictures. And that would have been one of the steps I would have taken if I was coming up dry. But I said, "Hey, this is a good opportunity to roam around the city and look at church doors." So, I did. I found one that I liked. It was actually not too far from where I lived. [Editor's Note: Woloch is referring to Park Avenue United Methodist Church on East 86th Street.]

I used it as a model. I took pictures, I took the Polaroid camera with me or maybe the Nikon and I shot pictures of the door. And I gave them to Bill Finneran at Manhattan Prop Works, and he built it and did a beautiful job. And he made hinges too. The hinges weren't any good though. They didn't look dungeon-y or castle-y enough. They were a little too small. I mean, they were old-looking, and they were well done but they didn't have the right flavor. We sent those back and he finally did that great big hinge that is going across, which is perfect.

You can see it on the back cover. It looks great.
Yeah. Also, the door was looking a bit too new and it was the wrong color. So, I sent it back and he changed the color and he beat the door up a little bit.

I think I've read you using the term "distressed."
Distressed is the word, right. I remember I said, "Bill, can you distress the door?" I think I then made a joke about being distressed ... (Laughs) Prop makers are always distressing things.

What about the circular knocker that has the rose on it? That must have been a specific request since it ties in to one of the song titles.
Yeah, "Under the Rose." We had two knockers made. The first knocker was no good. I think [it was made by] Bernard Vidal, the photographer who shot "Creatures of The Night" and he also shot a poster, "The Loudest Band In The World" — we shot that the same day.

What a great poster. One of my favorites.
Yeah, with the moon back there. Yeah, it's cool. We shot that the same day, about 40 feet away from the "Creatures" cover shot. Diana Ross was there that day. I still do work for her. After all these years, she still calls me to do work for her.

That's really cool.
Yeah it is.

Bernard also shot like a fantasy poster [of] the four guys. The poster was divided into four photos; it was like Ace standing at the controls of a spaceship or something. Peter was like in a jungle with a girl and like green leaves. Paul had pretty women hands all over him with big red fingernails, some roses. And Gene had the volcano. I have a picture of me and Gene with the volcano. That's a good picture. That's when the fire department came — that's another story.

(Laughs) Those are great images.
Bernard [Vidal] had done some stuff for KISS. There was one with Gene and a gargoyle standing on a ledge, with his tongue sticking out. [There was] like a big cement sculpture thing that you would find on the side of a cathedral or something. He knew some prop makers, for some reason, I don't know how it happened, but he said, "Oh, I'll get a knocker made for you." I said, "OK. Fine." And he had a knocker made and it was terrible. It was a piece of shit. It was like somebody took a big fat rubber hose and they bent it to a circle and then they took like a plastic flower that you would find at a five-and-dime store and stuck it on. And they sprayed it gold.

Yikes.
It looked tacky. It looked really bad. And Paul got one look at that and he said, "Noooope." I said, "Yeah, I know. It's not too good. So, let's try again." I guess we went down to the guy who made the door because he had done such a good job on the hinges and the door. And he built one. I guess we looked at some books and what have you. My only thing to him was that it had to look authentic and it had to have a rose on it because we wanted to be "under the rose," *sub rosa*.

How about the gatefold? Opening it up, we see a dark room with a long table, some ornate chairs and a candle.

There is?! I spent a couple of days roaming around the city again and I knew one place off the top of my head, it was called Newel Art Galleries. They are still there. They are on 55th Street, off of York, possibly 53rd. It's called Newel Art Galleries — [they have] basically antiques and stuff like that. I think that's where I got the big oak table, but I couldn't find anything else in there unless I got the chairs there too. I don't remember... I know I got the little candle holder thing in some other joint. Some other place on the West Side. I was just in the phone book, the Yellow Pages, calling places all day long. "I'm looking for an old, old candle holder, something that looks like a candle at a castle." And you know, they'd say yes or no or whatever. And I would have to go down there and look at it and it would be no good and I'd have to go someplace else. A lot of leg work...

Between the church door, a prop company, chairs, tables and candles, it sure sounds like a lot of legwork.
That's the way things went back then. There was no other way to do it really. And I couldn't trust anyone else to go shopping for me because it was too important that the stuff looked right. I may have gotten the chairs and table at Newel. But something tells me I had to go to three places to get those things. I just don't remember where the chairs came from. But it was just me renting this stuff. It all had to go back.

In the center of the gatefold, there's a faint orange light — a "Dark Light," if you will — that's looming in the background. How was that achieved?
We lit it that way. There was sort of a brown, no-seam paper all around. And there was a light back there with an orange gel on the light, or maybe just a white light and we made it look orange. Probably put an orange gel on it to keep it nice and warm. I remember describing it to David Spindel, who took the picture. David had done a lot of work for me over the years for all other kind of clients. And I knew he could pull that off. He was good at that sort of thing, so I went to him.

You were present at "The Elder" shoot?
Oh yeah. I was there for the door, there for the inside, there for everything.

There's an outtake of the door session where you can see Paul and he has a funny look on his face.
Yeah, David took those. I do remember.

What happened was we shot that with somebody else's hand. I don't remember who, a model? I don't know ... I can't remember whose hand it was originally. Anyway, Paul didn't like it. He says, "My hands are nice." I said, "Yeah, OK."

So nice that it's airbrushed?
Oh yeah, absolutely. So, I said, "Yeah, OK Paul. Meet me at the photography studio." Or we went together, I can't remember. And we shot it and then we did the other stuff on a different day. The only thing I retouched on that interior thing — I think I had to add a little background in because we didn't have enough to fill it. But the flame on the candle is retouched. You can see that. But I wanted it to meet exactly that design on the chair. I wanted that symmetry.

Hard to imagine that all of this was done without the aid of a computer.
I know. Yeah, well some stuff was tougher than others. You can imagine, when I did "Creatures of The Night," I was doing sketches by hand of the band in a jungle, the band on a hilltop, all kinds of different things. Every time they'd say, "Gee, I don't like that. Can you make it more blue or whatever?" Then you'd have to go sit down and re-draw it again, even if they wanted just the lettering to be a different cover. You had to sit there with your T-square [ruler], your triangle, your drawing table and your Magic Markers and all the rest of that crap and you had to do it.

Whereas today you would do that with the click of the mouse in Photoshop.
One click. That's it. And then you're done. That's right. Back then you were inhaling fumes.

There's no photo of the band at all within the album's packaging, which is certainly an anomaly. Was there a discussion about a photo of the band being featured in the final art?
I don't recall. But if you look at it backwards, the fact that they're not there anywhere definitely was done on purpose, by design. It was probably talked about very briefly. It was kind of a taken for granted thing that they wouldn't be [featured] because it's the soundtrack to a movie. You know, they're not in the movie so I think they wanted to keep it ambiguous so that it wasn't, you know, these guys dressed up in their funny costumes. It was the soundtrack to the movie about a kid being mentored by Elders. They've been here since the beginning of time, blah, blah, blah.

There are some photo shoots from the time featuring the band in their "Elder" costumes. You would have been present at these?
I don't know. What were they?

There was a session with a laser in the background.
Yeah, Barry Levine [shot those]. We were just shooting pictures for publicity really. Just to have pictures because you have to have pictures. People ask for pictures all the time. And you have to keep them updated so you try to shoot pictures as often as possible. So yeah, I remember that day.

What about the other materials used in conjunction with "The Elder"? There is the ad that has the headline "The New KISS Album" and there is a light coming out of the gatefold.
Yes, like the door is opening and the light is coming out.

How did you achieve that effect?
I don't remember. It wasn't done by retouch. We probably literally put a light in there somehow. That's the way we did stuff.

I like that ad.
Yeah, it worked out. David Spindel shot that.

What about the clear album sleeve? It has the album's credits ...
And you can hardly read them, right?

Against the vinyl, it is difficult.
Yeah, that was a failure, I think. You know, somebody had that wacky idea ... I know that was not something I thought of. Somebody probably suggested it to me. I don't know, it just didn't work.

Overall, are you pleased with the album art?
(Pauses) You know, half and half. I look at it now and I really probably would change things. The back cover, I think I'd do a little different. The photo I would leave alone but the type and stuff like that, I think I'd try to do something else with that somehow. And the logo. The front cover, I have to cut myself a little slack, because we didn't have computers. To achieve that glowing type effect, that was not something that was easy to do. Now, [with] Photoshop you just do it. But back then, that was hard to do. I don't even remember how the hell I did it.

Pat yourself on the back, Dennis.
(Laughs) Yeah. I don't remember how the heck we did that. It was hard.

So, who ended up taking possession of "The Elder" door?
They probably took it when they took everything else, after they sued my boss. Not before though because it was laying around the office. It was falling apart after a while too, kind of falling apart a little bit.

Paul and Gene have distanced themselves from this album over the years. But obviously, at the time, they seemed to be pretty positive about the project.
Well, they have to be. I mean, even if they're not. What are you going to say? "We made an album. I think it sucks. Don't buy it."

In Chris Lendt's "KISS and Sell" book there is a great depiction of the album listening party for label staff and other members of the camp. Were you there?
I may have been. I went to a lot of them. I could have been drunk...

(Laughs)
I was drunk a lot back then ... you know, trying to ease the pain of working with these guys. I don't remember [that particular] listening party, but I went to a lot of them. Hey, I went to the listening party for "Saturday Night Fever." Can you believe that? That was the best-selling album of all time or something.

Where was that?
The guy brought it up to our office and played it in our office and he played it in our conference room. It was unbelievable. (Sings) "Staying alive, staying alive." I had no idea what I was listening to. I knew it was the Bee Gees — I know their sound, but ...

After the listening party, Chris Lendt recalls an exchange with Howard Marks in which Marks described the whole "Elder" project as "asinine." And Lendt says Marks requested that his ad agency not appear in the album's credits. Do you recall this?
I don't remember that, no I don't. Well, Howard was one who I think would say, "If it ain't broke, don't fix it. Why are you screwing around with this wacky stuff? Make another KISS album."

I think that's exactly where he was coming from. According to Lendt's book, Marks said, "This album doesn't sound anything like KISS, and no one is going to buy a KISS album that doesn't sound like KISS."
Yeah, he was right actually. (Laughs)

I think he was right. I mean, it was a vanity project, you know. You know, Bruce Springsteen is doing Bruce songs. And all of the sudden, [what if] he does a whole album of, I don't know, Woody Guthrie or something? Alright, if that's what you want to do. But most of your fans don't give a crap so ...

Dennis, you oversaw so many iconic KISS albums. Where does "The Elder" rank?
I don't know, let me see. Let's do a quick rundown. The first three I didn't do anything with, those were done by the record company even though, the first album, I was there for that shoot and I did get somebody to help them with their makeup because their makeup was very bad.

Peter's makeup is very different on that one.
Yeah, well that was ... it's not better. But we gave him a silver nose, which he kept. Anyway, I was at that first one and I did help with their makeup. I had nothing to do with number two and nothing to do with number three. And then, of course, "Alive!" was the first one I did from scratch and I did at least 18 in a row after that. I never missed one. They just kept giving them to me to do so ...

What about "Double Platinum"? That's always been a striking presentation to me, with the mylar.
In my opinion, Howard Marks wanted to do mylar because it was the most reflective material but all the printers that we were talking to, to produce this thing (especially one guy) kept saying, "Mylar is plastic and it has a memory. When you emboss in it, that embossing is going to shrink and shrink and shrink because the material wants to go back to its original state." It doesn't want to hold the emboss, it wants to lose the emboss. We did a lot of samples on silver paper and silver cardboard and stuff, which I thought looked beautiful and better really. But Howard Marks, he was my boss for 22 years. I had arguments with him constantly about matters of taste and design. And as far as I'm concerned, he didn't have a lot of taste when it came to graphics and art direction. But he was the boss. I had to beat my head against the wall sometimes, to convince him, and I was always

doing double work. I had to do it his way and my way, just to show him. And if it wasn't for him, I wouldn't have to be doing double work all the time.

So, he won with the mylar, and yeah it's cool, because it's all shiny and everything. But it sure as hell didn't hold the emboss very well. When it was first embossed, it was really nice and high. After two weeks, it shrunk down ...

It'd be interesting to see your treatment.
Yeah, they were nice. Really high relief, really good. Just not as reflective. I love the solo albums, if you want to talk about artistic achievement.

Absolutely, they're iconic.
They're iconic. I think the solo albums are great. I think the best albums are, in no particular order, well I love "Alive!" because it was my first one. And it has the notes inside and a couple of little cute things.

It's such a great package.
Yeah, it's a nice package. But I think "Destroyer," "Rock and Roll Over" and "Love Gun" — those three right in a row — are really strong. Real strong. And I like all three of them. "Double Platinum," it is what it is. It's cool because of the material, I guess. After that, I don't know if it has much going for it. And then, I think "Creatures of The Night" is a good cover. And I think that's about it, right there. I think the other ones ... they're OK. A lot of people hate "Asylum," I don't hate it. I was trying to do something that Paul wanted me to do.

That was based on a Motels [album] cover?
Yeah, that's right. You can look it up, you'll see the high-contrast face. You know, black-and-white kind of face with some paint splattered on it. That's the one he liked.

What do you remember about the "Lick It Up" cover? That's just a photograph with a white background.
Yeah, that's one of the few things I wasn't there for the photo. And they kind of just went and did it.

How do you view the state of album art and design creativity in the digital age?

I'm no expert to comment. I can't even think of any current CD designs that are out there now. I wouldn't even know where to look. Who do you look at? Who is popular now? The music today leaves me cold ... totally cold. What'd you think about "Sonic Boom"?

There are a few songs that I like. The album design I didn't particularly like.
Yeah, that's Michael Doret, who did "Rock and Roll Over." But this is a case, see these guys have had no contact with me since they fired Howard Marks. And frankly I don't know why.

That's a natural question.
I don't know, because they're assholes, maybe. Could be. (Laughs)

You know, I think in their mind ... and they were all friendly with me. I had no problems with any of these guys. I mean, privately I had a couple of problems with Gene. I wanted to beat him up but thank God I didn't. But he doesn't know how close he came ... at least twice. (Laughs)

They fired my boss; I guess they wanted nothing to do with anything from that era or that office. If you notice, all their interviews, and their KISStory, and all the crap they put out about themselves, they don't mention the agency. They don't mention Howard Marks or Dennis Woloch. They don't. And I'm someone who worked slavishly hard for almost 15 years, you know because half the time there was a KISS project on my drawing board.

The other half the time, I was trying to do my other work, which was the advertising agency work. So, they got the best of me and I tried really hard for those guys. I think I did very well under the circumstances but they're like [trying to] rewrite history. It's like, "Oh, that never happened. What are you talking about?" Where do you think you got all that creativity and all that marketing stuff, that didn't come out of their heads. That came out of the agency's head. It came out of the agency. When did they take off? When "Alive!" came out. Who did "Alive!"? The agency, it was the first one we did. It's not a coincidence.

With some interviews that Gene and Paul give nowadays, they really don't mince words when talking about Ace and Peter. That is difficult for some fans to take.
Yeah, yeah. I mean I think Peter and Ace were really impossible at times. They were part of the original thing and nothing can change that, and they

always feel that they have to put them down somehow. I just think they've just ignored us in their history. Which I guess they have every right to do, but they can't misrepresent because if they do that then they're just being wrong. But they should give credit where credit is due, I think. But they don't.

My take has always been that KISS have gone a long way, but they had a lot of help along the way. A lot of help.
They most certainly did. They had a lot of help from Bill Aucoin, who was a creative guy. They dumped him after a while, and us. But we were the guys that got them there. We really were.

Neil Bogart and Casablanca, too.
That's right. Neil really believed in them. He was very excited, and he did his thing. I liked Neil, I didn't know him well, but I knew him a little bit. I went out to his house in California one time, he invited us. He was a nice guy.

Howard Marks passed away in 1990, correct?
1990. Yes. That's when he died. The office closed very shortly after that because we just had no business at that time. He was sick for a couple of years, so he wasn't around a lot. Roseanne Shelnutt, that was his girlfriend, and the other vice president of the agency and me, who was the creative director and vice president — we tried to get business and tried to hold it together. But basically, it was just a money pit, paying very expensive rent there on Madison Avenue. And you know, we had no clients, so we just had to close it up. So, we did [close] after he died. That was sad man, it was the end of an era.

Bill Finneran

The first-ever conversation with the man who constructed "The Elder" door

Greetings, Bill. First, it's interesting that we're having this conversation because I don't believe KISS fans know who actually built "The Elder" door. So, this is a bit of an exclusive detail that we're uncovering here some 30-plus years later! Back in 1981, you were working at the Manhattan Model Shop. What did the company specialize in?

Bill Finneran: Well, we've made props for major television commercials and all kinds of print advertising for more years than I would care to reveal. And you know, we don't get credit for that any more than the guys who work on making the cathedrals in medieval Europe. But we did ["The Elder" door]. I remember doing it. I was a hero with my children for a short period of time after having done that.

The company is still in business?

Oh yeah, absolutely, I can tell you we are not trying as hard as we were back in 1981. But we're working on a job this week. We started business in 1974 and we're still going. It's a greatly changed environment. ["The Elder"] album cover was made in what I would consider to be the sort of classic period of model making. It was before any kind of digital manipulation of images was possible. If you wanted to do a tabletop in those days, you pretty much had to deal with our company or one like it, whether you liked it or not. (Laughs)

Dennis Woloch, who was the art director for "Music from The Elder," mentioned he got in touch with you to work on the project. Do you remember anything about your initial conversation?

Yeah, he was a big tall guy. We talked on the phone first and then he came down to the studio and we talked about what he wanted to do. From our point of view, [the job] was very straightforward, in terms of the technical aspects of it. It was like a lot of props we had made. We were not technically involved in doing album covers. It was rare that anyone wanted to make a prop for an album cover. You know, they were almost always location shots with talent. It was an unusual thing, but we were quite interested in doing it. The techniques we used we had used in other similar projects. The nice thing about our business for all the hundreds of years we've been doing it is it's rare that the same thing comes up twice. The projects are always quite unique. They share certain technical categories with other similar projects but they're all very different. And this one was the same, it was very different. We never did anything like it again. I don't think we ever did another album cover, to be honest with you. I can't think of one.

In terms of direction for the door, Dennis mentioned that he went around and took pictures of church doors. Do you recall him showing you sample photos?
Yes. He had some samples that he was interested in duplicating and we interpreted that. I would say generally what we do with a prop like that is to bump it up a bit. In other words, make it a little more intense than it actually is in reality. If you were to go out and photograph a real door, it would be a little bit less aggressive. I don't want to disappoint anybody, but the hinges and all those metal parts are made out of Plexiglas.

No kidding?
Yes, it's easy to carve. The hammered little divots [were] made with a high-speed die grinder. It's been such a long time; I don't remember exactly where we got the patterns for those. It might have just come out of my head.

You wouldn't know it's Plexiglas from looking at it. They look real.
That's just sort of true of everything we do. It's all made out of materials that are routinely and [is] utterly fake.

But the actual door is wood, correct?
Yes, it's wood. It was white pine wood. It's soft. Typically, a door like that would be made out of a hard wood, like oak or ash. But this was easier for us to manipulate. And we're not looking for durability; we're just looking for "a look."

The studs on the door, how would those have been beaten in?
Those are actual little nails that have special heads that we made. All those heads, we made a mold and cast the heads. We made one pattern and then made a little rubber mold and cast all those heads. Actually, I think we made about five or six different ones so that they wouldn't all come out looking exactly the same. And then we made them in gangs of five or six and drilled little holes into the door and inserted the nails and just stuck them in there.

In looking closely at the pattern closely, they seem to be a bit crooked, likely on purpose?
Yeah, right. The art director had brought a certain amount of scrap as reference for us. But we looked at a lot of stuff from our history. Both my partner and I are schooled in visual arts — I was a professor of arts for quite a while — so we had a lot of books that showed famous cathedrals in Europe ... places like that that have those kinds of big heavy doors. Now the other thing, the knocker as I recall, I think that wasn't part of the original job.

That's right. Dennis mentioned that they had attempted to make the knocker independently. But it didn't end up working out, so they went back and asked you to do it. Would the knocker be made of Plexiglas also?
No, it's actually mostly cast out of automotive body filler, a polyester resin material. We use that quite commonly; you know the stuff you fix a car with. But we have our own little way of juicing it up, and we've been making stuff out of that for years. So, you can build with it directly, which a lot of that knocker was built directly onto an armature. We just added an armature into the rough shape and then sculpted the surface of it with a polyester resin. The same way we made up the flower, we just sculpted it ... and sanded it with traditional sculptural tools. That's how we made that.

How long would it have taken to sculpt the rose?
Probably took me a day. A full day. And then the surface is painted with an automotive lacquer.

It looks like a bronze color.
Yeah, in that bronzy color. I don't recall the discussion exactly. I recall objects much better ... [but] let me say, first of all, that during that period we were doing typically three jobs at a time every week, and pretty much all through the year. It's not easy to keep them all sorted out. (Laughs) It's possible that the techniques, not so much the images, but the techniques overlap a great deal. You know, we used the same technique to do an awful lot of different things. So that process was quite common to any number of things we might have made. And it's directly built over an armature. And I believe that the armature we used was metal window-screened and [the knocker was] bent into the appropriate shape. That's how I believe we did it.

Can you approximate the dimensions on the door? Was this a full-scale door?

It was pretty big. It wasn't a whole door; obviously it was a section of a door. I think it was 4 feet across, 4 feet square. It wasn't bigger than that. It was right around 4 feet square.

From start to finish, how long did it take to finish the entire door?
I think we probably worked on it for a little more than a week. But the thing is, like almost every project, there's a certain amount of work and there's a certain amount of interaction, and then revisions. I started out in life as a fine artist, I made paintings and sculptures. That's totally driven by your original intent and it was hard for me at first when I went into business with my partner, who actually happens to be my wife. She was doing it a number of years before I was. It was hard for me to come to understand that this is a very collaborative way of making art. It's not typical of the way we perceive artists to work, you know individually and sort of controlling every aspect of it. Every job that we do, and this job included, there's a lot of back and forth between the art director and between, sometimes, other personalities. In this case, I don't remember anybody else being involved except the art director. But he might have had interactions with ...

Likely the band members and the manager, Bill Aucoin.
Right, we would do something and then we'd say, "What do you think about that?" There were some changes [with the door] as we went along, and I can't honestly remember what they were. Because it's always the case. It's never ... well I won't say never ... it's almost never that a job is perfect the way it is, and everybody loves it. And particularly that's true when you're talking about a thing that's being made up. A lot of model making, a lot of the work that we've done over the years, is copying things that exist. In that day, we made a lot of work making large tubes of toothpaste, large toothbrushes [and] large pills because there was no digital retouching in film and photography and so things had to be very perfect. So, the way to do that was to make them large and then to photograph them and they'd be reduced in size, so they looked really crisp. So those things tend to be pretty straightforward. You know, an aspirin pill is an aspirin pill. But toothpaste nurdles, the little squeezed out things on the tops of toothpaste which are carved out of Plexiglas as well, are treated like little fine sculptures. And for some jobs, you just want to say, "Oh for Christ's sake, cut me some slack here, will you? It's just toothpaste!" There's a lot of interaction back and forth, and the same was true of this job. But I can't give you the details because it's just been too long ago. It seems to me it might have had something to do with the hardware, but I honestly don't recall the specifics.

That's some fascinating insight into your world, Bill. When the job was completed, do you recall being happy with the finished product?

Yeah, I thought it was good. A lot of people ask us that kind of question. I just thought it was an interesting project. That's what I thought about it. It was kind of unusual for us to do. As I said we didn't do album covers. That wasn't our thing. We're used to dealing with different kinds of clients, mostly advertising clients. And this was very different. It was more artistic. It was more focused on the artistic aspect than it was on selling product.

And I have to ask, when the project came to you and they said it was for the group KISS, were you familiar with the band?

Oh yeah, I was. I'm not going to tell you that they were my favorite band. (Laughs) I'm more into a different vein of music from that period. But you had to be impressed when they show up ... you know, they were a very famous group. We were saying, "Hey we're working on an album cover for KISS!" And my children, who are all now grown now, were pretty young at that time. They were just getting into the period when they knew all about that — my son was into rock and roll and actually played in a band for a while. So, that was a big deal [for them].

People are fascinated by our business, in the way that you wouldn't be fascinated by somebody being a really successful attorney. Because first of all it's perceived of as being fun to do, which I can tell you for the most part it's not fun. (Laughs) And it's also thought of as being creative and unusual. Working for KISS was like that. It was, "Wow, we're working for this rock and roll band that everybody in the world knows."

Bill, it's funny you use the word unusual because this album proved unusual for KISS. I'm not sure if it was explained to you, but this album was actually a concept album and quite a departure for the group. So not only was it unusual for your company, but it was unusual all around.

Yes, I understood that too, at the time. The art director explained it. We didn't have interaction with anyone else, other than the art director. But he was really into this and he worked on this kind of business quite a bit as I understood it. He was a different kind of art director for us to work with.

I know we're going back 30-plus years, but what would have been the final cost for the work on "The Elder' door?

We might be able to find that out for you, but I would have to ask my partner and that would really piss her off. (Laughs) My feeling is that this might have been in the $1,500 to $1,800 [range], something like that.

That's including all the parts and labor?
Yeah. I would think it was something like that. Around $1,800. In those days I think we were typically making about $4,000 a week, and there were overlaps. Like when we were doing [the door] there were other jobs in the studio at different stages of development. So that would be my guess.

If we did the job today, it would be like a $5,000 job, $6,000 job. You know it's funny because that would be probably cheaper than $1,800 then. The business has changed a lot. In the days when that prop was being made, nobody much cared what things cost to be honest with you. I am sure somebody cared, but at our level and for most of the people we worked with, they would just say, "How much is this bill?" And we'd just say, "It's $1,500 or it's $2,500." And they just paid it.

The work is something that an awful lot of artistically skillful people could do but there were not very many people doing it at our level, maybe four or five small companies on the East Coast like ours, and the reason is because we didn't fail. You know, there was no, "The dog ate my homework." Thursday is Thursday. When people are going to get together to make a half a million-dollar television commercial and there are over 100 people involved in the production of it, you don't want to find out that the guy who is making the pills didn't get them done. That's what we were and are still as a matter of fact: completely reliable. Artistically reliable.

You know, the phone rings and somebody says, "Can you make us a quilted rhinoceros?" And we say, "Sure." And then we look at each other and say, "How in the hell are we going to do that?" We have to be able to say, "Yes, we're going to do it. And we're going to do it by a certain date." And I guess the way you get to that is pure force of will, you know, you refuse to fail. Just by doing so many jobs, when a job like this one comes along, you say, "Oh, you know this was a lot like this. Remember how we did the metal on that other one? Yeah, we could do that." That's how we do it. It's sort of a muscle memory.

Who knows, someone may now call to order an exact replica of "The Elder" door?

Well, we'd do that. (Laughs) I don't think we'd do it for $1,800 but we'd probably do it, sure. We would do it for the equivalent of that.

After "The Elder" came out in November 1981, do you remember getting a final copy?
We saw the album cover, yeah. I'm not sure how we came to have it. Tower Records was right around the corner from us so we might have just gone there and looked at it or gotten one. In those days, any person would have hundreds of albums, I don't even know where my albums are now (laughs) or if we ever saved any of them. Most everything is on a little iPod [today].

Would you have any production photos of the door?
We wouldn't. The only kind of photos we ever took were not production photos of us working on stuff, but they would be of finished things that we suspected that we wouldn't get any record of from the people we were giving them to. For example, part of our business is making prototypes for people of various products. Now, they're not going to be used in photography but are actual prototypes for products that are going to be marketed. So, we would typically photograph those in house before they went out. But a thing like this that was clearly going to be photographed by a professional photographer, we would not waste our time trying to duplicate at an amateur level a product that we were fully expected to get a copy of when it was finished. So, the answer is absolutely no, I'm sorry to say.

Bill, did your company promote your having done "The Elder" door?
It was in our book for a long time, so the answer is yes. I think it was probably in some of our advertising. Our advertising in those days was in a vehicle called the creative black book. See, this is before all this kind of information existed online. You proved that you were a serious player — whether you were a photographer or a prop maker or whatever — by proving that you could take a two-page ad in the creative black book. And people would look at it and say, "Well, if these guys can pay this whopping amount of money for this ad, they must be OK." Instead of showing one or two very large images like most photographers would do, we had to be all things to all people so our ads were a whole bunch of images and our style of making those two-page ads has to treat it as if though it was like a bunch of tear sheets thrown out on a table, so they were all sort of scattered around. That way we could get lots and lots of images into the ad. And it also had a unique sort of casual look to it that nobody else used. And I'm

pretty sure we used the KISS album cover in one of our ads for one of the years in there. Because we saw it as a pretty big deal. It wasn't so much a big deal, you know $1,800 in those days, it was a good job, but it wasn't a bell ringer. A bell ringer would be a $5,000, $6,000, $7,000 job. This was less than that. But in the scheme of things, it was a good typical model job, in terms of the complexity and the payback. So, it was something that we felt good about and we wanted to show we had done it.

Did you work solely on this project, or did you have any assistance?
I am sure both [my wife] Kathy and I worked on it. At that time, we had two assistants, younger people who we had around. But I made most of that. I remember making it. It's not that Kathy couldn't have made it, it just happened to be a job that I worked on. I remember pretty much making every part of that. Kathy may have worked on the rose. She might have worked on the armature for the rose. She probably wouldn't have worked on putting the polyester material on it because I've been "Mr. Goo" all these years, so when it's time to work with goo, I'm usually the guy that gets called. (Laughs) But I think I pretty much did it all.

David M. Spindel

Still life photographer recounts a different kind of photo shoot featuring a door, table, chairs, and a "messenger"

David, prior to 1981, had you worked with KISS?
David Spindel: I worked with Dennis Woloch on a lot of the albums, doing photos [on] KISS "Alive!" and I can't even remember the names ... I wasn't that much into music; I was totally into photography though. I did some things for "Alive!" and a couple of the other albums. I did a lot of photography for promotional things that they would put out.

What do you recall about getting asked to work on "The Elder"? Who contacted you?
That was Dennis Woloch. He was the art director. I had been working with him for years, not just on KISS, but on other stuff for the ad agency that he worked for, which I believe was called Howard Marks.

"The Elder" album photography shoot took place in 1981 — do you recall a specific date?
Usually when I did stuff with Dennis, it was a month or two before the finished product would get done.

Where did you photograph "The Elder" door and the tables and chairs?
That was in my studio in my Manhattan. It was 18th East 17th St. on the second floor. I was there almost 30 years.

Do you recall who was at the shoot? Obviously, Dennis, Paul Stanley ...
That's it. [There was] no one else, because Paul wanted to have his hand on the door.

Did you have an assistant?
Oh, I probably did. I don't recall who it was at that point. A lot of assistants worked for me, then they felt they knew enough to go on their own and then they found out it wasn't that easy. (Laughs)

David, "The Elder" represented a complete musical departure for KISS. Do you recall the fact that this was a concept album being explained to you prior to the shoot?

Not really. Dennis just told me the props that were needed — finding the table was unbelievable. We both went to different prop houses and we found what we wanted and then I had to figure out how to get it up into my studio because it was kind of big. (Laughs)

Dennis mentioned that you found the table at Newel Art Gallery?

Newel Art Gallery, yeah. There were a couple of different places [we went to]. Encore Photo was the name of another place we got stuff from. [We went to] Newel Art Gallery because they had a lot of antiques there. They sold antiques but the art department would rent things from them.

In addition to the table, the gatefold setting has some chairs that are medieval-looking, and there's the candle.

I don't remember where we found that.

The album cover is literally a door and a hand. From a photography standpoint, were there any challenges in shooting the cover?

Well, not really. For me, I pretty much can [photograph] anything. I'm very lucky. I saw the door [and] I loved it because I knew I could light it and get a lot of texture to it. And I actually didn't realize that Paul was going to be there [so] it was kind of neat meeting him. Because at that time, most people didn't even know what any of the KISS guys looked like. When the doorbell rang, I thought maybe he was a messenger or something, because I didn't know who he was. (Laughs)

(Laughs)

Dennis said, "That's Paul Stanley." I said, "Oh, OK." (Laughs)

What type of lighting did you use for the door?

Well, I used strobes. For something like this, I kind of cross-lit it so you got that texture. [There were] little nubs that are on the door, because Dennis had the door custom-made. Some people think it was a copy of a door on St. Patrick's Cathedral. Dennis would remember where he got the idea from, and then they got a model maker in New York to make the door for them. It was like a 4x4 panel. It wasn't a whole big door.

About half of a door?
Yeah, about that, maybe a little less.

We actually spoke with "The Elder" door maker, Bill Finneran of Manhattan Model Shop.
Yes, that's it.

In "The Elder" gatefold, there is also a faint orange light in the background. Do you remember how you achieved this?
I had a strobe under the table with a color gel on it. It was actually sort of a brownish seamless, but I put an amber gel over the light to give it that kind of glow, just to give it a little more dimension because Dennis was mentioning that he wanted to use type on the top so he wanted it dark. I said, "That's not going to have any pop to it." So, I said, "Let me put in a little light behind the table and the chairs to help emphasize the design of the chairs and give a little more depth to the shot."

Even though the gatefold was a different presentation for KISS, the setting really jumps out at you when you open it. Did you shoot everything in the same day? About how long did the shoot last?
Well, the principal photography was just a couple of hours.

Pretty quick, huh?
Once I see the concept, I take the shot in my head half a dozen times before I even do it. And I figured out the way I [wanted] to light it. Since I understood the concept behind it, I wanted to have that sort of rich quality to the image and give a spiritual feeling to it.

Do you remember photographing anything else for "The Elder" album, something that was not used?
No. Dennis was pretty specific with what he wanted to do. We didn't try a bunch of different things to see which would work. I'm sure he showed the concept and sketches to the guys in the band for their approval. At least I would think so, because this was something really different.

I've seen an outtake from the session with Paul.
Yeah, with his hand over his face.

That's the one.
Yeah, he said, "No one will know who I am so I'm going to hide my face here." I still have a copy of that photograph.

That's a fun photo. The natural question is: Are there any other outtakes from "The Elder" session?
Well, I have all the shots. I have the shot of Paul with his hand in front of his face. Somewhere I have the shot of his hand on the door. I'd have to look through my files again because I keep filing stuff and then I file them under different things and then I lose them. (Laughs) I pretty much have all the stuff I ever did for them. I definitely have the transparency of the inside gatefold. I've already made some 11x14 prints that some friends of mine liked. They framed them and hung them in their homes.

Is there anything that stands out from working with Paul Stanley that day?
Nothing specific. You know, it was 30 years ago! I remember some things so specifically, and other things I have absolutely no memory of. There are certain things I can remember, and other things are a total blank. When I talk with friends, sometimes I'll bump into an art director through the Internet and he'll remind me of things that we did, and it will bring it back. I remember [Paul] was very soft-spoken, very nice. He wasn't there that long. We got the shot done and he had to take off.

And actually, I only went to one of their concerts. My son was a big KISS fan, so he convinced me to go to a concert. I couldn't hear for a week! All their concerts are incredible, I mean I love watching them on TV, but I had no concept what it was like to be at one. Now that I have 50 years of experience behind me, and I had plenty of experience even then, I'd love to go back and be able to photograph them. We sat up in the balcony somewhere. It was neat. I remember taking candid shots from up in the balcony and I had a roll of 35-millimeter shots, but when I moved to Arizona, I don't know what happened to them.

This concert was in New York?
Yeah. My son Jeffrey is somewhat of an artist. He works with autistic children but he also [paints] and he did a lot of paintings of KISS that he decorated his room with.

Do you still keep in touch with Dennis Woloch?
As a matter of fact, I've called him a couple of times. When you called me, the first thing I did was call him and he said, "Oh, I just spoke with Tim." It's a small world.

In 2010 a book came out about John Lennon, "Starting Over," by Ken Sharp. And when we were talking, it came up that I [had] worked with KISS and [done] photography for them. So, he said, "Oh yeah, I interviewed an art director named Dennis Woloch and he told me he worked with this crazy photographer on 17th St." I said, "Guess what? That was me."

(Laughs)
Dennis called me a couple of weeks ago ... and so yes, we do still keep in touch. I've known him, perhaps, the longest of any of the art directors I've worked with in my career!

David, you've photographed many luminary figures, like John Lennon, Joe DiMaggio, Willie Mays ...
Duke Snider, Eli Wallach, Anne Jackson, Marty Allen. One of my favorite friends was Chuck Connors the rifleman.

Aside from John Lennon, Liberace and KISS, are there any other musicians that you've photographed?
That's pretty much it. You know, I wasn't that too much into music. I didn't think to get more involved because I was basically known as a still life photographer.

You're now out in Arizona. How long have you been out West?
It's going on over eight years now.

Do you like it better than New York?
Totally different life. It's a lot easier. I mean (laughs), in New York I had a $5,000 a month mortgage. Here I have no mortgage. We bought the house outright ... And I switched from photographing baseball players to photographing cowboys. (Laughs)

So, what projects do you keep busy with nowadays?
I have a company coming out to see me soon. They want to use my baseball stuff and create product that we'll sell in different shopping malls. And another company contacted me; they make giant prints on canvas. Someone

told them about me. They're interested in my John Lennon and my baseball [photos] and some of my other still lifes. They make 30x40 prints or larger to hang on walls in corporations and in people's homes. I'm always trying to network and do something. In today's world it's very difficult because no matter who you contact, no one wants to speak to you directly. You have to always leave messages or send emails and hope someone will respond. Being your own agent is difficult. I called up a book publisher — I've designed six books — and they said they'd like to speak to my agent. And I said, "I'm the agent." They said, "We don't speak to an artist who is his own agent." I said, "I've been doing this for 50 years and been very successful. I've never even found an agent that was good." (Laughs)

(Laughs)

I just keep plugging along. That's what makes every day interesting. George Burns had a great line. He said he would wake up in the morning and read the obituaries. If he didn't see his name, he would shower and shave and go to work.

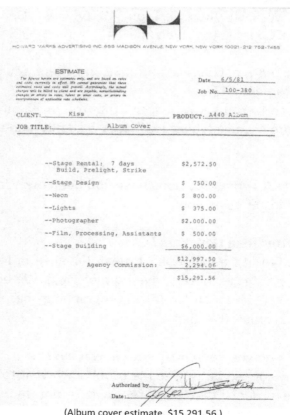

(Album cover estimate. $15,291.56.)

Waring Abbott

Renowned photographer of many iconic KISS photos recalls his "Elder"-era sessions

Waring, a majority of "Music from The Elder" period photos in "KISS: The Early Years" are from two video shoots, "I" and "A World Without Heroes." Do you recall if those were two separate shoots?
Waring Abbott: I remember going at least two days and maybe three. It must have been sometime in 1981 when the album was released, no? Both the shoots were right after each other.

Do you have an approximate date for these shoots? And do you recall them being long days?
My daybook for 1981 says Oct. 31 and Nov. 1, 12 noon until late each day. No location [is listed], but it was somewhere on the West Side between 44th and 57th St. in a large video studio. All video shoots are long, long days. Everyone did seem to be in a good mood, particularly the fans who were selected to be in what I assume was the "I" video with the weird backdrops. There are some photos of them carrying the band around in the book. The band was very good with them and it seemed as if they all knew each other. Some of them were most likely relatives of management office or road crew people.

The "I" video actually never aired so it's a bit of mystery. The backdrop has been described as "American Bandstand meets Mars." What do you recall about the backdrop?
I thought the backdrop was just very science-fiction and I had no idea what it had to do with the song, but then again, I can't honestly remember the song itself.

Did you ever see the finished video for "I"?
Never.

"A World Without Heroes" is known for the ending where Gene Simmons sheds a tear. What are your recollections from this shoot?
I recall that very well since I took a ton of photos of the management guy putting the "tear" on Gene's face. The "tear" was some sort of glycerin that

would stay in place during all the takes. Personally, that is one of my favorite songs of theirs and every now and then I take '"The Elder" out and play it all. Not more than once a year though.

"The Elder" in moderation can be a good thing. Waring, you were also present to shoot the band as they played live as a trio from Studio 54 in early 1982. What do you remember about the general atmosphere given that Ace Frehley was not present?
We were all down in the basement and I had brought a bunch of studio strobes, a backdrop and an assistant so I was thrilled that Ace was "delayed" — I used all that time to do individual shots of Eric, Paul and Gene, and some NYC cops who were hanging around in the basement as well. Personally, I was pretty surprised that Ace would be a no-show. I would have thought by that time that he would have had a "minder" to make sure he showed up. Plenty of other people I shot had some sort of PR/management person with them all the time.

The story that day was that he had been stopped by the highway patrol going the wrong way on some road in Connecticut. Don't know what the truth was. To me it was nothing short of miraculous that they could get away with doing a "live" telecast without ever showing the lead guitar. It seemed to work, and no one was throwing fits, including the fans in the audience.

This period is a strange one for the band in more ways than one, including "The Elder" costumes. As someone who photographed the band in their earlier days, what did you think of their "Elder" look?
As I said, I'm very fond of "The Elder" [musically] and as for the costumes, no problem there as well. Anything flamboyant and graphic is good for photographers, but then again pretty much everything they wore fit that description.

Do you have any "Elder"-era outtakes that were not used in "KISS: The Early Years"?
Plenty of them. I have always wanted to do a part two version of the book using all the stuff that would not fit in the first one, but Gene and Paul have no interest in it. [I] also wanted to do an e-book version of the first book, but no joy there either.

Did you take any other "Elder"-era photographs of the band?

Not that I remember.

Following "The Elder" shoots, did you ever photograph KISS again? If so, when?
Don't think I ever saw them again until the book came out. The Bravo studio photo session was probably before the Elder. I rarely if ever socialized with any of the musicians I shot.

From what I've noticed, response to "KISS: The Early Years" has been positive among fans. Were you happy with the way it turned out? And was it a pleasant experience collaborating with Gene and Paul?
Until I read an article in "The Wall Street Journal" that stated that 95 percent of all books released sold less than 5,000 copies I thought we were not doing well. Since Crown printed 100,000 copies and sold most of them — that made it a success.

We did not do a lot of "collaborating." I did layouts and sent them to Gene and Paul, they then wrote their captions and I of course wrote mine, along with the introduction. They only had a few small changes to make and they had no requests to "take this out, put that in." I was the only one to make any changes and my idea was to make it an accurate and honest visual record of what really happened, while still being graphically interesting. If it came to a choice between history or graphics, I went for the latter.

You mentioned that you rarely socialized with bands you shot. From a work perspective, did you have a favorite KISS member?
I liked Gene and Paul since they have always had long and intimate relationships with cameras. I doubt if they ever met one they did not like. And for a photographer, having subjects who like what they were doing and usually thought up their own "ideas," what could be more perfect? All I had to do was push the button and change the film. Many other musicians regarded photo sessions as roughly akin to a root canal — they loathed and despised them. Not Gene and Paul, or at least in those days. If they were not loving it, they were doing an awfully good job of pretending.

Personally, I liked Ace and Peter just as well and always wanted to shoot them whenever possible, but they were just more low-key and often not around. When we were on the road, I never seemed to be able to locate either one of the two of them, and they did not hang out at night. The exceptions would be when I shot them at the Makeup Center —the photo of

Ace reflected in his makeup box mirror — or Peter running up and down the football field in Cadillac banging those big cymbals. They were not totally introverted, just not as "out there" as Gene and Paul.

Rob Freeman

Decorated producer/engineer offers a fascinating account of KISS' pre-"Elder" sessions at Ace in the Hole Studio in early 1981, meeting Bob Ezrin and how the project ultimately relocated to Canada

How is it that you got to work on the project with KISS?
Rob Freeman: The first project I worked on for KISS was Ace's solo album for Casablanca Records, "Ace Frehley," which I recorded and mixed with producer Eddie Kramer in 1978. The album achieved a good degree of commercial success, with multi-platinum sales and a hit single, "New York Groove." It also garnered critical acclaim. But I believe it was the distinctive sonic character of the album that drew the attention of Ace's bandmates and others in the KISS organization to my work. I'm in no way meaning to understate Eddie's unique contributions. Over the ensuing couple of years, I worked on a variety of smaller projects for the KISS organization such as radio spots and demos. Also, during that time, I was fortunate to be given the opportunity to design and install a 4-track home studio and a state-of-the-art home theater system in Paul Stanley's uptown NYC condo.

Then in December 1980, someone from the KISS office rang me up and asked if I would work with the band on a new recording project. I heard it might be for a new album, and naturally I was thrilled at the prospect of working with KISS again. In early January 1981, I began recording tracks with KISS at Ace in the Hole, Ace's home studio in Wilton, Connecticut. There was no producer-for-hire present, just the band and me, as recording engineer. These were the first recording sessions to feature Eric Carr's extraordinary drumming.

What was Ace in the Hole Studio like?
Ace in the Hole was bunkered into the hillside adjacent to Ace's house. John Storyk, of the renowned Walters-Storyk Design Group, did his usual exquisite job designing and constructing the facility. Ace had genuine love and respect for the recording arts and seemed to have spared no expense when it came to the acoustic quality, technical layout, and cosmetics of his studio. Ace in the Hole may have been a private recording studio, but it was as professional and fully functional as many major commercial studios of the day.

The studio complex included a spacious control room and a large, open recording room. The control room was appointed with lots of wood, but had enough acoustic traps placed throughout to effectively reduce sonic reflections, making for more accurate recording and mixing. The studio room was also abundant with wood and featured a mirrored wall and a construction glass wall built at odd angles to each other so as to disperse standing sound waves. The acoustic characteristics of the wood, the mirror, and the glass combined effectively to give the room that sought-after "live" sonic quality. There was an acoustically deadened booth like area designed for recording drums or other instruments that might benefit from a tighter, less open sound and some large "gobos" [movable baffles] for creating smaller areas of deadened acoustics where needed.

In addition, there was a tile and mirror bathroom that was wired for recording or for use as a live reverb chamber. For the latter, sounds could be selectively fed from the control room into the bathroom, played out through a speaker [adding natural bathroom reverberation to the sound] then miked and returned to the control room. At one point I put a guitar amp in there to capture one of Ace's solos in that lively acoustic environment. We might have also recorded some of Gene and Paul's background vocals in there as I can recall the sound of their voices singing and cracking jokes from inside that bathroom.

Apparently, Ace's studio was outfitted with the latest technology of the time. Do you remember any of the gear you utilized?
Ace in the Hole had an MCI 600 series automated console, not one of my favorites, but very popular in the day, an MCI JH-16 2" 24-track tape machine with full remote, and two MCI 100A 2-track tape machines for mixdowns. An outboard equipment rack on wheels sat right next to the console and another multibank rack was installed into a large cabinet behind the engineer's seat. All the rack spaces were filled with a good assortment of signal-processing equipment-compressors, noise gates, equalizers, filters, effects generators, etc. — some of them with warm vintage tube electronics. Sitting on top of the console was a LARC remote for a Lexicon 224XL digital reverb and multi-effects unit, truly a state-of-the-art system at that time. All the acoustic spaces and electronic tools for making great recordings were there.

The mic closet at Ace in the Hole was filled with a fine selection of popular mics, among them condenser mics by Neumann and AKG and dynamic mics by Sennheiser, AKG, Beyer Dynamic, and Shure. There were also plenty of direct boxes for recording guitars, basses, or other electronic instruments directly into the recording console.

Then there were Ace's guitars and amps! During the "Ace Frehley" album sessions at Plaza Sound Studios, NYC, Ace had his extraordinary collection of guitars and amps all lined up in the studio. At Ace in the Hole, he kept only a few choice guitars and amps set up but would often duck out and return with another and another and yet another guitar or amp. Ace's collection wasn't just for show, although it was truly fabulous to behold; it provided a palate from which Ace could choose just the right combinations of touch and sound. As oddball, humorous, and lovable as Ace could be, he was dead serious about his instruments, his amps, and his studio. I felt so privileged to be the one running Ace in the Hole for him at that time.

What were the sessions like at Ace's studio?

The hour-long commutes to and from Ace's studio were a heady mix of the beautifully serene and the terribly treacherous as I zoomed up and down the pristine Merritt Parkway and through the curvy, well-moneyed hills of Wilton in icy winter weather. I often arrived at the appointed hour before any of the band members, including Ace, whose slight commute — a short walk from his living room down a flight of stairs, through his KISS memorabilia-laden playroom, and down a long, sloping gold-record-adorned hallway with skylights — gave him few excuses for tardiness. Someone in the house would buzz me in and I'd drive around back and park, hoping that Ace's fearsome-looking dogs were secure in their kennels. Once inside the studio, I'd busy myself with setups and calibrations, or playbacks of previous sessions until the band members all trickled in. Gene, Paul, and Eric would arrive in matching — in style, not color — Porsches, which made the studio parking area resemble a high-end car dealership when their cars were all lined up. I was told that Eric's Porsche was one of many band-joining gifts bestowed upon him by the others.

The sessions continued on and off throughout January and February and ran like marathons at all hours of the day and night. Since there was really nowhere else to go once you were there, we were all happily "trapped" together in the studio. When a session ran particularly late, I'd just sleep on the couch in Ace's playroom rather than risk the commute home in an overly exhausted state.

We recorded in highly energized spurts but would take long breaks during which Ace might disappear into his house for what seemed like hours, leaving the rest of us to either carry on without him or pass the time chatting or watching live KISS concert footage — over and over — on the television set installed in the wall between the control room speakers. Paul had a terrific sense of humor — as did all the guys — and during breaks, he'd sometimes record comedic bits to play for the others. On occasion he brought his acoustic guitar into the control room and played Beatles songs. That was a side of Paul I loved — and would enjoy again during the making of the "Lick It Up" album — but I suspected few of his fans got to see. Ace would return from his upstairs respites sometimes decked out in outlandish outfits but invariably with snacks or meals in tow. No matter what tensions might have been present in the studio, when Ace arrived like that, one could only smile and get on with the session.

Were all of the members of KISS present at Ace's studio?

All the band members of KISS were present at all of the "basic track" or "tracking" sessions. Basic tracks, in this case, consisted of drums, bass, and two guitars performed live by all four of them playing together in the studio. As we got more into the overdub phase — replacing and/or adding guitars, solos, vocals, percussion, etc. — the studio thinned out at times with one or more band members opting not to show up for certain sessions. As a result, some sessions were considerably more low-key than others with only a single band member and me working together in the studio.

How was the studio set up for recording basic tracks?

For the recording of basic tracks, the four band members were situated fairly close to each other in the studio, maybe 10 feet apart. The drum kit was set out in the open room. I placed close mics on the individual drums and cymbals and an array of "room mics" about 10-15 feet away from the kit to capture its sound in the room ambiance. Gobos were put around the guitar and bass amps in an effort to keep their sound from bleeding too much into the drum and room mics. Gene's bass was recorded through a direct box in addition to having a microphone in front of his amp. I also set up a few vocal mics that were used for communications, cueing, and reference vocals. The band members all wore headphones with a mix of instruments and vocals that I set in the control room.

Any recollection of band members switching instruments: Gene on guitar or Ace or Paul on bass? Do you remember anyone playing keyboards?

The band members mostly stuck to their designated instruments. Gene played bass on all the tracks, but he might have added a guitar part on "Feel Like Heaven." Ace and Paul always had terrific interplay between them when they laid down guitar tracks at the same time. They'd work out the parts together — chords and lines — and then divvy them up, sometimes doubling parts, sometimes playing off each other. I could count on lots of wonderful "stereo" guitar moments by splitting their tracks hard left and right in the mix. No keyboard parts were added to any of the tracks we recorded for this project. I have a fond recollection of a well-known studio percussionist, likely the late, great Jimmy Maelen, stopping by to overdub a shaker and a backwards cymbal on "Feel Like Heaven."

How would you describe the vibe and interaction between the band members?

Overall, the sessions maintained a good-natured, pleasant vibe. A lot was accomplished amidst plenty of goofing around. But truth be told, I did sense some tensions brewing within the band even as we started the project. At various times they were all vocal about not being happy with this or that. The management people who sometimes hovered around the sessions had their own set of issues as well and often engaged in long "private" discussions with band factions. This was a time not too long after Peter Criss left the band — or was asked to leave — so nerves were still raw from the splintering. There were a few times when I thought things might heat up enough to grind the sessions to a halt, but thankfully that never happened. Whenever the time for making music was at hand and the red record light went on, any discord among the band members melted away, and they worked together in harmony.

You said the band members all had a terrific sense of humor. Got any stories you'd like to share from those sessions?

Throughout the long hours in the studio, you could always count on Ace to come up with entertaining ways to help keep moods light. He would bring in remote-controlled toys and gadgets of all kinds and even various types of weapons. Ace had a video that was just a close-up of one of his friends wearing tons of shaving cream all over his face doing a rather decent impression of Ed Koch, New York's mayor at the time. It was actually quite funny, and Ace reveled in playing it over and over again. He played a variety of other videos, too — not all in the greatest of taste. What can I say? Ace was, well, Ace.

Gene and Paul kept us in stitches with some weird song they kept singing for days on end. It resembled an American Indian chant and featured developing ever-more-depraved lyrics poking fun at certain members of their road crew. It was brutally funny.

The studio bathroom, wired for sound, was also the source of some amusing moments. Paul was prone to singing, sometimes in funny voices, as he used the facilities. It was always interesting to hear what might be leaking [literally] through the studio's reverb system.

Unfortunately, Eric Carr passed away in 1991. What do you recall about working with Eric during these sessions?
Eric was a sweet, talented guy, and working with him was always a joy. I felt that he and I related very well together. During those sessions Eric confided in me about how he considered himself the luckiest guy in the world to have been accepted into KISS. He would say, "Last month I was playing in a Long Island bar band, and now I'm here, recording with KISS. How unbelievable!" He talked about the new Porsche the band had given him and how they set him up in a great condo in NYC, all expenses paid. He was truly humble about his recent change in fortunes. Fresh at the beginning of his time with KISS, Eric also expressed a touch of insecurity about his place in the band. I reassured him that from everything I'd heard his bandmates thought the world of him and truly respected him as a musician and as a person. It's interesting to note the change just two short years later during the "Lick It Up" sessions at The Record Plant, NYC. Although he still remained very amiable, by that time Eric seemed to take his status as a member of KISS more in stride.

Eric had an abundance of positive energy and was always ready to play. He'd arrive and go straight into the studio to begin tweaking the drum kit and warming up. When it came time to record, Eric would lay into his drums with everything he had, as if on stage in front of thousands of screaming fans. He was lucky to be in KISS and they were lucky to have him.

During the sessions at Ace's studio, the band were working on material that was more straight-ahead rock compared to what resulted on "Music from The Elder." Is that what you recall?

Most certainly, yes! Eric brought renewed energy to the band — his bandmates all said it — and those sessions afforded them all a chance to let loose and really rock out. I remember sitting in the control room listening to them playing together and thinking, "Wow, this is one smokin' band!" Whether rehearsing or recording, they played with tremendous energy and sounded rock solid.

Rob, according to my notes, recording for the new KISS album initially ensued in March 1981 at Ace's studio. Does that sound about right? If you had to guess, how many weeks did you spend recording until Bob Ezrin showed up?

I've always suspected that some of the basic tracks I recorded during those sessions ended up on "Music from The Elder," although I've never confirmed which, if any, those might be. If that were the case, then January 1981 would be a more accurate start time for the album, even though producer Bob Ezrin and his concept for the album were not yet in place. If not, then I suppose the actual album could have commenced sometime in March, though in Canada, not at Ace's studio. Either way, I believe it was in late February that Mr. Ezrin first appeared during one of the sessions at Ace's studio. I don't recall him participating in that session. Very shortly thereafter, Mr. Ezrin, the band, and the multitrack tapes I'd been working on all upped and headed north to Canada. Unfortunately, I didn't go, since Mr. Ezrin had his own engineers awaiting him there. That was ostensibly the end of my involvement with the project that later became "Music from The Elder." Happily for me, there would be many more great recording sessions with KISS to come.

How did the project end up at Penny Lane Studios and how much work did you do there?

The decision to take the project to Penny Lane Studios might have been made in order to give Paul, Gene, and Eric, all of whom lived in the New York City area, a break from the lengthy commutes to Ace's studio in Connecticut. Penny Lane had a wonderful Trident recording console and well-designed recording and control rooms. I had recorded several projects there prior to bringing in KISS and was always very pleased with the experience and, more importantly, the results. Because it was primarily a radio jingle production house operated by its parent company, Radio Band of America, Penny Lane Studios could be booked at very reasonable rates, but only after hours, and that meant overnight through dawn sessions.

The songs we worked on at Penny Lane were "Nowhere to Run," "Feel Like Heaven," and "Love's A Deadly Weapon." Since the basic tracks and some overdubs had already been recorded at Ace's studio, all that was left to do at Penny Lane was a final round of overdubs, including lead and background vocals, and then mix. For some reason, we never got around to recording guitar solos on "Nowhere to Run" or "Feel Like Heaven," so the solo sections of both of those songs remained open.

It was at Penny Lane that I developed a deep appreciation of Paul's incredible vocal abilities. Paul routinely delivered amazing, flawless vocal performances in a single pass of the tape — one take! Many singers, even seasoned ones, would be happy to record through the first chorus of a song only to stop before carrying on or trying again. Paul could visualize how he wanted his vocals to sound then commit them to tape, spot on, every time. Sure, we may have opted to fix something here or touch up something there, but for the most part Paul's vocals sounded polished just as he sang them — a remarkable talent, indeed!

Finishing overdubs and mixing the three songs at Penny Lane would take only four or five sessions.

Do any of these song titles sound familiar: "Deadly Weapons," "One Step Too Far," "Bad Reputation," "Heaven," "Feel Like Heaven," "Nowhere to Run," "Don't Run," "Every Little Piece of Your Heart"?
We worked on quite a few tracks. Some of them were complete songs presented by Paul or Gene and some seemed to develop spontaneously out of unfinished bits and pieces or studio jams. As I mentioned, the only songs we completed to any degree were "Nowhere to Run," "Feel Like Heaven," and "Love's A Deadly Weapon." Others on your list may have been among the batch of songs we recorded, but I wouldn't recall them by name as many remained untitled and unfinished at the time.

One note: Over the years, someone circulated the songs I recorded with KISS during those sessions on the Internet. Without exception those "Pre-Elder Demos," as I've seen them referred to, sound like they were sourced from someone's cassette copy of a cassette copy — in short, the sound quality is pretty dreadful. It's so unfortunate because the master-quality versions of those songs sounded totally awesome!

Can you pick your favorite song, or the one that stands out the most to you, from the sessions you did with KISS in 1981, and why?

That's easy. I particularly enjoyed working on "Nowhere To Run," not just because I thought it was a great song, but also because the enormous dynamic range of the arrangement — from loud to louder to quiet to even louder — posed a real challenge to record and mix. The song's dynamics served up its greatest payoff. "Love's A Deadly Weapon" and "Feel Like Heaven," though quite different from each other, were both fairly constant dynamically speaking; once a good balance of tracks was established in a mix, levels for those songs stayed pretty much the same throughout. Not so with "Nowhere to Run." The intro hit like a ton of bricks. From there the song built to a huge peak before dropping down to a delicate bridge section comprised only of a beautiful falsetto vocal and a sparkly acoustic guitar, both tenderly delivered by Paul. Out of that section, the track swelled again and slammed into the end choruses — with yet another ton of bricks — and then continued growing bigger and louder even as the fadeout consumed it. I came up with a hooky background vocal answer idea for the "Nowhere to Run" choruses and was really pleased when the guys liked it enough to commit it to tape. I suppose that's another reason why I'm somewhat partial to that song.

"Feel Like Heaven" — at least the version that circulates among fans — has some rather nasty lyrics. Was that the version you recorded with the band or did you work on a proper track?

"Feel Like Heaven" was one of Gene's songs. I believe the version you're referring to was Gene's original demo recorded in his bedroom closet 4-track studio. The 24-track version I recorded with the band was a smokin' dance/rock recreation of that demo, but with perfectly civilized lyrics. It was, as you say, a proper track.

Do you recall a working album title for these pre-"Elder" sessions along the lines of "Rockin' With the Boys"?

I don't recall any working titles for an album at that point. We weren't in the process of compiling an album, more just throwing tracks together to see what stuck. One advantage of working in a private recording facility like Ace in the Hole is that you can spend inordinate amounts of time writing and tinkering without worrying about the clock ticking away expensive studio hours. And spend time we did!

Do you remember there being any discussions at all at Ace's studio or at Penny Lane about constructing a concept album?
No, I never heard any discussions about a concept album during the sessions at Ace's studio or at Penny Lane. That's not to say there weren't such discussions going on, just that I wasn't privy to them.

Had you ever met Bob Ezrin prior to this experience?
I had never met Bob Ezrin prior to his appearance at Ace's studio in late February 1981. But the level of his success and the quality of his work preceded him, as did his reputation for being highly demanding in the studio. I recall looking forward to meeting him, but with some degree of trepidation. This feeling justified itself at one point when Mr. Ezrin was walking out the studio door and into the parking lot. I was inside the control room with some 30 feet and lots of acoustic baffling between us. I heard him snap something to me about packing up the 2" master tapes and sending them to an address in Canada that he rattled off just as he stepped through the door and his voice faded into the outdoor ambiance. I bolted after him and quite innocently asked if he would repeat the address so I could write it down. He just muttered something to the effect of, "If you didn't get all that, you shouldn't be working with me," got in his car, and drove off. That was the last time I saw Mr. Ezrin.

The other engineers credited on "Music from The Elder" are Kevin Doyle and Corky Stasiak and the "Recorded by" credit reads Brian Christian, Rick Hart, Robert Hrycyna, and David Brown. Remember any of these gentlemen?
I may have crossed paths with one or two of them back in the day, but no, I can't really say I know any of them except by name.

Chris Lendt, who worked for KISS' business managers, recalled the "Music from the Elder" listening party as a bizarre experience in that the label personnel couldn't believe what they were hearing was actually KISS. Do you remember there being an element of surprise at the listening party?
After "Music from The Elder" was completed, KISS held an album listening party at, if memory serves, A & R Studios in midtown NYC. People from the KISS organization and their record company were there. Food and drink were in abundance. I have no doubt that some people were flabbergasted by what they heard, but I, for one, thought that hearing the album blasting out from some fine studio monitors was an awesome experience! I was never one to get caught up in music biz politics or in any of the controversy

surrounding that album. I was just happy to know that I had contributed some creative input to the band and their music.

"Music from the Elder" is arguably the most controversial album in the KISS catalog. While some fans love it, others would rather forget it. After listening to this album so many years later, and as someone who worked on "Lick It Up" and Ace's '78 solo LP, what's your take on it?
I liked much of "Music from The Elder." I thought it was a gutsy attempt at something intriguing that delivered enough outstanding moments to far outweigh any not-so-memorable ones. Granted, it didn't ooze typical KISS sound but rather was subtly infused with it like a nice flavored vodka. It possessed an understated elegance and passion that lurked just beneath the surface of it all. Apologies if I waxed poetic.

If I were to conjure any criticism of the album, it would be that it was too tightly controlled, manipulated even, with few opportunities for spontaneous moments of "studio magic" to occur. At times it seemed like the album's concept steamrolled right over the band — which should never happen with a band as strong as KISS — leaving them pacing through their performances, unable to break free. It can surely be said Paul's vocals, although impeccably executed, lacked some of the unbridled fire we all know he is so capable of.

A couple of technical questions, if I may: In the guitar solo for "Under the Rose," starting at 3:19, there is a strong use of delay to achieve a mirror-like effect. Can you outline how this would have been technically achieved in 1981?
The early '80s were not at all technologically challenged when it came to creating spectacular effects of all kinds for guitars, other instruments, vocals, or anything else. There was no lack of delay-producing options back then. Certainly, whoever was playing that guitar solo — presumably Ace — could easily have kicked in an effects pedal set with a long delay [also known as "echo"] while playing. But more likely, that effect was created in the control room after the fact during the final mix or perhaps committed to tape sometime prior to mixing. They could have used any number of DDL [digital delay line] units that were around in those days; Eventide, Lexicon, and others made them. In a purely analog realm — as were my recording roots — that effect was easily achieved using "tape delay," a common process in which a sound was fed from the multitrack tape to a secondary tape machine, recorded and played back there resulting in a delay — the

delay time being dependent on the speed of the tape as it moved across the record head and on to the playback head. The delayed sound would then [be] mixed with the original sound yielding anything from a short "slap" [a la Lennon vocals] to long, sweeping echoes. Tape delay could also be fed back onto itself creating an on-going loop of delays.

Now, as to which option was actually employed for the effect in the "Under the Rose" solo ... I haven't a clue.

The breakdown in "Mr. Blackwell," starting at 2:52, is extremely odd. There is an almost violent use of panning, eerie vocals, percussion, and general sonic mayhem. Can you offer some insight into what's going on, studio trickery-wise, during this section?

Quite an interesting mishmash was created for the "Mr. Blackwell" breakdown. There's the wild panning you mentioned, with tracks split wide across the stereo field. Not being present at the sessions, I can't say for sure what else was done there. However, upon a quick listen, I hear a flanged high-hat cymbal, a variety of vocal effects including backwards vocals, Eventide Harmonizer or possibly "vari-speed" [variable tape speed] vocals, or vocals through a vocoder, percussion instruments including wooden blocks and ratchet, whammy bar guitar effects, and overdriven and heavily compressed bass guitar plucks swimming in reverb, a similar dose of which can be clearly heard at the beginning of "The Oath." What do you hear?

John Storyk: Designing Ace in The Hole Studio

Legendary studio designer details the story behind the construction of the Spaceman's underground laboratory, Ace in The Hole Studio, which was utilized for some of KISS' 1981 recording sessions

John, how did you come to be contracted to design Ace Frehley's studio? Was it through Eddie Kramer?
John Storyk: Yes. I'm 99.9 percent sure this is correct. At the time Eddie was very involved with KISS as you know. He did a number of their albums and I think he was pretty close with Ace. Ace had, more or less, just gotten his new home in Connecticut, right on the Connecticut-New York border, and wanted his own studio. And Eddie and I, of course, had been friends since 1969. He's my daughter's godfather. Basically, Eddie said to Ace, "This is the only guy to do it." And Ace said, "Great. Let's do it." And I remember he sent a limousine to pick me up and I went up to his house up in Wilton, he had already moved into the house. And he basically outlined that he wanted a private home studio.

According to "KISS and Sell," a book authored by KISS' former business manager Lendt, "Ace's dream was to have a recording studio in his home." Was this how you recall the project being described to you?
100 percent. You know, it's kind of funny because artists having their own studios at home now is like buying a loaf of bread. It's an everyday occurrence. It's not a big deal. Then it was a slightly new idea for an artist to have a "commercial-grade" studio. When I say that, I mean a glorified recording studio. There was nothing noncommercial about it other than the fact that it was not going to be a commercial studio. And also, it [wasn't] a giant studio — [Ace] didn't need a giant studio. He needed room for three, four musicians. So, the idea of having that was a little newer then [than] it is now.

It all took place in a relatively short meeting. I knew [KISS'] music, liked some of it, didn't like other parts of it, but enjoyed the energy. I knew nothing about any of the members personally. To be honest with you, I didn't even know what they looked like, from the makeup. I got up there one morning and met Ace and he reviewed very quickly what he wanted. What he wanted was of course not what we ended up building, and that might segue into the next question.

In this case, I can only go by what I have read. Initially, I believe the initial budget was in the neighborhood of $60,000 and the studio was to be more "modest," according to Lendt's book. Do you recall this initial budget?
Well, that's true, but that was not the dynamic discussed at our initial meeting. That is true and I'm sure that a business manager would present that from that perspective because that's his job as a business manager. My guess is somewhere between Ace's vision and the business manager watching the money, that's what they started out with. And you're absolutely right, they didn't spend anywhere near that money. It was closer to 10 times that amount when we were done.

From my perspective, our meeting started in a very different way. Which was that Ace had very quickly described what he wanted, which was basically a modest-size studio, [and] budget was not discussed, basically to handle three, four, five musicians, mostly himself, practicing, recording ... maybe the guys would come over, et cetera, et cetera. And now comes the big point, he wanted it in his basement. He wanted it in the basement of his house. I said, "OK. That sounds like a good idea. Let's take a look at the basement." At which point, literally, and this was very quick — I don't think I spent more than one hour there, maybe two — I looked at the basement. And it took me, even though his was a long time ago, about 19 seconds to basically turn around to Ace and tell him "this was not going to happen. At least this is not going to happen with me in the basement. Because first of all, your basement has only got 8-foot ceilings. Plus, it's got pipes and wires, and this and that." Actually, it was big enough, and there was enough of it, because it was a big house, but I turned to Ace, "There's no way we can isolate this in your basement. It's impossible. You don't have enough height. And also, it's a wood building. It's not going to work. It's going to be very loud obviously. You're going to wake up your wife. It's not going to happen. Maybe I can think about digging down, but it'd be a major project [and] I have no idea whether it's even possible."

And this conversation lasted a very short amount of time. And you know, it was almost like I've got a job and I'm talking myself out of a job about as quickly as I'm meeting Ace. But I had to tell him that, "This is the truth." At which point, I had walked around the property — I think he had like five acres — and I came into the house. I said, "You know, Ace, you're up here on a beautiful [piece of property]. Why don't you just build a small little barn in your backyard? Build it out of concrete block, side it with wood so it will look just like a house or anything you want, and then you just walk to the studio and you can make as much noise as you want and everything will be perfect. This will be really easy." At the time, I had just finished doing the project for Albert Grossman in Bearsville working on Bearsville Studios [in New York] and I had a lot of experience with those [type of studios]. And that's exactly what we did — we basically made a concrete block bunker look like a wood building. And I said [to Ace], "This would be so much simpler. To try and do this in the basement would be impossible." And he just looked at me and said, "No. I'm from the Bronx. I don't want to walk outside to my studio. I want to just get up, put on my slippers and go out to the studio." And I said, "Well, you know, Ace, what do you want me to do, you want to put the studio underground and connect with a tunnel to your house?" I said this as a joke. And I remember this almost exactly — I was literally joking, and I was half-kidding with him. I was trying to see if I could flush out some kind of solution. At which point, Ace turned to me and said, "That's a really good idea. Let's go do that."

No kidding? (Laughs)
He said, "You can keep the limousine for the rest of the day." He walked out of the room and I never saw him again. That is the story. Period. End of conversation. Nobody was angry. He just said, "That's a brilliant idea. Let's go do that. Work out the details." And he walked out of the room.

How far underground was the studio ultimately built?
It was built about 6 feet underground. I literally never saw Ace again. I worked with Eddie to get the basic specs that he needed. I mean nobody knew more about recording him than Eddie because he had been working with Ace. So, it was easy to get all the equipment specs and the needs that he had. And basically, that is exactly what we did. The land kind of sloped — it's hard to explain. The side of his property — the land sloped down. It was easy to basically put the studio into the ground. It was under the ground, but then one part of it basically day-lighted out. At that was the only part you saw. It was a big giant concrete curved box, actually it was pretty. [It] was one of my favorite studios [and] favorite designs. It was pushed into the ground, 6 feet lower.

The bottom was 6 feet lower and the base was level. So, we made a hole in his basement and you went through a small tunnel that actually had a skylight in it, believe it or not. You went down and then you entered the studio, which had a modest-size control room, about a five-man live room with a small iso booth. And one edge of the studio was a floor-to-ceiling glass block wall. That wall you'd see from the ground, from the land as you approach the studio. When you went into his property, you took one turn to go to the house and another turn to go to the studio. That's what we ended up doing. The studio was solid concrete — it was basically a giant basement and the roof was concrete.

On a scale of 1-10, how challenging was this particular studio design?
For me, at that point in my life, it was a 10. Now it would be a 5. But I was much younger then, [and it] was before I met [my wife]. My company is Walters-Storyk Design Group. Walters is my wife, Beth Walters. It's kind of like I have two careers, before Beth and after Beth. But [this job], it has to be [more than] 25 years ago.

Again, based on what I have read, construction took about a year and wrapped in late 1980. I think we're talking mid-to-late 1979 that this project would have started.
Yeah, that's possible. I could easily look it up; I have all the original files. I've kept every drawing I've ever done since 1969, including Electric Lady Studios. I have those drawings. And I have one great photo of the outside of [Ace's studio]. It's still to this day one of my favorite photos. I never really got any pictures of the inside. But I have the original drawings.

Once you had that initial meeting with a client like Ace, what would have been the first step of the process in designing his studio?
Well that project happened in a slightly unusual way because, as I said, I never saw Ace again. At that point, and this was not so good, it was a little bit goofy, I think we dealt with Eddie. Eddie became the mouthpiece between me and Ace and that was fine with me. Ace, you know, had his own qualities and stuff. I've been around a lot of celebrities and stars and that stuff doesn't interest me that much. I was happy to deal with Eddie. Eddie is very grounded and he's an incredible engineer and my friend. So, I did my drawings and then I took them to Eddie, and he would have feedback, et cetera. And they would either be his comments or Ace's comments. The actual design was pretty quick because everything happened in that 10 seconds. I mean that's the real story. That's what happened. I jokingly said,

"What do you want me to do? Put it underground and connect it with a tunnel?" And he said, "Yeah, that's a great idea. Let's go do that." And that was it. Just like that.

The real pedal to the metal came [when] we finished the drawing, then we went out and found a local contractor. I forget how we found that contractor — it might have been the person that built the house. I don't remember. I would have to go to my file to find that and that requires some work. But one way or another we finally got a builder — a real local builder — who had never built a studio before but knew how to build concrete foundations and stuff. And then of course, the prices came in and I do remember the business manager saying that it was "going over the budget" but Ace basically wanted it. And the business managers ultimately do what their clients want them to do.

That is the scenario Lendt describes in his book, that the price escalated.
Ace didn't care.

Exactly. According to Lendt, Ace's reply was, "Aren't I a millionaire?"
And that's exactly what happened. I'd only seen the basement boarded. I think we ended up busting it apart. I think I remember the construction was something like $250,000, [which was] a lot of money for 35 years ago. But you know, he was making that kind of money. That was in an era when they made so much money, those guys, and sold a lot of records.

In an interview with engineer Rob Freeman, he detailed some of the gear in the studio: An MCI 600 series automated console, an MCI JH-16 2" 24-track tape machine with full remote, and two MCI 100A 2-track tape machines for mix-downs.
We had tape machines ... I forget the gear; I'd have to look that up. But I think the drawing — sometimes I'll pull it up in a lecture presentation on "stranger" studios, "unusual" studios, [because] this is one of them. I remember seeing the drawing. And I remember seeing the tape machine and at that time MCI was one of the leaders and they were of course bought by Sony. But the equipment was probably handled through Audio Techniques and Ham Brosious, who was my friend and buddy at the time, and one of the great pro audio dealers of all time, and they were the MCI dealers. My guess is that the gear was all sold and brokered through Audio Techniques.

And this recording gear would have been considered top of the line for the time?
State of the art. It was a commercial studio. It just happened to be at his house. And that's what he wanted.

As you said, you had no other interaction with Ace. But according to Lendt there were "constant meetings" with you in lower Manhattan. These meetings would have taken place at your Union Square office ...
Absolutely.

Despite Ace was not being present, there was still a series of meetings?
Yeah, but they were all between me and Eddie. And I also remember going [to Ace's house] quite a bit when it was being built. It was a challenge to get it built because it was so different. If you were to see the shape you would realize that it was kind of an odd shape.

Would you have been onsite for all of the construction?
No, no, no, no. I went there maybe once every two weeks. We were involved in the process, but we didn't go there every day. But there were [a lot of] phone calls. Even today, we are always in the middle of the present project. And we'll get some projects where we get calls daily. Sometimes we get pictures sent to us. Of course, everything is different now 30 some odd years later. Now, we've got cameras onsite, Skype conversations and live video chats. Then, it was not quite as fluid because we didn't have the technology we have [today]. But I was working [and] living in New York City, 30 minutes away, so it wasn't that hard for me to go visit, and I did on occasion.

Apparently, a bathroom was added at the last minute, and some walls that were erected had to be torn down and done over again. Does this ring a bell?
I don't remember ... the bathroom kind of got thrown in there. It was sort of part of the tunnel. The tunnel was not really a long tunnel. It was almost like a 10-foot connector but, to tell you truth, I don't remember the bathroom being a last-minute effect. It might have been last-minute in design, but it was always on the original drawing. I'm going off of my memory, because I don't have the drawing in front of me, but I think that I remember that it was always in there.

Once construction ensued, how smooth would you say the process went?
Given that it was being built by a non-studio builder, because there really weren't that many studio builders then, I think it went relatively smooth other than the fact that it just kept costing more than everybody thought it was going to cost. I don't remember any nightmarish moments. Other than this bathroom story that I'm really hearing for the first time, it's not like whole pieces of the project had to come down and be built back up. It basically just got built. It was a concrete box in the dirt. Basically there was a giant hole and imagine building a foundation that had some very strange shapes to it and then instead of putting a wood floor on top of it, they put a concrete floor on top of it like a commercial building and then they put two feet of dirt on top of it and grass. That's the box. And once that was done, the inside was more conditional — it was a two-wall system with multiple layers of sheetrock and drywall. The studio construction was a little more atypical than what we were building at the time. It went relatively smoothly.

When work was finally completed, what was your immediate reaction? Do you remember being satisfied?
Oh sure. I only got to see the studio once after it was built and then I never went back. But it did pop up in my life again because the house got sold.

That's correct.
Now there's a lot of stories that I heard. Ace, more or less, got asked to leave the community. Not because the studio was making [too much noise], the studio was 100 percent soundproof. But I think he kind of got caught using the studio for commercial purposes because of the traffic that was coming in and out.

His house wasn't cleared for commercial use?
No, no, no. It was totally noncommercial, but he ended up using it for commercial use, but he didn't get caught because of the noise. He got caught because of the traffic. That's what I heard. I can't verify that, and I have [heard] some [other] stories about that ... anyway, none of that interested me, it wasn't my deal. But I did get a call from the future owner, from the person who bought [the house] whose name I completely forget right now. I did get one call because he was thinking of converting it into some kind of studio and wanted information and "could I help him?" I think I said yes but nothing ever became of it. I have no idea what became of the house or the studio.

According to Lendt's book, the studio was ultimately "gutted" and made into some sort of recreational room. I think we're talking sometime in the mid-'80s. With all the work that went into the studio, from your perspective, do you think that's unfortunate?

I don't think about it. I mean, I don't mean to not answer your question, but I've done 3,000 studios. I move on. Studios don't generally have a very long life. Stone churches last for 5,000 years; studios have an average life of four years. They come and they go. There are some that have lasted a long time and it's actually fun to kind of think about them, like Electric Lady Studios, ironically my first studio. Not only does it still exist, it's flourishing. It's fun to be associated with that but most of the studios that I've done, they arrive and they're there for a while and then they go. Some have lasted longer. [Ace's] didn't.

Ace's studio was absolutely designed as a state-of-the-art commercial studio. He just wasn't allowed to do it. What he should have done was ... pay a little more attention to when people arrived and observing the community and whatever, because you are allowed to have your own private studio. But basically, I just think somebody didn't want him in that community. That's a pretty uppity community, that Wilton, Connecticut. But I don't know all of the particulars of how he left and why he left.

Would you be at liberty to divulge the fee you would have been paid for your work?

I don't mind divulging it, I just completely forgot. [It was] not that much I am sure.

John, as you said, you've constructed 3,000 recording studios and the very first one, Electric Lady, becomes both a legendary studio and a landmark. Talk about making a big splash the first time out.

Yes. It was a very interesting turn of events that happened and changed my life. Among other things, I got to meet Eddie and got to work with a genius, which was fun, and started a new career. I was a musician. I was actually thinking of being a musician, but I had studied architecture so two loves in my life kind of got combined very quickly right out of school. It was just one of those strange turn of events. Just within a few months my life changed around and put me on a different path.

How much did Electric Lady cost to build?

It cost somewhere between $1 and $1.3 million dollars, in 1969 dollars. There have been a number of interviews and articles about Electric Lady. There's been the Electric Lady 35th reunion and there was an Electric Lady 40th reunion and I've been on panels. They recently have a new owner and they have a terrific young manager who has really kept that studio alive. It's fun that it's still there. It's one of the most famous studios in the world.

You mentioned your company, Walters-Storyk Design Group. When was the company founded? And how active are you today?

I've been designing since Electric Lady and then 26 years ago Beth Walters came into my life. And I met her and fell in love with her. She's an interior designer and fabric designer and very quickly, almost within a year, we became partners and everything. Actually, we became business partners before we became married. We formed Walters-Storyk Design Group. She runs everything. She's not only in charge of the interiors; [she] has changed a lot of the look of some of the studios, but also runs the business. She's an amazing woman. And now the company [has] five offices around the world, it's a much bigger company.

I am still extremely active. I work every day but other people are now very seriously involved in some of our activities, even to the point where over the last five years we've sort of tried to change our name to WSDG because we want people to know us just by our letters. I've tried to get it to where not everybody has to talk to me. I can't be hands-on with every project. It's impossible. It's a much bigger operation then when I was doing Ace Frehley's studio.

Michael McCarty

Uncredited engineer sheds some light on KISS' sessions at Phase One Studios in Toronto, shares fun recollections of Gene Simmons and Paul Stanley, and offers a personal snapshot of Bob Ezrin

Michael, you are not officially credited in "The Elder" liner notes. How do you fit into the album's picture?
Michael McCarty: Well, I was working for Bob as an engineer and associate producer and started off with the project. He was alternating working on "The Elder" and the second Kings' album. I was the associate producer on the Kings' record. Actually, Ringo [Hyrcyna] and I both engineered and co-produced the Kings' independent record. And when Bob heard that record, he got very excited about the band and got them a deal with Elektra and then we redid the record. So, Ringo and I were engineers and associate producers.

So then [Bob] took the job of doing the next Kings' album and "The Elder" at the same time. I don't think he consciously did that but that's just the way it worked out. I mean, it's hard enough for a producer and an engineering team to work on one album at a time. Working on two at a time is really, really daunting. (Laughs)

The Kings' album would have been "Amazon Beach," correct?
That's correct.

Some documents from this period outline KISS' schedule of rehearsals and recording with and without Bob, and they specifically list that Bob was working on the Kings' project. This was late May, early June 1981. As you inferred, it had to have been tough on Bob and the recording team?
Yeah. I'm amazed that you got that kind of information. (Laughs)

I'm not sure how widely known it is among fans that Bob was doing-double duty at the time. Michael, another colleague described Bob around this period as a "very intense" guy who liked to "be efficient." How do you recall his demeanor?
Well, he was a very intense guy. You know, he still is. He's a whirling dervish of energy and ideas and I tell you, especially at that time, it appeared he had

a lot of interest in entertainment and media beyond just music. I think it's probably safe to say that he was a bit burnt out on music at the time and was very excited about various other projects, I think some film projects.

Bob is one of the most brilliant people I've ever met in my life. He has interests and ideas way beyond mortal human beings. (Laughs) And so I think at the time, not only was he sandwiching two recording projects simultaneously, but he was also sandwiching his music interests in with other interests he had at the time.

He was intense, but he was fairly hands-off. He wasn't showing up a lot and he wasn't a good delegator. I'm not saying he didn't show up, he was showing up late, [and] he would try and delegate large chunks of the project — either the rehearsals or recording — to people around at the time and he was never satisfied with the work that anybody did, and probably rightfully so. You know, it's hard for me to say and judge. The delegation thing wasn't working well so he got frustrated with that. It was a bit tense because of the two projects going on at once and also we were, I don't want to say rebuilding the studio, but we were revamping the studio to try and bring it up to the kind of level, technically and ergonomically, that would suit these two projects.

Bob was looking for a new home; I guess you could say a home base to record in. He was using a studio called Phase One, which was in the outer suburbs of Toronto. Bob had to basically tear out rooms and build a dining room for KISS. We spent a considerable period of time going over all of the technology and making sure that all of the signal paths were clean. I can't remember if we upgraded any gear — I don't think so. But we just sort of tore the studio apart and made sure everything was up to snuff. It was a good studio to begin with. We were just trying to make sure it was going to be foolproof when we were working there.

This was Phase One?
Yes, Phase One. It still exists. It's now in sort of the inner suburbs of Toronto. But then it was the outer suburbs, out on the edge of the city, near the countryside. It was in an industrial mall, sort of a like an L.A. valley industrial mall.

There's a guy named Rick Hart, who ended up a film mixer. [Rick] ended up working on The Wall live tour, and I think Bob met him at the Producers'

Workshop, which is where they mixed "The Wall." And it's where [Fleetwood Mac's] "Rumours" was mixed and it's [also] where we mixed the first Kings' record. And that's when I met Rick. And Bob ended up taking Rick on the road with The Wall tour. So Rick, myself and Ringo were charged with assessing Phase One, determining if any technology changes had to be made, any wiring upgrades, that kind of thing. If I recall, that was probably two or three weeks that we were doing that — this was before we even started recording with KISS or the Kings.

And Bob had his famous Stephens tape recorder then. It was a 24-track machine, a very boutique firm [was] making it and it was very cutting-edge and it had a lot of elements in it that made it probably the best 24-track tape recorder in the world. And there was only a handful of them. I think one of them was at Producers' Workshop, that's where Bob heard about them. Wherever he was recording, he would have it shipped there, so we had it installed at Phase One. A bit of a funny-slash-extremely sad story was we were there for a few days before Ace showed up. And I think that we were just getting sounds and that kind of thing. He showed up — apparently, he was a recording equipment enthusiast, and he had a fairly elaborate home studio — I was in the control room when he arrived. He arrived at the door and without saying anything to anybody or noticing anybody; he saw the Stephens machine across the room. He got very excited and made sort of a beeline across the room to come over and check it out. In many studios, control rooms have two levels: there's the level where the board's at and then usually there's a sort of sunken pit in front of that. And this tape machine was right on the edge of the upper platform. And Ace was leaning over looking at the tape recorder and marveling at it and lost his balance and fell into the pit. (Laughs)

Ouch.
And [he] jumped up immediately, almost like a routine you'd see Dick Van Dyke or one of those famous old-school comedians do. He had sort of like a "what happened?!" look on his face.

It's interesting to note that Ace really wasn't creatively invested with "The Elder." When all was said and done, he was absent for most of the sessions and "flew" in a lot of his guitar work from home, sending the tracks back to Bob. Do you recall this dynamic?
Ace appeared to be the odd man out. There's probably other issues [that were] going on there that probably aren't appropriate for me to comment

on. He definitely seemed to be the odd man out and seemed to not be very in the loop as to the songs or what the chords were. Our observation was he was sort of disinterested possibly for other reasons; we didn't pick up any tension that there were creative differences necessarily. The [other] band [members], particularly Gene, were pretty frustrated with his playing. It could be that they did have some fundamental core creative differences on the project and that caused the sort of emotional disconnect for him. Regardless of what the reason was, he definitely wasn't up to speed on the songs. Gene was quite frustrated, and they ended up letting him go take long breaks and they would record when he was taking a break. It wasn't particularly clear whether Ace knew they were recording when he was on the break or cared.

How would you describe Eric Carr's attitude?
Eric Carr was extremely enthusiastic. It was a big deal for him.

It was his first album with the band.
That's right. They were all excited to have him in the band. He was a real go-getter and very enthusiastic and quite easy to work with. [He was] happy to participate in whatever length of time it took to get drum sounds.

What are your recollections of Gene and Paul?
There was an interesting dynamic between Gene and Paul. Gene was definitely the most enthusiastic about the project, Gene and Bob actually. And I guess in hindsight, it was kind of their project and the others were participating with varying degrees of enthusiasm. Paul was participating, but he seemed a bit skeptical. And I remember one time, they did a number of takes of one of the songs, I can't recall which one it was. They were all back in the control room listening back and Gene and Bob were dissecting the merits of the various takes and really focused and zeroed in on it and [they were] debating which take was best. And at one point, Gene turned to Paul and he said, "Paul, what do you think"? And Paul said, "I don't give a shit. I'm rich already." (Laughs)

(Laughs) Well, you've hit on something interesting. Though Paul and Gene both have distanced themselves from the project, it seems Gene was much more emotionally attached to "The Elder" compared to Paul. But even recently, neither of them has many good things to say about the album. In a way, it's sort of become the bastard child of KISS albums.

Yeah, you know that's probably why I remember those of us working in the various roles, I think that we probably had an intuitive feeling that it was a very odd direction for the band. Certainly, I know in my mind, I was having a hard time reconciling what they were doing with what I knew KISS to be. Although, I did leave before it really started to take much shape, so I didn't really have a solid idea of how it was turning out.

I'd say the number one recollection I have of the time I was working on that project was I came away with an enormous amount of respect for Gene. This may sound disrespectful, but I thought he was the best businessman and worst musician I'd ever worked with. (Laughs) And when I say worst musician, I don't think he was bad. To say his strength was business is doing a disservice — his strength was he was a visionary media guy, and an expert in human nature and communications and media and how it all worked together. To that degree, Bob is as well. The two of them together were a pretty formidable team when it came to the intellect they brought to those areas.

I remember one day we were sitting in the lounge of the studio, watching TV, I think we were having lunch or something. There was a soap opera on TV, one of the daytime soaps. And Gene said to me, "You know why soap operas are so popular, don't you?" And I said, "Not exactly. Why?" And he went on a 10-minute, Ph.D.-level thesis as to the appeal of soap operas and why they were so popular and such a powerful thing. I was just blown away by it and you could just tell that was the brain that helped conceive KISS and take them through to that level. He also delighted in talking about business and talking about [how he] owned the trademark in the money bag symbol. Is that something you're aware of?

Yes. That's definitely something that Gene has spoken about and he has incorporated it into a logo.
He was talking about how that occurred to him. He said that early on in his career he started signing autographs with the S in Simmons, turning it into a dollar-sign by putting the two slashes through the S. And then eventually he just started enclosing it in a bag, sort of similar to a money bag in "Monopoly." That's where he got his inspiration from, he said. And then one day, as he started to become more aware of and involved in the intellectual property aspects of his business, he said, "Gee, I wonder if anyone's got the trademark on that thing?" And he had his lawyers investigate and the answer was no. So, he went out and trademarked it. And I remember he

said, I don't know if this is true, but he certainly said it to me at the time that as a result he then approached "Monopoly" and said, "You're using my trademark," and ended up licensing it to them and making a royalty off of every "Monopoly" game. I don't know if that's true, but that's what he said.

That I haven't heard. However, it would not surprise me. Those are some great stories about Gene. Do you recall any conversations with Paul, or was he more distant?
Yeah, he wasn't around as much. As the driving force of the project, Gene was there all the time. I don't recall very much of note of [my] conversations with Paul. They were really generous about sharing their space with anybody who was working with them. We all would often have lunch or dinner with them in the dining room that was made for them at the studio. And that was really a fascinating time to hear the talk in there and the interaction. So, I don't remember anything that Paul said at the time that was particularly noteworthy other than that comment that he was already rich and didn't care. (Laughs) It was definitely a joke. He was basically saying, "I'm not sure what you're doing here but the consequences aren't going to ruin my life."

Michael, "The Elder" ended up moving around a bit, in terms of recording studios. How long were you actually involved with the project? And did you go to any of the other locations?
I wasn't at any other studios. It's hard to say exactly how long, because of the two projects happening simultaneously. The plan was to do two weeks of one and two weeks of the other, so alternating in two-week blocks. I definitely recall the initial get the studio ready phase, then I recall a KISS phase and a Kings phase, at least one each. I don't know if it was two each. I'm not sure. I'm pretty sure that we did KISS the first phase, and then the Kings, because I ended up leaving in a Kings phase. It was either KISS, Kings, KISS, Kings, and then I left or KISS, Kings [and then] I left.

Why did you ultimately leave the project?
I had been working nonstop in the studio, including my education, which was the music industry arts at Fanshawe College, the world's first recording/engineering/production-accredited course. I had been working there for three years, nonstop 24-7. I was working for Jack Richardson at Nimbus 9, where I met Bob. Bob used to be a partner there. And I segued into working for Bob directly and the sort of high level of intensity and craziness that was going on with those two projects just finally got to me. I

just needed a break really, really badly. I ended up leaving the Kings record partway through after we'd had enough dealing with Bob. He didn't show up for quite a while and when he finally did, he didn't like the work we had done, and he said we were going to have to work the weekend. As soon as he said those words, I saw my first weekend off in probably six or nine months going down the drain and I just couldn't take it any longer.

The studio was on the edge of the city, near the countryside. I remember just walking out through the countryside trying to figure out what was going on and get my head together and figure out what to do. And Bob and his wife at the time came looking for me in their jeep, they were driving through the country roads and finally found me a mile or two from the studio. I was on my way back then and they offered me a ride of course. I said, "No, I've just got to be by myself for a while." By the time I got back to the studio, everybody had basically left and so I tacked up a sign on the control room wall that said, "Gone fishing," and signed it. And the next day I was on the beach in the Bahamas, trying to sort out my life and trying to cool off.

That's quite the story. Michael, earlier you mentioned Bob being interested in film and media around this time. There was discussion at some point of "The Elder" being made into a film. Do you recall any talk about a film?
Just vaguely. What you're saying rings a bell, but I don't remember any of the details about it. But Bob and Gene did seem very ambitious and they definitely had a very large vision. You know, don't forget Bob had come through "The Wall," and there was a very sweeping grand plan for that project that worked out pretty well. I think it was an attempt ... they certainly were inspired by that, I think.

And unfortunately for KISS, things didn't work out in a similar fashion. While "The Wall" was a huge success, "The Elder" was a commercial failure and KISS spiraled to their lowest point. That said, the album has become a bit of an underground fan favorite.
Yeah. Well, certainly there was a lot of time and thought and effort and vision put into it by Bob and Gene. There was definitely a story and a theme there, and characters and it no doubt resonates with some people.

Speaking of "The Wall," I did a little bit of work on the "The Wall," some minor stuff, again that I wasn't credited for. But Ringo and I actually both worked on it a little bit. And Ringo ended up going to Los Angeles to

Producers' Workshop for the mixes and had some interesting stories about those. But we did some of the sort of theatrical things, like I remember recording the groupie that comes to the hotel room. She flips and sees all the guitars, and says, "Are these all your guitars?" So, we did stuff like that. I was supposed to do a lot of guitars but for some reason they changed the schedule and didn't do the guitars at Nimbus 9 in Toronto. Bob used the studio time that was booked to do some of the theatrical things and a lot of rough mixes, that kind of thing. I just remember one of the most eye-opening, inspirational, thrilling — and add another string of adjectives — moments in my life was when Bob first put the multi-tracks up for "The Wall" at Nimbus 9 and started to do some rough mixes. I remember thinking I never had heard anything like it in my entire life. It felt like you were on another planet.

That must have been quite an amazing experience. While you were at Phase One, what do you recall accomplishing for "The Elder"?
I just remember a lot of bed tracks. Drums, bass, guitars, rhythm guitars, some keyboards.

Do you recall Bob playing at all?
I remember overdubbing some of Bob's piano work there, yeah.

Would any of the choir or orchestral tracks had been recorded there?
Not during my time there, no. You know, Bob was very into choirs then. (Laughs)

Do you remember any discussion about adding those elements?
No, I don't.

Another component that was added later was narration from Canadian actors Christopher Makepeace, Robert Christie and Antony Parr. Do you recall any discussion along the lines of, "Hey, how about we add some spoken word dialog?"
Not that I recall. But you know, again Bob and Gene were always huddling and talking about the vision and how various components fit into it. So, to them it was sort of self-explanatory, the context that they were talking about these things, and they didn't explain a lot of the bigger picture to us.
Do you recall Lou Reed being around at all?
No, I don't remember Lou being there.

Lou co-wrote a few of the tracks so I'm curious if he was around at that time.
No. Of course, Bob had produced the "Berlin" record which is one of ... you know Bob has got several records that he's produced that are among the greatest records ever made. And that's one of them. And obviously, he produced the earlier KISS record ...

"Destroyer." He actually remixed that in 2012.
Bob remixed it?

Yes. He mentioned that he was very excited at the opportunity.
That's great. Bob has so much knowledge of every element of making music that it's really incredible. He has this amazing combination — [he] can go to 30,000 feet and look down on everything and pick out the core intellectual elements of what motivates people to make music, what about music appeals to a listener and the connection between them all. And he's extremely well-versed in all the technology. And then he can get down and be a great musician himself. And he's an artist, and he understands it all from so many different angles and [he has an] his ability to analyze a piece of music — he's also an incredibly astute judge of character and human beings and knows how to motivate them and read them. So, he's amazing at the psychological aspect of being a producer, and the technology aspect — from writing to everything.

Bob can do it all. Are you still in touch with him?
Yeah, quite often. There was a long stretch where we didn't so much, but say the last 10 years, we keep in touch often. He lives in Nashville a lot of the year now. I see him frequently when I'm in Nashville and when he's in Toronto. He seems to be excited about music again and making records, which is good.

Definitely. What do you know about Bob, going back to before he got into record production?
You know I think he was about 17 or 18 years old, something like that, when he first did Alice Cooper. That's remarkable. He was a real child prodigy in many ways. One of those people that I think accelerated, skipped half the grades in high school and ended up in university at an abnormally early age, ended up with abnormally big responsibilities at that university. People immediately realized he was a genius and sort of set him loose. I think one of the interesting things about him, you talk about his other interests in film

and theater and that kind of thing, he's always obviously brought a cinematic and theatrical approach to his productions. And he first got involved in music by being involved in musical theater. And one of Jack Richardson's partners, Al McMillan, who was an arranger by trade, was arranging the music in this musical and Bob was a sort of a stagehand or something. And because of the era and the need to appeal to young boomers, they had incorporated a rock band into the show. Bob was sort of inserting his opinion into the guidance of the rock band. I guess [it's] the kind of thing [that would] be annoying, for a stagehand to pop up and tell the musical director what to do with the band. But Al very quickly realized that Bob knew exactly what he was talking about. And he suggested to Jack that they hire him as a trainee producer.

That's interesting.
So that's how he got involved with Jack. At the time, Jack was one of the top independent producers in the world. First of all, there weren't that many independents, most producers were staff A&R people at record labels. And secondly, he was hotter than a pistol. He discovered, financed and produced the Guess Who and had big hits with Bob Seger. Bob got to follow Jack around for the better part of a year and watch him produce and he learned the methodologies and the gear. He was trained by the time the Alice Cooper project came along. They were after Jack to produce Alice and Jack didn't want to do it. He actually sent Bob to see an Alice Cooper show in New York with the hopes that Bob would declare it bad and that would be the end of it all. But Bob came back from New York raving about them. Jack said, "You're so excited about it, you produce them." He went to [Alice's manager] Shep Gordon with a plan for them to do it together but really, he just sort of oversaw a little bit of it and Bob did most of it. He just brought such insight into what Alice Cooper was all about and how to tighten the whole thing up and make it commercial and mold Alice into a character. That was a really big part of what Bob brought to it.

Bob definitely played a similar part with KISS, in terms of shaping and defining character songs on "Destroyer." Michael, let's go down some of "The Elder" credits and see if you recall anything about them. Brian Christian was credited as the associate producer.
Brian was Jack's engineer for the better part of his career. And because Bob was Jack's protégé he sort of became Bob's engineer early on. He engineered the first Cooper stuff, so they were used to working with each other quite a bit. Brian got involved in the project after I left though.

David Brown and Corky Stasiak.
I certainly know who Corky is, but I don't know the other person. I think he was a Record Plant guy.

Tom Laughlin is credited as chief technician.
Don't know him.

This is probably the KISS album with the most credits in terms of recording and studios. According to some reports, the album cost in the neighborhood of $1 million.
Really?

That's quite the sum for 1981, isn't it?
Are you kidding? I'm really shocked. That's amazing.

Michael, do you have any recollections about when the album finally came out? Were you curious to hear it once it was released? Or had you just moved on?
No, actually I was quite interested to see how it turned out. I didn't personally enjoy it and I wasn't surprised that it turned out the way it did based on where it was headed when we were working on it. It was one of those sorts of noble projects where everybody reached for the moon and it didn't happen. Did they unmask themselves them on that album?

No, that was a couple of years off. KISS unmasked in 1983. A couple of folks have asked the same question, so it could be that there may have been some rumblings in the studio about it?
Yeah, I was going to say, because I seem to recall them discussing that. Actually, I forgot about that. It certainly rings a bell. It was very interesting to see them when we met them because you hadn't really ever seen a picture of them without their makeup. So, you felt like you were really on the inside of a state secret. (Laughs)

MEMORANDUM

DATE: August 13, 1981

TO: HOWARD MARKS
          ROSANNE SHELNUTT

FROM: William M. Aucoin

RE: KISS LP TITLE

Please be advised of the following KISS LP title suggestion
made by Bob Ezrin and the bandmembers:

(music from) THE ELDER

Please get back to me with any thoughts and/or comments
you may have re the above.

Thank you.

WMA/kd

645 MADISON AVENUE NEW YORK, NEW YORK, 10022 · 212/826-8800

Kevin Doyle

Award-winning engineer shares his vivid memories of recording "The Elder," including capturing Gene Simmons' vocal performance on "A World Without Heroes," recording multiple days of spoken word dialog and how the album ultimately evolved into "Bob Ezrin's show"

Kevin, you graduated from Fanshawe College in London, Ontario, in 1980 and the next year you were working for KISS. How did first meet Bob Ezrin?

Kevin Doyle: I knew Bob from a colleague's son I went to school with at Fanshawe. The man I knew was Jack Richardson, who manned Nimbus 9 Productions. He hired Bob originally. I think Bob was about 20 in the [early] '70s and he approached Jack with this act called Alice Cooper. And Jack basically said that the powers that be at Nimbus 9 didn't think it was a good idea, but Jack gave him the OK to go ahead and spend the money and do the recording [anyway]. And the record did phenomenally well as history says. Bob did very well with Alice. And then Bob went on to do Peter Gabriel. You know Bob is a Toronto boy and he used to do a lot of his recordings in Toronto. [With] Jack being his mentor, I knew him from Jack Richardson.

Initial album sessions commenced for KISS in 1981 at Ace Frehley's Ace in the Hole Studio in Connecticut. Were you present for those sessions?

No. They were probably just pre-production demos. Bob was doing some writing with the guys and I would imagine just kind of finalizing the concept of the album. I mean you have to understand; I think a lot of the idea for "The Elder" was probably from Bob because Bob had just coming off doing the "The Wall" with Pink Floyd.

That's right. So ultimately recording moved to Toronto and New York with Bob. Which sessions were you present for?

I was at most of the ones in Toronto at Sound Interchange where I was a staff engineer and I went over and did some work at Manta Sound where the album was being mixed. And some of the recording and pre-production was done up at Bob's farm, outside of the city.

That's Ezrin's home studio?
Yes. The interesting part is Bob had brought up a mobile; I think he brought up the Record Plant mobile, and he just parked it on the farm.

Do you recall any of the specific gear that would have been utilized at these studios?
It was an old vintage Neve at Sound Interchange that was being used. We also did the choir there, the local boy's school, St. Robert's Choir. And I was involved doing a lot of the vocal stuff, like I did the lead vocals with Gene on "A World Without Heroes." I think that's the best one on the record.

I think it's one of Gene's best vocals in his career.
And I think Lou had a bit to do with the writing of that song, Lou Reed.

That's correct. How often do you recall Lou being in the studio?
In and out periodically.

The choir was based in Toronto?
It is. I think it's based in the northern part of the Toronto city. It was a kid's choir basically.

How as the choir tracked?
The choir was approximately 20-30 members and they sang into three Sennheiser 421 [microphones]. They all sung as one performance.

Do you recall on what songs they were specifically featured?
I think they might have been in a couple of other places, but I don't know that they ever made it to the final mix.

Left on the proverbial cutting-room floor. As you mentioned, Bob was just coming off the mega-successful "The Wall." What are your general recollections of working with Bob during this time?
Well, Bob is Bob. I've known Bob for a long time. He's cooled down a bit now, but he was pretty intense. Bob's a pretty intense guy. He likes to work quickly and efficiently. Bob's a great guy, a really, really smart guy. You know, Bob kind of met his match a bit when we did the narration part, which was with Antony Parr and Robert Christie.

Kevin, you bring up an interesting lost piece of KISStory. Parr, Christie and Christopher Makepeace are credited on the album but there is really only one part of narration featured on the final album, and that's it.
Yes, I believe so.

So, more was recorded?
Yeah, there was tons recorded — a lot of narration. The idea of the narration was supposed to bridge some of the songs together, with some orchestral and choir underscoring. And basically, more or less, in keeping with the idea of "The Elder" as a goal of being a seamless concept idea, almost kind of like "Dark Side Of The Moon" where side A is not really a bunch of songs, it's one continuous play with no ending. That was one of the goals.

Unfortunately, that goal was never realized with regard to the finished product. What do you recall about the decision to discard the narration sequences?
I have a funny feeling [that] this was the first album that the guys were going to do it without any makeup. Is that correct, Tim?

It could be, but I can't say definitively. Ultimately, KISS kept the makeup on for "The Elder," and in 1983, just two years later, they unmasked. Perhaps it could have been discussed around this period?
OK. I was under the idea that this was a transitional record for them in their career. And [they were] utilizing Bob's experience from "The Wall" [to form] this concept idea. But from what I remember, I don't think Gene and Paul [were] totally committed to the idea and that it was probably straying too far away from what their dedicated fan base would want.

Well, to this day, Paul and Gene don't mince words about their feelings regarding the project. So, it's interesting that you would have sensed that back when they were recording the album.
Yeah. Well, I'll tell you, I guess I'll go on record, I remember doing some of the vocals with Paul. And vocally, [the songs] were really challenging for him. I mean, you've got to admit that Paul and Gene aren't the greatest singers in the world, but they're accomplished if they stay within the parameters of what they know they can achieve. I think Bob presented some ideas and an orchestral concept where Paul would be singing falsetto and really challenging his vocal techniques. And I'm pretty sure Paul was ... I'll tell you right now, there was one song, I can't remember. Paul had a hard

time getting past the first couple of lines because it was such a foreign way for him to sing.

You might be talking about "Odyssey," which is heavily orchestrated and a song he doesn't feel is his best performance, vocally. In hindsight, he's commented that his singing the song was "tragic."
Yeah. Paul couldn't keep the timing and the meter. I remember very distinctly because you're talking about guys who are used to having steady drums keeping the tempo and the meter. And now you're asking them to get the meter and time out of orchestral [instruments]. In hindsight, I think Bob would have been better to put down drums for them to sing to and then take them out of the mix.

You know, it's like asking Ace to go play a violin in an orchestra. I mean Ace is an accomplished musician, but it would be kind of a challenge for him so ... this was a very challenging record, vocally, for these guys. I was really pleasantly surprised that Gene nailed "A World Without Heroes."

He really did.
We did that song; he didn't wear headphones. We put the music through the speakers so he could hear the song more acoustically, which is a departure from proper studio techniques. I remember setting up speakers for him and he needed an intimate sound. He needed to sing a lot softer. I mean, here's Gene Simmons, the romantic vocalist, coming out in this song. You know, he nailed it. I think he did a great job doing it. It took us a while to make him comfortable with the approach and the environment of doing it, but he did a great job. We weren't so lucky with Paul.

With regard to Paul's performance, what comes to mind when you hear "Odyssey" now? (Plays sample)
Well, Paul double tracks the main vocal to create more power in the performance. Double tracking creates the idea that the vocal is more pontifical. It is understandable that the key of the song is too low for Paul — Paul's vocal power is in a slightly higher key.

Another song Paul has expressed displeasure with regard to his vocals is "The Oath," particularly the falsetto. Your thoughts? (Plays sample)
The key is too high for Paul, which explains the lead vocal double. It is falsetto, which is about vocal control, which Paul is limited. There are intonation problems in the higher notes. When Paul descends in pitch his

real vocal sound stands out, which has more sonic mid-range and is not pure and clean, which is the goal of falsetto singing. The turning point where Paul goes from falsetto to his natural range is quite evident and maybe a little embarrassing. [It's] not one of Paul's best vocal performances.

You've cited "A World Without Heroes" as an album highlight in terms of Gene's vocal delivery. In listening to this with fresh ears, what else stands out? (Plays sample)

Gene delivers a very subdued, intimate and well-executed vocal performance. The verse is controlled so the story is well-stated and the chorus is projected and sung out to give the message of power and passion. The solo is very melodic and well-constructed. Obviously, the technology of today would make for a better sonic mix.

How about another Gene track, "Under the Rose"? Would that be the choir singing in the chorus? (Plays sample)

With Gene's vocal in "Under the Rose," he double tracks the verses and adds harmonies in the choruses. Because he is using tremolo and vibrato in the verses the double track is needed. He also layers the choruses and sings out more in the choruses to give them more power and character. I don't believe the choir is used in the song. When the choir sings, they add much more harmonic content.

You've intimated that you sensed some misgivings from the band about the project. How did that affect the overall atmosphere during the recording sessions?

I think there was a lot of positive energy, just from stepping outside and looking at it from a bit of the distance. I kind of have the idea that no one really had, [except] maybe Bob, and I don't even know for sure, an idea of what the total concept was going to sound like. So there was a lot of experimenting, a lot of challenges and I think Bob probably had some really good ideas about the concept of what he was trying to achieve but he was limited, basically, because of the capabilities, especially the vocal capabilities, of Gene and Paul. Bob's vision was really great, but when it got down to executing it, I think Paul, more than Gene, was a little uncomfortable. "It might be great, Bob, but it's not really the KISS that we want." I think Paul and Gene were willing to go somewhere different, experiment and things like that but [they said], "We can't really go so far that we're so far removed from our basic dedicated fan base." Does that make sense?

Sure. But in the end, it seems that they did stray too far.

Another interesting thing that was going on in my career at that time, I was also working on Glenn Gould's "Goldberg Variations," which was regarded as one of the greatest classical piano recordings ever. You know, here I was going from an incredible musical genius in Glenn Gould to KISS. I'm not undermining KISS' expertise. I could see where there was an accomplished artist and I could see the guys in KISS really wanting to elevate by transitioning themselves but not knowing intimately how limited they might have been at the time. And I think that was scary for them.

Can you give a general picture as to how the songs were tracked?

The orchestral stuff was layered towards the very end of the record. I think a lot of the orchestra stuff might have been done at Manta. I can't say for sure. But usually the bass and drums and the bed tracks were done first and some overdubs missing. And then we got to doing the lead vocals and the backup vocals and the choir.

Do you recall about how big the orchestra was?

I can't imagine it being that small. It would probably be more like a 60-piece orchestra. You know, knowing Bob.

Eric Carr was the new addition at this point. Any recollections of working with Eric?

No. I think Eric did the initial sessions and from what I was led to believe he was no longer involved in the concept and direction of the album after his drumming was done. And I can probably sympathize; he was the new kid on the block. He's not going to overstate his welcome or overstate anything. I think he was basically, with Gene and Paul and Bob, [saying,] "I'll do a good job. I have no idea where the album is going but I'll do what you guys need me to do."

Drummer Allan Schwartzberg subbed for Eric on a couple of the album's tracks, "I" and "Odyssey." Do you recall him being around?

No. I think Allan was recorded in New York for some of the songs, definitely at Bob's request. [Editor's Note: Allan Schwartzberg has said that he recorded drum tracks at Ace in the Hole.] [He was brought in] because Bob had worked with Allan before, I think with Peter Gabriel and maybe some of the Alice Cooper records.

Allan has actually stated that Bob made him double his drum parts. I've heard of doubling guitar parts and other instruments, but doubling drums seems very challenging.
I think it was just to make the sound bigger. And especially when there is going to be orchestration added later.

Ace has been said to have been absent from a majority of the sessions in Toronto. Apparently, 24-track masters were sent to his home in Connecticut and he recorded his solos there. Then Ace's solos were sent back to Toronto where Bob apparently went through them and decided what to keep. Do you recall this dynamic?
I think that early on [we] didn't need Ace. But Ace wasn't really brought up in a lot of the sessions.

Ace certainly was not enamored with the direction of the album, which surely explains his absence.
Yeah. I have to agree with you. If he was really digging the record, he would have been more involved. And basically, it got to be Bob's show, Bob Ezrin's show. And I think with the fact of Gene and Paul realizing a lot of their earlier success was due in part to Bob, they were going to let Bob run with it until they became uncomfortable. Bob came from the Jack Richardson school of music production where bands came in and they virtually didn't know anything about the recording process, and you had to dictate total control.

Well, Bob worked with KISS on "Destroyer," which is still considered a classic in the KISS catalog. And with "The Elder," he played perhaps an even more integral role.
I'm pretty sure Bob co-wrote quite a bit of the record with the guys.

He did, he co-wrote more than 50 percent of the songs. I want to go back to the spoken word component since there is little known about this part of the project. Robert Christie and Antony Parr were two of the actors who contributed spoken word passages, most of which, as previously mentioned, were left off the album. Do you recall how these actors were recruited?
They were actors ... we have a city called Stratford about an hour's drive out of Toronto that is very famous for a lot of Shakespeare plays. And they were part of that actor's guild there. They're very much from the English Shakespearian school of live performance acting.

Bob would have brought them in?
I believe Bob hired an agent and we listened to demo reels and the agents got a hold of them and they came in and read from scripts.

Do you recall which roles they played? There's the boy, the role of the Council of the Elders representative and there's Morpheus.
Chris was the boy. He was a lot younger. The older guys were Robert Christie and Antony Parr.

In the one spoken word portion that was kept, there seems to be an effect on the councilman's voice.
The effect on the voice is an Eventide Harmonizer tuned down. I believe the sound effects were added in the final production at Manta.

So, you recall quite a bit of recording of dialog and an initial plan to include it on the final album?
Well, I think the story was going to be between the songs. There was going to be narration between the songs.

KISS fans wonder who has these recordings? Maybe Paul, Gene and Bob?
I remember everything distinctly going to Aucoin Management. The tapes would have gone there.

Some of the studio professionals credited on "The Elder" are Corky Stasiak, Brian Christian, Rick Hart, Robert Hrycyna, and David Brown. Remember any of these gentlemen?
Brian Christian was initially hired by Jack Richardson. Brian's from Chicago. He was hired when Jack was first producing the Guess Who. And when Bob needed an engineer, he just asked Jack if he could just use his engineer, which was Brian Christian.

The album is said to have cost more than $1 million. Do you think that this is accurate?
I could see it costing a lot of money, yeah. Especially when you hire the orchestra in the States, that was expensive. I wouldn't be surprised because there was a lot of recording done that never made it to the end. We spent a good three or four days recording all the narration and those actors don't come cheap. I think if they added in all the narration, I don't know if they would have gotten everything on a single album back then. It would have had to gone to a double album.

Well, there may have been initial talk that it could have been a double album so this might explain something.
Exactly.

Are you still in touch with Bob Ezrin?
I stay in touch with Bob once in a while. I did see him at Jack Richardson's memorial [in 2011].

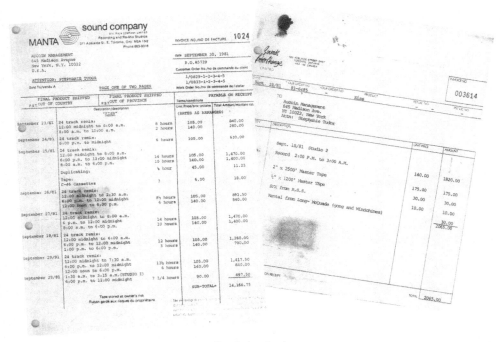

(Studio invoices)

Corky Stasiak

Engineer goes on the record about his work on "The Elder" during the final overdub sessions

I did know that your credit on "The Elder" was for a very brief interaction, though I wouldn't want to call it minor since it was part of your career! Could you give us a quick overview of what you were doing in 1981 with KISS?
Corky Stasiak: Of all the records I did with KISS, I worked on this one the least. Maybe, maybe a couple of weeks. This project was done mostly in Canada; I just worked on a few vocal overdubs. Bob called me up at my home and he said, "Listen, we're coming to New York to do some more overdubs for KISS, for the new album, and we want you to be a part of it. The guys want to work with you. We're going to be over at The Record Plant. Are you available?" And I said, "Yeah!" So, I showed up. That was it. I don't even think I worked two weeks on this album. And it was just vocal overdubs.

So, this is really the very tail end of the project. They've got most of the back recording done at Ezrin Farms studio up in Toronto and they're coming back to New York just to finish?
Yeah, they were just in town. When you work with KISS, they'd put out a couple of albums per year, which was very different from many groups because they wrote a lot of songs. They were prolific songwriters and they were on the road all the time. It wasn't uncommon to start an album with those guys, and then put it on the shelf for a few weeks, until they go to Japan for a few weeks, or until come back from Australia, or they have to play certain dates or [are] promoting something. And they'd come back, and we'd have a couple of weeks to work with them. And then back on the road so we tried to get as much done. I don't remember what their schedule was at the time. This was the last album I worked with them, the album before that was "Alive II." It was a double-record set and I think I only worked on one and a half sides of that album. But this album I worked less than two weeks. So, it wasn't unusual, if they were going to be in town, "Oh, let's go to the studio we're comfortable with, work with the people we're comfortable with, and add on as much stuff as we can, and let's move along."

Would that be why they would have picked The Record Plant for the final work, because they were comfortable with the place?

Yeah, because they're in New York. When they started to work at The Record Plant it was with me and it was "Destroyer," and then "Rock and Roll Over." "Destroyer" was done with Bob Ezrin and then with "Rock and Roll Over" they changed producers. Eddie Kramer, who was the producer, probably wanted to bring the work to Electric Lady, but they were comfortable at The Record Plant and said they wanted to work with Corky. But they all had a meeting and decided they wanted a different venue to record the basic tracks. They wanted to capture the sound that they had live so they rented out the Nanuet Star Theatre with The Record Plant remote truck. When we got all of the basic tracks, and some of the overdubs, we came back to The Record Plant and finished it. And then the next album was "Love Gun," with Eddie Kramer, and we did it all at The Record Plant.

To the uninitiated, how do you define the role of a studio engineer? What was your job in the studio for those who don't know, particularly when working with Bob Ezrin?

In 25 words or less?

(Laughs) In as many words as you want to use to explain it!

In 25 words or less, you're painting with sound on a canvas made of tape.

That's a highly concise answer. That's wonderful!

The role of an engineer is: You have a guitar, an amplifier, an idea for a song and you come into the studio and it has to go through the engineer, the electrical wiring through the board to the engineer's ears. And the engineer and the producer say, "Hey, that's a great sound," or "it needs a little more bass," or "a little more treble," or whatever, and you put it on tape. And then after all the information, so to speak, is collected on the tape then the engineer and the producer and the artist sit down and try to paint the canvas with sound and put it on two-tracks, left and right, stereo. So basically, it's what I said earlier.

In terms of KISS coming back to New York to do vocal overdubs, how was it different working with them in 1981 versus the first time with Bob?

Before I ever met them, Bob came to me and said, "I've got these four guys. Have you ever heard of this group, KISS?" And I said, "Yeah!" I was a big music fan and had been in bands myself. I watched all the rock shows of the era. Back then there was a show called "Hullabaloo," another called

"Shindig!" which I liked very much. "Hullabaloo," I think came from New York, and "Shindig!" from California, and these were the music shows of the late 1960s and early 1970s. And Don Kirshner's "Rock Concert." Those were the three shows that if you were a fan of music, be it pop music or rock and roll or whatever was going on, on the radio, then you were in tune to those three shows on television if you followed it like I did. I saw them on Don Kirshner's "Rock Concert" so I was aware of the band.

It was very rare that you would hear, back then, any of their records, before "Destroyer," on the radio that much. Because they walked in to do "Destroyer," and I don't believe their live album had been released yet. They were at the end of their contract with Casablanca with the live album delivered and Bill Aucoin ... I believe, from the stories I've heard, he mortgaged his home to do this album. And he was going to pay for the production of the album rather than a record label. He was going to shop this album to other record labels — when I met them.

A lot of contracts back then were three albums and an option. The deal was when you sign with a record label you do three albums and the record label has the right to request two more after that if they want you. And I don't know the details of their deal with Casablanca, but if it follows most of the contracts signed back then they probably said, "One more because you're not really selling records." I think they only picked up the option for the live album and were then going to drop KISS after that. They weren't going to pick up the fifth record option. So, when these guys came into the studio, they were a bit down and out. Bob even told me that, he says, "These guys really need propping up. They're really down and out. They've got a great live show." I'd never been to one of their concerts, but seeing them on Don Kirshner's "Rock Concert," they did a couple of numbers and there was pyrotechnics; they were a great theatrical act with rock and roll sensibilities. He says, "They just need a hit. If they get a hit this group is going to go into the stratosphere. So, let's do whatever we can do to prop these guys up and help them out." They walked into my studio paupers and walked out millionaires!

(Laughs) I guess that's right!
During the recording of "Destroyer" the live album came out and, "Bang! Zoom!" They were a force to be reckoned with. And now this record is just going to put them over the top because the real legwork had been done with the live album. I've worked on a lot of live albums: "Frampton Comes

Alive!" — that was his do-or-die album. And do-or-die studio albums like "Born to Run." That was Bruce Springsteen's third album, his do-or-die album — they were going to drop him. It just clicked. The albums that I worked on, those albums just did the legwork and brought all the other records into a higher sales category. So, they came in and their attitude was, "Ah man, we're trying this, we're doing that," but like Frampton or like Bruce, they weren't sure of themselves. They were sure of themselves before, and they thought they had something good and they did, but people weren't buying them. Maybe the record company wasn't supporting them, or whatever, they weren't getting the right breaks. It just happened for them and "Destroyer" went through the moon.

That's right, all their albums before "Destroyer" were only selling like 100,000 copies, so there was a real disconnect between how their live shows were resonating with the public and how the studio albums were performing. In late 1975 there's desperation as they're starting to work on "Destroyer." In 1981 was there desperation as they're coming of the pop and failure of "Unmasked."
Well there was only a partial desperation [in 1976], but as soon as the live album kicked in, they had more confidence. And that was towards the end of the recording of the record. With Bob Ezrin at the helm you couldn't ask for anyone better for that album. When it comes to "The Elder" I had lost touch with those guys. From "Alive II," we did that at Capital Theatre [in Passaic, N.J.], which was a theater that was crumbling. Again, they wanted to do a live record, and have it sound live, so we brought The Record Plant truck in again and we cut some tracks there. But then they cut some other tracks elsewhere, but I wasn't a part of that for the rest of "Alive II." We did some overdubs for "Alive II" back at the Record Plant.

Versus "Destroyer," "The Elder" is something of a disowned album by the band because it was a commercial failure.
Yeah, [of] the things I worked on, I said, "Boy, this is different!" But that was a Bob concept album kind of thing and you know concept records — they can go either way.

Yeah, you either get "The Wall" or you get "The Elder" I guess.
(Laughs) There you go. Brilliantly put.

What do you remember in the studio? You may not recall song titles, but what stands out in your mind working with them and what they were trying to accomplish through this overdub process?

I don't remember much, just being there and doing the overdubs. Brian Christian was there as well, and I remember we were in Studio C. Now we're talking attitude, it didn't have the attitude of any of the other albums that I had worked on. There was a different vibe in the studio.

But it wasn't about attitude, was it? It was "art" and Ace wasn't really around?

I didn't see Ace at all. Gene and Paul were the only two people that I worked with on that album. Every other album I worked with all of them, but with that particular record I only worked in the overdub situation with Gene and Paul and I believe the majority of the things we did were vocals.

Do you recall a different attitude from them working on this than back in 1976?

Honestly, I don't remember — it was so long ago, and it was just ... what I'm telling you is what I felt. It just felt very different. And I didn't work with them that long and I hadn't seen them in a while. There was a lot of time between "Alive II" and the recording of "The Elder." I'd also changed my look. I had a mustache and a beard when I worked on most of their albums, but when they worked with me on that record, I had short hair and no mustache or beard, and they didn't recognize me. They almost walked right past me in the studio at first. Don't forget they recorded all the tracks and overdubs in Canada, and just came down here to do little piece work. I wasn't "getting down" with them and hanging out and putting in hours and hours and hours. As a matter fact, as I remember now, Bob Ezrin didn't even show up for the sessions we were at. It was just me and Brian Christian.

So, were you working under your own guidance, or were Gene and Paul fulfilling the producer's role when Bob wasn't there?

Bob called in a couple of times. I think Brian took over the whole production end of things when Bob wasn't there.

I think Bob was working on other albums at that time as well.

You know what he was doing?

I think it was the Kings' "Amazon Beach," and Murray McLauchlan.
He wasn't even there. I loved working with Bob. We worked really well together. I liked Gene and Paul too. When I got the call and Brian Christian showed up, and he said, "No, Bob's not going to be here. He's back up in Canada doing something." I don't know. I figured I'd see him the next day or so, but that never happened. The difference was those sessions for "The Elder" that I worked on were truncated sessions. The guys would come in and maybe work on one or two vocals and then leave. There wasn't working 10 or 11 hours together on those sessions. I don't know if this is true or not, but it just seemed like they were probably in New York in between something, and were like, "Hey, let's just throw something on tape." It was like doing a commercial. When you work with an advertising agency recording something, you work from 9 in the morning to maybe 3 in the afternoon and go home. When you're doing rock and roll, every session I did with KISS was minimum 10 hours a day.

So much more of a hit and run kind of thing. Coming in for a particular thing or focus?
That's right.

Back in 1981 did you listen to "The Elder" when it was completed?
Yes, I did.

From a professional point of view, what did you think of that album when you first heard it knowing what KISS was and had been?
It was "different." It probably affected me like it affected everyone else. They just took a wrong turn getting to their destination.

I've spoken to some other people who knew Gene and Paul in the post-disco era, and there's kind of a feeling that they wanted artistic recognition. Knowing them and having worked with them in a professional capacity, do you think that that's where they went wrong, trying to get artistic validation? Or was it just a concept album that didn't work?
It was probably just a concept that didn't work.

So "The Elder" was your final record with KISS. Why did the relationship end? What happened to Corky and KISS?
I did quite a lot of records with KISS. My name shows up on their records more than anybody else's, I think, as far as in that capacity. They moved on. That's the nature of the business. You work with an artist and do a couple of

records. It's kind of like going out with a girl. The wanted to branch out. They worked with a different producer who requested different engineers.

After Bob Ezrin they worked with Michael James Jackson.
Yeah, and he doesn't know me. He probably had people he could relate to and had worked with before. I was totally honored that they wanted to work with me through a couple of different producers. The producer could have said, "No, I don't want to work with him." But they were adamant, I believe, and I was very lucky to be able to work with those guys. They were terrific guys to work with and we made a lot of good music and their legacy will live on forever. The music business ... you go with a different producer and he goes, "I'm going to produce this record — I know an engineer." Then they go to another producer and somebody he's worked with. But my career took off in a different way.

So, which direction did your career go?
After that I did Blue Öyster Cult. I did the Clash's first American release. I did Lou Reed. I did a lot of stuff. One thing leads to another. Some heard me on a record and wanted to use me for that. And so forth.

When someone wants to capture a sound in the studio they think of the engineer in the studio as well?
It all depends. Back in those days, you get signed to a record label and the record label goes, "Listen man, I heard you in that club and you sound great. I know just the producer. ..." And the record label turns you towards somebody and that guy says, "I worked with a bunch of guys and engineer 2 is the guy I can work with to do you." I can't recall a group who used the same engineer throughout their whole career, can you?

No, because a band's producer, studio, and other factors change, like you said.
Yeah, because you want to try somebody new. You hear a record and you go, "Wow, what's that! I want to hear that. Who did that!" And then you try and seek that person out if you think that they're right for you. It's just like a house painter or a construction guy who's going to redo your kitchen. You hear from somebody, or you see somebody's work, and you go, "That's nice, who did that?" And that's the way it is. And as engineer you move from project to project like that. And sometimes you work on multiple albums. I've done multiple albums with a lot of groups.

That's right, your non-KISS discography is impressive, and you've work with a ton of acts — a diverse group of artists.
Yeah, I've been lucky. I was very lucky. It's great when an act says, "I want to work with him again."

Talking about the producers, rather than the acts, where does Bob Ezrin rank for you for those you've worked with?
Oh, number one. Without even thinking because he was the one who got me to see sound differently.

That was his innovation early on, wasn't it? He came in almost as a prodigy producer and changed the way things were recorded.
He made me see audio. He wanted to see audio — he didn't want to just hear it. He wanted to paint pictures with sound. He wanted to make motion pictures for the ears.

I think he said in another interview years ago, something like "aural tapestries" for the ears or something similar. An audio canvas with layers upon layers of sound. Very Beatles ...
I never heard that, but we talked about it a lot. We sat down and he told me that he wanted to make "Technicolor" recordings. He wanted to be cinematic.

And that's where he was very successful in the 1970s ...
Yeah, and I said, "Whoa, wait a minute now! Oh my God, that's amazing!" One of the things along those lines, there was an article in one of the audio magazines that I used to subscribe to, and it was about binaural recording. I read this article like three times and I said, "This fits right into what Bob and I were talking about." Do you know what binaural recording is?

Yes. [Editor's Note: Binaural recording is a method of recording that uses two microphones arranged with the intent to achieve a 3-D-like sensation for the listener.]
So, I posted this article to him and he said, "I've never heard of that. What is that?" So, I explained it to him and found a copy of the magazine and gave it to him. And the next thing I know two or three days later, he had walked in with something that he got from Sony — a binaural microphone with a dummy's head. It was just a dummy's head, with no eyes, but it wasn't really detailed. But what was detailed were the ears, and the ear canals were made exactly like a human ear canal would be. And what you'd do was take

these binaural microphones, which were shaped like a stethoscope, and put it in this dummy's ears and put the dummy's head somewhere that you wanted to record somebody and those microphones would pick up the sound as the human ear would hear it.

When we recorded something like that, we recorded the intro to "Detroit Rock City" and we used my car. I had a Toyota S5 and we took the wires from the studio ... the studio was on the ground floor that we used, and we put extensions on the wires, and we put them outside and connected them to the binaural microphone. We put them in my ears, and I started the car up. We had a cassette of "Rock and Roll All Nite" in my cassette player in the car. We couldn't drive because we were connected to the board, so luckily it was a stick. I had the clutch all the way down and [imitated accelerating and shifting]. When we came back from recording and played it on the speakers it was so-so, it didn't kill us. It was going through the queue system and I hooked up headphones and listened to it and it blew everybody away. On speakers you can't really get the feeling of the binaural recording but put on headphones [and] you are that head.

It's kind of like you're getting it all focused ...
And it's eerie. And Bob said, "Oh my God, I want to do this!" So he went out and got in my car in front of 321 West 44th Street in Manhattan, that's where the studio was, and he put the headphones in and he did one and he started to hum along with the song ["Rock and Roll All Nite"]. And when we came back and we played it back, [and] put on headphones, it was the creepiest thing you've ever heard because it sounded like you were humming. When you listen to that, on that cut, put headphones on, you'll be freaked out because you are in the recording. And that's what he wanted to do. He wanted to paint pictures. He wanted to make a movie that was just audio.

And he did that to connect the songs. You go to the end of "Detroit Rock City," the car crash and screeching tires leading into "King of The Night Time World."
Yep, if you remember it faded into a woman doing dishes listening to a radio. And that woman was one of the secretaries and we got a bunch of dishes and went into one of bathrooms and we filled the sink up with water. Andy was one of the engineers there and it was his girlfriend, Anne. And she was around, so we were like, "Can you do me a favor? Can you put these headphones on?" So, Bob and I explained the whole thing to her. She put

the binaural [microphones] on and was doing the dishes. And Bob had recorded a little piece that we put on a mono tape machine that we played through a little radio that we put in there. We hooked it all up to the control room. Bob read a news piece, but that's his voice on the radio.

Right, that's the newscaster that some people think is Gene, but is Bob. Gene's said so, Bob's said so, and now you're saying so!
That's Bob. So, she's doing the dishes ... Gene and Paul weren't even there during this whole thing. They were on tour some place or doing something. This was a little add-on that Bob wanted to do. The car, the crash, and she had the binaural [microphones] on and you listen to the end of the song with headphones on and you'll be creeped out because you're doing the dishes.

I'm going to have to try that!
You should, it's amazing. And that is where the binaural [recording technique] really comes alive. We panned the radio all the way to the right side, and she's there doing the dishes, and she has on the binaural microphones so you're hearing everything through her ear canals.

One last question on Bob. How was Bob different between 1976 and 1981? Five years had gone by. He'd done "The Wall" and a lot of big albums in interim. They brought him back in to have his name associated with the album because they're on a bit of a downslide. You've said he was not around the studio a whole lot ...
I didn't see him. For the week and a few days that I worked on "The Elder," I didn't see Bob. So, the last time I saw Bob was, I think, when we did Peter Gabriel's first solo album, [with] "Solsbury Hill." I was over his house a few times for dinner. I think we did one other project together which I can't remember. And the CB craze was big, and we took a drive. He was really into CBs and he bought me a CB and we hooked it up in my car. He got one in his car and we drove around town talking to each other on CB radios. Of course, Eddie Kramer then did "Rock and Roll Over," "Love Gun," "Alive II," and then [for "The Elder"] Bob phoned in, when I was there, he phoned in his requests to Brian what he wanted to do. It was just vocal overdubs, and anyone could have produced those. The guys knew what they wanted, so the guys really produced it, Gene and Paul. So, I couldn't really tell you what he was like after that because I haven't seen him since.

So that was your swan song with Bob?
Yeah, that was it. We didn't get together because he was off doing different things and so was I.

KISS has been going on more than 40 years. You were there for the classic era, 1976 – 1981. Are you surprised that they're still out there on the road?
No. You see, they have a theatrical act. To make it in the business you have to have a certain equation to have longevity. And that equation would be image, songs, and show. There's a lot of groups that haven't made a record in a long time and they're there still playing. Because they have show, they have an image, and they have a fan base. And these guys knew that right away, they have deep spikes in the ground with the KISS Army. They knew what they needed to do to keep doing. They had the image. You could paint lunch boxes with their image. Cartoons. Other people can be them. I'm not surprised at all.

So here we are 35 years later, and someone's interested in their least successful album!
That blows my mind!

DATE: February 3, 1981

TO: ALL AMI PERSONNEL
            ALL GMI PERSONNEL

FROM: George Sewitt

RE: KISS RECORDING SCHEDULE

Please be advised that the KISS recording schedule is as follows:

SUNDAYS, MONDAYS, WEDNESDAYS AND THURSDAYS

12:00 Noon - OPEN

TUESDAYS

10:00 AM - 5:00 PM

FRIDAYS & SATURDAYS

OFF

The Frehleys ask that you please keep phone calls to a minimum, however, if you must call, please contact Jayne for the correct number.

-IMPORTANT-

All mail and other deliveries for the band coming from AMI and GMI should be consolidated into one package and coordinated through Jayne. The packages will be picked up by John Harte.

Since travel time to the studio is 1½ hrs. each way and other pick-ups must be made in the morning (ie: food, supplies, etc.), one day's notice must be given to Jayne in order to insure delivery. Also, in order to limit the amount of packages going to Connecticut, please send only that which is absolutely necessary. Obviously, in the event of an emergency, this does not apply.

Your cooperation in this matter will be greatly appreciated.

GS/jg

cc: Ace Frehley
        Gene Simmons
        Paul Stanley
        Eric Carr
        John Harte
        Tom Holmes
        Tex Holmes

645 MADISON AVENUE NEW YORK, NEW YORK 10022 · 212 826-8800

Brian Christian

"Music from The Elder" associate producer goes on record about how KISS fans were ultimately not ready for the album, his music industry experience and his good fortune in working alongside Bob Ezrin

Brian, you had the privilege of working under the late legendary producer Jack Richardson, who was a mentor to Bob Ezrin. Did you meet Bob through your work with Mr. Richardson?

Brian Christian: The first time I met Bob I think it was when we were doing this small Canadian group and Bob came in with them. He was like [an] early 20s, long-haired hippie guy with an acoustic guitar, but extremely, extremely talented from the very beginning. We sort of met at the beginning of his production career. I did meet him through Jack, and eventually he went to work for Jack. He and Jack did Alice Cooper together and then Bob took over Alice Cooper after one or two albums that they did together. Jack Richardson was a sweetheart of a man and he was a mentor to a lot of people. I met Jack when he was doing the Guess Who. They needed me to remix some stuff and then I just started working and doing everything Jack did. And then Bob came in the picture and I started working with Bob and Jack. And then there were different times in my life when I worked with Jack and then I worked with Bob.

How would you describe your relationship with Bob? Was it strictly professional or were you friends?

Yeah, we were very close. I spent more time with Ezrin than I did with my wife. (Laughs) And throughout some of the years, we were constantly busy doing KISS and Peter Gabriel and "The Wall" and all those other things that we did. He's a great guy.

Fast-forward to 1981, what do you recall about being approached to work on "Music from The Elder"?

I was thrilled to be working with KISS. I didn't even know what the album was until we all got together, and we started recording and listening to all the stuff. You know, at that time, KISS was, and still is, a very popular band. I just loved rock and roll and they were a great band. Not only that, they're nice people. Actually, I ran into Gene Simmons [recently] at a volleyball tournament his daughter was playing in [with] my granddaughter. We got a chance to say, "Hello. How are you? What's going on?" and all that stuff.

Brian, when fans think of "Music from The Elder," Bob Ezrin immediately comes to mind since he was the album's producer. But you are credited as associate producer. Can you summarize your role?
Well, I worked really close with the guys. Sometimes Bob was there, sometimes he was not. But I had a chance to work really close with the band. And that was a lot of fun for me, working with Gene and Ace. I had quite a bit of freedom on that album, working with the band. And I think the album turned out really good. Obviously, Bob Ezrin always has the last say in these things. But we did a lot of good stuff and he liked it. And we did some things that he didn't like.

Bob was juggling two projects at this time, "The Elder" and an album by the Kings. Do you recall that dynamic?
You know, I do not. I wasn't aware of that because we were at Ace's house up in Connecticut. He might have been doing some pre-production work, but I really wasn't aware of him doing anything else other than "The Elder."

Were you up at Manta as well?
I'm not sure that I was up at Toronto to do the stuff they did at Manta. I probably was since I was the associate producer. But [our schedule was a] day here and a day there. Especially towards the end. I think they were getting ready to start a tour. I think that was the album that they intended to do and then tour without their makeup for the first time.

You're not the first person who has mentioned to me that the band was planning to take off their makeup.
I think that was the plan. I don't know why that sticks in my head, but it does. I think that's why there was a departure from the old KISS stuff. You know, it was a little bit different. And I think that was the reason.

In hindsight, there may be something to that. The album was a complete departure, and coincidentally there was no photo of the band anywhere to be found within the album's packaging.
It really was a left turn for them.

There were a few other studios utilized for "The Elder." Do you recall working in any of the other studios?

Yeah, we did some work at the [Record] Plant. I can't recall ... there was maybe three studios that we worked at. I think we even did some work in L.A. You know, it's been so long, I'm not quite sure. We used to travel like crazy when we were doing that stuff.

There was Sounds Interchange, Phase One Studios. There was also a mobile truck brought to Bob's house.
That's right. I'd forgotten all about that. You know, I worked a lot with Gene. He also had a large hand in producing the album.

Well, the concept of the album is based on an idea by Gene.
Right. For me, it was a good project. There were a couple of songs in there that I thought were really good. I really, really enjoyed working with all of those guys. That's when they brought in the new drummer.

Eric Carr.
Eric, right. That was the first time that he had worked with the band in the studio.

Correct.
They were a pleasure to work with. There was no craziness. I mean there is craziness always in the studio. ...

Speaking of drums, Allan Schwartzberg was brought in to play on a couple of tracks. Do you recall Allan coming in?
Yes. Allan was a studio guy.

He played on the songs "Odyssey" and "I." That was Bob's call?
I'm sure there was some kind of circumstance with Eric. Maybe he wasn't available. I'm not sure how that worked. But Bob and I worked with Allan on a lot of stuff. He was on the Gabriel stuff. He played on some of the later Cooper stuff, after Cooper and the band kind of disbanded. He was a studio guy from New York. He was very, very talented. Just a wonderful drummer.

Lou Reed also played a significant part on "The Elder." Do you recall Lou being around?
I do not.

Lou co-wrote three songs, including the lead single, "A World Without Heroes."
Right. No, I don't recall him being up at Ace's house or at any of the studios in New York. I think they just wrote together; I don't think he was in the studio with us. If Lou Reed was in the studio, you'd remember.

(Laughs) The American Symphony Orchestra was contracted to help add some sweetening to songs such as "Odyssey," "A World Without Heroes" and "fanfare." Do you recall the charts being written?
Bob probably wrote them. He was very good at that. I am pretty sure we recorded the orchestra in New York.

It would seem to have been a large orchestra, I've heard upward of 60 pieces.
Right. And I think that it was recorded at the old church. I think it was a CBS studio, and it was a church if I'm not mistaken.

A church? Interesting.
You know, there was also Michael Kamen. It wasn't Bob [who wrote the charts], it was Michael. But he always collaborated with Michael. Michael was an extremely talented guy who went on to do some big movies. Unfortunately, he passed away at a very young age. And I think if you look further at the studios, [the orchestra was recorded at a] church. I think it was CBS that owned the church on Broadway down ... I don't know, [on] 32nd.

I don't believe a church is listed on the album, but it's interesting, nonetheless. Brian, what about St. Robert's Choir? What do you remember about this choir?
(Pauses) I think that it wasn't ... you know, it's been a long time. My recollection is that it was just a bunch of people and they came in and did one or two songs. But it was very, very big and boisterous. I think [they are on] "I."

During the chorus, there sounds like a big group singing the refrain.
Right. So, I think that's what it was. I'm not sure it was a formal choir or if they just called it that.

Christopher Lendt intimated something along these lines, that it was just a name placed on a group of singers.
Yes. I'm pretty sure that's the case.

I would guess that the choir can also be heard on "fanfare." There is some "chanting" that seems to be in another language, maybe Latin. Either that or its source music.
I don't know. To be honest with you, I can't remember that.

(Laughs) We're turning the clock back a ways.
The more I think about it, it wasn't a formal choir. It was more of like a group of people. And they just named it.

I'm curious if St. Robert's has some sort of tie to Bob?
I have no idea. I can guarantee you, none of us were saints back then. (Laughs)

(Laughs) You alluded to working closely with Gene Simmons. What about Paul Stanley? Do you recall him being as emotionally vested in the project as Gene?
Yeah, you know those guys were pretty close. They worked really well together. I remember Gene being at all the sessions for the vocals and lead guitar stuff. Gene was always kind of hanging out. Paul was very much vested in the album. I'm surprised that they were not as enthusiastic about the album because I actually thought it was a good departure from what they had been doing. But obviously it didn't work as well. The fans didn't seem to accept it as much as they did their other stuff and the stuff that came after. I think the whole idea of taking off the makeup was part of why that album happened. That's something you'd have to verify.

Brian, Ace Frehley was absent for a majority of the album's sessions and Paul Stanley ended up playing quite a few solos. Do you recall Paul playing, or anyone else?
Yeah, Paul played some lead. I think it was just a matter of style, you know where [the songs] fit his style. Ace had, I think, three or four leads on the album.

That sounds about right. But it seems Paul played quite a bit of lead guitar.
Yeah, it was more legato stuff rather than hard rock stuff, which suits Paul's style more. You know, the studio was actually at Ace's house, so we were in

the middle of Connecticut and it was very quiet and there was not much to do. I know every weekend I went to New York just to get to civilization. (Laughs)

Was the entire band up at Ace's studio?
Yes.

When "The Elder" moved to other studios, Ace, for the most part, stayed behind and flew in some of his guitar work. Apparently, tracks were sent via FedEx. Do you recall this dynamic?
Yes. That's exactly what happened. I think we were in Ace's studio; I'm just guessing, I think we were there for a month. And then we started going into the city and working there.

The story goes that Ace was not happy with the direction of the album. Do you recall that being the case?
I never heard him mention it. He seemed like he was into it as much as Ace would get into it. I mean, he had his own deal going on so ... I just kind of think that that was his style and he was kind of detached. I didn't think anything of it; no one seemed to think anything of it. It was just the way it was. It worked. You know, we got some stuff out of him. We were there, we did all his solos.

On tracks he did play on, he sounded great. His playing on "Dark Light," which was a Lou Reed co-write, is quite spirited.
Right. And I'm sure we did that at his house.

Ace has mentioned that he has uncovered some tapes featuring some of his "cutting-room-floor Elder" guitar work.
Yeah, that could be really possible because he literally recorded all his parts there. After we left, like you said, he didn't follow us.

Brian, is there one song that you recall being a great challenge to capture in the studio?
You know, back then it was ... fun. I don't remember ever having a hard time with a song. Just being in the studio, working, doing that kind of stuff, it was fun. It was very fulfilling. This album was no different than any other. We all had the same idea; we all wanted to make a great album. I didn't find anything difficult. I think if we were having trouble with something, we replaced it.

So, you don't recall banging any heads, creatively, with any of the band members or with Bob?
Well, it happens, but I don't recall anything. You discuss things, "Let's try this. Let's try that." It either works or it doesn't. It was a pretty open and comfortable session to do.

In terms of the album's concept, did you have any input?
No, that was more Gene and Bob. I think they were looking for a departure. The idea was to change what they did and take the makeup off ... and all that. I think the album is great, but I don't think their fans were ready for that kind of change. It was a huge departure from what they had done. I think it was very, very good stuff but people, they just weren't ready for KISS to be that band.

Some fans see the album as a direct attempt to be more like Pink Floyd, rather than KISS.
Well, I don't think there's a comparison between "The Wall" and "The Elder." I do, however, think that it was something that the band wanted to do. They felt like it was time for them to do that kind of thing. And like I said, I think it was really good. If fans are comparing it to "The Wall" and saying, "Well, Ezrin, Christian did that" ... that means they didn't [want] KISS to do it. If it was another band, they probably would have bought into it because it's very good.

I think that's a valid point. I think if another band released this album it would have been better received. People had a pre-conceived notion about KISS and what their music sounds like, and "The Elder" wasn't it.
Yeah, I mean people go to see them because, obviously, they make great music, but they put a show on. They have the costumes, the masks, the pyrotechnics — all that stuff. It reflects in the albums they put out and "The Elder" didn't have that urgency to it.

Canadian actors Christopher Makepeace, Robert Christie and Antony Parr were brought in to read spoken word portions that were designed to help thread the concept between songs. What do you recall about the spoken word component?
You know, I did not do anything with that. I think Bob did that and, like you said, they were Canadian actors, so it was probably done up there. And I, in fact, don't recall that as part of [the album] so it never happened as far as I know. But it's not on the album.

There's only one piece of dialog that ended up making it onto the final album. It's a brief sequence that actually closes the album. But engineer Kevin Doyle has said "tons" of dialogue was recorded.
Right. I really didn't have anything to do with that. So that was done up in Canada, and it seems Doyle did that with Bob. I don't even recall listening to it.

Who knows, maybe it's out there somewhere?
Doyle might have it!

(Laughs)
You never know, you know what I mean? Things just show up. I know that I have some stuff in my archives that are very interesting to me and I'm sure people would like to get their hands on it. But it's stuff that is put away and not for other people to have. He might have that ... you know, that's a big part of [the album's] history. I guarantee you; someone has something on it, but I just don't.

One criticism that fans have is that the album's concept is confusing. What's your take on it, Brian? Is the concept well underlined throughout?
No. I think that concept albums like "The Wall" — you get the story when you listen to the album. I don't think that's true with "The Elder." That's my opinion. I think it's a good album; it's a good bunch of music. I just don't think it's clear ... and maybe that's one of the reasons why they wanted to do some spoken word stuff?

It would seem likely. Kevin Doyle specifically mentioned that was the focus of the dialog: to thread the songs and help illuminate the story.
Right. I don't think people "got it" as a full-out concept album. Nor was it ever marketed as such, to the best of my knowledge. It was just "The Elder." (Laughs) No one said, "Here's the concept." So, I think that, as a concept album, it fell short in that regard.

Brian, you've described a positive atmosphere in the studio. Do you recall spirits being high when the project wrapped?
Yes. I think everyone was proud of what we did. And I think we were all feeling really bad about the fact that the fans didn't accept it. I mean, we worked very, very hard on that album. That was not something that was done flippantly. We worked very hard and long hours. And everyone put in 100 percent. When you're doing stuff like that, you have to feel attached to

it. And we all did, as a group. We were all attached to it and felt really good. I thought the guys played wonderfully on the album.

I think the band really upped their collective musical game on "The Elder." There's a lot of fantastic ensemble playing.
I agree. Everyone worked hard and they were willing to do things again. It was a great experience working with them. And we came up with what we thought was a great album. The fans weren't ready for it. That's all.

I think that's an important point. At that time, the KISS fan base was on the younger side. I don't know that this album, with this presentation, was going to reach a 12- or 13-year-old kid.
I think that's true. You know [how] "I" was very uplifting? I actually made a copy of that and played it ... I was not on the coaching staff, but my son was playing linebacker in high school. And I was part of the group of guys on the sideline that helped with the guys when they got hurt, so on and so forth. Before each game, that song was played. Very loud. And people loved it. The kids at the time were 17. It was a varsity team [and] they were the older guys at the high school. It was inspirational. ["The Elder"] had some really good stuff on it. Like you just said, their group of fans, their demographic, was not ready for that.

And I think there is a segment of fans who did not like it at first but have come to appreciate it through the years. Maybe they've gotten older and opened up their horizons musically.
I agree. Sometimes you're just ahead of your time.

You're not the first person I've spoken with who has intimated that.
It showed some really good musicianship and it showed their personalities, what their real personalities were, I think. And not the facade of all the makeup and this and that.

Do you recall the album failing to storm the charts? Do you remember speaking with Bob about that?
Not really. We were really busy. We were obviously disappointed in the performance of the album. You just go from one project to another. But you do obviously keep track of what you're doing. And yeah, we were disappointed in how it performed.

The album's packaging is very much an anomaly by KISS' standards. Do you have a comment on the packaging and whether that had some sort of effect?

You know what, KISS albums had a very certain look to them with the band always prominent. And I think that's one of the things that might have hurt the album. It was too obscure. You know, it was this mystical thing and it [hardly] said KISS anywhere. I think that could have hurt the sales as well. It's kind of like any other band — people will buy everything [released] from a band. But I think that album was very hard to find. It didn't have the same PR push that their other albums had. I mean, that's my feeling. But again, I was busy doing other things, moving onto the next project. You know, KISS albums have KISS all over it and the band all over it, and that didn't. It did, however, suit the album's concept, but it didn't suit the band's image.

Do you recall any conversations in the studio about this project being made into a film?

No, I was not ... I was really just dealing with the music and the guys and making sure all the bass parts were done [and] I was really taking care of the business in the studio. I wasn't really part of any of those conversations.

Brian, do you own a copy of "The Elder" in your music library?

Oh yeah. I have [the] vinyl. I used to take two or three copies and put them away and not open them. So, I probably have more than one copy of it. I'd have to look through my records ... I've got so many records. (Laughs)

No CDs or digital downloads?

I do have a [iPod] Nano that has no space on it. So, I do download. Right now, I make computer games.

Are you out of the music industry entirely?

I've done a few little things. I worked with Nils Lofgren on his [2011 studio album "Old School"] — I did one song with him. I really loved the music business; I did it for a long time. I would not hesitate to get back to it if there was an opportunity.

Can you tell us a little about your career in gaming?

I've worked out several different game companies, Interplay, THQ, Rockstar, D3. I worked with Konami. I was the vice president of product development for D3 and for Konami and I was a director at the other three places, and an executive producer. And now, I do some consulting work.

But if someone called me and said, "You know what, we want to get that sound that you used to get back in the day," I would love to do that! You never get that out of your system. Being able to work with groups like KISS and Peter Gabriel and Pink Floyd, it was a thrill and a pleasure and an honor. Not only that, it was something I loved. My career started way back, doing John Lee Hooker and B.B. King and all the blues guys in Chicago. And then I went on to the rock and roll business with the Guess Who.

You are from Chicago, correct?
Yes. I moved out to L.A. in 1972.

I can still detect a Chicago accent.
Well, you can't get Chicago out of the kid. (Laughs) It's even worse when I go there. I just fall right back into it.

(Laughs) As someone who worked on "The Wall," do you consider that to be the biggest milestone in your career?
Yeah, that was huge. I mean, obviously it was huge. Working with Peter Gabriel, doing his first [solo] album, the one with "Solsbury Hill" was [also] huge for me. I was such a fan of his. But you know, when you're working with bands like the Guess Who, you fall in love. You fall in love with the music, with the product, with the people, and it's a great feeling to be in the studio with a bunch of guys and just create. It's just a great feeling. When we were doing Alice Cooper, and Dick Wagner and Steve Hunter and all those guys were in the studio, we were creating music. I mean what could be better than to be able to say, "I'm creating music"? Not much.

As someone who worked closely with him, how do you assess Bob Ezrin, the musician/producer?
Well, Bob is a really good pianist. I'm assuming he still is. He played piano on a lot of the tracks. He can write. He can read music. He's extremely talented. And he puts the time in. He doesn't take that talent for granted. He's really a nice guy. He treats people right. If you look at his body of work and you sit down and listen to it, you can hear him inside that body of work, you know? There's definitely a Bob Ezrin style and sound, so he created that. He's a very talented guy.

Do you still keep in touch with Bob?
You know what, it's become less and less. But yeah, we keep in touch. We talk every once in a while. It's been awhile since I've spoken with him. I think

he's in Nashville now. He's doing his thing in Nashville. I kind of left the music business in 1990 and in '94 I got into the game business.

What was it, Brian? In 1990 were you just fed up with the music industry?
You know what, I wasn't ready for the digital, let's do everything sampled [environment]. I loved going in the studio with six guys, setting everything up, tuning the drums, and making music. By the time [it was] 1990, we started "manufacturing" music. It was different. And I just didn't enjoy that as much. I mean, sometimes you wouldn't even see the drummer but for one day. And it took forever and ever to create the drum tracks. It wasn't like, "Let's sit down and play." That's the direction it looked like it was going for me.

I think since then; it's turned around and guys are actually starting to play again. But that's the reason why I walked away. I did it for many, many, many years. And I'm going to say that I loved every minute and ... it just happened. You know, sometimes things in your life just happen. I'm not quite sure how it happened but it did. And I made a great career in the game business and I enjoyed that equally well. But for some reason now, I really miss the music business. You know, the feel of six guys, seven guys in one room, all with one goal in mind: to make a great album. I mean that's what the business was all about back then. Bob was one of the guys that was part of that.

Charles McCracken

American Symphony Orchestra bassoonist Charles McCracken recalls his brief moment in KISStory

For a rock band that once proclaimed themselves "the loudest band in the world," KISS sure have an interesting history with orchestras. Of course, there is the 1976 classic ballad "Beth," a song offering the first taste of an orchestrally sweetened KISS. The mixture of lush symphonic touches, a perfect Bob Ezrin arrangement and Peter Criss' streetwise crooning yielded a monumental hit.

In 2003 KISS married black tie with black leather for "KISS Symphony: Alive IV," a concert that coated nuggets such as "Forever," "Sure Know Something" and "Shandi" and electrified classics such as "Black Diamond" and "Love Gun" with a powerful orchestral makeover, courtesy of the Melbourne Symphony Orchestra.

Sandwiched in between these orchestral bookends is 1981's "Music from The Elder." For this grandiose concept album, Ezrin and KISS contracted the services of the New York-based American Symphony Orchestra. Ezrin collaborated with late award-winning composer Michael Kamen for a set of dynamic arrangements that were meticulously performed by the ASO. The results added rich instrumental depth and sonic color to tracks such as "Odyssey," "A World Without Heroes" and "fanfare."

Current ASO principal bassoonist Charles McCracken, who played contrabassoon during the orchestra's recording sessions for "The Elder," had this to say about working with KISS:

"I remember a little about that session. It was scored for a huge orchestra [and] I was one of two contrabassoons on that session. We were squeezed into one of the larger recording studios in New York — I don't remember which one, and I'm certain it doesn't exist anymore. I remember the music as being loud and repetitive. And that's about it. I'm not sure if any of the members of KISS were there; if they were, they probably stayed in the booth and kept a low profile.

That's about all I remember, it was a long time ago and a lot of the record/jingle/film recordings I did from the '80s, '90s and early 2000s sort of run together.

But I do get to say that I recorded with KISS! Not too many bassoonists can claim that!"

(A 76-person orchestra was used for "The Elder," versus 28 for "Destroyer.")

Bruce Gowers

Emmy-winning director of Queen's iconic "Bohemian Rhapsody" video chips in his recollections of working with KISS

Bruce, as KISS released "Music from The Elder" in November 1981, a channel called MTV had just debuted three months prior. Prior to MTV, how would you characterize the purpose of music videos?
Bruce Gowers: What really happened, in terms of groups in England, if [they were] touring the Southeast or touring Australia or whatever, but equally at the same time, the record was released in the States, they had no means of promoting it. And there was no great liaison at that time. And this was really in the mid-'60s, because I, as a cameraman, remember doing at least three videos with the Beatles in like '65 or '66. It was no big deal. There was no great "Tura, tura! Here's a Beatles video." (Laughs) But they put it on tape, and I guess they used it as promotion. But it wasn't until like the early '70s or the mid-'70s when videos really had an impact. It was like a safety net. "We're touring Australia. The record's going to be released in England. What are we going to do to promote the record?" And they'd do a video.

In fairly short order, MTV would go on to revolutionize the music industry. Do you remember thinking this channel would have a sizable impact?
No, I had no idea at all. And it's funny, when MTV started [broadcasting], I think the majority of the videos shown were English ones. There was very little done in the States at that point.

Professionally speaking, in 1981 you were a partner in Gowers, Fields & Flattery. Did the company specialize in music videos exclusively?
That's absolutely correct, yes. We were all co-owners of the company. We all came from the original company, Jon Roseman Productions.

Generally speaking, how would a band like KISS have approached you?
Obviously, we had a show reels with videos we had done for bands. And really the one that kicked it off, as you say, was Queen. And once we did, actually *we* didn't do, I did the Queen ["Bohemian Rhapsody"] video. (Laughs) There was no company that did it. Once that happened, the door was open. Everybody wanted a video. There were lots of reasons why "Bohemian Rhapsody" was so successful. A, it was six minutes long. B,

everybody said you can't release a single that long. C, they could not perform it live because of the complexity of the audio. It was released around Christmas in England, and at that time, once you got into December the charts didn't alter because there were no returns. The record was good. And [it] was played on "Top of The Pops." "Top of The Pops" couldn't avoid playing it ... so every week they had to play the damn thing. For that reason, the video stayed at No. 1 for like 14 weeks. I'm not saying that the record wasn't wonderful and brilliant, it was. But there were a lot of circumstances. And "Top of The Pops" always boasted on playing this No. 1 record. But it was normally live. They didn't even consider a video because there was no way Queen could go on and do a live version of "Bohemian Rhapsody." I'm not blowing my trumpet at all ... (laughs)

Well, your accolades speak for themselves, Bruce.
There were a lot of economic reasons and whatever that that video got played so much. And once that got played, other bands in the States at the time thought, "Oh my God. That's amazing. Let's get one of those." Then I had calls from the Bee Gees and Rod Stewart and whatever. It kind of flew from there.

Coming into the KISS shoot, would you have been aware of the type of project KISS were undertaking? "Music from The Elder" was a radical departure for them in being a concept album.
Well, certainly. I looked at the video you sent me [for "A World Without Heroes"] and the one thing that I recall was the tear shot [with Gene Simmons]. You're right; it was a totally different thing for them. I mean, it wasn't like an out-and-out rock track; it was a very emotional, moving track.

With the tear shot, I believe that was achieved by putting glycerin in his eye.
I'm not sure if it was glycerin or Visine. It was one or the other. Let's say it was done to emotionally help him. (Laughs)

In terms of the treatment of the video, would your team have fleshed out the treatment exclusively? Or would KISS have had some say?
I'm quite positive that they would have had major input into what they really wanted.

And there likely would have been meetings between your team and the band and their team?
Yes, sure. I think, back in the early days, we would have a very brief meeting with the band. If it was Queen, we would have a get-together with Queen, and we'd talk about what the record was. Or with John Cougar, we'd kind of get together and talk about what we were going to do. Sometimes, because we were in L.A., and the band might have been on the road or in New York, [some meetings] would be over the phone. But we certainly got together with [KISS] before we rolled any video tape.

How many cameras would have been utilized for the shoot?
Most videos were shot with [multiple] cameras. We would do like two or three takes. Maybe alter the angles on one.

When you watch this video all these years later, what are your thoughts on the finished product?
I was amazed that I didn't remember more about it. That was a time when we were flying between L.A. and Chicago and New York and cranking out maybe three videos a week.

What would have been the going rate for the work on two music videos in 1981?
Around that period of time, we did three videos with John Cougar, who is now John Mellencamp. We [did] three videos for $15,000.

(Pauses) Well, that seems pretty reasonable.
(Laughs) It's more than reasonable. And the Queen video, the one that begat all these videos, was done for 3,000 pounds.

Shifting gears to the other video that was filmed for the song "I." Frankly, little is known about this video, because it has never been released. Do you recall anything about the "I" video?
I don't even recall that one, forgive me.

If you shot it, would it have been edited and finished for release?
I do believe it was completed, yes. I have no idea, whether it was the record label or whether the band didn't like it for whatever reason. Maybe it wasn't released as a single?

It was released as a single overseas. One theory is that because the album didn't perform well from a sales standpoint perhaps it was decided to put a pin in the album and move on. Bruce, these videos were shot over Halloween weekend in New York. Do you recall the exact location?
I think it was just a sound stage that was available. Don't forget that a lot of these shoots were put together, literally, at the last minute. I mean, we'd get a call, "Can you do a video in New York on Thursday?" And that was like Tuesday.

In terms of an entire production team, how many from your camp would have been on the premises?
No more than two people from L.A., which is where we were based, would fly out. Everyone else was local, whether it was New York, Florida or Chicago, or whatever.

Any specific memories of the specific band members or the band's manager, Bill Aucoin?
There are some things. (Pauses) I have to be very careful because it was a long time ago. I know that, at the time, (pauses) Ace had a major problem.

Well, at that point, Ace was very disenchanted with not only the direction of this particular project, but his place in the band.
Yeah, I mean, I don't want to ... I was just aware that there were some problems with Ace. And I just played it very cool, that was all.

According to a 1981 report in "Billboard," PolyGram and MTV could not come to an agreement, and as a result videos from the label's artists were not featured on the channel, at least initially. So, I wonder if "A World Without Heroes" was even shown widely at the time?
At that time, a lot of labels had a problem with MTV. When you go back to it, MTV was programming material; they didn't have a single cost. And they got the videos for free, and they were on the air 24 hours a day! And if they didn't play your video, as a label, you got pretty pissed off, I would think.

With regard to your career, after directing many music videos you moved into television specials and live events. What made you want to quit doing music videos?
Having done about 200 or 300 videos I kind of faded to black and went back to my usual kind of work, which was network television. I had done something like 300 videos, and I had really had enough. (Laughs)

Given your expertise and professional history, how do you view the state of the music video medium today?

Oh, I don't know. (Laughs) I mean it's got so bizarre with so many fast cuts and ... a lot of women. I don't know. It has certainly changed from when I started. (Laughs)

Paul Flattery

Producer from Gowers, Fields & Flattery fills in some blanks regarding the conceptual treatments for KISS' videos for "A World Without Heroes" and "I"

Paul, MTV debuted in 1981 and in a quick time span revolutionized the music video medium. Prior to MTV's debut, can you paint a picture of the music video industry?
Paul Flattery: Well, I don't think there was much of a difference in intent when it first started. Have you read the book "I Want My MTV"?

I have. It's a good book.
The thing is, primarily, when we were doing videos before MTV, they were being used overseas mostly. So, a lot of our commissioning came through the international departments, because there wasn't much of a use for them here. And gradually they tried different things. There was an in-store point-of-purchase type of use for them, but that didn't really work out because the record stores complained that people just watched the videos and didn't buy records. Then there were some TV shows that used them and we — our company at that time when I first came over was Jon Roseman Productions — and we actually had a television series on the air called "Juke Box," which was hosted by Britt Ekland. It was a syndicated show, and quite selfishly, we only showed videos that we made to encourage people to get us to do their videos.

What the record companies were doing with all these videos that we did is hard to say. But mostly, they were shipped overseas. I remember being in Germany once, visiting a friend of mine, and there was 15 minutes of filler, because in those days there wasn't the ubiquitous channels that we have now. They would use [videos] as filler — they ran three Rod Stewart videos that we had done.

When MTV happened, they called us looking for videos. I mean it was that naive. And we said, "We don't own them. We do them for either the artists or for the labels. So that's where you're going to have to go." And some artists who did own their own, like Rod Stewart, he gave all of his library to them and he was given a lot of favor in later years because of that loyalty. Ultimately, as you know, because it's a visual medium, it was more successful when people were visually appealing. You've got that whole thing that came about, the '80s hair bands kind of thing. That's why some people wouldn't do videos. Like Steve Miller ... Christopher Cross. We did "Ride Like the Wind." We shot it in the Roxy in the day. And I'm sure you're familiar with the very famous Michael McDonald lines in that [song]. We didn't have Michael McDonald; we had this keyboard player lip-syncing to [his] lines. It was a little ludicrous. And of course, Christopher Cross didn't have the most visually desirable image so, as you can see, he didn't make a lot of videos.

In 1981 you were a partner in Gowers, Fields & Flattery. Did the company specialize in music videos exclusively? And was business robust at the time?

Business was great for us, yes. We were doing a huge amount of the available market. We were only doing [music videos] at that time. Bruce Gowers was a television director. He, me and Jon Roseman all came from London, we came from television. I was sent over here to open up the company. And Bruce was actually doing a show, "Headliners with David Frost." Before I even came out here, we were basically telling the record companies, because they were looking for Bruce, and we'd say, "Oh, this is Bruce's protégé! This is the guy he's bringing up." (Laughs) And Bruce would have to kind of go along with that. We would use other directors in England, and when I came out here, we found Russell Mulcahy — he was actually found by Virgin Records. They said to us, "You should look at this guy. He's Australian." So, we brought him over to England and actually then he and I went to America and the first video we did [here], in New York, was the Cryers, and that was for PolyGram. I remember that, and basically we just worked through a lot of these things. We had David Mallet.

I know his work. He did a video with KISS later.

He would come over and we did the Stones' "Emotional Rescue" and "She's So Cold." At the time, the record companies used to have these conventions, and then in '78 Warner Bros. asked us to do ... I think something like 10 videos, all for their artists, because they were going to show them at their convention. It was like Van Morrison, Steve Martin ... that's what they would use these things for. When MTV came along, obviously when they got this exposure, everyone wanted to get onto MTV. So, there was an explosion of doing videos. We did a lot of concepts. Bruce did Toni Tennille's show; he was still doing TV. And we would do our shoots on the weekends [when] he was available. That kind of stuff.

Do you have a recollection of how your firm came to work with KISS in 1981? Do you remember who approached you?

I honestly don't recall in that instance. I actually didn't do go on that shoot, just because of the economics. It might have been Bill Aucoin, it might have been Len Epand [from PolyGram]; it might have been Phyllis Chotin [from Casablanca]; it might have been somebody else. I remember a lot of people [from various labels].

What would happen is, they would say, "We've got this KISS video. We've got this amount of money. And we want some ideas." So basically, we would do the ideas and then I would write [them up] and we would send them, and we'd send the budget. And then they'd say, "OK. You're going to do it. Here's when we'll do it."

This particular KISS album, which was titled "Music from The Elder," was a radical departure for the band in being a concept album. Coming into working with them, would you have been made aware of the "different" type of project KISS were undertaking?

Yes. Which is why I think you see in "A World Without Heroes," it's a very muted presentation of them.

Let's get into that video. You have mentioned that the film "Excalibur," which was released in April 1981, was an influence on the "A World Without Heroes" video treatment. What was your thinking in drawing that connection?

Well, because the costumes KISS wore were like armor. And ... if you actually go back to the first-ever video album [we did] with Blondie with David Mallet, we shot every track on it in New York. David, if you looked at his videos, he would always fade to white and he loved tweaking the video to almost blow it out. With video you have much more of an on-the-spot ability to tweak the imagery as opposed to on film. And we did them on video, because video was cheaper. It's a bizarre thing, but in England in the early days, when we were working on TV, the unions determined that video was shot inside the studios and film was shot on location. So, if you actually went and looked at some very old British dramas, if they went outside it went to film because it was a different part of the union. So basically, we were mainly "inside" people, so our medium was video. When we would shoot bands in these studios — we called [them] "cheap and cheerfuls" — because they would have a cycle ready and the lights would be up, you'd just have to adjust them, and the equipment was there. And we would shoot the drummer and the bass player for one pass and we would roll that back and put the singer and the guitarist in, in front of them. On two or three cameras, you could get a thing done in an hour, setting lights, [and a] two-hour shoot, you could do them for a few thousand pounds. That's why we were on video. When I saw "Excalibur," with the armor, I thought that might be a good look for KISS.

I've seen that film. And one of the things that I recall is scenes where the knights' faces are illuminated, with an almost glowing effect. And it seems that effect was also borrowed for "A World Without Heroes." In some of the solo close-ups, the band members almost look divine, due to a glowing effect.
Yes, yes. Honestly, a lot of the time, we took our influences from other mediums, from TV and from movies.

That makes sense. Paul, would part of your process have also entailed listening to the track you were shooting the video for, to help inform your direction?
Oh yeah. That's exactly what we would do. They would send us the tracks and we would listen to them and would see what came out. A lot of the time, in the early days, a lot of it was performance as opposed to conceptual stuff. But we did do some conceptual things.

Gene Simmons is filmed at the end of the video with a tear in his eye. Do you recall that part being in the treatment?
I can't claim that. I honestly don't remember if it was in the treatment, or whether it was something that came up at the time.

In this video, there are shots where the band is in the background and Gene Simmons is superimposed in the foreground. Can you expand on how this would have been achieved in 1981?
It would have been planned to do it that way in post-[production]. So [Gene] would have been positioned to one side and the others to the other [side]. It's just basically a dissolve, it's just a superimposing — combining two shots.

In hindsight, "A World Without Heroes" is tastefully artistic but still powerfully leverages the band's image. In other words, it's not uncomfortable for the change of pace it represents. In watching all these years later, are you proud to be affiliated with it?

Oh yeah, absolutely. I think maybe the Fortress of Solitude[-inspired video] a little less so. (Laughs)

Let's shift gears into the video for "I" then. Little is known about this video, frankly, mostly due to the fact that it has never been released. So, am I to understand you were inspired by "Superman" in putting together the backdrop for the "I" video?
Yes. [The thinking] was [to] inform that these guys were ... remarkable and a positive force.

That certainly ties into the song's message of self-empowerment and the album's concept. What are your recollections for how that set was built?
You know what a glass shot is, right?

I don't know that I do. Can you please elaborate?
Well, for instance, one of my most famous videos is "Billie Jean" [by Michael Jackson]. If you look at the shot of the street corner, all of the top of that [scene] was painted on glass that the camera shot through. The set itself was only 10 feet. And this is Russell Mulcahy, he brought this back. If you look at Fleetwood Mac's "Gypsy," again that was done like that. Eric Critchley was the guy, he was quite famous in this world, doing this kind of stuff.

So, it's quite possible Eric Critchley had something to do with the "I" set?
Yeah, I would think so. He would have painted it, and done a glass shot to shoot through. He would have done that.

According to a "Billboard" news report from 1981, 100 extras were brought in — both actors and friends of the band — to participate in the "I" video. In looking at some photos, it seems these extras served as the audience and were also used as far as propping the band up on their shoulders. Would you recall working in extras to the treatment?
No, I don't. I don't really understand the connection between an audience and the Fortress of Solitude. They go against each other, don't they?

Well, again, I think part of the problem is that we're flying blind in that there is no finished video out there to have a look at. "A World Without Heroes" was completed — can we assume the video for "I" was edited and finished as well?
Oh yes.

So, there was a finished product and for some reason it was not released.
Yeah. Usually, videos would be shot like two at a time, or three at a time in some cases. Even more sometimes. I remember doing like six Santana songs in one session as well as two for another act, which Columbia made us do on the same stage. And we did an entire album by REO Speedwagon onstage in one day. They used to shoot these ... but of course if the album was a flop, there was no reason to put the videos out.

All signs would point to that for "The Elder." The album was released in November 1981. By early 1982 it was clear that the album wasn't performing to the level the band had hoped. It may have been a case of cutting losses and moving on. And the "I" video could have been shelved as a result.
Exactly.

But the video has to be out there somewhere out there?
Well, here's the thing. When Bruce, Simon [Fields] and I broke up, essentially it was very acrimonious. Simon had brought in Steve Barron and essentially ... the videos that Steve did under our joint banner; he was subsidizing them with our money. So, he was getting a better product then he could have done for the budget. Then he left. He said, "We're gone." I was actually best friends with Simon, so I was blindsided by this. And when we closed the company and we got a check for a dollar each, Bruce was pretty pissed, as I was. Bruce had his television career; I had basically nothing. I was in the music video world and didn't have anything [else]. I had to start all over again.

I started my own company and eventually ended up with a director called Jeff Kohl, who was really good. And PMI approached us. We went in with PMI and that's where I met Jim Yukich. And we formed our own company and all that — we formed Split Screen and it became FYI. I didn't have the wherewithal or the money for offices at that time. I worked out of my own place. There was no point in me of trying to get a hold of all those masters. Plus, there was no point because I didn't have those directors. And that's what the reels were. ... Simon, when he opened Limelight ... he had the library. So, what happened to it?

What year did Gowers, Fields & Flattery fold?
I've got a timeline because I'm writing my own book. It was 1983.

A couple of final questions, Paul. For the KISS videos, again your offices were based in Los Angeles and the shoot took place in New York. The reason you didn't attend was strictly a budget decision?
Yes.

Can you give a ballpark for how much these videos would have cost?
Probably about $30,000.

For both?
Yes, for both.

Can you guess as to how many cameras would have been utilized for these videos?
Well, it depends on what the concept was. If it was a performance, we would do two or three because if you have multiple cameras you can't change the lighting. You can't favor any individual lighting if you're doing multiple cameras. So, the KISS thing was probably two cameras.

How much post-production would have been involved? Can you walk the uninitiated through the general process that would have been undertaken in 1981?
In those days, we would do offline and then online. ... It was expensive to go in to post houses so what we would do is we would go in at night when they didn't have the big demand from the networks. So, we would get a cheaper rate at night. [Also, in Los Angeles] at the time, we used to use a mobile truck from a guy called Bob Stivers. He did "The Circus of The Stars" and he did "The People's Choice Awards." He had this small truck that we would then take to a studio and we could then shoot the three cameras and do kind of a live mix as we went. And when he wasn't using the truck, he would put the video tape machines into an edit bay thing that he had. We went to him and he said, "Why don't you have offices here for free? You can use my truck; you can use my edit [bay]. You can pay me for that. You can pay me for the phones. But otherwise, you can have offices here for free."

We did and we used to edit down there in his bay. If you look at one of our most famous videos, "Jack & Diane." How that happened, when we were shooting the video for that, we had done Cougar before he even had a record label. We shot him in England at the Marquee. We had this relationship with Billy Gaff, who was his manager, and he said to us, "Look, there's a track the record label doesn't believe in, but I do. Save one role of film and we'll do one take and I'll give you some of my own pictures, and will you make a video for me?" We said, "Of course." So that's what we did. We shot all of that video, the film, and the stills, we projected them on the edit room wall. And we did this for free-ish, because we bribed the editor and tape op with cocaine to get in there at night. (Laughs) And the tape op was a guy called Kirk Morri, who still works for me. Because he was Korean, and he was doing the handclaps, we put those white gloves on. That was Kirk Morri clapping.

Anyway, Stivers is dead now, but he was very helpful to us. And that's where we did most of our post-production. So, we must have done [KISS] there.

Paul, have you run into the band in later years?
Oh yeah. I produced "Rock Honors," which honored them, for VH1 [in 2006]. For that, I interviewed Paul and Gene. I've run into Gene now and then. He was desperate to get into acting or television. And I did a show [in 1987] called "The Return of Bruno," which was a fake documentary — what we called a mockumentary — of Bruce Willis' career. You can find it online. And we interviewed ... because we knew so many stars, we would get them to talk about Bruno as if he was a real person. We got Elton John, we got Ringo Starr and we got Genesis, because we worked with all them. And they didn't know who Willis was. This was when he was still doing "Moonlighting." For anybody else that we went to, they would ask, "Well, who else do you got?" We'd say, "Well, Ringo Starr, Elton John, Phil Collins." And they'd say, "OK. I'll do it." And then KISS did it. I don't know that Gene did it, but Paul Stanley did it for us. They would help come up with a conceit as to what their relationship was with this character Bruno. I've run into them at various times over the years.

Jerry Watson

Director of photography puts the spotlight back on the KISS videos for "A World Without Heroes" and "I"

What was your employment status with Gowers, Fields & Flattery in 1981?
Jerry Watson: I did all of their stuff. I was the director of photography, which includes the lighting. I did all the music videos that Bruce did. They had found me in Miami doing a Bee Gees [video] and they liked it so they flew me out in '78, I guess. And then for four or five years, I did music videos for them.

Typically, in those days, how would you have learned about forthcoming assignments, such as these KISS videos?
I'd just get a call from probably Paul [Flattery] or one of the other producers at the time, and they'd tell me they had a KISS video going in New York and gave me the dates and locked me in.

Would you have been part of the planning meetings to discuss the treatments for the videos?
Sure, I would have. We would sit down and discuss the look with the production designer, who basically was the scenic artist as well. Basically, [for the "I" video] they were on a stage and he did some macabre background stuff. And it was basically them performing in front of this background. It wasn't much of a set. It was a small stage in New York with this fantastic scenic background.

The production designer would have been Eric Critchley?
Yes, that would be Eric, who is no longer with us.

Given their image, a band like KISS seemed perfectly suited for the music video medium. What were your impressions of the band?
They all seemed to be very cooperative and willing to do whatever they were asked to do. Which mainly, there wasn't a lot of acting. It was a straightforward performance that we shot. They just did their thing and got comfortable with it. Naturally, we shot multiple, multiple takes from different angles and different sort of setups and specials to capture "a

moment" within the performance. They basically knew how to play and mug the camera to stay within what they were known to be. (Laughs)

This particular album, "Music from The Elder," was a radical departure for KISS in being a "serious" concept album. Coming into the video shoots, would this have been something you were cognizant of?
Not really. They wanted to have that, for that time, gritty look, [an] in your face performance. And that's basically what it was, an "in your face" performance. So as far as conceptual stuff, I would not call them concept videos. We put them in front of a nice scenic background for ["I"]. To me, the whole thing was Eric Critchley. I thought he just did a fantastic job creating an environment for them to play in [that fit] in with the tone of the song.

The videos were shot over Halloween weekend in New York City. Do you recall why it was decided to do two videos?
I think what used to happen frequently in those days, the record company would say, "We'll do two." They would choose which one they thought was going to be the hit that they were going to run with, because at that point they didn't know. It didn't come out before the album had really come out. They really didn't know. And a lot of times record companies really blew it. I remember a thing with John Cougar Mellencamp. The biggest song was "Jack & Diane" and that was a throwaway. We did three [videos] and they said, "Just have him lean up against a thing." And that got turned over to me because they thought, "Well, it will never get shown so you just direct this and shoot him up against this thing. He's going to get a bunch of old footage from home movies. Create something with it." Which was pretty challenging. And then all of the sudden, that was the big hit. (Laughs) I don't even remember the other two songs. I think one was "Hurts So Good." But record companies, they would kind of roll the dice on the couple songs they thought would be the ones. With the KISS project, I don't even know if they aired them.

How many staff would have been on the premises for the KISS shoot?
As far as crew and staff, let's see, probably about 12 to 20 people. I mean if you don't count craft service. (Laughs)

How many cameras would have been used?
I believe it would have been four or five in a setup like that, with multiple takes. So basically, when you're done you wind up with 40, 50 angles

because after they get a take they like, we move on and reset cameras to different positions. So, it would look like there would be 25 cameras. Doing those music videos, man, I would remember this song would get grounded in your head and it would take all the way until the next music video to erase that one and replace it with the new one that was stuck in your head. You'd hear the playback track 30, 40 times and it would just lay on you. Now a lot of it was shot in segments. You'd shoot a segment, "We're going to do up to this point and cut." You don't run through the whole thing, or you kill them. You'd take a section and set up for that. And another section and set up for that. Then go in and do some specials that would be within those. Generally, there would be a wide master that you were happy with. As long as they lip-synced fine and [KISS] didn't have any problem with that, I recall. Some people do. I was doing a thing with the Stones and Jagger had to have somebody walk behind the camera with the lyrics. (Laughs) He couldn't remember the lyrics to his song. But [KISS] were very clean with that. There was no problem with lip-syncing that I recall.

Would you describe these as grueling shoots?
Oh God, yes. All day and night. Getting the setup was one day. Then when we went in to do the two songs, I remember it was about midnight when we wrapped, and it was Halloween. And it was in New York and Eric [Critchley], who was great, he had never been to New York and he was there for Halloween. And he was a party kind of guy so he just couldn't wait to get off. Ordinarily, we are probably on-set at about 7 or 8 in the morning going until about midnight. That was a typical music video.

Do you recall the location?
It was some small stage in New York. It was in Manhattan. It wasn't very large. We didn't need a large stage for it. It's not what I'd call a working film stage. It just happened to be that they put some risers and a stage in this place. And since you're not dealing with lights and sound, you don't need a proper sound stage.

How would the songs have been played back in those days? Did you bring in a big sound system for the playback?
Back in those days, it was a Nagra. They'd sync the Nagra with the camera. They had a Nagra which would have been played through large speakers. They'd get a balance of each guy's monitors, the way he wants it. It's like a typical live performance even though it's to playback. It was very loud.

Paul Flattery mentioned that the film "Excalibur" was an influence on the "A World Without Heroes" video treatment. Does that merge with your memory?
No, that doesn't ring a bell with me. But you know, I wasn't in on that discussion. (Laughs)

Gene Simmons is filmed at the end with a tear in his eye, which was achieved by putting glycerin in his eye.
Oh, I recall that! Makeup comes in with a little squirt of glycerin ...

This would have been part of the treatment, yes?
I don't think it was improvised. I don't know if it came from the band. A lot of times something like that comes from the band. "Hey, I want to do this." "Fine, do that." It doesn't [look] something like something that Bruce would have designed, initially. It sounds more like it came from the band, but I don't recall specifically.

In hindsight, "A World Without Heroes" is a striking video. It's tastefully artistic but still powerfully leverages the band's image. It really captures the band nicely.
Well, that's nice. They were pleased with it. At the time, we were doing so many music videos, back to back to back to back because there really weren't a lot of companies that had a director like Bruce. Bruce was pretty brilliant; having done "Bohemian Rhapsody," which was basically what started music videos. He and David Mallet from England ... it's really funny, I did an AC/DC music video with David in February. Last month we were at Wrigley Field and did an AC/DC concert. It was done film-style, video, film cameras ... the way I like, the good way, the old way, like the film days. It was pretty big, like 20 cameras and they plan to sell it to networks and various countries. And once they've exhausted that, put out a DVD. They were kind of pocketing that while the guys could still get through a whole show. They're getting old but boy they really do crank it up there. I don't see how they do it.

I really don't know where the [tear shot] came from. I don't really recall. Often times I would be so busy with lighting and getting camera angles set up, and stuff like that. It was fun. It was a wham-bam deal. We went in and loaded in. Eric started on his scenic background. I came in about midway through the day on the first setup day and started hanging lights and all that stuff. And then we went until quite late in the setup. Because it was all setup in one day and then shot the next day and night.

So, one day for setup and then the next days for the filming.
Right.

Jerry, let's watch the "A World Without Heroes" video and I'd like to get your commentary.
(Plays video) Most of what you see is I think the brilliance of Bruce. He's a great director; he knows how to get right movements. I see the spotlights you were talking about. Those were rear spots. You can really get a hard crown of light on them without contaminating the whole stage.

It's a simple, effective contrast with the spots and the black backdrop.
Yeah. As I'm looking here now, Bruce was great at split screens. I've always thought those we're really good. You've got the close-up of [Gene] singing. That's right. I did have rear spots only because you can't see if they cross across other guys' backs and stuff like that. Besides that, this song was pretty etched in without movement. I think this is the only one that I had those because those we're actually locked off. They weren't operated spots; they were high-power lights because the guys were meant to be nailed down. But it gives them wonderful crown of hair light. Also, for filtration, we used behind the lens filters so that you could get that sort of halo glow where it just sort of fogs it out. It makes it kind of dreamy.

Right, that's exactly what it achieves. It really adds a nice effect.
Just cheap old filters. (Laughs) That's how we got the glow off the neck of the guitar. It looks like [Paul's] got an aura around him. That was the whole point of it: to create that "halo" around them. And as you saw [there are] so many angles in it. Now this one, not as many as the other one because it really moved a lot more. It was a lot more upbeat. In fact, in this one you don't even see the backdrop. We went to black; I'd forgotten that. We did one song in black and the other we did with [Eric's] great scenic in the back.

So, the backdrop was likely there, but just darkened out for this video?
Yeah. And then it's all lights. You have to be delicate and know what you are doing with your exposures in a way because of the fact that they're in white face [makeup] and they're up against a very, very black backdrop. Putting the filter on would help in any overexposure in the white, to make it kind of

just glow. That was sort of the thing. Do it against black in white face, put a filter on it and they'll just look they're emanating an aura.

Well, it seems that this video went according to plan. The video really fits the nature of the project and seems to really tastefully capture the essence of the song.
Well, that's really good to hear all these years later. It looked to me like, I don't know, German Gothic expressionism, if you want to take an artistic look at it. To me, that's what it felt like. It was the black and white and the heavy shadows drawn in. It was like [the 1920 silent horror film] "The Cabinet of Dr. Caligari," with more of a black theme instead of the white theme in the movie. I guess we all have our own interpretation. To me, it was like that German industrial-type era look.

If we get into the video for "I," there is no video available to view. Little is known about this video, frankly, mostly due to the fact that it has never been released. The backdrop for this video has been described as being inspired by Superman's Fortress of Solitude. Paul described it as being as glass matte painting.
Yeah, we had a glass matte. But you had the background painted and then you put a glass matte around it, so it feels as if it's three-dimensional.

It definitely achieves that effect, going by the pictures.
And yes, now that I see this, it was a very crystal-like, Superman thing. I think "Superman" had come out around this time. He had the crystal pillars of his lair, or his cave or whatever it was. That's correct. He painted the crystal look on the floor as well. What we'd generally do, while he was painting the background, we would start hanging our lights and getting our tables running. The guys getting all the lighting and the cameras and all that stuff. And then he would wait to paint the floor until we were completely done, so he didn't have to get ladders on the stage to get all the lights and all that stuff. He would be the first to come and the last to leave, so it could dry overnight. The floor would be the last element done so that it could dry. And then the guys could come in and scuff it all up. (Laughs)

How big was the backdrop?
I would say it might have been 60 feet with a cove curve to it. It probably was; we wouldn't have taken something small because you don't have much of a cross-shot angle. It just falls off because you don't have a side there to paint.

Of course, with today's technology, everything can be achieved via CGI. But matte paintings used to be very prevalent. It's amazing how matte paintings could really achieve a realistic effect.
Yeah. That's a complex thing in a lot of ways. It takes a real good scenic artist to do that. And they need a little hole for the performers and the background just ties in. And you make them small. You shoot them head to toe and it looks like they're in this huge cave where this is all around them. Because they have to stay in focus, you've got a glass matte in front of your lens about 2 feet away, and that has to stay in focus. So now you really have to put a lot of light into it, even though it doesn't look like it, and then stop down so you're depth of feel will cover what's in the foreground on the glass and what's in the background view of the talent. So, you may shoot the thing at like a 2.8, but when you do the glass shot you've have to boost everything up so you're shooting at about 16 or 11 or something. Whenever those glass shots came in, I was like, "OK, basic free light." But it's got to look the same but you're just adding more light from the same angles.

Would there have been any colored lighting for the "I" video?
Nope. I think we stayed pretty much monochromatic throughout. That's the reason the set was monochromatic so I would have stayed away from that. The only color I used — it wasn't really a color; it was just lack of color temperature correction like you saw in the rear spots. It was just a cold blue white overexposed. That would be the only color, only because it was daylight instead of a tungsten.

In looking at a 1981 Billboard report, it seems extras were brought in — both actors and friends of the band — to participate as the audience in the "I" video.
Oh, [a crowd] is always a mess. (Laughs) But you've got to have them because it was supposed to be this intimate concert type of thing. I call them shrubbery. You have heads to shoot over and you kind of top light them, you know they're there. I would imagine Bruce probably got reverses to get frantic faces as well.

Also, it seems at some point in the video, perhaps the ending, the audience members put the band members on their shoulders.
Yes. I think we shot that element. As I recall, that was actually on film as well. When I saw [the picture you sent], I thought, "Oh yeah, I think we actually shot that." But not posed like that. It was like they picked them up and that was that. But this particular frame was not in the music video. It

was a kid's thing; they're smiling and all bright and everything. It was like [Ace] being hoisted up on shoulders.

Were the same number of cameras used for this video?
Yes. I don't think that they had any problem. As I recall, there was a massive crowd outside. They didn't have to pay for an extra audience, that's for sure. As I recall, sometimes that gets pretty hairy when they have too many. We've done that many times. In fact, this thing we did in February with AC/DC, they were winners of AC/DC's fan club. From around the world they flew themselves here just to be in this very intimate little club and they came from Brazil, from Amsterdam, it was crazy. I thought, "Are you kidding me? There are really fans that rabid?" It blows me away. That happens. But as I recall, that was a similar situation. There was a line of kids outside and at a certain point you've got to cut it off because the fire marshal will only allow so many people in at a time.

Once the shoots wrapped, the videos went into post-production. Did you participate in the post-production process? Or is your job finished once you walk off the set?
Often times, I am. I will come in and I may edit one of the songs or something because we were pretty busy at the time. It could be a situation where Bruce says, "OK Jerry, you edit this one. I'm done with this one. I've got to get onto this project." He would be prepping another project; I could finish the other and I could come in and join with production on the next one. But I think Bruce [edited these] — I don't recall editing these at all.

Did Bruce ever farm out the post-production to another company?
[No,] that would have definitely been Bruce. Bruce was very picky about anybody editing his stuff. (Laughs) I did several of them for him, but he didn't want anybody else really touching his stuff. If I did edit things, I would edit them and then get his approval and he often times would come in and say, "That great. That's fine." Or he'd make a suggestion, "Let's go back, right there." He may change a little thing or something. It made it easy for him because I would basically do a step above a rough edit and he could come in and just do the polish and make it his own in a way.

So "A World Without Heroes" gets completed and released. But the video for "I" is completed and just sits on the shelf. Why do you think the "I" video never saw the light of day?

It would have been completed. (Pauses) That's a good question because there may be a reason. They may have said, "This is the one we're going to go with. We're only going to go with one." I would hope and think [it was edited] and that the raw stock would be there. I don't understand why it [wasn't released]. It had more elements in it than "A World Without Heroes."

I think the popular theory is that the since the album didn't perform well from a sales standpoint, the label and/or the band decided to cut their losses and move on.
That sounds like the kind of thing record companies would do. It's like, "Hold on to that [video] and let's see how this album does. We really like ['A World Without Heroes'], we think this is the [single] that will do it." But if the album flops, it's like, "What's the point? We're beating a dead horse. It would have made it by now." Like you say, if it's already dead in the water, why [release it]? So that's one way the bean counters thought. (Laughs)

Assuming it's out there somewhere, who do you think would have a copy of the "I" video?
I would only think it would have to be the record company. The record company would have held on to it. Unless Gene said, "I want this footage for

archival stuff. And maybe one day I'll do something with it." I don't know. That just depends upon, at that point, who had the ability to call a shot like that. And the record company could say, "No, it's our property. We bought it. We paid for it." Nowadays, it's more convoluted because the bands oftentimes put up a good chunk of the money. That's why they were originally called video promos. When we were doing these before ... was MTV even on yet?

MTV had just debuted months prior, in August.
OK, we'd been doing it for about three years. There was Don Kirshner's "Rock Concert" and "Saturday Night Special." I remember seeing [Kansas'] "Dust in The Wind" and a few other videos. But for the most part, these were played on "Top of The Pops" in England. And Australia had a show that played [videos]. Until MTV came along, it wasn't really all that viable in the U.S. to make them because there was no outlet. Where were you going to go to go see them? It's not like communications nowadays; you know social media and those things. (Laughs) If one of the big networks didn't air it ... so along comes this little cable company and I'm telling you; MTV was little. There were about four guys and all they did was plug tapes in to a player. (Laughs)

It's interesting to note that some labels had an issue regarding compensation with MTV in its early stages. MTV's argument was that the videos should be handed over for free, since they were promoting the label's product. The label's argued that they should be compensated to play the videos. One of the labels that initially withheld their videos was PolyGram.
That's the kiss of death. Until it caught on here ... see, they wanted to be compensated because of there were live viable network-type shows that were showing [videos]. At the time when MTV came along, they were a little cable company. They didn't have any money to pay anybody. They had nothing. So, if they didn't get it for free ... and I think it was very short-sided because look where MTV took it. I mean, it was the best way in the world of getting free publicity. My God, that's free advertising. Why be compensated? What do you spend in your advertising budget? Well, look what you're getting for free. And I always thought that was really stupid, because I was aware of that. They'd say, "We don't let our stuff go on MTV." I thought, "That's ridiculous. You want to sell albums!" If people see it, they get a feel of the music and a feel of the concept. That may be what sells them, the visuals along with the music. I always thought that was really

stupid. And in the end, you see how MTV won out. It was like everyone wanted to get their stuff on for free. It was like, "Yeah, take it."

According to a 1981 "Billboard" report, PolyGram was withholding their artists' videos. So, it is quite possible "A World Without Heroes" was not seen until years later, if ever. I know I never saw the video on the channel.
It's very possible. You know, it could have aired on "Top of The Pops." I don't know how big KISS was in England.

They had a solid following overseas, actually.
Yeah, so [the "I" video] could very well be in "Top of The Pops" archive, you never know. Because they archive all their shows.

Well, Bruce and Paul claim to not have it. They thought Simon Fields might have it, but they also mentioned that there was a bit of a falling out there.
Oh boy, yeah. When you said that, I went, "Oh ...." I think the sour grapes is more on Paul's side than anyone. I don't think that Simon had any kind of bad feelings at all. That company, Roseman Productions, went under at the time. And then came along Gowers, Fields & Flattery, and Simon left and went to work for a big music video company ... I forget the name. And he did quite well and became a movie producer and all that. And now he also manages Jennifer Lopez's film work and stuff like that. Simon's a good guy. We were roommates for a couple of years. I really like Simon. I really think the negativity — I'm not saying he's wrong — is more coming from Paul, but not necessarily from Simon.

Would Simon have been in New York for the KISS shoot?
If Paul wasn't there, Simon was. To be honest, Simon went to most of them once he came onboard. And that's one of the reasons why the bitterness might be more coming from Paul because when Simon came in, he pretty much took over most of everything that Paul was doing. Simon was very good, and I think that always has been a sore spot with Paul. There are all kinds of background you don't need for this. This is another book. (Laughs)

I've got to tell you, there is a book just in the world of doing music videos because along with the cocaine that was flowing rapidly and the way producers would buy crew by not paying overtime, they'd get them an 8-ball. All that got ... I was strict with my crew because I wasn't going to send somebody up in the rafters to move a light when they're all jazzed up. If it came down to it, I would not do a shot because I'm not going to get them up there [and risk injury]. There's a lot of weird stuff that went on in the early music video days. And it was a small family too, it was really Mallet and Bruce and there were a couple of others, but basically those were the big ones. There was MGMM in England, which was [Russell] Mulcahy, [David] Mallet, [Scott Millaney,] and Brian [Grant]. And there was Gowers, Fields & Flattery. Up until 1983, 1984, it was basically Gowers, Fields & Flattery that did them all.

Did Eric Critchley handle a majority of the matte work for videos in those days?
Yes, he did. He was kind of one of the only ones who knew how to do it. That came from a very good designer, who moved back to Australia, Bryce Walmsley, who took on Eric Critchley as his scenic designer. Bryce is a production designer. So, he took Eric on and Eric saw what Bryce was doing and most of the things he did [involved] a lot of graphic work and scenic work. He didn't have the art history background that Bryce had but he sure as hell was an artist ... he did some really crazy, amazing stuff. I always thought he was the best scenic artist that I ever, ever worked with. I worked with a lot of them — I'll never see anybody like that again. And he generally did it on a fifth of vodka. I could never understand it. He had a little shopping basket that he'd have on set with his paints and all of his other stuff and a little ice chest, with a couple of fifths of vodka and some orange juice. He never even slurred. It was kind of strange. Although, the way he died, he got out of his car and fell down a knoll by his house and hit his head on a rock. It was bizarre.

That's terrible. Do you recall what year he passed?
I would say that was probably around '85 or '86. It was a long time ago. He had just made it big, big. He was starting to get called in on commercials and little feature stuff. He was really, really zooming, in more ways than one unfortunately.

In terms of cost, what would you ballpark as the budget for the two KISS videos?
In that time, you're looking at between $26,000 and $35,000.

For the two of them?
Yes. Because you'd [charge] by day. That's reason why a lot of times you'd load up, "Look, you're going to have the crew there, you're going to have the stuff there. Let's do two. It's not going to be anymore cost, except to edit."

We'd have a big video once in a while; back then a big one would come along and be maybe $50,000, $55,000. For the most part, the average range was right in there, like between $26,000 and $35,000 maybe. I mean, they would work the crew to death. I mean they got them on flats; it wasn't union. So, they'd literally kill a crew and instead of paying them overtime they'd go invest in some cocaine, which was cheaper than paying them for the overtime.

Finally, this was Halloween weekend in 1981. Do you have any fun memories or anecdotes of working with any of the band members?
No, I really don't. We got out of there at midnight. The only funny thing involves Eric Critchley and it was pretty strange because he'd never been to New York. And this guy, he was from Birmingham I think, a kind of a steel-working town in England. He was like a poor boy. He was in New York, and he said, "We've got to go out, mate!" So, we went out and I had finally wrapped it up. I was beat from working all day. He never got beat. I went and crashed at the hotel at around 3 in the morning. I get a call at about 6 in the morning from security asking if I knew this guy named Eric Critchley. He had gone out and gotten himself a couple of prostitutes — the people at the hotel knew these were professional women. But he had left his key in his room, so he went to the front desk to get a key. He didn't have any ID on him, he didn't have anything. They said to me, "He was about to take a couple of prostitutes to his room, which we don't have anything to say about, but he gave us your name to vouch for him that he's staying here." (Laughs) And I said, "Yeah, that definitely sounds like Eric Critchley." He was a sweetheart of a guy. He really was.

It sounds like he had some fun in New York.
He burned the candle real hot. And he burned it right out well before his time.

<u>MEMORANDUM</u>

DATE: March 3, 1981

TO: HOWARD MARKS

FROM: William M. Aucoin

RE: ROB FREEMAN / ENGINEER

Rob Freeman and I have come to a mutual agreement that
he has worked a total of 160 hours with KISS (though it is
my feeling that he has worked in excess of 200 hours).

Based on top engineering fees, and not taking into consideration any of his involvement in co-production, I
think $50 is a reasonable fee.

If the group is in agreement with this, would you please
pay Rob the sum of $8,000.00.

Please let me know your thoughts.

WMA/kd

645 MADISON AVENUE NEW YORK, NEW YORK 10022 · 212/826-8800

Ida Langsam

Publicist pro discusses working with KISS during a challenging time in their history and trying to get word about "The Elder" out to the masses

Ida, I see you started at Ren Gravatt Associates in '74?
Ida Langsam: Ren Gravatt, yeah. That's actually my first full-time, paying PR job. I actually started as the New York City area secretary for the Official Beatles Fan Club, which was an unpaid voluntary position while I was in school.

Oh, how fun. So, by 1978, you were with MJL Management as director of PR, and the following year you were with the Howard Bloom Organization and they handled Peter Criss' solo album PR in 1980. Could you tell us about your background, and how you entered the publicity field?
Well it was through my love of the Beatles. I knew I wanted to do something related to the Beatles — anything I could do to work for them, and I didn't know what that entailed. When I graduated high school, my father sent my mom and me to Europe for three weeks. The first stop was London, and of course, that's all I wanted was to go to London, so it was 10 days in London, nine days of which I spent standing outside Paul McCartney's house, waiting for him to come out and, you know, talk to the fans and sign autographs and take photos, etc. And my then best friend was with me, and so when we came back to New York, she wrote a letter to Mal Evans, who was Beatles' road manager, roadie, whatever you want to call him. He actually wrote back, so we were so excited about it that we went up to the Beatles' fan club headquarters. Living in Manhattan, it was a very easy thing to do. We could just find out where it was and go there. We showed them the letter that Mal had written, and they kind of set us straight and said [that] he does that to everyone. He tries to pick up girls! So, we were very innocent teenagers — we had had no idea!

We just started hanging out there after school, volunteering and helping by stuffing envelopes, or doing whatever crap work was needed. The fan club was divided into states. Each state had its own area secretary who was responsible for answering letters from dues-paying members. Another responsibility was writing a newsletter, once a year, which the fan club would [then] mail out to the fans in that state. New York and California had two, because the area was so big. New York had New York City and then the rest of New York State. The girl who was the New York City-area secretary had to resign because she was going out of state to college, and the head of the fan club asked me, "Would you like the position?" And I was like, "Yeah, I think so. I'll take it!" So, that was really my first taste. I didn't know that it was really publicity, but that's what I was doing. I was answering fans' questions that they sent in by letter. They would send letters and I would answer them and send it back. They would ask stupid questions like, "What kind of toothpaste does George Harrison use?"

That sounds like not much has changed for the questions fans often ask!
Really silly stuff! Then instead of doing a newsletter once a year, I did it four times a year, just because I was that enthusiastic! I worked there until the fan club closed down because George Harrison decided that the Beatles really didn't exist anymore — 1971 or so. There was no reason to have a fan club. In the late '70s, when John and Yoko were living in New York, and the government was trying to throw them out of the country an organization was formed. It was a non-Beatles' fan organization, a political organization fighting the government, and it was run by a very small handful of very active political activists — they weren't Beatles' fans. They just didn't want the government to be able to throw John out of the country. They got in touch with me and asked if I still had the contact information for all of the Beatle Fan Club members. I still had all the info, so they asked me if they could have it and I brought it in to them because they wanted to send petitions to them — so that these fans could get their friends to sign the petitions, and then the petitions would be sent to the government. That was the theory. So, they offered me a job to work up there to really file the petitions and organize the office. It was grunt work. But I also worked as an assistant to the woman who was doing the publicity, so that was my first taste of real public relations and organizing a press conference and so on. So, that's how I started.

Mailing lists are gold! Let's jump into your move to Aucoin Management International. When did join AMI?
January 1st, 1980. I think.

Was there anything in particular that made that position particularly attractive to you? How did you end up working for AMI?
When I was working at the Howard Bloom Organization, I was the senior publicist, and they gave me the difficult acts to work. Peter [Criss] had

parted ways with KISS... I don't know if it was Bill [Aucoin] or if it was Peter's record label who hired Howard to handle the solo campaign. I was the publicist that was assigned to it. There were about six publicists and like four assistants. It was a fairly big organization, a fairly big company, and I'm not sure that he put individual publicists' names on the [press] releases, but we all had individual clients. We didn't really share clients. I was doing press for Styx, and they were on tour constantly, so I had one of the assistant publicists, as my assistant. She was responsible for tour press, and I was responsible for national press, because there was so much going on at the same time. It was like at the height of their success. So, anyway, I was the person who handled Peter's solo debut. I got him the interview in People Magazine, which was a couples' piece, with him and Debra. Peter had a house in Connecticut, and I'm pretty sure that's where they did it. I think Aucoin was so impressed with the fact that I was able to secure a feature for Peter in People that Bill approached me and asked me if I'd like to come and work directly for Aucoin Management, and for KISS.

You basically went from working with Peter — who had just left KISS. And yes, your name's actually on one of those Howard Bloom releases — the Peter Criss schedule for the taping of the "Tomorrow Show:" "Ida will meet Peter at the NBC Building." So, Oct. 22, 1980...
There you go. If that was October 1980, then that would mean I started at Aucoin in [early] '81.

What were essentially your primary responsibilities at Aucoin and where were you in the overall reporting structure? Did you report to Jayne [Grodd]?
No, I reported directly to Bill.

Were you specifically given KISS to work with or were you working with any of the Aucoin represented acts?
I was responsible for press for all the artists signed to Aucoin, any events that they had, and for Aucoin Management itself in terms of corporate press. I was the only publicist there. I had an assistant, and it was just me and her.

That must have been a lot of work then, with the size of their roster at that time?
Yeah, it was pretty intense, although it was always understood that KISS was No. 1, 2 and 3! Everybody else came after that.

Can I throw some of the names from the era out at you and just say what your relationship was with them? Let's start with Ric Aliberti.
Ric and I were on an even level in terms of hierarchy. He ran his division and I ran my division. My division was the PR, and his was promotion — radio. He had one assistant and it was the same thing.

Rosanne Shelnutt?
Rosanne worked at Howard Marks, which was the financial management company. She didn't work at Aucoin. I didn't have that much day-to-day contact with her, because I didn't have anything to do with the monetary situation of the band. So, if I needed something monetarily, I would have to go to Bill, and then he would go to Howard, and secure whatever it was, if I needed a certain budget for a publicity campaign.

That makes sense from the financial organization side of the band and their business. I won't even mention Howard Marks then. Jayne Grodd, where does she fit into the picture?
Jayne had the office right next to mine. We shared a wall. Jayne was already there when I started working at Aucoin. She'd been there for a few years, and she was KISS' "God" — like their right, left and middle hand. She just took care of everything for the guys individually and coordinated everything that they did, both business-wise and personal. She was super, super involved in everything.

The keeper of the schedules and everything that goes with that, no doubt.
Everything. When Gene was building his apartment, he had bought the air rights on a building on Fifth Avenue and like 64th Street or something. At one time it had been a mansion, and it was broken up into floor level apartments and he bought the air rights to build his own apartment on top of the building. It was only like a six-story building. It wasn't like a skyscraper or anything. As I understand it, when he bought the air rights he was going out with Cher, and she had her architect design the space. By the time I was working with him, he was with Diana Ross. When the apartment was being built the band was on tour — this was before I was with them — so Gene wasn't there to supervise. Jayne did everything. She supervised everything, she bought whatever he needed. I remember she told me it was Christmastime and people were asking her, "what can I give Gene as a present?" Or maybe it was like, "what can I give him as a housewarming present?" And she was the one who told them, "he needs a down blanket, he needs pots and pans, he needs, whatever!" She was practically living in

the apartment, taking care of whatever needed to be taken care of, so she told people what she needed.

That's hilarious. She knew exactly what had to go in there.
She was cooking there, so she needed whatever. They didn't have microwaves then, but like a double-boiler, so she told them that Gene needed [one] — Gene never cooked! So that's just a pretty funny aside. But that just shows you that Jayne absolutely took care of everything: Doctors' appointments, hiring limos, getting them airline tickets... You know, you name it.

Two more names: George Sewitt?
I didn't have that much to do with him, because he was mostly out on the road with the band.

Chris Lendt?
Chris, I also didn't have that much to do with. He kind of signed the checks. He also worked at Howard Marks, not at Aucoin.

Ken Anderson, was he still around at that time?
Ken had the office next to Jayne, so it was like, Ken had the big office, then Jayne had her office and then I had my office. And then Stephanie had her office, and then Bill's office. So, we were all against the same wall, so to speak. Nothing that I did directly impacted Ken, and nothing he did directly impacted me, but he designed all of their stage show.

Let's move on to Bill Aucoin. What were your general impressions of Bill at this time?
Being in the industry, for several years at that point, I knew who he was, and I was well aware of his status and his part in the KISS history. It's not like I went in there not knowing who or what he was. He was always a gentleman. He was always soft-spoken, always very personable and friendly. I never had a problem with him. The one thing he scolded me on was that I didn't hang out with the rest of the office crew often enough after work, going and hanging out at some Japanese restaurant for dinner.

That's a very minor complaint then, isn't it?
That's it. Because I don't drink. Everybody else were the pretty big drinkers. So, there was no reason for me to be hanging out until 2 in the morning drinking when I didn't drink. That was the only reason that I didn't hang out

with everybody. I had other things to do. I'd rather be going to a party or a concert or something than hanging out with a bunch of people getting drunk.

Do you remember what was the first major project you worked on when you transitioned from Howard Bloom to KISS?
They had started working on "The Elder." So that was my project.

"The Elder" project essentially ran from January 1981 through to April 1982. Doesn't that pretty much dovetail with your time with Aucoin?
Yes.

So, you were there for the whole "Elder" period.
Yes.

A lot of the other people we've spoken to have recounted the members of KISS were often around the AMI offices. Do you recall meeting them for the first time?
Yeah.

Let's, let's do a quick word association then with each of the members at the time. Let's start with Gene.
His reputation preceded him. Look, I had been in the music industry at that point for maybe 10 years or something. So, I wasn't starstruck. I was a little nervous because I knew he was my new boss, but I wasn't afraid of him. He's very imposing just because he's so big. I mean, I'm 5'10", but he's bigger than me. He has this aura about him of being large so that was a little intimidating at first. He takes up the room, so to speak.

When you opened the door to Aucoin's office there was a reception area, and the receptionist. Then there were glass doors. To walk into the office space, when you opened those doors, my office was immediately across from those doors. I could see everybody who came in and went out. You couldn't really walk past my office without saying, "hello." You know, looking in and waving or something. I knew that he had been born in Israel and I'm Jewish and I know a smattering of Hebrew. So, one day he came by to say hello, and in Hebrew, I said to him, "*Ma nishma*?" Literally it means, "What's new," but it's used a greeting for "hi, how are you?" And he looked to the right and looked to the left, and made sure nobody was in the hall, and then he answered me in Hebrew. That was just a connection I made with him.

What about Ace Frehley?

Oh, Ace. When you say Ace, all I think of is his cackle. That was Ace. He was kind of oblivious. He was always in a haze. He was pretty much on a different planet, Space Ace.

Paul Stanley?

I'm fighting for the right words here. I don't know. I don't know how to explain Paul. He was very serious about the success of KISS, the business end of KISS — doing the right things, making the right moves and the right decisions and coming off correctly in public to journalists. Saying the right things [and] making sure that the right information got across.

So very focused and driven, in particular?

Very particular. He wasn't easy to get close to.

That's something that I think a lot of people have alluded to — that he kept a lot of people on the periphery, kept them at arm's length and didn't really let them in close to him.

When I started there, I requested to meet with each band member individually, so that I could get to know them and just spend like an hour or so with them talking, getting to find out what they're like. The way I learned to do PR is by focusing on the musicians' personalities. If you, as a journalist, can get to like the musician as a person, then you're less likely to slam their work. I learned this from Howard Bloom. I was all about finding out about the person. What makes that person tick, what makes them an artist, what influenced him, his life story, etc? Paul was pretty hard to pin down. He was up in the office a lot, but he was in and out of there. You know, he did what he had to do and then he left. He didn't hang around. So, I kept saying, "I need to talk to Paul, I need to talk to Paul, I need to talk to Paul!" And one evening, right toward the end of the day, he came into my office with his dinner — they were always ordering meals for the guys when they were up at the office — and he sat in the chair opposite my desk and put his feet up on the chair and said, "okay, what do you want to know?" And I was told afterwards that if he ate in front of me, he must like me! I never developed a particularly strong relationship with him. I think of any of them, I would think probably my most comfortable relationship was with Eric and then with Gene.

So, let me ask about Eric Carr? Obviously, he's very new to the band at that time. He's just been in the band I think for five months and he's done a tour with them. But he's still very green.

Well, he was more experienced with the band than I was at that point. But he was the easiest to deal with on a personal level because he was still so amazed at his good fortune to have been chosen to be in the band. He was kind of still naïve and wide eyed. Everything was new and exciting for him.

I think we'll add Peter Criss; obviously, you'd worked with him. What would you associate with him?

Not the sharpest pencil in the bunch. He was okay. He would basically do what you told him to do, without too much resistance. And I guess once in a while, he got into a snit. But that's pretty normal, most people do.

So, let's talk about 1981. You've met with all the members of the band. They're not really recording until I think April or May, and that goes through to September and they're hopping around from New York to Toronto, and maybe a couple other places. How are you approaching PR for the band in that time while they're basically constructing the album that becomes "The Elder?" What are you trying to do to keep their name out there? Or is it that's just what you're trying to do; keep their name out there?

We were trying to get some buzz going about the forthcoming album without giving away too much of the detail. I think we did let the news out about it being a concept [record]. If I recall, we were calling it the "soundtrack to a movie that had not yet been made" so that you would get the impression that if it was a soundtrack to a movie — then there was as story behind it and not just individual tracks, like their previous albums, or like anybody else's album. The concept albums weren't as plentiful as non-concept albums. The band was going through turmoil. They were questioning everybody. "Should we take the makeup off? Should we leave it on? Should we take it off? Should we leave it on? We're going to take it off. No, no, we've changed our mind, we're going to leave it on! No, what do you think? Should we take it off?" It was like every day there was a different decision. I was kind of restricted. There wasn't a lot that I could really tell the press because everything was in such a state of flux.

I don't know if you ever put these press releases out. There was a stack of them along the lines of "Paul pulls a tendon," "Gene's burglar alarm mystery — it's a pigeon going through laser beams." And "Eric Carr goes

roller-skating." That sort of stuff... Were these just ideas, or did any of those actually go out to the, go out to places like "16" or any of the other magazines?

I don't really remember. I know that I had done a bunch of sample press releases and again, that goes back to how I approach press. Anecdotal press releases to get across the personality of the individual artist, so that the reader — ultimately the fans, but the intermediary being the journalist — would know something about their lives, could relate to them, could feel like they know them, which makes them feel closer to the artist. I wanted to do a whole series of these kinds of anecdotal things. And certain magazines were printing anything that you said about the band, anything that they could find out about the band. They were just hungry for any bit of information because up until then, the band had really kept their non-KISS lives and activities pretty quiet [and] out of the press. They didn't want that information out there, but they were aware that they were at kind of a low point in their popularity. It wasn't a high point and they were anxious to get back into the media in a much more spotlighted way.

Gene's got a relationship with Diana Ross and I believe Paul Stanley had a relationship with Donna Dixon around this time. So, they were getting mentioned in the press.

Paul wasn't with Donna Dixon when I was working with him, at least not that I recall. Paul read all the "People" magazines, all the gossip kind of magazines, and I'm not saying this in a negative or a nasty way, but he really wanted to be in them. He wanted to be talked about like those celebrities, and so he came to me one day and said, "You read the Chatter column?" [It] was the back of the book gossip items. They weren't stories. They were just so and so was seen at this and this place with such and such. He said he wanted to be in there. He was going out with Patti LuPone and he wanted that information out. All right, what do you do with that? You call up somebody and say, "Hey, guess what, Paul Stanley's going out with Patti LuPone." I called the writer of the Chatter column and I said I just have a piece of gossip for you: "Paul Stanley's going out with Patti LuPone." And the guy said, "Oh, write it out in a press release and send it to me." So, I wasn't sending it to anybody else. It was just him. I told him it's an exclusive. I wrote something up and I sent it to him... The next issue of People had an item that said something along the lines of, "Paul Stanley is so impressed that he's going out with Patti LuPone that he had his publicist send out a press release."

Ouch. That's pretty nasty!
Yeah. That was horrible. I was embarrassed. Paul was embarrassed. It was terrible. He tried to make light of it with me, but I know he was upset, and I was upset. I apologized to him a million times and I explained, you know, exactly what happened, that the guy had said send me something in writing. I still have a poster that they signed for me. Paul wrote, "After 'People,' I knew it would, could only get better!"

That's very painful and must have hurt him quite badly.
It was also one of the first things I did when I started working there. So that was not a great foot to start on.

So, KISS was doing an album. Was there any discussion about the album around the office about how you guys were going to do PR for an album that at first starts off as a regular hard rock album which then becomes a concept album? Was the direction of the music ever discussed in relation to the PR?
Of course, what else was the PR going to hook onto? That *was* the angle. There was no other way to approach it. They wanted it known as a concept album. It was this big amazing, creative thing that they created, that it had a storyline and it had a young boy [who] was a hero, and conquering negativity — so many things that went beyond the music, that the music and lyrics were meant to express. There was no other way to do the press campaign. That had to be it.

Were they playing any of this music, while they were recording it, around the office for you guys to get a feel for what they were doing?
Not for me. They may have played it for Bill. We did have a listening event where everyone in the office sat in the conference room and listened to it once it was done, but I don't remember hearing things in advance. I may well have, but I don't remember. I do remember going up to Toronto for an afternoon to interview [Bob] Ezrin. I came back the same day, but I don't think he played me anything.

You just touched on the listening party. Paul's alluded to it in his book that when they did the listening party or he played the album before it was released for anyone at his apartment that he demanded like silence and seriousness, or gravitas. That it was so important musically. Was the listening party like that, seriously presented?

It was really supposed to be perceived as a serious work of art. It was meant to be very serious, not to be laughed at, [and] not to be made light of. It was not a frivolous album. It wasn't a comedy album. It was to be taken seriously.

What did you think of the album when you heard it?
I liked it. I really liked the whole idea of the concept. I think it was very ahead of its time because it was all very "Dungeons & Dragons," and "Star Wars," and you know, this whole concept of good versus evil.

It's kind of your traditional plotline, good versus bad?
Right, but it had a whole story that seemed to be a little futuristic and yet a little medieval.

That's what we get out the documentation, that it blended the medieval with the modern and with the futuristic, especially the screenplay treatment. Do you remember there being spoken word dialogue separating the songs when you heard the album?
I hadn't thought about that, but I think so.

It was ultimately cut out of the album before it was released, and you know we're trying to determine how much of that was recorded. We know Bob spent the day in the studio with all the spoken word actors and only one tiny little bit survived on the album at the end. We've got the script of what they recorded, but we don't know where any of that dialogue would have fit in, in between the songs.
Wow, how'd you get that? That's amazing.

What were your best outlets for KISS related PR? I would think that every band's got certain "go to" places that most of their listeners kind of gravitate to depending on age group and whatnot, but were there any particular outlets that you knew would be winners every time that if you put PR out, they'd pick it up?
At that point, certainly in the U.S., "Hit Parader."

Charlie Crespo was at "Hit Parader," I think.
Charlie was one of the writers. He wasn't the editor, but he was one of the writers. At that point in their career, it was mostly European. England still loved them. As a matter of fact, we flew over to the States the editor of "Kerrang." His name's Dante Bonutto. [We] sat him down in the conference

room to listen to the album all the way through way before it was released. We wanted his feedback. We wanted to know what he thought of it as a huge pressman. He and I are still friends.

How did you guys measure the success of your press campaigns and what you were doing?
How many clippings we got.

So like that press report that I have a copy of that has 270 press appearances for KISS in a certain period, you'd have someone going through newspapers and keeping track of that sort of thing?
Well, there were a number of ways to do it. If I set up an interview, I knew who was going to write something. So, I would always ask them to send me a copy, but there were also clipping services. You paid them a monthly fee and more or less gave them a list of all the outlets that you serviced, and they had staffers who got hold of those publications and read through it to see when the name KISS appeared. Then they would charge you, I don't know, it might've been 50 cents a clip, and they would then send you a package of those clippings.

For "The Elder" period, that's November of 1981 when the album comes out through April 1982, when they've basically given up on the album to go to Los Angeles. I think the press report notes 270 press appearances for KISS in that period. Where would that sort of number be considered for a band of KISS's stature? Would that be good, bad, indifferent or what for the release of a major album?
Well, that was good. We didn't have as many outlets. We certainly didn't have [the] Internet. We didn't have blogs. So that was a very good number.

Right and I guess I'm kind of leaning towards the question of do you feel the press campaign for "The Elder" was a success in that you got the word out about the album exactly how you wanted to and that you were satisfied with the effort/results?
We certainly got the word out. The reception was not what we wanted, but that's not something we can control. We can only present the focus of the campaign in the most positive light in the way that we want it to be perceived, but we can't make anybody like it. So, at that point in their career, they were not being taken very seriously as a band anymore. People wanted them to take the makeup off. It was enough already. Nobody goes around disguised in costumes. They were being told you have to get real.

"People don't, don't respect you." They were being told all kinds of stuff. Like I said, they would come into the office every other day. It was we're taking off the makeup. No, we're not taking off the makeup. Yes, we are taking off the makeup. You know, back and forth. They didn't know what to do. The fact that the commercial press wasn't overwhelmed with the album was disappointing, but not surprising.

How did the mood in the office change? I mean it becomes apparent pretty early on that the album's not performing. Was there, was there any panic; that they have to try and do something to drum up interest in the album? Were there any disaster planning sessions to try and inject some life into the album?
I think a lot was hinging on a tour. Are they going to tour? If they tour, are they going to do the whole album as concept. Are they going to mix in their hits? Are they? I had no part in deciding that.

Right and they're going back and forth on that throughout the year. We know they went Mexico on that quick visit. Just a PR visit to try and improve their image, basically, and they were talking about that they we're going to maybe go to South America in early '82. Then they're doing budgets for various permutations of tours, maybe hinging into going into the U.S. and elsewhere, but everything's got a loss attached to it. So, it sounds like they didn't really have a tour they could do. At some point, they're talking about synthesizer players...
They wanted synth players so they could do tracks from the album, and they just were not popularity wise and income wise at the same level that they had been previously. So it was, under normal circumstances, a KISS tour was an enormous financial undertaking. With all of this in mind, that the press was not lapping up the album [and] ticket sales had fallen... So, with all of these things going on simultaneously, it was very hard. They knew you made money from touring and you made money from selling albums. It was kind of a pre-merch era where they had, I don't even know if they were selling merch at concerts at that point.

They were. They've been doing that from 1976 onwards.
OK, but it certainly wasn't the way it is now where bands basically make their money off the merch. You can't make money off albums anymore.

No, KISS was well ahead of the curve on the merchandise side of things. They basically built the model everyone else does now. By early 1982

they'd given up on the synth idea from the sounds of it and budgeting for a guitarist, so I guess Ace had fallen out of the picture by the end of January. Literally.

For the San Remo broadcast he doesn't show up and we see the press releases that he's sick. We hear the other stories, that he's just not willing to do it anymore or not able to.

That's when they did the performance at Studio 54 for a live satellite feed to Europe and, up until the last minute, Bill was saying, "He's on his way, he's on his way," you know. We didn't have cell phones, although I think Bill had a phone in his car, but it wasn't the same thing. It wasn't like you could just pick up a cell phone and get anybody. And right up until the last minute, we thought he was going to be there. I was panicking. What the hell am I going to tell the brass? "Ace is not here." Oh, we'll have to say he's sick, but...

For the first ever satellite link up to the San Remo Festival with an audience of — I think it was 22 million.

Yep.

Did you attend the video shoot Halloween weekend shoot for "A World Without Heroes" and the "I" videos?

Yeah you can barely see me in the crowd, only from the back, and I knew it was me because I knew what I was wearing. We were there for both.

These videos would've been useful publicity tools. That format is starting to take off. I know that PolyGram initially wouldn't let MTV use their artists' videos, because they didn't want them financially benefitting without themselves being paid. Do you remember why the "I" video was abandoned? It was just never used, never sent out to anyone and it has only just surfaced this year.

I don't remember why. There were very few places that you could use it. I remember going over to PolyGram and meeting with the publicity person there about MTV and him just telling me, "If MTV wants a film clip of KISS" — I don't know if they were calling them music videos yet — "they have to pay for it."

Right, that wouldn't be resolved until mid-82 when PolyGram finally agreed because they saw the benefit all the other labels were getting from having their artist's videos shown.

Yeah. Hello! You [the labels] should be paying them!

So "A World Without Heroes," I think it only really gets used on "Flo and Eddie," and a clip of it on "Entertainment Tonight," and on "Solid Gold." Did you handle any of the PR on the visual side as? They didn't seem to get a lot of appearances on TV to support this album? That's pretty much the sum total plus San Remo. It didn't seem like much of a push visually.

Well, no, I tried to get them on whatever shows there were that had live rock performances and I got them on "Solid Gold." I know we went out to L.A. for a couple of days.

They did "Solid Gold" at KTLA Studios in L.A.

So that must've been it.

"Solid Gold," which was national, but seemed to be not the right sort of demographic for the band. So obviously, you're limited in the number of outlets, but where there any kind of attempts to get them elsewhere that fell through?

Well, I do know that anything that was on the air, I attempted to book them on, but I don't remember which shows they were on and which ones turned it down.

Was their popularity just at such a low that it was an impossible task to do publicity for this time?

It was really difficult, not only because their popularity was at a low point, but also because their music was not popular; that style of music was not popular at the time. You know, people were listening to other things and they were still hiding behind makeup and costumes, and people were kind of all right, we've seen that already, what else is new.

Right, new wave and post punk are taking off and obviously, metal has got a different direction starting to emerge. Ace is out of the picture. How are you guys talking about handling that? Was there a discussion in the office about Ace after San Remo and did he ever come back or was that basically the end of him?

I think that was kind of the last straw. There were things all along. He just he was so out of control. I remember picking him up once from his lawyer's office to bring him back to Aucoin.

So, his lawyer was on 57th Street and like Sixth, right near Carnegie Hall, and the office was on 60th Street and Madison Avenue. It's like three Avenues and, and three or four streets over. It was a very short distance, and he had his car. But he was driving back to the office and I got in the car with him, and I think we made, we got there in like a minute and a half. I was afraid for my life. I didn't think I was going to make it!

Not surprising with what he later did on the Bronx Parkway.
Unbelievable.

During this period and Paul stated in his book that the relationship with Aucoin became strained. Obviously, the album wasn't a success, but he's also said that Aucoin was focusing too much energy on other bands on the AMI roster. What's your perspective on the dynamics in the office about the suggestion that Bill's was becoming, apparently, a bit wild, in his personal life and that there's just too many other bands?
They were very upset at any attention Bill paid to Billy Idol. They felt Bill, Bill was spending too much time on Billy Idol and not enough on them.

Billy Idol, of course, was emerging big time, but I think Paul also questioned Bill's personal and professional behavior and said that he was a bit erratic. It's kind of tough to talk about Bill since he's no longer here, but was there a strain and was there any perception that he was perhaps going a bit off expected behavior?
There was.

Did it make the office stressful? Was he becoming unreliable?
It felt more like there was no one steering the ship.

Did Diana Ross ever come into the office?
No! I had one meeting with her. I mean [we crossed] paths. I went to bring something to Gene at the studio. I don't remember what it was, but it was something that he needed, and she was there, and Gene introduced me. She was sitting on the sofa in the studio and Gene introduced me, "Diana, this is Ida Langsam, our publicist," and I went to shake her hand and it was like a dead fish. She was just better than anyone. She was too good for anyone, you know.

We, we kind of get the impression of that from talking with others and hearing the "Ms. Diana Ross" stories.
Ms. Ross, yes, Ms.

Must refer to her as "Ms. Ross."

Jayne [Grodd] had a better relationship with her because any time Diana needed to get hold of Gene, she had to go through Jayne if he was on the road or, you know, "What hotel is he at and where can I reach him." So, she had a better relationship. But I heard the story that she was living at the Sherry-Netherland Hotel at the time. They have apartments and that's where she was living. [It was a] very fancy, expensive hotel, kind of across, catty-corner, from the Plaza Hotel, and I think she'd been there for a while already. She wasn't a new resident, and I understand that as a Christmas present, she gave everyone on the staff an autographed photo. That was her Christmas present, no money.

An autographed photo?
Yep, and I'm sure they loved that.

A shame they didn't have eBay back then.
Exactly.

As we look at this period particularly in relation to KISS and your expertise in PR, is it true any press is good press?
I never believed that. I still don't believe it. I don't think that's true.

Because it's such a throwaway phrase these days, you know, that as long as you get your name out there, it doesn't matter what the context is.
I don't believe that, and I think that's been proven that it's not the case. I mean you can, with the Internet now, you can look [everything] up. A case in point, everything you've found, everything you've looked up and, and uncovered and discovered, it's a different world, and when you have celebrities, quote, unquote, and you know, everybody that's a bad girl or a bad boy, being able to turn all that -- I don't know, I would consider it negative information about them -- out there into celebrity, maybe it's different now. Maybe now there is something to be said for any press is good press, but I think it depends what you want to be known for.

Right and from what you said earlier about Paul's press release, about his dating, he certainly wouldn't agree that any press is good press, would he?
No.

Do you remember anything about Paul having surgery on his ear during this time? I'm trying to figure out whether this occurred during "The Elder"

era. He was wearing his purple headband, probably to hide his ear -- that sounds so "Spinal Tap-ish" to be asking, but...

I think so. I do believe that he had surgery at around this time. It was sort of whispered about in the office. That was not press, press release material!

Paul going to New Hampshire, nope, but it would've been the ideal time with what wasn't happening on the band's schedule.

Yeah, well if it were today, then maybe it would be talked about.

TMZ would have a cameraman on site.

Oh, please. The publicist would be calling them and telling them to go. Maybe they can squirrel their way into the hospital and get some shots of him in bed in the hospital bed.

In April 1982 you leave Aucoin? Did you go solo at that time?

Yes. I didn't leave by choice. KISS fired Bill. Since they were basically funding the office, Bill didn't have the finances to keep the staff on.

Billy Idol's not taking off enough at that point?

No, he wasn't bringing in enough money yet.

So where did you go in your career after KISS and how did the experience of working with them either help or hinder you?

Well, at the time, it helped because any time you're working with a band that has name recognition on that level, people assume that you're responsible for getting them that recognition, whether you're responsible or not, you know. It can work both ways, but Bill approached me as soon as he'd made it known that he was going to be closing down the various departments. He told me that he had a new band he was working with and he would like to hire me to work PR for that band, and I could stay in my office and if I wanted to take on additional clients, I could. So that's how I went independent.

And you've been independent ever since?

I have.

So where does KISS fit in your personal catalogue? You worked with the Ramones, I think, for 9 years?

Yep.

Who else have you worked with and where do they kind of measure up in, in terms of where you feel your professional accomplishments were?
Hmm, I don't really know how to answer that.

Obviously, it was a challenging period for the band, and you did the best that you could to get them as much publicity as you could. Did you ever face a similar period like that with other bands like the Ramones? Did they ever have a down period?
The media did not like the Ramones. The legitimate press didn't want to have anything to do with them. The only press that loved the Ramones were the underground press. It wasn't until the band broke up and, and then when Joey died, all of a sudden, the Ramones were the most brilliant thing that ever happened in the world. But when I was working with them, it was like pulling teeth.

When did you get involved with the Ramones?
One of the first things I did with the Ramones was a photo shoot, the one and only photo shoot that they did with Clem Burke. They did one photo session with Clem because they had gotten rid of Richie and Mark hadn't come back into the band yet. So, they approached Clem and he was a little wary of it, but he said he would do it. But after a very short period of time, he said, "You know, I can't commit to you. I'm in Blondie. I can't commit to being in the Ramones." I guess they were hoping to steal him away.

The power of Google, Elvis Ramone.
Yep, I was just going to say they couldn't figure out what to call him because it was Joey, Johnny, Dee Dee. It had been Richie and Markie, and what are they going to do? Clemmie? So as a joke, they said, "How about Elvis," which also had nothing to do with the ending, but they were going to go with "Elvis Ramone."

So, what other acts have you worked with?
Oh, my God. Barry Manilow, Linda Ronstadt, Steve Martin ... I'm trying to remember everybody!

That's a heck of a résumé right there.
Yeah, I can't remember. I mean there are things that at the time were hugely popular. There was an artist named Randy VanWarmer, who had an enormous hit record called "Just When I Needed You Most" and I did his press. He never had a follow-up hit and then he became a producer instead

of a recording artist. A few years ago, he actually passed away from cancer. I [also] worked with Rick Derringer.

Oh, well, after, after KISS, I kind of began working with, up and coming artists rather than big names. I mean always said if Madonna called me and said, "will you do my press," I wouldn't say no, but I wasn't going out and soliciting those kinds of accounts because after some of my experiences, not necessarily with KISS, but with other big name artists. After Bruce Springsteen was on the cover of Time and Newsweek in the same week, all these other artists wanted to know why they couldn't be on the cover of Time and Newsweek in the same week! It became a real pain in the ass to try and work with those kinds of artists. So, I found it much more rewarding to work with "newbies" because they're starting off from Ground Zero, so you have so much information you can give them and so much you can teach them. [They have] so much they have to learn that it's much more rewarding, then again, not talking about KISS, but working with someone who had been at the top of their game and was now not, but acting as though they still were and wanting to know why they weren't still getting features in Rolling Stone.

Exactly, sort of the elevator going up versus the elevator going down.
Yeah.

My very last question is what would be your advice to someone wanting to work in publicity in the Internet age?
Hmm. It's very different from when I started back in the dark ages.

Is it still the mailing list, you know, still contact driven, that that plays an important component, that you want to accomplish something, you know someone, or you know someone who knows someone?
It's certainly a very important component. It's not the same as it used to be. Now, because information is instantaneous, a lot of the gatekeepers are gone or no longer have the status and importance that they used to have. You can get online and put something out there on your own instantly. If you have a million followers on Instagram, you can get the information out there without anybody. You can just do it directly yourself.

Exactly, but on a weekly basis you see people, you know, sports stars, music, or personalities putting something out on Twitter that they quickly delete, but it's too late and out there forever.

Right, they're not always the smartest.

They probably shouldn't be their own gatekeepers.
Well, if you're somebody like, Taylor Swift, you're okay. She's almost bullet proof, but it took her a while to get there. It wasn't an overnight thing and she has such a love-love relationship with her fans. Then you think about somebody like, not a music artist, but someone, what made her famous, a very rather personal sex tape. You know, years ago, that would've been scandalous. It would've ruined somebody, not made somebody's career.

Now it becomes a line of perfumes.
The role of a publicist has really, really changed.

It must be somewhat depressing to see how it has changed when we've just mentioned that particular case?
Well it depends on who your client is and what their aim is. What's their goal? It's one thing I always ask potential clients when I have a meeting with them. What is your goal and what is your expectation for PR? If they have unrealistic expectations, nothing is going to satisfy them, and if their goal is, "Oh, I want to sell records," [then] that's not a goal. That means nothing. You want to sell records. There are people who sell records that you've never heard of. I always tell the artist you have to treat it [as] a business. It's no longer a run in the park. You have to have a business plan. You need a goal. You need to have stages of development. You need to have financial considerations. You really have to make a business plan. It's not just fun and games anymore. So, it's quite different.

And that is a perfect way to end this. I think that's fantastic and I appreciate you giving me this time to tell me about your experience within the industry and working with KISS as well.
I should tell you one story because I just thought of it. This does point to what the band was like. This particular situation was with Gene. At one point, he had a lot of things that he wanted done on his behalf and he gave a list of directions. He gave me something specific that he needed taken care of, and I was working on it. I don't remember what it was. Whatever it was, I was working on getting the information he needed, and he called. It was fairly early in my working there. He used to say, "Are you smoking?" because I was smoking at the time, and he could hear me smoking on the phone.

He would say, "If you're smoking, I'm hanging up," because he didn't want me to smoke. I would have to either pretend I wasn't or put the cigarette out, but that's just an aside. So, he called to find out if something was done, and I told him the progress I had made, what I was up to in getting whatever information it was, and he got completely bent out of shape. "Is it that hard to do? I gave you one thing to do and I told you where it was, and I told you how to get it, and why aren't you doing it, and this is inexcusable!" And just he like went off the deep end, and I was so rattled when I hung up the phone. I went in Stephanie's office and I was so upset that I started crying. Stephanie called Gene to find out what was going on, and it turned out that he thought he had given me something to do that he had given someone else.

Oops.

I had no idea what the fuck he was talking about. He had wanted somebody to go to his mother's house and dig through all the old boxes of press clippings and press stories in different magazines. I think they were doing research on costumes. They wanted to take some elements of old costumes and incorporate it into the new stage set. It might have been a money saving factor. He needed someone to go through all the old pictures to see about the costumes and he thought he had given that to me to do, but he had not. So, when he called me, he didn't understand why I hadn't already gone to his mother's house and gotten all the clippings. But that's not what he said — he wasn't specific. He just said, "I gave you one assignment to do and why can't you do it." I was just devastated. So it turned out that we were at cross-communications, but that's an example of how on edge they were in terms of wanting to get things done, and needing to get, and looking for the right angle, and trying to decide how to handle it. Everything was pressure.

It sounds like a pretty unpleasant period, to actually have been working with the band.

It wasn't the best. I mean he did apologize. [They also had] a baseball game between Aucoin and Howard Marks. You know about that?

Yeah, there's a press release for that!

I took pictures there. I actually have some photos, but you know, I was not allowed to use them except for my personal use because it had Gene without his makeup on. I don't play sports, so I said instead of being on the team I would be the professional photographer because I have a degree in photography. Gene said he wanted the [game] filmed. He had whatever the latest video film camera at the moment was. So, I had to meet him at his house early that morning, and he was going to show me how to use the camera. That was his way of apologizing.

Some fun times as well, right?
Yes, there were. It's just overall it wasn't the best period in their career.

No, it was the lowest ebb for them there, their nadir, so. That's probably why we're so interested in it.
Yep. The last time I saw Gene was a long time ago. There was a party for his solo album. It was maybe 10 years ago.

Oh, his "Asshole" party.
Yes! And he came in with an entourage late to the party and of course, everybody was crowding around him and I kind of waited until the crowd was a little less. I went up to him and he was talking to people, and I said "Hi, Gene, it's Ida," because I didn't think he'd recognize my face that quickly, and he went, "Ida Langgggg-sam, how are you," and I was, I was thrilled that he like even went so far as to remember my last name and pronounce it. It's a German name, so he even pronounced it properly.

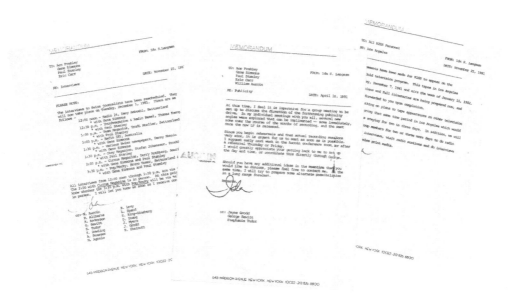

(Some 1981 memos and PR from Ida)

Melanie Chartoff

Multitalented actress looks back on a "Fridays" adventure with KISS

Melanie, can you touch upon how you came to work on "Fridays"?
Melanie Chartoff: I was a Broadway actress moonlighting as a stand-up at the Improv club in New York and Los Angeles and they brought me in to read, then later for a screen test in which I was asked to improvise with other aspirants. I got the offer a couple weeks later. I'd known Larry [David] and Bruce [Mahler] from the NY Improv club — they felt like cousins to me. The others were all new collaborators.

KISS performed on the show on Jan. 15, 1982. What was the preparation like for the cast for a typical show?
We rehearsed six days, taped the dress in the afternoon in case of technical difficulties, and broadcast live to the East Coast at 8:30 p.m. from Los Angeles. The East Coast got the unedited live show with all our flubs, the West Coast had a 3-second delay and the editors beeped out the curses and worse.

What do you recall about the audience reaction to KISS' performances?
Some were wildly enthusiastic fans; some were pretty nonplussed and didn't applaud or respond at all.

And what do you remember about getting to introduce them?
I see from YouTube they dressed me way outré and trendy to set up the wildness of their performance.

Part of the band's mystique was that they were rarely seen unmasked. Do you recall seeing them without their makeup?
I saw them at the party afterward without makeup or costumes and they were regular nice guys, rather like Alice Cooper without his rock and roll persona. I saw their onstage characters as puppets, and they were the puppeteers.

KISS made a brief cameo in "The Hollywood Cubes" sketch. You also appear in this sketch, playing Marina Oswald.
And Charo and Barbara Mandrell too.

(KISS on "Fridays," screen captures from the "Best of Fridays" DVD set)

Do you have any recollections of this particular sketch?
Oh, yes — the finest of green-screen acting for its time, as we all pretended to be relating to others who were not there. It took hours and hours to

shoot it, not only for our many make-up, hair and costume changes, as we all played several different celebrities — except for KISS who played their professional selves in the masks of their characters — but for the video effects, which were very innovative for their time. I believe we all worked separately in the pre-taping that day, as we were all confined to the same box in different positions. We were keyed into those positions in postproduction — there was no actual Hollywood cube that could spin like that without killing some very expensive personalities.

During one of the two endings to the show, you were next to Gene Simmons. Any memories of being alongside Mr. Simmons?
Only from watching YouTube, I see I was a bit reserved. I wasn't a big fan of the extended tongue routine; I didn't prefer the unfamiliar nude men groping me action. I was being classy, which was my trademark, and he was being crassy, which I guess was his trademark.

Following the show, you went to the aforementioned party at the Hollywood Hotel, hosted by Paul Stanley. Can you give us any memories that stand out from the party?
It was relatively low-key — we were all exhausted from performing that week. I think the sedateness, with Paul on his best behavior on a date with Donna [Dixon], was one of the interesting contrasts. He was toned down to his hamisha, nice, normal person self.

Do you recall if Donna Dixon was also at the "Fridays" taping?
She was probably there with my press agent, Susan Patricola.

Aside from your recollections of Paul, any observations about Gene at the party?
He was very aggressive! I kept trying to shove his impressively long and flexible tongue back in his mouth.

Ever run into any members of KISS following the "Fridays" episode?
I wouldn't have recognized them without their get-ups — we were in L.A. — weren't they New York guys? When I went back home to New York, I was in the theater scene, rather than the rock music scene.

"Fridays" aired from 1980–1982. Despite the brief tenure, the show has maintained a cult following some 30 years later, evidenced by the 2013

Shout! Factory DVD release. When you think of "Fridays," what immediately comes to mind?

Wildly intense and innovative — we took some big chances and scored some groundbreaking successes. We gave exposure to some incredible, bleeding-edge music groups. I loved and miss every cast member. Only half of our many talents got exposed, especially for us women who were relegated to ensemble and supporting the guys most of the time. I [recently] visited Maryedith [Burrell] in Asheville, N.C., and visited Larry after his "Fish In The Dark" performance on Broadway last spring — he was hilarious and he is much beloved by the theater crowd.

What more do you remember about some of those great music acts who were on the show?

I had a crash course in contemporary music and on-the-job training on "Fridays," which, besides KISS, featured breakout groups like the Clash, the Boomtown Rats, Stray Cats, and Devo on the show. Mark Mothersbaugh and I became collaborators on all the musical numbers we performed in our years doing "Rugrats." The crew would dress me, tell me where to stand, put a light on me, and have me introduce incredible artists in their ABC TV debuts — it was a true privilege having that momentary association with the most revolutionary groups of our time in that last Millennium. I was thrilled to hang out with Bonnie Raitt and Al Jarreau, Joan Jett, and Jean Luc Ponty's group and attend their live shows at other venues, when I wasn't changing clothes or preparing for my next live sketch. I rarely got to see the groups perform during the taping. I'd catch up later and watch the shows at home via my Betamax to see what had actually happened.

Do you look back at your "Fridays" experience fondly?

Immediately after, we were all very burned out. But now we all recall only the best of times and adventures.

Ty Tabor

King's X guitarist discusses being one of the proud few who liked "The Elder" upon its release and the simple reason why the album didn't catch on with the majority of KISS fans

Ty, from a fan perspective, what do you recall the word on the street being about "Music from The Elder" in 1981?
Ty Tabor: To be honest, I had heard a lot of people badmouthing it and I was thinking, "Wow, there just seems to be a very strong opinion about this record," which made me want to hear it even more. So, I went out and bought it immediately. I had the opposite reaction. When I started listening to it my first impression was, "They're really getting serious with this one," as far as branching out with the songwriting and everything. I personally was floored by it when I heard it. I couldn't understand why people weren't getting it, because I thought it was killer.

You were a big KISS fan growing up, correct?
Oh, heck yeah. When I was 15, KISS came to the Jackson Mississippi Coliseum. A friend of mine and I went to the show. Of course, we had been fans since "Midnight Special," that's where I saw them first. I freaked on them, I thought, "Wow, this is unbelievable." Of course, KISS "Alive!" — My whole age group, everybody had that album. I was the perfect age for when they happened in the '70s. I was a huge KISS fan, just all through the early albums and up to "Alive II." "Dynasty" is where I started kind of losing interest a little bit. But up to that point I was a diehard.

As a guitar player, Ty, would it be safe to say Ace was an influence?
I was certainly influenced by Ace heavily because I always thought he was the most underrated lead guitarist in rock. Every time they put out a new album, I couldn't wait to see what his solo would be on a song because he had such vocally melodic solos. The kind of things you hum when you hear it back. And that was just a big influence on me, that solos weren't just some kind of show-off moment. He was, and he is, very musical with his solos. But the truth is I was a fan of the whole band, I was a fan of everybody, and certainly caught up in the whole hysteria just like every kid my age at that time. (Laughs)

What would be your top five KISS albums?
"Destroyer", "Music From The Elder," "Alive!," "Alive II," and "Rock And Roll Over."

Getting to "The Elder," were you even aware that KISS was doing a concept album?
I didn't know about it until it was out, and people were talking about it.

What do you remember people saying about it?
The only thing I was seeing was very negative. In the press, it just seemed like people were writing it off immediately. However, there was enough information in these little things that I saw that intrigued me to hear it because some of the things they were saying about it were the reason I wanted to hear it, despite them not necessarily being fans of it. It was obvious that they were going into a direction they had never gone before and they were cohesively trying to put — I hate to compare it to something like the Who — but the fact is the first time I heard it, like the one part where Paul is singing, "I am just a boy," it hit me as almost straight out of "Tommy." Not as a comparative, not to say they were copying, but to say the same magical feeling I got when I was listening to "Tommy," I started feeling when I was listening to this record. That was what surprised me. That's when I started feeling like, "Well, I wonder why people aren't getting this because to me, it seems to be one of the most magical things they've ever done."

Were you able to pick up on the album's concept right away?
I don't think so, when I was younger. I think it was more a matter I was aware that was going on, but I was so intrigued by the music, by the melodies, the different writing styles, the not being afraid to go there kind of stuff. That's the thing I remember the most about it. Not really following the story as much as being blown away by the branching out of ideas.

What format did you purchase it on?
I had the vinyl.

What do you remember picking up in terms of the packaging? It was the first album not to have a photo of the band.
Right. To me, it just made the whole thing more mysterious. The whole project just seemed mysterious. This just came out of nowhere as far as I was concerned. I didn't know it was happening. And it was so impressive to

me as a change for them and having the balls to go there and do it well. The packaging didn't matter, [it] made it that much more mysterious. It made me wonder what the hell this was about that much more.

Were you aware this was the first album for Eric Carr?
I don't think I was actually thinking about that at that moment. Maybe I was. I don't remember to be honest.

You mentioned "Tommy," were you a fan of previous concept albums, in particular?
I don't think I'm a fan of really anything just as a genre. To me, there are good concept albums and there are pitiful concept albums. So it's not that I'm a fan of concept albums, but I'm a fan of concept albums that are done well.

And you think "The Elder" is done well?
I do. I think it's done very well.

What are some of your favorite tracks on the album?
There are several songs that struck me as heavy as can be. That one song that has the galloping rhythm [sings rhythm guitar figure in "The Oath"] ...

"The Oath."
I remember that one blew me away. There are a couple of Gene songs that are super bad too, really heavy. But believe it or not, some of the more adventurous Paul stuff really intrigued me too. I guess it was both because for me I got the KISS out of it I wanted to get out of it because they did do some rockin' stuff on the record that was right up the alley of what you'd expect from KISS but at the same time it was flavored with all this other stuff that I don't know, when the heavy stuff came in, it made it even bigger and better to me. There was a day and night between things. There was comparison. There were low points, high points. For instance, there are certain songs where it's more like the parts of the songs and where they choose to go are what struck me as amazing.

For me, "Under the Rose" seems to fit that description, in terms of dynamics. There are quietly sung verses by Gene and then the it builds with the choir vocals, and then before you know it there's a sledgehammer riff.

Exactly. It's weird because I don't even think of the album as individual songs. I think of it as putting on a movie and going with it.

Personally, I think Gene shines the most on "The Elder." The lead single, "A World Without Heroes," is a song you would not expect from Gene Simmons. But that's the lighter shade you were talking about.
Yeah, exactly. Also, "Mr. Blackwell" is a contrast to that. I love that one too. That would have been a great single.

That's part of the reason why I think Gene is the star of the album. On that track, Gene gets into the mindset of the album's antagonist. He doubles his vocal with octaves to create an evil effect. Musically, the track is so dissonant. And the breakdown is positively eerie. Classic Bob Ezrin.
Yeah, I'm a big fan of a lot of Bob's stuff. Anytime you hear KISS with Bob Ezrin, you can expect greatness.

Paul and Gene really don't have many kind things to say about the album nowadays.
Really? That's too bad.

Whenever "The Elder" comes up, Paul especially does not mince words.
Well, it just goes to show you that artists aren't good gauges of themselves. I remember John Lennon actually said that there's one song called "And Your Bird Can Sing" that was an early Beatles song that had the first dual harmony guitar leads of any song I'd ever heard before. It was one of my all-time favorite Beatles songs growing up. And I saw an interview where people were asking John about songs, and when they got to that one the only thing he said about it was, "Yeah, that was a throwaway." (Laughs)

Did you own Pink Floyd's "The Wall"?
I didn't. I don't know why I didn't ever buy it, I heard it so much on the radio I almost didn't need to because it was back in the old days of true FM radio. The radio FM station in my town I was growing up in, they would put a whole side of the album on regularly. I was familiar with the record without even having to buy it. So, I never did actually purchase it.

Obviously with Bob producing, there are all sorts of ingredients foreign to the KISS sound — choirs, symphony orchestras, harpsichords, and the like. How would you rate "The Elder" from a production standpoint?

I think it's great. It's on the level you would expect from Bob Ezrin, because to me he is what made the Alice Cooper band magic. He took a bunch of ragged stuff, because I've heard their material before he was involved, and I'm telling you, it wasn't that great. (Laughs) Once he got involved it was just the magic combo, so I've always had a great respect for his vision in production and how he brings things to life. For me, it's just another one of his very great works because there are too many albums that he's been involved in that are important albums to me. That's a credit to him that he just does good work, period.

Of course, he helmed "Destroyer," which is considered a classic.
Yeah, that was my personal favorite album of all.

Are you aware "Destroyer" was remixed in 2012?
No, I didn't know that. But I'd be afraid to hear it remixed because I like the original so much.

Of course, "The Elder" ended up not performing well, commercially speaking. You're actually part of the minority being a fan who liked the album at the time. Ultimately, why do you think the album did not resonate with the KISS fan base? Was it just too much of a left turn?
Yeah, I think so. The fact is the stuff that has worked for them is the stuff that has been more directly to the core, more straight-ahead — right to the melody, right to the chorus, to the excellent bridge with an excellent solo. They had delivered so many powerful blows in that fashion that when this came out, I imagine a lot of people were just close-minded to it because it wasn't what they were expecting. It's just that simple.

Do you think that because the album was released by KISS, it was not given a fair shake? In other words, if a band like Pink Floyd or Rush, who had more progressive pedigrees, released "The Elder," would people have had a different reaction to the material?
I think they would have had to because by that point everybody had their own idea of what they believed KISS was in their own mind. And it's hard to break loose of that once people have formed their opinions. I think if they had not existed as a band ever until that moment and that was the first thing they did, I think people would have been extremely impressed.

As an artist yourself, have you ever found yourself straddling that line between creativity and trying to deliver what your fans expect?

I can honestly say that I'm too one-minded [and] focused when I'm writing to even really think further than that. I don't ever know if anybody is going to like what I'm doing as an artist. I just try to do what makes me happy and I hope that they like it. I know I went through a brief period of time back around the time King's X did the "Ear Candy" album, which was mid-'90s or so. And I remember I went through a period during that time where there were people trying to influence us to write more commercial and things like that. And I remember that was one of the only times I've thought about it that way and considered what other people wanted, and it was miserable for me. So, I personally made a choice after that to try and not second guess what people want. You know, the people who come up with great ideas are people who just come up with great ideas and people like it. There's no way to ever know what fans are going to like. So that game is a game of insanity that I can't allow myself to go into. I just try to be happy with what I write.

After "The Elder" KISS recorded "Creatures of The Night." Did you continue following the band? And was there a point when you stopped following them in the '80s?

Well, I was sort of already off the KISS train when "The Elder" happened. So "The Elder" kind of brought me back in. Then "Creatures of The Night" came out [and] of course I paid attention to that. I thought it was a good rock record, and I dug it. But I was also getting older and very busy with King's X. King's X in the '90s would go out up to nine months on a tour. I was getting caught up in our own little world of insanity there for a few years and really kind of lost touch with following lots of bands just because we were so busy.

What KISS albums do you have in your collection? Did you get "The Elder" on CD?

I do have it now. I've got the original vinyl, of course. But now I've got everything on CD, I have everything up to "The Elder," except for "Dynasty." I didn't buy "Dynasty," but I have everything else, including "Double Platinum."

All the classics. Ty, correct me if I'm wrong, I don't believe King's X have ever opened for KISS?

No, we have not. Even though I've spoken to Gene on the phone more than once and we've met. But we've never toured with them.

Can you share a story about Gene?
Yeah, he actually called me to ask King's X to be part of the "KISS My Ass" album.

That's right. What track were you considering?
Well, we actually never got to the track. It's kind of a long story and it's kind of silly actually. But the truth is he called and asked if we'd be interested and I said, "Of course!" And we had a long talk that night about all kinds of different stuff that was very hilarious to me; it was a very fun conversation. We talked about everything from motorcycle racing to him saying he wouldn't get in a single-engine plane or anything like that that would keep him from walking onstage the next night. And he was like chastising me like a parent, like I really shouldn't be doing this stuff because I was racing Supercross at the time between tours and stuff. He was pretty much telling me that I was crazy. (Laughs)

We had a really great conversation that night and I said, "OK, we'll talk again in a few days. I'll go back to the band." So we talked again in a few days and when he called back the second time he said, "Well the truth is we have so many bands that are wanting to be a part this, we've had a great outpouring and it's just overwhelming and awesome so what we're going to do is start asking bands to pair up together to do stuff." And he said, "We'd like to pair you guys up with the Galactic Cowboys." And here is where the problem was. They had asked the Cowboys before they had actually talked to us and the Cowboys instantly went into the studio to record a song for the record. They already had something done on their own because they had been asked. Gene asked me if we'd pair up with them and I said, "Well, the truth is I don't have a problem with it but ..."

It's really a long story, at that particular moment in time; the Cowboys had done several tours with us. Because we had the same management and were from the same town, the press was constantly comparing them to us. And they were trying to make a very serious conscious effort to get out on their own without the comparisons. And it had become a point of contention, a real problem to them. When Gene asked me that, I said, "I'm sorry Gene. You have no idea how much we would love and be honored to be part of this, but we really can't do it with the Cowboys because they've already recorded something, and they are trying hard to disassociate themselves with us right now." So, I said, "We respectfully are going to be the ones to have to back out." And I think he was not very happy with that and pretty much canned the Cowboys.

Do you recall which track they recorded?
I can't remember what it was to be honest.

In hindsight, if you had the choice, what song would you have picked to cover?
I was considering maybe something off "Rock and Roll Over" — one of the high-energy heavy tunes from that period between "Alive!" and "Alive II." We were kind of looking at songs from "Love Gun, "Rock and Roll Over" and "Destroyer." We had decided on something from "Rock and Roll Over" ... [it was] "Calling Dr. Love." I think we started out thinking about doing "I Want You" and then we talked about doing "Dr. Love."

I have a trivia question for you. Both King's X and KISS have songs on one particular album. Do you remember which album and the song titles?
Oh yes, I do. The song KISS did was "God Gave Rock and Roll To You," the Argent song. And the song we did was, I may be wrong on our song, but I think we did "Junior's Gone Wild."

You got me. And the album?
The album, was it a "Bill & Ted's" soundtrack?

That's right, "Bill & Ted's Bogus Journey." I remember going to pick that up in 1991. KISS is on there; your track is on there, Megadeth, Winger, Slaughter, Steve Vai. So much for stumping you Ty.
(Laughs) I actually [remember] becoming close friends with Eric. It was a cherished friendship I'll always really appreciate, no doubt.

It's hard to believe he's been gone for more than 20 years.
I know, I know. He was just a sweetheart.

Ty, you're a fine guitarist, so we'd be remiss not to ask you about KISS' guitarists. I'm going to name each KISS guitarist and if you could say the first things that come to your mind in terms of their playing and/or your favorite solos, if anything. Ace Frehley.
Oh yeah, one of the all-time great [Ace solos] is "Shock Me." I remember the first time I heard it, me and a best friend of mine, a guy named Marty Warren, we were very excited because there was a new KISS album coming

out. We actually heard "Shock Me" on the radio and we were like, "Check out this KISS song with Ace singing!" And then it got to the solo, and it was quite possibly the greatest Ace solo ever recorded. It's just a really great solo.

Any thoughts about Paul Stanley as a guitarist?
Yeah, I dig Paul. As a matter of fact, his solo album was the one I liked the most of the four, by far. Again, some other of my best friends, we all had the albums and the one that we played constantly was Paul's.

Do you remembering getting all four of the solo albums in '78?
Oh yeah, absolutely. Everybody did!

How about the guy who replaced Ace Frehley, Vinnie Vincent?
Well, Vinnie's a great player. He's a killer player, no doubt about it. I have to say every guitarist that they've had since, I mean Bruce is a great player. They've not been any lacking for having a great lead player at any point as far as I'm concerned. I'm more partial to Ace because he's a little bit different kind of guy than the rest. He's not the type of technical player that they kind of ended up with later, which I have nothing against whatsoever. I'm just saying sort of the rough edges and the dangerousness of it with Ace was what I liked so much. So, I'm very partial to Ace.

It's hard to argue with that. Ace's guitar is a big part of the classic KISS sound. When players like Vinnie came onboard, the sound morphed into a different direction. Of course, Vinnie became known for his otherworldly guitar chops.
Right. Technically killer. Technically proficient. For me, I'll be honest, even though I totally appreciate how good he is and have nothing negative to say about him at all, the whole vibe of what the solo became in a KISS song at that point changed to a different kind of thing. Because it used to be the melody and style when it was Ace. And then it became more like real guitar solos as they had guys that could do amazing things.

Do you remember Mark St. John's at all? The guitarist who played on "Animalize."
I do. But I don't remember much about [that album] to be honest.

You mentioned Bruce, who is fantastic player.
Yeah, Bruce is awesome. He's great.

Nowadays, are you familiar with Tommy Thayer, who plays in the band today?
I heard the name, but I'm not really familiar.

He was in the group Black 'N' Blue in the '80s.
Yeah. I'm actually familiar with Black 'N' Blue, but I haven't heard what he's done with KISS.

You also own a recording studio. Ty, aside from King's X, what else do you keep busy with nowadays?
Yeah, I am always recording. I've been extremely busy. I play in a sideband called the Jelly Jam, which is made up of me on guitars and vocals, John Myung from Dream Theater on bass and Rod Morgenstein on drums. We did two albums together under the name Platypus and then we changed the name of the band to the Jelly Jam. And we've put out so far three Jelly Jam albums and a fourth one that we've already recorded most of it ... I'm also right in the middle of a new solo album, because it's been a couple of years since I've put anything out solo. So right now, I'm in the studio every second of the day that I'm not out here touring.

Chuck Klosterman

From the packaging and the meaning of "Odyssey" to analyzing Paul Stanley's disdain for the album, New York Times bestselling author dissects "Music from The Elder"

Chuck, you got into KISS in second grade, correct? What's your introduction to KISS story?

Chuck Klosterman: It was an amalgamation of things. I know I saw "KISS Meets the Phantom Of The Park" and an episode of "20/20" where KISS was prominently featured. I think it was mostly the "20/20" broadcast, to be honest, because I recall going to school the next day and "playing" KISS at recess. It was probably my idea. You had to have moon boots in order to play, which seems like the kind of weird playground bureaucracy I would have demanded as a second grader. Obviously, at that age, my interest was not musical. I just thought KISS was cool, especially since I believed no one knew who the band members actually were. I was somehow under the impression that it was possible to be super-famous and totally anonymous at the same time.

Around fourth or fifth grade, I started listening to regular pop music on the radio — Eddy Grant, Madness, Huey Lewis, Van Halen's "1984." Around fifth grade, I became completely obsessed with Mötley Crüe. They were the only band I cared about. But then my brother-in-law ended up with an unwanted "Animalize" cassette through the Columbia Record Club —he failed to send in the little "selection of the month" card. He gave me this copy of "Animalize," based on the premise that KISS was "the Mötley Crüe of the '70s." I liked it immediately, except for "I've Had Enough (Into the Fire)." I was really into the idea that there were two singers who didn't seem to write songs together, so it was almost like getting two bands for the price of one. "Animalize" led me to "Lick It Up," and then to "Destroyer" and "Love Gun" and "Alive!" and "Alive II" and eventually to the "KISS Exposed" VHS tape. That was the real game-changer. From that point on, I would just read about KISS constantly.

Where does "The Elder" rank on your favorite KISS album list?

Oh, it's definitely my favorite KISS album, but that's based on a whole bunch of confusing factors. "Music from The Elder" is the most fun record to think about. But it's not the best KISS studio album — those are "Love Gun," the first record, the second record, and "Rock and Roll Over." I think about half of "Creatures of The Night" is pretty good; if you took the five best songs off Creatures and combined them with the five best songs on "Dynasty," you would have one excellent album. I'd make the same argument for "Asylum" and "Crazy Nights." "Destroyer" is a little overrated. "Unmasked" is a little underrated. "Dressed to Kill" is up and down. I also love the solo records, except Peter's. Those are fun to think about, too.

When did you actually acquire "Music from The Elder"?
Not until it came out on CD, which must have been around 1989. It was almost impossible to find on cassette. I only saw the tape once, at Mother's Tapes and Records in Moorhead, [Minnesota]. But I couldn't really afford it. I only had enough money for one tape, so I got Ratt's "Invasion of Your Privacy" instead.

When you first listened to "The Elder," what was your immediate reaction?
My main memory of playing "The Elder" is that I just kept thinking to myself, "So this is it. I'm listening to 'The Elder.'" I'd read so much about it that it seemed meaningful to simply possess the artifact. I knew that it was supposed to sound unlike any other KISS album, so I unconsciously exaggerated how much that difference would be. I probably thought it would sound like free jazz or something. But it still seemed like KISS to me. It didn't sound anything like Pink Floyd or Jethro Tull, which is what I'd been told. I suppose the very beginning of the album is a little like [Jethro Tull's] "Locomotive Breath," but that would have never occurred to me at the time. "I" seemed exactly like a good mid-period KISS song, except for the part where Gene directly criticizes people who get wasted. But that was a known thing about KISS. They were totally overt about their sobriety.

What did you think of the album's packaging?
I thought, "Hmm. So that's what Paul's hand looks like." But I don't think it's actually his hand.

As you open the package, there's a brief text description, which begins, "When the earth was young, they were already old." Do you remember that initially intriguing you or confusing you?
It reminded me of the prologue from "Star Wars." The crawl at the beginning of "Star Wars" begins with the words, "Long ago," even though

the movie employs technology that could only exist in the future, so the narrator's distant past is our distant future. Relative to that concept, "The Elder" made sense to me. I was like, "Oh, of course these characters were already old when the earth was young. That's totally reasonable." I suspect "Star Wars" played a bigger role in the narrative construction of "The Elder" than the band has ever admitted. KISS always viewed themselves as the "Star Wars" of arena rock.

When is the last time you listened to the album?
Yesterday.

Chuck, what is it exactly about "The Elder" that fascinates you?
If you like a band, you appreciate all the things they do well. But if you *love* a band, the parts of their career that truly fascinate you are the aspects that go wrong. Artists are best understood through their reaction to failure. So, if you love Black Sabbath, the record you want to think about is "Technical Ecstasy." If you love Oasis, you want to think about "Be Here Now." And if you love KISS, the record that's most compelling is "The Elder." It's not even close. "The Elder" helps you see the psychopathy of KISS. You can still see how the experience of this album changed the way they look at themselves and how it galvanized some of their pre-existing opinions about the world.

The thing is, KISS always tries to convince themselves — and the rest of the world — that they don't care how critics view their work. But this is clearly untrue, and especially during this period of their career. I think they thought releasing a critically appreciated album would reinvent their perception and cause people to rethink the meaning of their previous records, which might have a commercial benefit. It also seems like they came at the "The Elder" from a paradoxical artistic position: They assumed making a concept record would be relatively easy, despite having no idea how to actually do so. So, they hired a cocaine addict to teach them, and they never said "no" to any of his insane ideas. When you listen to "The Elder," you can hear that awkward combination of insecurity and arrogance that most interesting artists possess.

That said, I do think Paul and Gene were extremely proud of this record, at least initially. But when the response was so unilaterally negative, they were forced to reimagine how they felt about it. The reviews were slightly better than they'd been for the previous albums, but not significantly so. In fact, the marginally positive reviews were worse, because it made them seem desperate. To KISS, this became proof that trying to please anyone except your core fan base was idiotic and wrongheaded. It galvanized the fictional persona they had once tried to project and turned it into their actual worldview.

How have your feelings for "The Elder" evolved over the years? Has the album aged well for you?

It sounds like an album conceived and recorded in 1981. But I like that quality.

One criticism levied against the album is that the concept is not entirely tangible from the songs. What are your thoughts?

That's a useless criticism. Concept records are supposed to be a little obtuse, because every individual listener is supposed to manufacture their own version of the concept within his or her mind. If anything, "The Elder" is too clear about its narrative intention. I mean, it's not as explicit as [R. Kelly's] "Trapped in The Closet," but it's more straightforward than something like [Radiohead's] "Kid A." I feel like I know what the rough story was supposed to be. I know there's an island that needs to be escaped from.

Have you ever pondered the meaning of the song "Odyssey"?

To me, this is the song where — if there had been a movie — the protagonist from "Just A Boy" would have traveled through time. I have no idea why the little girl is wearing a sundress, and I don't know why the stallion and the mare are on the mountain? For most of my life, I thought the lyrics claimed it was a stallion and a bear, which makes less sense but is probably a better idea. I like that song, though.

Which song do you feel is the most atypical KISS song on the album?

"Under the Rose." It's the only song that couldn't fit anywhere else in their catalog, except maybe on side two of "Carnival of Souls." I suppose the least KISS-sounding track is technically "Odyssey," but that's sort of in the vein of some of what they did in Wicked Lester. "The Oath" sounds like the type of music they would have made if they were just trying to make a regular pre-glam metal album and get on FM radio, except they spent an inordinate amount of time on the lyrics.

Which band member do you think shines the most on "The Elder"?

That's a difficult question. Probably Eric Carr.

Interesting. I personally think Gene Simmons is the MVP on the album. Can you elaborate on why you choose Eric?

Eric Carr was a complete drummer who knew how to take direction, and this was a wholly directed album. The guy who would have really excelled in this situation would have been Bruce Kulick, had he been around at the time. I suppose you're right about Gene being the most personally invested in "The Elder," but I don't think this record is necessarily the finest reflection of what he's good at. He's better at stuff like "Ladies Room."

In the video for "A World Without Heroes," Gene Simmons sheds a tear. This song features a delicate Simmons vocal, showcasing his "serious" side. Do you prefer this side, or the "I want to put my log in your fireplace" Gene Simmons?

Somewhere in-between, but I lean more toward the serious side. I like it when Gene writes about capitalism and social class — "Cadillac Dreams," "She's So European," "While the City Sleeps," "The Streets Giveth ...," "Deuce," "War Machine," that sort of thing. He's such a nihilist.

You once described "The Elder" as the "most advanced hard-rock album ever." If you said this to Paul Stanley, he might offer to take you to a hospital for a psychiatric evaluation.

If you ask Mick Jagger what his favorite Rolling Stones songs are, he inevitably gives the most banal answers possible. He'll say "Satisfaction," "Jumpin' Jack Flash" and "Start Me Up," based on the argument that those are the most popular Stones songs among casual fans — so they obviously must be the best. It's like Mick Jagger doesn't believe his own perception matters; he has conditioned himself to view his work as a pure commodity. KISS is the same way. They've come to believe that thinking critically — or even caring — about your own music is somehow missing the point. And it was "The Elder" that galvanized this.

Speaking of Paul, whenever "The Elder" is brought up in interviews nowadays, he doesn't have positive things to say about the project. Going back a few years, he's was quoted as saying it was "a good album but not a good KISS album." As a fan, why do you think Paul has grown to seemingly despise the album?

I think it represents a terrible time in his life — a period where he was publicly experiencing an existential crisis about who he was as an artist and a celebrity. I think he's embarrassed that he overreached and tried something that didn't work the way he imagined, and I suspect he hates how certain people like me always want him to talk about projects that failed commercially and critically. It's the same situation with "KISS Meets the Phantom."

Of course, the album was produced by the legendary Bob Ezrin. Bob added elements such as an orchestra and a choir and helped the band stretch their creative boundaries. What do you think of the album's production?
It's good. Ezrin's a great producer and a specific type of genius. His force of personality is massive, and he obviously has vision. But the downside to sophisticated production is the degree to which it ties an album to the time and place of the technology that was employed. Like I said before — this record was made in 1981, and it sounds like it was made in 1981. It will always have a 1981 feel. But the KISS albums that Eddie Kramer produced sound like they could come from 1975 or 1995 or next summer.

In listening to the album's first track, "fanfare," a regal mood is quickly established with the entrance of the theme. I've always pictured the members of the Council of the Elder taking their places at the table featured in the gatefold. What do you picture when you hear this track?
A lot of straws. But no milkshakes.

(Laughs) "Dark Light" is notable for containing a lyrical reference to Sodom and Gomorrah. A stroke of brilliance? Or is this what Paul is getting at?
I don't think referencing "Sodom and Gomorrah" is particularly brilliant or particularly obscure. I mean, is "Modern Day Delilah" obscure? It's not that KISS fans don't read books. On balance, I would say "Dark Light" is the best track on this record, or at least my personal favorite. The guitar solo is the fourth best of Ace's career, after "Strange Ways" and "Rip It Out" and the live version of "Strutter." I really wish Vinnie Vincent had covered this song. The repetitive nature is right in his wheelhouse. It would have been interesting if Lou Reed had written this whole album, frankly. [Did] Reed ever give an extended interview about The Elder? I would like to read that.

Not to my knowledge. Chuck, you've mentioned that it "wouldn't have mattered if "The Elder" had been "Sgt. Pepper's Lonely Hearts Club Band" and that "people viewed that music through the prism of how they understood KISS." In other words, are you saying that KISS fans *and* the general public are generally close-minded when it comes to KISS?
Well, yes. That's certainly true. But that wasn't my point. My point was that KISS had incredible success creating an image for itself that had a highly

specific meaning. In many ways, this is their supreme achievement: The band itself has a higher profile than the totality of their music, and that facade informs everything they do. It turns KISS into an idea, in and of itself. When people played "Music from The Elder," they were not hearing a collection of art-rock songs in a vacuum; they were always hearing art-rock songs that were specifically made by KISS. It's impossible to think about anything KISS creates outside of the context of who they are.

So, when people first heard "The Elder," they did not ask themselves, "Is this good?" They asked themselves, "Why is KISS doing this? What is their motive?" And that immediately changed the meaning. Lou Reed singing "Dark Light" signals something different than Ace singing "Dark Light." The song is interpretative, but the singer is not. One clear example of this process is the Hootie & The Blowfish song "Time": Coming from Hootie & The Blowfish, the idea of time not existing seems facile and meaningless. It makes them sound like college students trying to be deep. But if Jerry Garcia had written a song [with the lyrics] "I don't believe in time," that title would have become a bumper sticker.

You can't have everything you want, and you can't force people to think about your own work on whatever arbitrary terms you demand. You can't perform "Cold Gin" in front of an electric 40-foot sign that says "KISS" and also have intellectuals view your mythic fantasy as a serious piece of art, and you can't expect the kind of kid who loves "Cold Gin" to automatically engage with music that was consciously made to impress the type of person who usually listens to Kate Bush. That's not how public life works. Now, things might have gone a different way if audiences had believed KISS had been compelled to make this album for artistic motives that they could not repress. But KISS had spent the last 10 years convincing the world that they never thought like that, about anything.

Imagine an alternate universe where "Music from The Elder" surged to No. 1 on the Billboard 200 and won a Grammy for Album of The Year. How would KISS' career have changed?
Paul and Gene would have promoted "Hot in The Shade" by insisting, "It's our best album since 'The Elder.'" And Ace would be dead.

If you had one album to convince Jann Wenner of KISS' brilliance, would you pick "The Elder."

Why would I possibly aspire to do this? I don't care what Jann Wenner thinks about KISS. Look, there are some really smart people who work at "Rolling Stone." But that magazine was created so that Jann Wenner could meet John Lennon, and it continues to exist so that Jann Wenner can go skiing with John Mellencamp.

Say you are overseeing an "Elder" film project in 1982: Who would you cast in the roles of the Boy, Morpheus and Mr. Blackwell?
River Phoenix would have been 12 in 1982, so he could be the Boy. Maybe Leonard Nimoy as Morpheus. I have no idea who would make a good Mr. Blackwell. Perhaps Nick Nolte, although Gene would likely cast himself. The best move would have been to make an animated version.

You've authored several books. Ever given thought to writing an "Elder"-based book?
I have not. But I have considered writing a screenplay based on the Steve Miller song "Take the Money and Run." So, if any super-rich people in Hollywood are reading this lengthy interview about "The Elder" and want to produce a film project based on a narrative Steve Miller Band song, get at me.

Once a year, I wait for the murkiest overcast autumn day and dim all the lights, light a candle, grab the headphones and listen to "The Elder' in its entirety. I've attained "Elder" nirvana many a time following these steps. Do you have an "Elder" listening ritual?
I usually like to play the album in its entirety during Thanksgiving dinner. But my wife is always like, "Why not side 4 of 'Alive II'?"

(Laughs) I've read that you listen to the Vinnie Vincent Invasion debut album six times a year. How many times a year do you listen to "All Systems Go"? And second, how many times a year do you spin "The Elder"?
The only tracks off "All Systems Go" I regularly play are "Heavy Pettin,'" "Naughty Naughty," and the intro to "Let Freedom Rock." Sometimes I'll play "Ashes to Ashes" at the gym. I have no idea how many times I play "The Elder" in any given year. My iTunes suggests I play it twice a year, except for "Dark Light," which I evidently play five times.

No love for "That Time of Year"?
Oh, I don't know. I suppose. Were you a big "Back on The Streets" fan, too?

I do like that song.

There are parts of "That Time of Year" I like, but it seems more like a Slaughter song than a VVI song. In some ways it seems almost like Dokken. I guess I could never deduce what time of year Vinnie was actually describing. Is he talking about autumn? Christmas? Tax season?

One final "Elder" question to take us out, Chuck. Originally, spoken word dialog was planned to help thread the album's story between songs. It seems this component was left on the proverbial cutting-room floor. Ace Frehley has mentioned that he's uncovered his lost "Elder" guitar solos. And Bob Ezrin recently remixed "Destroyer" in 2012. How does the thought of an "Elder" deluxe-edition release with, say, a remix of the album and bonus tracks grab you?

I would totally love to give Paul and Gene my money for this. I mean, I've only purchased "The Elder" twice in my life. As a KISS fan, that's not enough.

(U.K. picture disc)

Bas Hartong

Phonogram International's A&R manager gives perspective on the state of KISS in 1981 and shares his recollections of Bob Ezrin's "Elder" presentation for the label

Bas, let's start with a bit of your background. In 1981, what was your official role with Phonogram? And how long had you been at the company?
Bas Hartong: I moved to the USA in 1982, but in 1981, and since 1979, I was an international A&R manager for Phonogram International in my native Holland. From 1973–1979 I had other positions, first at Phonogram Holland and from 1976–1979 I worked at Polygram's Dutch corporate headquarters in its legal department.

Polygram in 1981 had two international repertoire centers, i.e., Phonogram International in Baarn, Holland, and Polydor International in Hamburg, Germany. Like at the time in the USA, most countries had one local Polygram company which would deal with both repertoire centers and used the Phonogram label Mercury and the Polydor label. But in some of the major territories outside the USA, such as the UK, France, Germany, Holland, and Japan, there were local Phonogram and Polydor operations which would compete in these markets. My A&R job was with Phonogram International and thus the Mercury side if you will. I believe in 1979 or 1980, PolyGram bought Casablanca Records from Neil Bogart.

A 50 percent stake in Casablanca was purchased by PolyGram in 1977 for $15 million. The buyout was completed in early 1980.
Yeah. In any event, it was decided internally that Casablanca overseas was going to be channeled through Phonogram. Which made little difference in a lot of countries, but, as I explained, it did in several countries, because there Casablanca recordings would be released by the local Phonogram companies as opposed to local Polydor companies. It also meant international marketing would be handled by Phonogram International's Dutch head office rather than the Polydor office in Hamburg.

Phonogram International had its own A&R department that signed mostly established Anglo-American artists. This was mainly done because the size of the Polygram companies around the world, in terms of market share, was a lot bigger than PolyGram in the U.S. Even after Casablanca had become part of Polygram USA. Phonogram International needed additional Anglo-American repertoire, and before I got that job, other executives, in the '60s and certainly throughout the '70s, predecessors of mine, made outside U.S. deals initially with labels like 20th Century Fox and Sire and others. And also, British labels like Charisma, so the company had Genesis and Peter Gabriel and that label's other artists. When I got the job, we focused more on trying to sign established artists directly with whom we could build up a more lasting relationship. During the period before I moved to New York, we signed Lindsey Buckingham, Ronnie James Dio and Black Sabbath [featuring Dio] before that, and Van Morrison and Elton John and several other artists. And so, I started making business trips to the USA on a reasonably regular basis. I quickly started pushing to be moved to a U.S. office and did so in July 1982, but obviously still reporting to Phonogram International's Dutch management, which had agreed to establish this N.Y. outpost.

How would you describe the general state of the company circa 1981?
It was a difficult period, after the death of disco and the enormous successes of "Saturday Night Fever" and "Grease," which were virtually impossible to repeat. The company all of a sudden was in rough waters because it relied way too much, certainly the American company, on that repertoire. It was all about trying to trim costs and reducing losses. In the midst of all that, the company had to renew the contract with KISS because Donna Summer had already left. Casablanca had two huge stars: KISS and Donna Summer. One of them already had signed a deal with Geffen Records. So, it was essential that KISS was re-signed.

Were you involved in making that deal happen?
I was involved [internally] somewhat in those negotiations. However, KISS' attorney Paul Marshall and other more senior Polygram and Phonogram executives were actually handling this, but I used to go meet Paul Marshall and also used to know the band's manager Bill Aucoin and later Howard Marks. The situation with KISS was that [there were] various licensing agreements across the world between Casablanca and different local companies. So, let's say in Europe, one German company would release KISS albums in Germany and another company in France in France and so forth. There were all these different territorial deals and they didn't necessarily all expire at the same time. Also, the problem we had in Europe is that KISS really only broke on the disco rock single, "I Was Made for Lovin' You."

Before the "Dynasty" album, the band was not that big of a deal in Europe. So here we are. Finally, KISS did not owe any more albums under all these different deals with foreign companies and the band comes to Holland to be introduced to us. This was a *big* deal. There was a party in the Hilton Hotel to launch the "Unmasked" album, where we really couldn't have any photography because they had no make-up on. We weren't unhappy with ["Unmasked"] but obviously everybody in Europe was hoping it would have another "I Was Made for Lovin' You" on it, but that [ultimately] ended up being just a one-time thing. So "Unmasked" was really the first record that Phonogram International got its hands [and said], "Let's try and make this band bigger in the rest of the world than they have been before." We made strong efforts for that record. I don't remember how well it did, [in terms of the] mass public.

In the States, "Unmasked" only went gold, which was a cut below "Dynasty." And, as you mentioned, it didn't spawn a repeat worldwide smash.
"Shandi" was the single.

Interestingly, "Shandi" did extremely well in Australia.
Yeah, Australia and Japan always have been a little bit more attuned to the American market than Europe.

Jumping to "The Elder." There was a meeting you attended, during which the album was played back for various label personnel.
I did attend the meeting where "The Elder" was presented to the American company.

Bob was there. Who else would have been present? Would David Braun, the label head, have been there?
I don't even know if he was in that meeting, and he wouldn't have had a strong creative opinion about a record like that. That wasn't what he was doing. The thing is, in the A&R department, there was no one who actually signed this band. There was no person who had signed them or had been a point person, simply because [the band came from] Casablanca. It was a completely new situation for the band and the company. The head of A&R, I don't remember if he was in the meeting, was Chip Taylor. Chip was and is a renowned singer/songwriter and was brought in by David. I was just focused on listening to this [album] and taking notes. If I close my eyes, who else do I see? I would say Harry Anger was probably in that meeting; he was one of

the top marketing execs. After our initial conversation I spoke to Jerry Jaffe, who told me he did not attend. At the time, he was the head of the rock radio promotion department and he got very involved, later on, in discussions with the band, following the "Creatures of The Night" album. I can't remember if Gene and Paul were there or not. I believe it was the first time I met Bob.

Any way to recall when this meeting would have taken place?
I think it must've been sometime in the summer, or early fall.

What sticks out the most when you think back to the meeting?
I particularly remember — these are just little remarks you don't forget — two bands that Bob mentioned before playing a note: Pink Floyd and Supertramp. It's not unlikely that people were rolling their eyes a little bit, "Like really? Do you really think this is doable with this band, considering what they've done this far?"

What was Bob's demeanor like?
I remember him pacing up and down. He was not sitting down, as far as I can recall. And he looked very sharp. It's not like he came in with blue jeans and a T-shirt, or something. He almost looked like an executive. Some producers, obviously, can be wild and crazy, and he was not. He made a very focused presentation.

So, at some point, Bob starts playing the album.
He started playing it, and I started making notes because I had to report back to Europe. So that when I came home to Holland, I would have my notes ready to talk to everyone. I remember writing something down like, "This is a whole *different* deal. This may be a significant problem, because we just started with this band, to build what we were doing, and now they have sort of thrown us a curveball. It's just so different from what they've done before. And this could indeed be a big problem."

And so, we had a coffee break, and during that coffee break Bob Ezrin, by his own admission later on, apparently read my notes [when] I was outside the meeting room. In a very nice way, during the second part of the presentation, he mentioned my reservations and he said he understood them, because we were in a different stage of developing this band [in Europe], than the American company was. But [he said] to the others in the room that America should be ready for this band to make this step. But he did understand that for Europe and the rest of the world, this was a bit of a problem.

With regard to the recording sessions, Bob recalled, especially in those days, they were typically closed to label personnel. It doesn't seem that word would have leaked out the label that "KISS are doing a concept album."
With KISS it's not an abnormal situation because of what I said before. There was no affiliation with any A&R staffer that I am aware of and I don't even know if there ever was. I don't know if Casablanca, Neil Bogart or anyone there really gave them guidance or not. It wasn't necessarily like it had to be all a big secret, there probably wasn't a person who was close to them then.

Bob's recall is that the reaction after hearing the album was one of complete shock.
Yeah, it was like, "What is this??" And, "How are we going to market this?"

Do you recall there being spoken word dialogue interspersed between the tracks?
I do not remember if there was. I guess the copy I have here at home is certainly one of the early pressings. I mean, are you suggesting it came out and was changed?

No. Bob went into a studio and recorded dialogue designed to be interleaved between the tracks. The dialogue did not make it onto the final album. But it is unknown as to whether the dialogue was actually put into the album at some point. So, I'm curious if perhaps the dialogue was present during the listening session. And if it was, I'm wondering if it was the label that demanded it be cut?
My response to that is, and [this is an] assumption, I find it hard to believe that the label would have the right to do it. I mean, the status of the band was such that they likely retained creative control in the new contract. Any editing would all have to be subject to prior approval. In other words, it must have been persuasion by the label and not the label's legal right if indeed this was an issue.

I'd venture to guess that the label was none too thrilled about the album's artwork. It's certainly not the artwork you'd expect to see on a KISS album.
No, but to be honest, I looked at the artwork this morning for the first time in decades probably, and I was like, "Wow." I mean, if you hang posters up

like this, how do people figure out it's a new KISS record? I'm not suggesting it has to be an in-your-face photo with the makeup. But (pauses) I agree with you, it's different. It doesn't necessarily jump at you. Of course, you can you pay for space in the stores. Nonetheless, put yourself in the position of store owners and guys in Tower Records who work there. They probably would've preferred something that was stickered, you know? It could've been made a little bit clearer, from a design point of view, that this was a KISS album.

Obviously, the band and the design team felt this artwork gave the album the gravitas it deserved.
Well, as we're talking, I'm thinking about the whole thing. If you think about it, KISS was going to retain a number of their fans. That's a given, you know? You're not going to lose all your fans. But with the somewhat more casual fans, you're in jeopardy with a record like this. So then the question really is — and Bob must've been really confident, hot on the heels of that enormous success with Pink Floyd — "Can we bring in Supertramp and Pink Floyd fans, or even Genesis fans, to like this group instead of the casual hard rock fans we may lose?" And that's really an enormous risk to take.

It's really not important what my opinion is, but it was more a matter of, "What are we going to do with this record?" And, "Can we really sell this to a new audience — to a more *mature* audience?" To fans of acts that, at the time, the Ramones and all the other new wave acts and punk acts were rebelling against, really.

So, you end up going back to Holland and reporting back.
Yeah, I went back and probably said, "Guys, this album's coming, it's a complete different story. We're going to have to do the best we can." Nobody was upset; it's just, "Whoa," you know? Our first album was "Unmasked," and so we were hoping to get something that could repeat the "Dynasty" success, including a single that you could get on the radio.

The shock sets in and it sinks in that "The Elder" is the album that is being released. I guess the next step for the label is to figure out how to make it work, in terms of marketing it.
Yeah, and we always had a good rapport with KISS. Personally, I always tried to keep my relationships with management and the artists really good. I think we're there to serve the artists. In other words, I never thought or think the executives are more important than the artists.

In his book, Chris Lendt, said that PolyGram was mulling not accepting delivery of the album, which would've been within the label's rights. Perhaps you were not privy to such a discussion, but it's interesting to think that may have transpired.

It's conceivable. I mean, if you talk from a legal point of view, I don't see why Chris would've been making it up as he knew the contract's contents. But you have to understand; the reality is the band got a lot of money for this record, so for financial reasons alone there was a lot at stake for the label aside from other considerations.

Right. Regardless, the call was obviously made to go with "The Elder."

Well, you know, it's something the band did. It's something they tried — they wanted to try it, they tried it and they moved on. Instead of trying to do it again, they came back with "I Love It Loud," the first single off "Creatures of The Night." I remember being excited when I heard "I Love It Loud." I said, "This is great."

Of course, a tour to support "The Elder" never materialized, marking the first time KISS didn't tour in support of a studio album. "The Elder" was on the chart basically for a couple of months. In early 1982, it peaked at No. 75, and then by February, it was off the chart. So, we're talking a very short lifespan.

Yeah. You know, it's not necessarily wrong to try something different, but this was a 180-degree turn. And I'm not saying it was awful, I'm just saying that they went too far from one place to another. Maybe they should've gone back and made a much harder record, not a "Dynasty" kind of thing. If they would've come and said, "We're making a hard rocking [album] and a little less poppy," [that] might've been a better decision. And that might've happened if they would've worked with, fill in the blank, Martin Birch or somebody.

Maybe Mutt Lange?

Well, Mutt Lange, yeah. [He] did the AC/DC record ["Back in Black"]. But they chose Bob Ezrin for good reasons, because they worked with him before [and] they were familiar with him. But he just came off this whole concept thing and he must've played a big role in telling them, "You can do this, you're capable of doing this."

Before "Creatures" and "Lick It Up," there was a decision to do the compilation album for overseas, "KISS Killers." That album contained four new KISS tracks, which were in a harder rock vein.

Yeah, I remember that record. I have it. We were very much in favor of it because, at that time, the old licensing agreements that Casablanca had made with various overseas labels had all expired. Finally, the entire catalogue of KISS had become part of Phonogram's catalogue. So, there were two solid reasons for the release of KISS Killers: "The Elder" record not being successful and us finally having all of the KISS albums in our catalogue. To release the "KISS Killers" record with a couple of new tracks, that was even better of course. I do remember when that record came and we finally had all of the KISS albums in our catalogue, we were hoping that would generate some new fans or even fans since the "Dynasty" days, who would get this record and hear all these songs and say, "What album is that from?" And so forth. That album's release was an ideal way to introduce fairly new European fans to songs from KISS' older albums.

There were no "Elder" songs on "Killers."

No, but I think that makes total sense. I wasn't involved in selecting the songs at all, but it wasn't so much meant to be a career overview. It was more, "Let's take some of the best hard rockin' tracks that they have — plus some new songs — and reestablish them."

Jerry Jaffe

PolyGram's head of rock promotion on why "The Elder" had a scarlet letter attached to it and why getting KISS radio airplay in 1981 was a lost cause

What was your official role with PolyGram in 1981?
Jerry Jaffe: I was head of rock promotion.

And how long had you been with the company?
About 5 or 6 years.

How would you describe the state of PolyGram at the time?
You know, it's so weird because at that time the company was going through so many changes. I started off with Polydor. Then Polydor became PolyGram — well there was Mercury and Polydor running as separate entities, and then they came together as PolyGram. And then there was one promotional staff and then PolyGram bought Casablanca. And there was this brief period when it was called PolyGram Services, or something like that, where the company still existed. It was Mercury, Polydor and Casablanca, but there was one promotion staff. In other words, the companies only existed as A&R. And everybody else, like marketing, promotion and press, was all one company.

What were your impressions of the Casablanca label and Neil Bogart?
I knew everybody there. But I was kind of a rock guy, and they weren't known for their rock acts at all. I mean, I don't think that they had any successful ones other than KISS, and KISS had an asterisk because at that time was the rise of underground radio. Then it became programmed as AOR radio, and KISS never really mattered on that format. Even though, in retrospect, that was such an uncool, unhip, totally corporate format. For some reason the people who ran it thought of themselves as being like progressive and somehow KISS wasn't part of it, because they kind of looked at [them] as being some kind of dumb band. I'm from New York and the irony is I remember I used to hang out at those places [where] the New York Dolls used to play all the time. And there was the New York Dolls, KISS, Teenage Lust. But it considered so hip in downtown New York, and KISS was part of it. And then when KISS signed with Casablanca and started out, the first couple of albums went nowhere. And then somehow KISS was unhip.

Although, their origins were right there with the New York Dolls who never sold a stinkin' record. But [they're] somehow in the pantheon of great rock and roll to this day.

Anyway, when you talk about Casablanca, they had no rock credibility whatsoever. And I remember only taking one or two people from Casablanca. One who I absorbed in my department was Drew Murray, and I remember saying, "I got to keep Drew Murray because he must be good if he did rock promotion at Casablanca with the crap that they had." To this day Drew is a friend. He's a wonderful guy. And I guess he's the guy who probably promoted KISS at rock radio.

In 1981, how much of a priority was KISS in terms of promoting their new album?
To my way of thinking, there was no differentiation from whatever label a band came from. But the fact of the matter is when "The Elder" landed on our laps, it was already a defeated record. It wasn't like, "Here's 'The Elder,' it's coming out! Let's sit down and devise a promotion strategy." It had already been out and already had a scarlet letter on it, so it wasn't like, "Here's a new KISS album." I was familiar with the album and that it was going nowhere, even though one tries to keep their personal feelings about a record divorced from actual promotion. In the words of the great promotion man Al Coury, "Every record is a hit until proven otherwise." And that was my philosophy.

What are your thoughts on the choice of lead single?
Well, the lead track was a ballad, ["A World Without Heroes"]. And it was just a terrible song, if I may add my personal opinion. But listen, I promoted a lot of terrible songs that became hits, so that's not even the question. But the video was everything KISS wasn't.

The video was filmed by Bruce Gowers' company, Gowers, Fields & Flattery. Gowers is known for having shot Queen's "Bohemian Rhapsody" video.
Really? Between that and Bob Ezrin, [there was some] credibility.

And then there's Lou Reed, Michael Kamen and Tony Powers, all of whom played roles on "The Elder."
What did Lou Reed do for that record?

He co-wrote three songs, including "A World Without Heroes."
You gotta be joking.

Bob Ezrin brought Lou Reed in because he had worked with him on the Berlin album.
It's like news to me right now. Not that it would have mattered at radio because Lou Reed never got played on the radio. Believe me I'm used to rock and roll in New York, and I can tell you that that nobody ever bought the Velvet Underground record. They never got played, even on the rock radio stations in New York. I mean, Lou Reed wasn't somebody you brought in to have commercial success at that time.

A fair point. It seems Reed had more critical acclaim.
Right. Well, I think the band, from what I could observe, really wanted that kind of acclaim. They yearned for it. I mean, they had the money. They made this record, which in their demented minds they thought [was] something that people would love. What KISS did is just amazing. And yet, [with "The Elder"] they lost a lot of their commercial base. And there was certainly no critical acclaim for the record. I mean, to put out a song like "A World Without Heroes" and think that was going to actually get radio airplay? It was a pipedream. I thought that that song was a rip-off of — nobody agrees with me on this by the way — John Lennon's "Working Class Hero." That John Lennon song was certainly heartfelt and a very personal song. And then this thing comes out with Gene Simmons, with his tears, singing it in makeup. I'm not going to go any further than this, [but] KISS wasn't immune from taking part A from this record and part B from that record.

But having said all of that, there was an expectation, from the group and from Bill Aucoin, that now that the "the heavy hitters" from PolyGram were taking over, we were going to actually put this record back on the map. Casablanca couldn't do that. We somehow had more credibility than Casablanca. [And that] would make a difference. We had better connections with radio, I think that was understood.

Obviously, the music industry has radically changed since 1981. Can you bottle the process of how a track was promoted at rock radio in those days?
Well, you have the local promotion staff. The most important part is the relationship between your local promotion staff in every city and the programmers at the radio station. In those days, my main thrust was what

was called AOR radio, album-oriented rock. It was heavily formatted. It wasn't easy to get played. There were consultants; most notably someone named Lee Abrams, who basically made all the decisions. New acts and acts that weren't familiar on that format, when they did get on usually, they were banished to late night. Unless you had a name, you didn't just go onto the radio. I mean, there were certain exceptions that blew up big from the beginning, like Boston.

As a national person, I had relationships with a lot of the key programmers also. Plus, I wined and dined the consultants — you make appointments and you'd play the records for them. You'd tell them that this was a great priority and that the company was behind it and supporting it on the radio with time buys and toys and all the other razzamatazz. And then there are also independent promoters who give an extra voice to the record. I mean, at AOR Radio there weren't that many influential people at the time, nor was there any kind of sleaziness like Top 40. Basically, it was about creating excitement on a record. There were tip sheets for rock radio. There was "Billboard." There was "Album Network" that was starting. You'd take out ads when certain stations went on the record.

Almost all the time, when there was a real concerted effort at radio and then it went to us, for whatever reason, there was really nothing more you could do. I mean, the verdict was already in by the time we got the record.

Let me backtrack. Do you remember learning about "The Elder" and the fact that it was conceptual in nature?
I don't remember what was going on behind the scenes although, as a rock person, I wasn't thrilled that the company was doing a deal with Casablanca. All they had was KISS. The other stuff that they had was disco and Donna Summer and the Village People, and they had kind of seen better days. I could not understand why PolyGram (and this is from afar; I had no voice in it) were buying something that looked like it was completely over. Casablanca was run by a guy, Neil Bogart, who was a great character. I just thought he was a hipster, and he got lucky.

But anyway, by the time we got the album it was damaged goods. I don't remember whether the fact it was a concept album or not had anything to do with it. I mean, if we would've had one track that we could take fresh to radio and try to resurrect it. ... The most important thing was this record had already made the rounds, and the verdict from both the public and radio was in and this was *not happening*.

In hindsight, would it have made more sense for you and your team to initially steward the album's promotion?
I don't think it was in our jurisdiction. It maybe would have made sense but the deal with Casablanca wasn't totally put together. It would have been like working a record on RCA, another label that wasn't affiliated with PolyGram at the time. The fact that PolyGram owned a piece meant nothing. They were an independent label. And the other weird thing was outside of America they were distributed by a whole variety of different labels. So, it wasn't really like a worldwide PolyGram thing. I think that whole deal was formalized, and then it became worldwide. Would we have done a better job on it if we had it from the get-go? (Pauses) I don't know. I think the record was just flawed. You can sometimes get a shitty record on the charts. You can get airplay on it. But there comes a time when that record has to perform on its own.

The album was released in November 1981. In terms of the timing of the promotional campaign for radio, was the album promoted for a period of weeks or a month …
I don't remember. I do remember a meeting with Bill Aucoin and a guy named Ric Aliberte. I since became really, really good friends with Bill Aucoin. But Bill Aucoin's henchman was Ric Aliberte. He was saying, "These shitheads are losing on this record." This guy was just totally insulting to me. And subsequently I formed a friendship with Ric. It's amazing. I told him, "I didn't even talk to you because you were terribly rude and unprofessional in those meetings."

But he tried [to say], "I'm going to show these PolyGram putzes; I'm really going to let them have it." I was basically saying, "We did the best we can. Next." I liked KISS. I really did. I loved some of their records. I was intrigued by the whole concept. To me it was so Americana that these two Jewish guys from New York became these huge rock artists in America. What a story this made. I looked forward to working with them. I said, "Let's start fresh," and that's what my theory was. And Ric Aliberte was like, "Nah, it's not finished. It's a brilliant record. It's a great record." Basically, I was accused of personally fucking it up. And I was really offended by it. I remember once [saying] to Aucoin, "Can you call your dogs off? What is with this guy?" And I think I stopped taking his telephone calls.

Jerry, would you say your staff did their due diligence in promoting "The Elder."

That's right. We did what we could, yes.

In scanning the "Billboard" issue dated Jan. 23, 1982, "A World Without Heroes" hit its peak on the Billboard Hot 100 at No. 56. Not great, but not terrible. In looking at the radio section, I also found that the song was designated as a top playlist add at multiple stations nationwide, including Augusta, Atlanta and Birmingham.

OK, let's stop for a second. First of all, those are not the stations that my department promoted. We worked closely with the Top 40 department. Now, I don't know if that was the Casablanca staff or the PolyGram staff. If you had a rock record, you would try to get it to be huge at rock radio and then cross it over to pop, and most of the time, [with] even harder rock records, you couldn't cross over. And then we had that wonderful era of the power ballad, which was usually the second or third single. That was the one you crossed over to pop radio and for a lot of acts it was also the kiss of death. I think it cost Cheap Trick a good 10 years with "The Flame." I almost think that "A World Without Heroes" was KISS' attempt to do that without having it be the third single.

Would it have made more sense to go with something more up-tempo out of the box?

Absolutely. And that's in retrospect. I don't remember what my thoughts were at the time. But the problem with KISS being a credible rock act was that they had hits with "Beth" and "Shandi" and stuff that weren't rock records. They *never* got played at rock radio. "I Was Made for Lovin' You" was perceived as a disco record. I mean, they had no credibility at rock radio whatsoever. They had about as much credibility as Air Supply.

It would seem that "A World Without Heroes," and the fact the song was from a concept album by KISS, equated to a lost cause at radio, right from the start?

Exactly. And that's why I would sit there and take shit from Ric Aliberte. "You ruined this band. This was one of the biggest bands and you ruined it."

When I think of radio promotion, I think of artists actually visiting stations to conduct interviews and acoustic performances. Were those types of promotional vehicles ever discussed for "The Elder"?

I doubt it because nobody was interested. If there was something we could do, we would do it. I'm sure we knew which radio stations that maybe they still had relationships with that would still play the record, and we would go for ads. Let's say WRIF in Detroit was playing "A World Without Heroes," and it was a top request. We'd be taking out ads and saying, "KISS, 'A World Without Heroes,' Detroit, WRIF's No. 1 request, Top 5 sales." And then people would look at it and say, "Whoa, look at this! If it's a smash in Detroit, let's go with it." But you have to build the story. We didn't have anything to say; nobody was interested in the record. Nobody wanted to talk to the band at the time. They were on Casablanca and Casablanca was a Top 40 label. They had Top 40 hits. They weren't a rock band anymore. That was the prevailing view about the band at the time.

You said you vaguely remember that a second song might have been promoted to radio.
Maybe, yes. I don't remember.

There was a second video filmed for the song "I," which was more akin to an anthemic KISS song. Interestingly, the video never aired. So, I venture to guess that everyone involved said, "OK, we're cutting our losses and moving on."
Well, obviously it was paid for. At that point all you had to do was deliver it [to MTV] on a video. And basically, they were in the same neighborhood, just a walk down the block.

Apparently, PolyGram was one of the initial labels that held out from giving their videos to MTV because they thought the label should be compensated for usage.
Oh, right. That's vaguely familiar. But the point is that video promotion was basically nothing. It was just putting it in the mail or sending somebody over to deliver it. Again, as I said, I don't remember a second track off of that record. I was a huge vinyl collector and my whole house is filled with vinyl, [but] I've gotten rid of almost 80 percent of it because I know I'm never going to play it for the rest of my life. And I have every KISS record, but I don't have "The Elder" so that tells you something right there.

Back in 1981, rock bands made albums and went on tour to promote them. KISS did not mount a tour for "The Elder." In your estimation, did that play a part in the album's dismal performance?

I really can't say if it was coincidental with that record, but they were so cold that they'd overplayed so many markets. The next record was what?

"Creatures of The Night."
OK. There was a point where they couldn't tour because they were oversold in major markets. Their popularity had gone down and basically the only thing they could do was secondary and tertiary markets.

The "Creatures of The Night" tour sold poorly. Gene and Paul have acknowledged that they were at their lowest point with "The Elder" and that "Creatures" was an attempt to go back to a more traditional hard-rock sound.
Right. And guess who played a big role in that? The person you're talking to right now. I took it on the chin from Gene Simmons. That somehow, given my reputation in promotion and in rock radio, I should have turned ["Creatures"] into gold. And the fact that I didn't, somehow it was *my* fault. I was around when "Creatures of The Night" was being made and I was listening to it almost on a track-by-track basis. And I was so into it. This was the best challenge I'd had. I was going, "We're gonna really do something now. Now we got *the record*. I remember you couldn't get me and my staff more involved in a record than that track ["I Love It Loud"], and we only could take it so far. And that was the discussion: The only way we could get to the next level is to take the makeup off. And I think by that time "The Elder" was in the rearview window.

Multiple parties have said that the band was considering unmasking for "The Elder." It's interesting to speculate if that would have helped the band and the album.
I don't think so. Because when it was done, they had the album and the song ["Lick It Up"] to do it. ["The Elder" is] a shitty record. I think they got lucky by not doing it at that time. And even letting "Creatures of The Night" do what it did at least put back in people's mind that they were a rock and roll band.

Chip Taylor

PolyGram head of A&R and Hall of Fame songwriter on expecting to receive "the rock and roll record of all time"

Chip, you're a renowned artist and songwriter in your own right. How is that you came to be on the staff at PolyGram?
Chip Taylor: Well, what happened was I had a series of albums out in the '70s, for Warner Bros., for Columbia and one for Capitol. At the end of the one I had out for Capitol, I got a call from [PolyGram President/CEO] David Braun who I did not know. He said that Neil Diamond suggested that he call me. He said that he had a big job in front of him and he wanted to know if I could help him through figuring out how to get the label back in shape. I was flattered that Neil had suggested me and I knew David's history working with Bob Dylan and Neil and others.

I heard he was a very good guy and I just debated [my decision] for a couple of weeks. And I decided I would take a break. The original plan was I'd go over there and just see if I could help him form the roster a little bit and then get back to my music. I stayed a little longer than I expected to.

When did you come onboard?
It happened somewhere in 1980. My album ["Saint Sebastian"] was released on Capitol in '79. It would have been right after that.

With regard to your role, you were officially head of A&R?
Well, that's the title they gave me. And I had two great A&R guys, Peter Lubin and Stu Fine [who worked on my staff], that knew the ropes and had been around a little bit. They were young rock and roll guys. I relied a lot on them. They were *real* A&R guys. I was really a singer/songwriter coming over there to all of a sudden being an A&R guy. It was not such a comfortable position to be in obviously.

Was your role centered more on scouting new talent or working with existing artists on the label?
Well, it was a very tough period of time. We were just coming out of the disco craze. In rap we had Kurtis Blow, when rap had not kicked in. If they

were all smart, they would have paid a lot of attention because we were way before our time with [him]. It was one of these things where we're going out and signing with artists that could make hit records. It seemed like the best thing to do was find artists that were out there working and already doing something. But there wasn't a lot out in the field that you could go after. One of my big efforts was working with Blue Angel, Cyndi Lauper's band. I loved them and I was trying to figure out how to help them. From my point of view, I loved artists that stuck with the people they loved, and she wanted to stick with her band back then. And yet it seemed like the best thing for her to do would be to make a record by herself with the best producers around and show her off in her amazing light by herself. I had several talks with her, and the boys and I just couldn't quite figure it out. She was so ahead of her time.

Her career blossomed a little later in the '80s.
Yeah, you know that happens sometimes. So basically, the company was just trying to pull its reins in, and my job was to help David decide who on the roster should stay and who should go. And [also] try to develop [new talent], if we could find something. We were scouring the city and trying to find what we could find, but there wasn't anything that was really interesting. The one thing that did interest me when I first got onboard was that one of my A&R people investigated, I had worked with Cissy Houston on some of the recordings that I made. I loved her. We were friends and so when she was playing with [her daughter] Whitney, every label was passing on it. Clive [Davis] had passed on it, *everybody* passed on it. And then all of a sudden, I was in this position and I told David, "Look, I know Cissy. Let me go down and see what's going on with the daughter." I went and I saw her, and I really was quite excited about her. It happened to be that we had a rhythm and blues division at the company and Bill Haywood was just a wonderful promotion guy. Before I got there, he was ready to sign some other person that was in the same category and he was afraid of looking like a little lightweight for R&B radio, which she might have been. When Clive finally came back in, after I wanted to sign her, he signed her. Then he did all of that [for Whitney Houston], as only Clive Davis can do. I love Clive, but it's not the kind of thing that anybody in our company could have done. I certainly could not have.

KISS was among the acts on the roster. Were they considered a top-tier artist on the label?

Yeah, particularly at this point. The company had lost money and they were trying to figure out how they're going to survive and do well. One of the things David wanted to do was to find out what big star whose contract was up was out there. My interest was David Bowie. I thought it would be a very good signing for the company. But that didn't work out.

KISS was right up there. You know, an artist is coming through the system and your salesmen are projecting how many you're going to sell. KISS was projected high. The album that they just put out before, I guess, didn't do very well. But everybody was excited that Bob Ezrin was going to be involved. And he was hot as he could be at the time, and he already had success with them. It seemed like there was word within the company that this was going be the rock and roll record of all time. It was to be *straight rock*. You say to yourself, "How can you lose? You got Bob Ezrin, Bill Aucoin [and KISS]. This is gonna be easy." At the very least, you're going to get a record that's going to be so well received that you're going to go back to getting close to platinum or something like that. That was the feeling in the office.

Very interesting. To add some context, at that point KISS had come off of "Dynasty" in 1979, which spawned the huge worldwide hit, "I Was Made for Lovin' You." Their follow-up in 1980, "Unmasked," as you said, did not sell as well.
Right. But you know, even "I Was Made for Lovin' You," that was a big hit. At the time, it was an easy record to like for people. But because that was really losing its edge, [with] the connotations about disco, I don't know if that helped them like another big rock and roll record would've helped them.

Of course, KISS came in via Casablanca. What were your impressions of Neil Bogart and the label?
I loved Neil. When I was on the [Buddah Records] label, he had signed Spider-Man and Curtis Mayfield. When you walked in to see him, he had this big smile on his face. He was so nice to my children. I just liked his energy so much. I liked all the staff, Larry Harris, Bucky Reingold. In fact, I wrote a song about the whole staff and how much I loved them on my ["Chip Taylor's Last Chance"] album, "101 In Cashbox."

After I left, Neil had told me about KISS and his plans for them. He was so excited about them. This was something very special put together by some visionaries. Anytime I ever saw these guys, I always thought that they had a nice way about them. And they had a real street way. I was rooting for them from day one. Before this record came out, everybody was happy, you know.

All signs point to KISS looking to record a more traditional rock album in 1981.
Yeah, that seemed to be what was floating around the company. There was excitement like, "Wow, what do we have here? This is going to be so much fun. Not only the music, but we're going to sell a lot of records."

At some point, the hard rock direction was aborted, and the band veered into concept album territory, no doubt through Bob Ezrin's influence. After all, he had just come off "The Wall" with Pink Floyd. Do you recall how this news broke to the label?
It was like [we] were counting the days when [the album was] going to be delivered and we were going to hear it. Nobody was at the sessions so the buzz in the office was that it was going to be a hard rock album. I think what happened is acetates were delivered to the office and I ended up getting a few of them for my staff and myself. I do remember at some point hearing something with some talking on it. But I don't remember that being an issue for long, so I'm thinking somebody else would know better than me.

The dialogue is an interesting component. We've uncovered that recording for the album ensued in spring 1981 and went on at different intervals through the summer. And in September Bob recorded spoken word dialogue with a trio of actors.
It sounds to me, if the record was released in November, [the spoken word] was really last minute. It sounded like, "We better do this." I mean I'm not saying that's what happened. I'm thinking my original acetates came in without that on it.

What was your initial reaction to hearing "The Elder"?
I think I listened to it with one [or both] of my other staff members. And they were much more into rock and roll than I was. As soon as it started to play, they were saying, "What the heck?" And then I believe that there were acetates all over the place. The marketing and promotion department was very prominent in that organization. Bob Sherwood was really one of the movers and shakers of the company, so he was involved, as were the salespeople. All of a sudden, the buzzer rang. The office was like, "What did

we get here? This is nothing like we expected and not only is it nothing like expected; it's nothing we can sell. How are we going to market this? Jesus, there's no hits in here. Where is the anthem?"

For me, as an artist listening to it, I was trying to get into it. When I went to Warner Bros., they signed me thinking I was going make an album as a follow-up to the one I did for Neil Bogart on Buddha, which was kind of a rock/folk album. And when I went to make "Last Chance," I didn't tell anybody what I was doing, just like KISS didn't. I made a country album, in Boston. And I flew out to Warner Bros. and played "Last Chance" with my engineer and the whole marketing and promotion staffs, about 10 people in the room. We played the album from beginning to end. And at the end there was silence. Finally, the marketing head said, "Listen, Chip. I think I can speak for everybody here. That's a wonderful album but that's a country album, and we don't have a country division."

So, here we got KISS now coming in and I'm trying to listen because there were obviously a lot of well-done and interesting things on the album. And you give them the benefit of the doubt and everything, but as it played it just seemed — knowing what KISS had some success with — this wasn't the kind of thing that had sold KISS records in the past. For the rest of the company, it was more anger. It was like, "*What*? How come we were fooled like this? Why?"

But, you know, you wade through things and you try to figure it out. The way I always felt about record companies, they're a bunch of good people. They work hard on your music and they care. It's not like you're selling pieces of plastic or bottles of water, they are music people and they really love it and they want to be part of it, and they love to meet the artists, like they always did with me. They were nice people, and it was the same with this company. They were passionate people that couldn't wait for this album. They would've loved to have been able to say, "Boy, Bob, what a job!" And they're raising some flags that would've been some party, but the party was kind of ruined.

Perhaps David Braun would have had the difficult task of communicating the label's feelings to the band?
Yeah, David was a very artist-friendly kind of guy. He was there to represent the company, and the other people who worked for him were giving him advice and they told him what their feeling was and I guess he picked it up

from there with Bill Aucoin and those people and tried to figure out what to do. David asked me, "Chip, listen to this several times and just give me your advice as to if we have a hit here." And the song I did like was the one that was the single, "A World Without Heroes." I said, "To tell you the truth, it doesn't sound like anything they did before. But my honest opinion is it's really, really good. I could hear it on the radio." I think a lot of times record companies don't understand that. They try to predict the emotion of the listener by what happened before. And this one didn't sound like anything that KISS did, but it sounded very charming to me.

The song is very much a departure for Gene Simmons. He's more known for standard rock fare like "Calling Dr. Love," "Deuce" and "Rock and Roll All Nite." And here he turns in a plaintive vocal, backed by strings. It's interesting that this one stood out to you.
For me it was the only one that did. I mean, you hear all of the songs, even like "The Oath," that sounded KISS-like in many ways. The subject matter was sweet on this album. It was very ethereal, and it had nice messages, but it was very unlike what they'd done [before].

Chip, it seems there were a handful of changes made to the album after it was handed in. One of the alterations was the intended track sequence was jumbled. What's your recall on that?
I don't remember exactly but obviously the promotion department and marketing and salespeople felt like they had to get something at the start of those sides that, as far as they were concerned, could help it. I'm sure that was the suggestion that was put forward. Again, when it finally came through, David had asked me which song I thought was the hit and I told him, and maybe other people said something similar. So that was put at the front of one of the [sides].

I'll tell you something, you had some dissention and people were unhappy. Bill was upset. Bob Ezrin, I think got upset. They were good guys. I think Bill was a great guy and certainly one of the greatest managers of all time. And if somebody in the company didn't like something, I'm sure he was playing it for other of his friends, too, and fans. And he was probably not getting the reaction he wanted, and the boys were probably a little disappointed. From what I hear, Ace didn't like it. And the boys seemed to avoid it anyway, as it went on. It was an experiment. Everybody did it. They jumped in and after the reaction they probably said, "What the heck did we do?"

When it came time for the company to put it out, it wasn't like the company snuck this thing out as a bastardized thing. I'm sure there were conversations back and forth in the company. David probably said, "My people say this is the best way we can go with this. And if we do go with it this way, we can probably sell more records than we would with the other one." And my guess is also that because David was such an honest, artist-friendly guy, he probably offered something to them and said, "Let's get through this period of time. Let's unite on this thing and put it out this way. What can we do in the future? Do we add a couple of extensions on the contract? Let's do this, and we'll guarantee you this, and let's go forward." This is a guess on my part. But that's the way David would think. I am quite sure that when it was released, it was a "together" spirit. It wasn't, "Oh, they did *this* to us!" It wasn't like that.

As mentioned, the spoken word dialogue is one particularly interesting missing piece of the puzzle. It's unknown whether the dialogue was interleaved between the tracks, as intended, or if it was just left on the cutting-room floor.
I think I remember hearing it, but I think it didn't come first. That's my best guess is that it was like, "Well, what do you think of this?"

One of my theories is that perhaps the label said, "We need to dial back a couple of things." And the track order was one compromise, and maybe the dialogue was another.
I think that was right. I think it happened quickly. I don't think it was on the table for a long time. Again, that's my best guess. One of the things that I don't understand: In making records myself, when I deliver something to the record company, I don't just turn things over to them. I always have copies of everything. A group like KISS, they're turning something over to a record company, and they don't have absolute files of everything they ever did? I think I read that nobody had the [dialog] today. An artist, if they're doing voiceovers or something like that, they certainly would have files.

One other alteration that was made was a remix of sorts. I believe there was a comment that came in from the label along the lines of, "Where are the guitars? We need to bring up the guitars." Does that ring a bell?
It certainly wouldn't surprise me, given some of the hard rock people around the office that worked with me. You know, it sounds that maybe it was more like a marketing thing, or the promotion department that had to get the

records played. I never thought that when I was listening to it. And I don't remember that comment in my office with my staff.

As an artist, perhaps you're best qualified to answer this question: Do you think Bob Ezrin, Bill Aucoin and KISS would have had the power to veto any of these alteration requests? In other words, could they have stood firm and said, "No, this album stays as is."

Oh yeah, you have to understand what we're talking about here. This is a big management team, big producer, and big artist. You can't be pushed around. In fact, a big label won't push anybody around. And they make suggestions but they're not going to do anything behind anybody's back. They're going to say, "Is it OK if we do this?" And I'm guessing that Bob Ezrin probably said, "Yeah, maybe you're right. Let me move it up a little bit." Nobody did that without them. So, Bob, or maybe his engineer, called over to the studio and said, "They'd like a little more guitars. In this song, do it at this section and just bring it up." It happens all the time in the final mixing and final mastering.

Ultimately, was KISS recording a concept album was just too left-of-center of an idea?

I don't know that I'd say that. That's too general. It's just this one didn't work. If a concept album came in that all of a sudden had some other elements in it and a lot of what KISS folks and the hard rock people would really gravitate toward, I think it would've been different. And everybody loved "The Wall." But this wasn't that. And I'm not sure if [something like that] would have been right for them anyway. I mean, Tim, like you say, if all of a sudden, this thing did become important, maybe it puts KISS in a different direction.

Of course, there was no tour for "The Elder." This marked the first time the band didn't tour in support of an album.

It seems like they were saying, "Do we want to go around the world playing these songs?" I think one of the fears was that if they went out and promoted this, who was going to pay for it? What if their fans don't really come? I think that was a distinct fear. They're going to promote this and then all of a sudden there are reports that they got half a house and people walked out early and things like that. It's not just that you push a button and you spend money and go out and tour and that's the reason it didn't happen. I think it's way deeper than that. I think [the album] didn't sell terribly ...

Well, the album reached No. 75 on the Billboard 200. "A World Without Heroes" reached No. 56 on the Billboard 100.

That's not bad.

But by February 1982, the album and single seemed to vanish. "The Elder" didn't have legs, as they say. Without a tour and follow-up single, it seems the album just died.

I think you're jumping to conclusions, Tim. I think if it had something more than that, you would have seen in some territories some kind of cool little underground thing that surprised in sales or something, which would have generated a tour or something like that. I think it's which comes first, the chicken or the egg? But you know, I'm thinking it just wasn't the right album for the times to do much more than what it did. I think they did as much as they could with it, and I believe it was a total team effort. And they didn't want to play these songs in person. It was just a nice experiment.

Switching gears, Chip. You co-wrote "Rock Soldiers," the lead track on Ace Frehley's first post-KISS solo album. How did that come together?

He was recording at a studio of mine that I owned with a friend of mine up there in White Plains. I started the studio to do my last album for Capitol in 1978, and then it was an ongoing studio and some people came in. It was mostly a production studio for whatever I wanted to do, but Ace started working there. I would see him at the studio, and it was a really great studio. I don't remember how it happened, but somehow he told me the story of what happened to him and I wrote the song at home one day, came up to his house and we fixed it and changed it and we had a song within a few minutes.

Did you help like more with the music or lyrics or both on that, Chip?

I did both. I mean, he told me the story and then I wrote the music and lyrics, and then I came up there and played it for him, and then we adjusted it together.

More recently, Ace covered "Wild Thing" for his 2016 covers album, "Origins Vol. 1."

Yeah, he sent it to me. It's really good. The thing I love about Ace is he's all heart. He's not cerebral. So, he did "Wild Thing" kind of like I wrote it, and just added a little something of his to it. It's such a cool cover.

Finally, I wanted to offer my congratulations on your being inducted into the Songwriters Hall of Fame in 2016. What does this honor mean to you?
Thanks, Tim. I appreciate it. What does it mean? Well, I think of all the writers that I've known that have influenced me and that I've loved listening to, and some of them are not in the Hall of Fame. I feel humbled by all the people that did nice things to help me. I think about the guy that taught me three chords on the guitar when I was 14 years old. If it wasn't for him, I wouldn't be here. I think about all the musicians that I've played with. I put it in perspective, but in general, it's a very nice honor and I'm going in with some very nice people. It makes me think how fortunate I was to be able to be in this business doing what I love.

Christopher K. Lendt

Former vice president of Glickman/Marks Management recalls the state of
KISS in 1981 and an ambitious bid to redefine their career

**First, Chris, I've always wanted to share with you how much I enjoyed
"KISS and Sell." I know it's been many years, but belated congratulations
on your book. It is a spectacular read and a "must-have" for the KISS
library.**
Christopher K. Lendt: Well, thank you. I can never hear that too much.
You're very gracious.

**And it is a sentiment shared by many fans in the KISS community. The
book is well-written and your attention to detail is meticulous, whether
it's recalling the atmosphere of a particular meeting, what somebody
wore, a memorable quote, and so forth.**
Well, it's really for two reasons. First of all, I have a really good memory.
That's always something I've been fortunate to have, and it's served me well
in school and in business. The other reason, which is a little more colorful, [is
that] all of those events that happened in my life with KISS are forever
burnished in my brain. It was such an unusual experience that I absorbed a
lot of those details and I still remember them today because I felt like I was
sort of living in a movie. (Laughs)

I did pay attention and I was not, most of the time, inebriated or
incapacitated. And my job was to be the "detail man" for KISS. So, I carried
through that obligation professionally as well as in my private life.

**Getting to "Music from The Elder," prior to recording commencing, how
would you describe the overall health of KISS in 1981?**
Well, that was coming off of the Australia tour, which was December 1980.
That was the most successful tour KISS had done at that time. They were
treated like the second coming of the Beatles. And I recounted all of that in
the book. It was quite an event. They were really puffed up, and I say that
without any sarcasm. Their egos were really boosted by such a successful
tour. Their popularity was waning in the U.S., which they were aware of, but
a big tour like that, playing stadiums and creating "KISS mania," is a real
climate to bolster your spirits and put you back in a different mood.

Certainly. What do you recall about their initial studio album plans?
When they approached a new album, they had made a number of efforts going into the studio in 1981, recording different tracks [at] different studios. I don't know if there were other producers involved but I know that they tried a number of different types of records. The consensus that they got from the people in Australia at PolyGram at that time was that they should come back in '81 and do another hard rock album, because that was the essence of what KISS was and they felt that that was something that would serve KISS well. You know, the last advice offered that you hear from people who are in a position to have their advice listened to is often the advice that you go with. So that was their inclination: to go back into the studio and record a typical hard rock, heavy metal KISS album, which I think they tried to do, but it never coalesced. And [then] the thinking was that they didn't want to come out with another ordinary KISS hard rock album. Maybe it would have been good and accepted by the fans, but they didn't think it was really big enough. So, having their egos boosted by the tremendous success of the Australia tour, and with the influence of Bill Aucoin, they decided to go off in a different direction. And [they] eventually emerged [with] the idea of a "concept" album.

Right, which was a deliberate attempt to steer away from recording a typical KISS album.
Yes, rather than just a recording of 10 or 12 tracks that were all distinct and separate from one another, they decided to do something on a more elevated level, creatively. The concept idea became the operating idea.

Now, I can't really give you the day and date when all of this started to gel, but the idea was to do an album where all of the songs would be linked together and there would be a story. The next element was a story had to be created, and once the story was created, then there would be characters, like a movie. In fact, the original title of the album was "Music from The Elder." And that was intentional because as this concept started to mushroom, the thinking was it's not even going to be just an album anymore; it's going to be a motion picture. And this will be the soundtrack to a motion picture that will come out in the future.

This really started to move forward by leaps and bounds. This was no longer an album anymore; it was a concept album. And it wasn't just a concept album — like "Sgt. Pepper's [Lonely Hearts Club Band]" was a concept album — this would be a concept album that was the precursor to a movie. And the music would tell the story and present the characters who would eventually appear in a movie or an animated movie. That part, to my knowledge, never got any more concrete. The thinking really started to move by leaps and bounds.

Bob Ezrin was tapped because he was a producer who had worked on ["Destroyer"]. He was highly respected by the band. I assume he had a good relationship with Bill Aucoin, otherwise I don't think it would have gone forward. And Bob Ezrin had had enormous worldwide success with Pink Floyd's "The Wall." So here, on paper, this is one of those ideas that just seemed brilliant. KISS would come back bigger than ever. They would no longer be seen as simply a hard rock, heavy metal band with makeup and costumes. They were going to do something really ambitious and who better to carry it off than Bob Ezrin, who had a legitimate claim to being one of the most successful record producers at that time. He had a great deal of success as the producer, or the co-producer, of "The Wall," which has gone on to sell who knows how many tens of millions of copies.

So, everything started to fall into line and the pieces seemed to fall into place. And then as things moved forward, they developed the story, they developed the characters, they fleshed out the characters, [and] the songs and titles would reflect certain episodes or scenes of the movie and the musical script that the record would form the basis to. And one thing led to another and the group was largely isolated. They recorded some of the music at Ace Frehley's studio in Wilton, Connecticut. They used another studio — I don't really remember where that was. And Bob Ezrin kept everything under wraps and really nobody knew much except Bob Ezrin, the band and Bill Aucoin.

In your book, I believe you referred to the album as being "hermetically sealed."
Yeah, nobody really knew anything. You would get little bits and pieces of information but the band, I'd say primarily Paul and Gene, they were really almost in a rapturous state because they saw this as a huge opening where they could elevate themselves to an entirely new level of rock bands. They would now be a rock band that would be taken seriously, that could come up with something like "Tommy" by the Who or "The Wall" by Pink Floyd or "Sgt. Pepper's" by the Beatles. At least conceptually. They would be in that pantheon of great bands that made the transition from just being able to make rock and roll albums to albums that were, if not operas, then

conceptual albums where all of the songs written were connected [and] there was a story and characters — almost like a screenplay. And they would be taken seriously, and people would look at them in an entirely new light.

So, it was very tempting. And at that point they were really impressionable and that seemed like a very smart creative move. And here again, on paper, there was a certain sensibility to it, at least in their eyes. They didn't just want to do another album. They felt that they could do better. They felt that, as musicians and performers and artists, they could be more ambitious. And they didn't have to heed the advice of their critics to "stay with what you know," and "you'll never get out of that niche," and "be happy you're there." You know, they're artists so they wanted to expand their horizons and become a band that would be not so much a — I don't want to say joke — but they would be respected at a different level by a wider group of both critics and fans.

In terms of the album's concept, it is based on a story by Gene. But others who worked on the project have said Bob had a lot to do with developing the story. How much input do you think Bob had regarding the story?
I really can't give an opinion on that because I wasn't that intimately involved. But I think that you can't underestimate the role of Bob Ezrin and I think that Gene and Paul were very much captivated by this concept and they worked in a collaborative way. Who did more or less? I don't know. I know that Ace Frehley wasn't all that into it. And at that time, Eric Carr was basically a sideman, a supporting player.

In the book, you mention that the album ultimately cost PolyGram $2 million to finance. I've read an article from 1981 stating that it cost in the neighborhood of $1 million just to record "The Elder." Would this be an accurate estimate?
My recollection is that the album costs were somewhere in the mid- to upper-six figures, in 1981 dollars. Now if you recorded an album like that today and did the same thing, how much would it cost? Well I am sure it would be a million or 2 million dollars. At that time not too, many people were out there producing albums that cost in the mid- to upper-six figures. By the standards of the time, it was a very expensive production.

Indeed. Aside from the recording, the band employed the use of an orchestra, an arranger and spoken word actors.

That's part of what went into those costs. I mean, when you hire an orchestra, when you hire a choir, when you hire all the people that have to do the scoring, and everything, you're talking about tens of thousands of dollars. So just to go out and hire an orchestra, you have to have a big room in New York City in a big studio — you can't put them in some little room in a small recording studio. There are actually a fairly limited number of big recording studios in New York City that can accommodate an orchestra. There are physical limitations of where they can record. And you get involved with people, who are contractors for the players, and you have to hire people who write the music, and it's all union regulated. You know, it can easily go into tens of thousands of dollars for them to do a couple of sessions.

Chris, do you remember any details on St. Robert's Choir, and if they were Toronto-based or New York-based?
It might have been in Canada for all I know. After all, that's where Ezrin was. It may be that they gave the choir that name for that particular performance and it may have been a made-up name because they had to call it something. I don't know, I mean there's all kinds of reasons. It's not like the Mormon Tabernacle Choir, which has been like that for over a hundred years. It may have been a choir of singers who for that period of time identified themselves as St. Robert's Choir. And maybe a year later they disbanded, and nobody ever used that name again.

Originally, "The Elder" was to include spoken word dialogue designed to help carry the album's concept. The dialog was recorded but nearly all of this dialogue was ultimately scrapped. Do you recall who specifically requested the spoken word portions be removed?
That I don't know. I really have no idea.

Do you recall at one point there being more spoken word dialogue on the album?
Well, I assume that they recorded a lot of stuff that never made it into the final mix. But that's really up to Ezrin.

It would seem that the dialog exists, but it does so in a sort of "Elder" purgatory. One of the criticisms levied by some fans is that the album's concept is not transparent. So more spoken word dialog would have ultimately helped thread the concept.

Well, I think the idea of the spoken word was to provide some clarity to the story and enhance the continuity between the tracks.

Exactly. Lou Reed was brought onboard to contribute as a songwriter. Do recall any costs associated with bringing Lou Reed onboard?
That I don't know. I only found out sometime later that Lou Reed was a musician that apparently several of the members of KISS knew. He was also from New York. And I think they may have known him personally or socially or perhaps they crossed path professionally. I never met Lou Reed to the best of my knowledge, and I don't remember what his arrangement was except that he was a co-writer on at least one of the songs.

He co-wrote the album's lead single, "A World Without Heroes."
Right.

In the book you recollect that listening to Paul and Gene discuss "The Elder" was along the lines of listening to people who had just had "an epiphany."
Well, they were really hyped up about it. I can only tell you what I witnessed in terms of their reaction from talking to them and being with them and speaking with them either on the phone or at meetings. That's how they came across to me. I assume that this feeling was something that developed from working intensely on this project. And apparently Bob Ezrin, as the maestro, and Bill Aucoin were egging them on. And they had all convinced themselves that this was the idea of a lifetime. And this was a project that would redefine the entire career of KISS.

I don't say that in any disparaging way. If you're an artist, you have to believe in what you're doing. And there's no question that they were completely consumed by the project. They felt it was creatively ambitious and at that time they felt it was very fulfilling. Ezrin had a lot to do with the artistic aspects of what was going on in the studio. And I think Bill Aucoin was an equally willing partner. The problem, that everybody saw in retrospect, was that it probably would have been received differently by the public had it been produced by a different group.

Yes.
In other words, it's so much a departure from KISS. And it got some very good reviews in publications like "Rolling Stone," which was not exactly a fan of KISS' music over the years. But that's the problem: They created

something that had a lot merit to it — the whole idea was very clever and perhaps it was years ahead of its time. But that kind of production, that kind of creative work would never be accepted by a group like KISS in terms of how they had defined themselves to the public up to that point. It's just like movie actors who are consistently playing action heroes, movie after movie, and they are very, very successful at playing action heroes and daredevils and rough and tough guys. And then all of the sudden, they start saying, "I can do light comedy. I can be taken seriously in a romantic movie about a moody, withdrawn person." Well, it's not impossible, but it's not easy. Because the public has gotten accustomed to you playing certain types of roles, certain types of characters. All of a sudden, to do a 180-degree turn and give them something that they had never seen before, after seeing you year after year after year in a certain light, it's very difficult to pull off.

So that's why I say, if another group had done something like "The Elder," it probably would have been more widely accepted. But the audience for "The Elder" was the fans of KISS. And the fans of KISS didn't really see it like that. (Laughs)

I think there are some aspects of "The Elder" that are very much in alignment with the KISS ethos, particularly the comic book flavor of the story and the themes of self-belief and self-empowerment. Ultimately, it did not catch on with fans, largely due to the album's experimental nature. In other words, KISS fans don't want KISS to be experimental.
Right. And that's the problem that all musical artists have because, by nature, many, if not most, want to be more ambitious and want to go beyond what they've done in the past. But sometimes if they overdo it and it's too much of an about-face or a U-turn, it just seems out of place. It's not what you expect. It's very difficult.

It's interesting that in recent years Paul and Gene have expressed their dissatisfaction with "The Elder." I want to read you a fairly recent quote from Paul: "We became enchanted with the idea of becoming the darlings of the critics and proving some sort of credibility. For my money, we put out a pompous piece of pap."
Basically, the first part is exactly what I said in my book. They wanted to be taken seriously by their critics and their detractors. And they wanted to show the world that they weren't KISS, a gimmicky rock group that paraded in makeup and costumes, [but] that they were serious artistes. Why he

referred to it, in his words, as a "piece of pap"? That's how he thinks of it now. That's not how he thought of it then.

As a fan, there is a part of me that wishes Paul and Gene would acknowledge that the work is valid. Some have theorized that if "The Elder" had sold millions of copies and yielded a hit single, Paul and Gene may be singing a different tune.

Well I think what may have happened is that sometimes artists can be a little too conditioned by their fans in the sense that they have so much negative blowback from "The Elder," that rather and try and fight the criticism and the barbs that they suffered they just decided to go along with it and echo what's already been said about them by the people that never liked it in the first place.

In the book, you paint such a fantastic portrait of the album's "standing-room only" listening party. My takeaway from it as the reader was that it was a subdued, if awkward, atmosphere.

It was very awkward because it was such a different kind of recording. It wasn't something you associated with KISS. Most of the tracks weren't very upbeat; it was kind of mystical and moody. Like I said, if some other group did an album like that, particularly a group that wasn't so harshly or clearly defined as KISS with all the sharp edges, you might say, "Well, that's an interesting album." But people have prejudices based on what they're conditioned to expect from a particular album. And here's an artist that everyone in the room was very familiar with and they produced something that was so completely remote from anything they had heard in the past. People didn't really know how to react. Obviously, you're not there to criticize an artist. You know, you're working for the band. It not only would be impolite or disrespectful, it might cost you your job. (Laughs) So you're not in a position to critique them, so people were kind of awkward. They didn't really know how to react. It wasn't some hard-rocking album in the tradition of KISS. It was like it was recorded by a totally different band.

I mean, imagine if someone like Eminem went into the studio and he did a really great country-influenced recording. You'd say, "Well, maybe it's a great recording. But I don't get it that it's coming from him." Popular music is like that. It's all stereotypes. It's all pre-packaged images to a great extent. It's very hard to maneuver away from that.

"The Elder" was essentially a bomb. Was the album the final nail in the coffin between Bill Aucoin and KISS?

It certainly accelerated his decline. Any manager that is at the helm when the band records the worst-selling record in their history, their job is in jeopardy. And Bill Aucoin had been a champion of "The Elder" project. And he was very much associated with it in providing the moral support and the encouragement to go in that direction. Once it became a big flop, the band said, "Well, this guy's our manager. He's supposed to know better. He should have told us. He should have known better than to let us get carried away. He should have had better judgment." Is that fair? Not necessarily. But artists have to look for someone to blame because they're the ones that are going to end up suffering the worst [because] they don't have any more fans. I mean, there's got to be a fall guy.

Your boss, Howard Marks, labeled "The Elder," and I quote from your book, "asinine."

Yeah, he did.

And he refused to have his ad agency appear in the credits. Did Howard share his opinions regarding KISS' creative direction with Bill?

Bill and Howard communicated on a regular basis. And there may have been dozens and dozens of conversations between the two that I obviously wasn't privy to. But you have to know your place. Bill Aucoin is the manager, he's the creative guru. You can give your opinion privately. And I'm sure he did. Howard wasn't exactly a "yes man." So, it's entirely possible that he communicated his misgivings at some point about the recording. And I'm sure Bill listened politely. Bill had his own preoccupations and he was the one who was in the studio with KISS. And he was the manager. You can't really overstep your bounds. At the end of the day, we were "business managers." At the end of the day we were responsible for their finances, not for what producer they choose or what style of music they are going to record. That's not even really peripheral to what we do. That doesn't mean you don't have an opinion or he, from the standpoint of a marketing person, didn't communicate to Bill his thoughts on that. But at the end of the day, Bill's the manager.

Do you recall how far any discussions regarding an "Elder" film got off the ground?

I never heard anything about any movie. I do remember sitting in Ken Anderson's office once and looking at a stage set with the idea of presenting

"The Elder" onstage. And I mentioned in the book that we had a meeting in our office with [Lou Falcigno], who is now deceased [but] at that time was a big entrepreneur [with] — it's not pay-per-view, that's the term today — when you would go to the theater and pay money to see a prize fight live on the theater screen. That was the pre-cursor to what's called pay-per-view on your home TV today. And the idea was "The Elder" was going to be such a worldwide international success that everybody would want to see KISS live onstage in an "Elder" production and you would buy a ticket for it, closed-circuit TV. So, you would go to a movie theater and buy a ticket and see "The Elder" live because it was being staged in some spectacular arena somewhere else. And this would be an opportunity for everybody to see it in their local theater, if not, in an arena in a real live venue. There were some of these ideas that we pursued but it never got past that.

What do you recall about "The Elder" tour stage design? Was it elaborate?
No, it was really sparse. It wasn't like a real KISS show. Everything was black. It was kind of like a different group. It was mystical and much more along the lines of one of these video games where you're defending yourself against the forces of the universe and there are all of these ethereal concepts. In other words, I guess you can say it was ahead of its time, because there are many successful video games today that create that kind of world for their fans. But unfortunately, it had nothing to do with KISS. (Laughs) If there'd been some other group at that time, maybe Journey or somebody, I'm just throwing out names, maybe people would have accepted it more.

So, Ken Anderson oversaw the stage design?
He was the one who was on Bill Aucoin's staff, the director of production. And he was in charge of organizing the production elements for KISS' touring shows.

I've read Mark Ravitz was contracted to do the stage design.
He could have been. It may have been his [stage design]. I just remember being in Ken's office. I don't know who actually should get the credit for that.

A tour never came to fruition since the album performed poorly. In hindsight, is there anything they could have done to promote the album on the road?
No. It would have been an unmitigated fiasco.

MTV had debuted in August 1981. Do you recall any push to get "A World Without Heroes" played on the channel?

There was no interest. I can't speak on behalf of MTV, but I don't remember there being too much interest from KISS to promote that album. As soon as the album was a certified flop, they went in and did that record...

"KISS Killers."

"Killers," with the four new tracks and the old tracks. That was a priority. They went back to the makeup and the costumes, in a somewhat updated style. But "The Elder" was something they wanted to distance themselves from as fast as possible.

The band had also shot a video for "I," which was never formally released. Was this part of the mentality of "Let's cut our losses and move on"?

Yeah. It may have been released in some other country, but it certainly wasn't in any way pushed by anybody here [in the United States], that's for sure.

The album peaked at No. 75 on the Billboard 200 and spent only 11 weeks on the chart. Since Nielsen SoundScan was implemented in 1991, "The Elder" has sold more than 116,000 copies. Many fans wonder if the album has since crept passed gold status. What is your guess?

If it's sold 116,000 copies since 1991, and it was released in 1981, would it have sold 500,000 copies in the United States? I doubt it.

Of course, after "The Elder" came the more traditional "Creatures of The Night," which also underperformed commercially. What would you say was more of a failure for KISS: the left-turn conceptual album or the back-to-basics hard-rock KISS album?

Well, failure is a subjective term. "Creatures of The Night" sold more copies than "The Elder" at that time. So I think you'd have to say it was a better-received album, but when you come off of a really huge flop and a lot of your fans ditch you and time marches on, it would have really been quite a coup if "Creatures Of The Night" would have been a million seller.

Had "Creatures" come out in 1981, do you think KISS' career would have taken a different course in the '80s?

If "Creatures of The Night" had come out in 1981?

Yes. Instead of "The Elder."
It would have been better. Yeah.

Some fans go one further and say if "Creatures" somehow came out in 1980 and replaced "Unmasked," things might have been completely different for the band in the '80s.
Yes, that's also true. But groups experiment and they have certain ideas. And they want to do things differently and they are subject to the influences of their peers and the culture at the time. And that's why certain albums come out when they do, and some do much better than others. Some are ahead of their time [and] some are behind the time. It's very hard to get it right.

Chris, getting into your career. You are an adjunct professor of marketing at New York University, correct?
Correct. I teach at NYU and I have for 20 years.

What else are you up to professionally?
I do consulting from time to time for entertainment companies and artists. I managed an artist briefly with a partner of mine a few years ago. I also have private investments, which have nothing to do with music or the entertainment world.

It's been nearly 20 years since "KISS and Sell" was released. Are there any plans for a sequel?
No, never. No, I said what I wanted to say. It was a labor of love. It took me many years to write and more time to rewrite and find a publisher. It was certainly the most ambitious personal project that I ever endeavored to do, and I don't have anything to add to the book that would justify my writing another book. I think you always should quit while you are ahead. (Laughs) I don't have that memory anymore. You have to realize that most of that book was written in the very early 1990s when I was fresh out of my experience with KISS and all of those details were retrievable within my mind. And I go back at look at passages of the book from time to time and I don't remember some of those things. (Laughs) I mean, I remember that they happened, but I would never be able to remember writing them today.

In recent years, Paul and Gene have intimated that an officially sanctioned "KISS 2.0" will be a reality at some point in the future. In your professional opinion, do you think a "KISS 2.0" could succeed on any level?

Well, I assume you mean a KISS without Paul and Gene, just four people playing KISS?

Correct.
We always believed — certainly I did and the people that I worked for — that at some distant point in the future, whether it would be the year 1996 or the year 2026, that it would be possible to keep KISS going in a new incarnation. So, it wouldn't surprise me at all. It would surprise me if they *didn't* do it. How well it will be received by the public, I don't know. But I think that the KISS experience, the KISS type of concert, the KISS kind of show, and the KISS music seem to have an enduring value. And people seem to go back to it. And I think that there's a market for it. Will it be as big as the KISS from the '70s and '80s? Probably not. But I think it could be a very attractive business proposition. And I'm sure that's why they would do it.

Something can be a success on a smaller scale. Whether or not that's financially feasible, I don't know. And who knows, it could be like a Disney character that you can breathe life into every so many years. Look at all of these Marvel Comics characters. There's a demand for that. How big a demand and whether or not a touring group playing even theaters with a KISS production can be done economically, and how you promote it, unless you make new recordings, that I can't answer. But I'm quite sure they'll attempt to do it. And time will tell.

Mark Ravitz

Stage designer recalls working on what was at the time an unnamed 1981–1982 KISS tour design

Mark, let's just step back... You hadn't worked with KISS since 1976 when you designed their "Destroyer" staging. What do you recall about being approached in 1981–82 to come up with stage designs for their then-untitled tour?
Mark Ravitz: I can't really say what brought me together with them again other than probably Bill Aucoin reaching out. I don't have, honestly, a clear memory of who [exactly] set up that meeting [or who] I ultimately met with.

For you, it didn't have a title, such as "The Elder" tour — it was just a tour design, right?
Right. It was never referred to as "The Elder" tour. So, when people talked to me about that in the past, I've said I never had anything to do with it because in my mind, I never did. It was never referred to as that. I definitely did preparatory work for a tour, but it didn't have any particular name. They were just looking for a new look.

It was more in the brainstorming stage when you worked on it?
It's just something new. The "Well of the Unknown." I have a little sketch of the "Well of the Unknown." I know there's a whole bunch of different stuff that never got done for sure.

So, the 21 pages of notes are actually in your handwriting?
Yeah. I [still] have the originals. There were a whole bunch of Xerox copies that aren't very clear. The only thing I don't have is the actual color rendering [that] I did [Editor's note: It can be seen in KISStory]. I [also] have some kind of a little sketch of Eric Carr's drum riser thing that real bastardization of what I designed.

What about how the process started?
I had sketches. I'm really not sure of the process that brought me up to the point of the sketches themselves, although I took out my files to look at stuff from that particular tour. I have some notes of a broader scope of things

that I was trying to get to. I have this series of pages that I have various notes on those bigger themes.

Let's start with some of those themes?
The basic themes I was getting into, or at least the words, let me put it that way: One was "timeless," another "fantastical," another is "high-tech/militaryesque," another was "compact" and "portable," for the movement, and "powerful" and [finally] "variation in scale." Those are the themes that I was moving forward on. They're not like pictures, per se, but, [for example] "timeless" can be about a lot of different things, but it's not [just] today. "Fantastical" is the range of what is fantasy and bringing that [style] to life. For me, I like to do a lot of things in fantasy. When I bring fantasy to life, I make it a fantastic reality, just like the politicians! Then "high-tech/militaryesque" was something that I was looking around at the day and wanted to combine "Star Wars" and the kind of fantasy around the time. So, I just wanted to touch on some of that. That was it, the basics.

When working on these design concepts had you heard the album to assist inspiration in the creative process?
I never heard the music. [It wasn't] "Here, listen to this music," because it could be any music, you know? It was just a matter of coming up with [ideas]. In a sense, like what I did for David Bowie in '74 for the "Diamond Dogs" tour. I made lists of ideas, like a "Chinese menu" if you will, and just [came up with] a lot of different things. I would let my mind just run and put notes down. Sometimes with enough different fragmented notes you see a pattern, or some things hang together. This is what evolved. I still [have], in the back of my mind, a super tour design related to these things, but nothing evolved then. The idea of using the jet engines still burns in my head for a presence on stage with a lot of oomph to it.

Let's dig into some of the notes, like the "Keepers of the Light..."
"Keepers of the light, the light of truth." Now that's, you know, as a perpetual rock and roll group, I was looking for themes to keep moving them on in this timeless world. I even looked up in the Oxford English Dictionary what [their definition of] truth is, and I had a little definition written down. So, it was all about like acting out various scenarios that would bring the music to life or bring an experience to the audience instead of just standing up there and singing the songs. There's a little more action or interaction between the band members and the audience. It was, I guess you would say more "theater."

Right, a little bit more interactive. There were other bands who performed their conceptual material more as a presentation. Around this period that became a little bit more in vogue.

Right, exactly. That's one piece of it. Then I had another one: The "power of purpose, the purpose of truth." I don't know where I get all this truth from, but that was it. I do have a thumbnail sketch of, I guess you would say it's a tower, that had little cap roof to it, but it was more of a lighthouse.

Exactly, that's what it looks like to me.

And then you have that, it's not a balcony around there, you know, it's not a turret, it's a watchtower or something like that. It's the widow's walk or something like that so you could get up there as a staging area. It's multilevel but it could work as a lover's castle, a demon's castle [or] dungeon, a spaceship, and fox's lair. That was another thing I got into. I also had the stagehands and roadies as part of the stage [production] so they would be in monks' robes or [be] alien creatures. I wanted them in some kind of like costume or a fragment of costume if you will. Then I had them [the band] on their own asteroid or meteor traveling through time and space that would have been the stage.

Here's a nice one that I don't recall them doing but, they had the KISS Army they created. So, I wanted to make more of a ritual out of raising the KISS flag. Almost like today, especially in today's political environment, they would come out at the top of the show and have some moment, let's say "The Star-Spangled Banner" and have the American flag and then in some ways [because] KISS is Americana, raise the KISS Army flag. That's like it makes it equal, it makes it its own nation — the "KISS Nation," or whatever you want to call it. But that would be a nice moment. I mean, I'm looking [back] at these notes and they can be doing these things today and it's still valid shit!

When you're talking about the flag ritual, KISS actually went out with Mötley Crüe in 2012 and they entered the venue at the start of the show they did a solemn procession with flags marching around the outside of the audience and going down the middle up on to the stage. Very similar to what you've just described, the pomp and circumstance.

In 2000 I did the "Millennium" tour for Backstreet Boys and they had no kind of opening whatever, so I did something similar to that. The dance was whatever, you know, I forgot how many people in the audience with some kind of torches coming through. The music I picked out was the Chambers

Brothers' "Time (Has Come Today)." It has this rhythmic beat to it. So, they came in and inhabited the stage like that.

That's very useful device to really kind of like involve the audience in the show.
So then, [there was] the drum riser with the cannons sticking out, and rivets. It was more like a battlewagon with smoking cannons that were retractable, and lasers. [There was also] a swarm of killer bees, projection or animated, suspended, with sound overlay. They'd destroy them with the laser cannon. [There was] some fog with the stage, but that's nothing new there. A big power control switch like a lever from low to medium to high and I had thrusters on the rear of the stage

What other elements or effects were you thinking about?
Time capsules [that] could come down or some up from the floor and a freeze gun for Ace. I got into "cold" images opposed to Gene's hot image with fire, so I wanted to get into some kind of freeze gun for Ace. Then I had a periscope someplace; a big mirror effect with the light within. And the "Well of the Unknown." That was also above a trapdoor. [It was] a well with a crank on the end and a little bucket — a Midwest kind of thing — but the fantasies, it was really as a dramatic device with the fantasies emerging from the well. So, you go and you wish — it's a wishing well — but all kind of wishes come true and things come out of those wishes. Then I [came up with] the amps on wheels like artillery. You know how artillery has arm in the back that's really the tow bar?

That's right, the stabilizing arm.
Right, so that would be seen onstage too — heavy battle ware. I had a propeller... This is a beautiful note I have. Do you know what a caryatid is?

No, I don't.
In Greek architecture, instead of a dark or Corinthian column holding [a roof or other structure] up, it's a figure like a goddess [Editor's Note: The male equivalent is an "Atlantes"]. They were vertical and if you look it up online, you'll see they're in the Erechtheum. They're like people figures holding up the architecture. So, there it is. KISS [as] giant caryatids holding up the KISS "temple."

Right, I see those on page 9 of the sketches and the idea would have been a very impressive visual as part of the stage.

Yeah.

When you're brainstorming these ideas how do you "see" all these ideas? Are they kind of just a stream of consciousness — you're going for ideas, or are they different scenes imagine for during a show, different aspects to be represented; or are these just a whole bunch of different singular possibilities?
It's both. For example, when I did the "Glass Spider" tour for David Bowie he would give me like a few words [for ideas], but he wanted some kind of spider. OK, there's an idea of the spider. Now, I could have made the spiders some kind of like a prop that he held in his hand, but I took it, I made the whole stage [the spider]. I could take something like image like this and make it for a scene or I could make it the whole stage. So, these are ideas to bounce around and see what they like or don't like. The idea of a KISS temple, fuck, man, if you were a fan of theirs, what more do you want than go to the KISS temple?

Absolutely! "KISStianity" has irreverently been suggested! Did you know that they actually later did something similar to this with giant inflatable figures that were outside venues during the reunion in 1996? It's kind of hilarious to on one hand to be talking about this and here are the ideas in 1981–82 that later become parts of the show.
I didn't realize that but, I feel well used there! OK, on page 10 if you have these notes, then you see the wrecking ball. Tell that to Miley Cyrus or something! That was with the glowing orb that was like the "inner voice," all-knowing inner orb. The glowing orb, that's like a timeless kind of image, right?

Oh, absolutely. You immediately think of an oracle or something seen in the future. Something to that effect anyway, as you say in your notes, a dramatic device.
So, this is another variation on that. Then I have on page 11 a little more about the thrusters and stuff, maybe an aerial combat battle, but a little more detail on that.

Now let's talk about the thrusters for a second because you did a color rendering, I believe it's in the KISStory book, I think you mentioned that's the one thing you don't still have, and it shows the stage. You see the metal rivets, you see the metal flooring, you see the fire, the thrusters on the side, you see the lighting truss that goes up and, and around the drum

riser, the battle wagon. I'm going say that it's very imposing. Did you present this to the band?

No, I presented it to Gene. Gene was the only one that saw this. It was never a presentation to everybody there, so it was [just] Gene. He's the leader. Paul had a little more 2 cents to put in, but, at least from my experience at that time, Gene was definitely the dominant force in that.

Some of the key things that jumped out at me when I was going through these notes were the jet thrusters on the lighting rig, the moving the stage, and the drum riser part of the stage. There is one full page sketch out of the stage idea where you've got towers, very similar to what you did with "Destroyer," like the different zones for the players.

Yeah, but from what I recall that wasn't the final [concept]. The tower, I see you know in the sketches that I had something, but I don't recall in the final drawing that [the tower] was predominant or had much weight. I don't recall there was more about the lighting grid with the thrusters. When I first was getting into the idea the stage was a dreadnought battleship with the big rivets and stuff. That's where my head was really and that's what some of that reflection is there too. That's where I wanted to go there. That to me is heavy metal.

When you're showing this to Gene, is it a formal presentation or is this just two guys around a coffee table — "Here are some of the ideas I've been coming up with," and Gene giving you feedback?

This wasn't the time of PowerPoint! I forget where we were. I guess it was in some office someplace [Editor's Note: Likely AMI's Madison Avenue offices], but we had a meeting. It was informal in a way, sitting around and talking about stuff. But in the rock and roll world that is formal, you know!

Absolutely, that's formal enough when you've got Gene Simmons one on one. That's very formal!

There may have been somebody else there from KISS or whatever, a roadie or a road manager. I honestly don't recall. I don't think we were alone. Somebody else was [probably] there, but I don't recall who it was. I do not think it was Bill Aucoin.

So, how does that sort of presentation go?

It's pretty brief. This is how many years ago?

It would have been 35 years ago!

I tried to explain what the effects are. That's all he wanted, that was it.

Do you recall any sorts of questions that come at you when you're doing this sort of presentation? This must have been very early in the process. Are they asking about your ideas, costs or logistics, or is it just, "This is the vision I have for how you can do this?" Are they giving you any kind of feedback or suggestions how to do things differently?
No, it wasn't like, "How [are] we going to get this in the truck?" It's not that. It's concepts and the broader picture. Gene knows what he likes. But it was more you could expand your audience, but their audience has been good for them. As a designer I want to make new and bigger and better and more fantastic, but as a performer you have your likes and dislikes. You know your audience. You know what your comfort zone [is] or how you like to perform or what you feel you're capable of doing or not doing or have the energy to do or experiment with. In a certain way they play it pretty safe. The music changes a little, but the stage show basically hasn't changed from what I've seen. When they come over the amps and down the stage, that's still from the "Destroyer" tour.

That was going to be one of the things that wanted to ask you. Did you, in any way, go back and look at what you'd done for "Destroyer" as a starting point when you were thinking about the designs? I ask that in a way of looking at "zones" on the stage — "this" is Gene's area, "this" is Ace's area, "this" is Paul's area. Did you look back to how you'd done things in 1976 when you started looking at these ideas?
I didn't look back at that but knowing that each person onstage represents a different character within the group, of course I want to be mindful of that because that's their strength. Sure, I want to have things that play to that and if you go through the notes, there are various things that stand out for each one and I've thought about how to try and emphasize some of them. There's Ace "freezes" with no lasting effect, Eric "outfoxes," because I took that whole cat thing thinking, "Okay, a fox is a little bit like a cat," so I got into that being like outfoxing stuff. Gene was the blood and gore and Paul lives and loves wine, women and song. So, I still kept their themes and looked support them.

They're very much staying in character. I also note that you thought about a flying effect for Gene, which he'd started doing in 1979. Did they come to you and say, "There are certain elements that we have to have

incorporated," such as Gene flying to a lighting truss? Was there anything where they basically said, "We need to have 'this' in this concept?"
No.

Did they just say, "Mark, come to us with concepts?"
They didn't say, you know, "We need X, Y, and Z" at all; but knowing what we do and in rock and roll and onstage, [and] what they can do and what they're capable of doing. Some people you could say, "Oh, I'd love to fly," but some people don't want to fly and that's real. Some people are scared of heights so again in the "Glass Spider" tour, I put David Bowie coming out of the spider on top. I got on that when it was built... Fuck that! I was scared shitless. You're like 50 feet up in the air with a steel pipe behind your back and you have one of those big thick leather belts holding you. So, yeah, that's a moment! Not everybody is capable of doing that [sort of thing]. Even with the Backstreet Boys, they flew to the stage in the "Millennium" tour on these snowboards and with jetpacks on the bottom of them, whatever it was. I got hooked up to see what that was like and it's a trip to do, you know; but, it's not for everybody, that's for sure!

No, some of them want to stay firmly planted on the ground, don't they?
Yeah. I mean, you would think that would be for Ace, but I don't know, he'd be so high, I don't know if he could deal with it, you know.

I see that one of your ideas for Ace was a jetpack on his back.
The jetpack, because that's perfect for him. He's a space character and a rocket pack or rocket motif on his guitar [or a] rocket guitar. Fuck, that'd be great, you know.

That would've been a great. It would have been an advance on the previous tours where he'd been doing the smoking guitar thing for years; to have the guitar fly off rather than disappearing into the lighting truss would have been impressive to see.
Ports of call, that's another theme that could be used for scenarios. All of those are different calls for action or songs or whatever that may be. And then there is a letter. You get a letter somehow that tells you what to do or you could share what's in there [the letter] with the audience. It's another device. Those are the basic ones. That's the basis of everything I did for them at that time.

What I find interesting is you mentioned the monks in the robes, and I don't know if you ever listened to "The Elder" when it came out, but monks and chanting were part of the story. Did they tell you anything about the album they were hoping to tour for? I'm not going bore you with the story of "The Elder," but it's a quest so it's got a lot of fantasy elements incorporated. Did they give you anything really to work with and say this is our album, this is kind of the concept of the concert record that we're working on? Did they give you anything, any bullet points kind of to, to start working with?

I really have no memory of that. I have absolutely no notes [of any instructions], that's for sure, that they said anything to me like that. As far as I can recall, I didn't have any kind of input from them like that. But, you know, I'm also helping drive them and create for them. So, these [21 pages] are my notes. In all honesty, these are all mine originally. I don't have any notes at all from a meeting or a phone conversation that, "This is what we're looking for or [we're] thinking this direction," whatever. They're looking for new, they were looking for fresh, and that was it.

So, we look at this color rendering and it's, like you said, the dreadnought theme. The rivets, the heavy metal, the battle riser, they actually used that on their 1982–83 "Creatures Of The Night"/10th Anniversary Tour, because they ultimately didn't tour for "The Elder." It's one of the most distinctive stages of the 1980s. Were you aware of them basically using those elements and kind of like recycling a lot of these ideas later on?

I had no idea. I mean it's not like I listened to them in my leisure time, that's for sure. I'm not surprised. But they're like fragments. That's why I said it's a bastardization. There's a certain cheapness to what they do, you know. They don't spend money like other rock tours do or [like] David Bowie did or even Madonna, any of them, right? They didn't want to really get into it and spend a lot of money to do something. Once you have a strong concept you can work with whatever budget you have, but they moved away from it [and] took a fragment of it and that was it. When you tell me some things like the caryatids outside of the tour or whatever, no.

It's nice, in some ways, that for a tour that they were working on, I think they were talking about going to South America and then transitioning into an American tour. For something that never happened at the time, a lot of these ideas do turn up later on. Those caryatids made me think of Iron Maiden. They did their "Powerslave" tour in 1984–85, which had the

big Egyptian-type background with those sorts of elements. When do you find out that there would be no KISS tour?

When did I find out? You know, I don't know. I mean, from what I understood they didn't like what I had there and that was it. I didn't hear back from them again.

Communication essentially just stopped because obviously you don't refer to this as "The Elder Tour." This is just a KISS tour concept that to you has nothing to do with "The Elder," as far as you're aware. You're just doing a concept, correct?

Right, and if it's a timeless entity or environment, you can just apply it and it touches their characters. You can apply any of their music to it, if you will.

Absolutely, yeah.

So, I was designing for KISS. I wasn't designing for "KISS this" or "KISS that" because I helped make KISS. I know what KISS is, so I'm trying to just further that kind of imagery, and part of me is not surprised that they referred to [the concepts] over time. I don't love that I didn't get any compensation for it. I got, from what I see, a $1,000 in total for this work and that's it. So, they got their money's worth out of it if they used pieces of it, but they didn't get the full effect out of it because I didn't finish off the design. [If] I picked select things it would have been different coming from the original concept than when somebody else takes it and changes it. I'm not trying to be a sad sack about it, but it'd be different if I did it as opposed to somebody else doing it or somebody else milking it down and using it. I saw that with the Backstreet Boys, there was a piece of the "Millennium" tour that they didn't really execute under my watch and it was like throwing money out because they didn't like when there were some hanging elements over the audience. They didn't fulfill what the original intent was and so it's wimpy, it doesn't connect. I like to like get it all there at once if we can. That's the way life is.

At this stage you've just been paid to conceptualize. Had this progressed to the next stage, what would've been next for you as the designer? Obviously, there's a way to go before you get to blueprints, right? Do you build models?

Yeah, so the color rendering was an approach. One approach, and they could've said, "Oh, we like this and that, but can you give us 'this' or more stage here, or play up this more?" I would have done that, reconsider it, edit it or however you want to call it, redesign it. Once we had some two-dimensional agreements, because I had [only] started working in two dimensions here, I might've honestly gone into three dimensions and gone straight to a model to work things out because then I start to bring it more to reality. When I have a model then I'm working towards the finished end. So, if they say, from that rendering, "OK Mark, we want to move ahead," then we get more serious altogether with both money and intent. Then I put my head down and this is what I make that happen both through a model like the "Destroyer" tour, and then [make] blueprints from that. As you make the model you make a rough ground plan and elevation, and then you have the model. Once all of that is approved, then you start making detailed drawings of each of the elements and stuff.

When in this process do you really start thinking about a budget or materials and what it would take for the design to go on the road? Is that something that you don't worry about as the artist or designer or is that something that you'd turn over to Bill Aucoin and those who would've been involved in finance? Who thinks about those aspects of a stage design?
I definitely take it into consideration. I mean, I'm not there with a calculator thinking, "Oh, you know, this piece is going to cost X, Y, and Z." But I have an idea of how far to go in terms of what they might want to spend and how much things cost relatively. I'm looking to get a strong concept first because for me, once I have a strong concept, I could take it up and down in budget. You can make something out of plywood, or you can make something out of aluminum, so those are two different approaches. But, if I'm making a box, [if] you want a cheap box, you can make that of foam core or you can make it out of stainless steel, you know. It's still a box. Some tours leapfrog, they make two versions of it and they're setting up one in the next town, while they're ripping one down in the town they're just leaving. That's done on a lot of big tours these days.

You just mentioned something else that I was going to ask you as well. In the design phase, are you thinking about setup and teardown logistics for any of this, or is that going to be something that you're not concerned with and that they're going to have to figure out in terms of how the pieces go together?
I'm generally concerned with that because it's a tour and it's not just the whole thing about a tour. You know, it's up and down. So that from the get-go. There are variations of that in terms of some element might take a little more time than a different element, but it's all got to be setup up in a

certain amount of time. So that's worked out between me and the fabricator and the road manager.

Once you've got a stage, are you only concerned with the stage? Or are you also thinking about lighting, or is that something you turn over to a lighting director? Do you have suggestions for someone else for that part of the show?
I'll definitely have some suggestions or there are some things that I'll have a specific look I'm after. But then, you know, I'm not in there for every song and every move on stage, [so] that's also worked out with the lighting designer. I have to keep the lighting in mind and what kind of lighting rig [is designed], stuff like that. Sometimes it's me sometimes it's in collaboration with the lighting designer so it, it varies.

I want to jump back to 1976 for a moment. Where did inspiration for strong elements such as the lighting towers come from?
The lighting towers had a shape to them, and they were custom made. They had a certain shape to them styled after power towers in New Jersey. I was driving on some highway in New Jersey and they had all these electric lines going through the countryside and they were being held up by scaffold towers. The top of them had a certain shape so I played around with the base and gave that a little more of a dynamic shape, so they had a little more drama.

You can look at the model and easily see something like a mountain that Gene was standing on, which isn't immediately obvious when you're just looking straight on at the stage from an audience perspective. Are there things that you look at as a designer to design that can't obviously be seen?
Unless I'm looking to reveal something, it was to be seen. The stage itself didn't have so much on it, but the KISS logo, that's big. You want to see all that — that's upstage. Everything in front of that wants to be a little lower and not as prominent. The spike, the glowing spike for Gene, that was onstage but, unless it's lit up, you're not really aware of it. When it's time for each of those characters to come alive, the set pieces supporting them came alive. Otherwise they're dialed down and something else is highlighted. That's just theatrics.

I do want to touch on 1973. Your history with the band goes right back to the beginning of their professional performances, doesn't it?

I built their first logo in what is now my living room.

That logo made its debut at the Academy of Music on New Year's Eve, 1973–74. That was, I believe, a surprise present for them?
I honestly don't know about that, if it was a surprise to them or not. I know that it was a big deal. KISS was signed to Casablanca as the first group and there was a lot of hullabaloo about that at the time. That was all good and that helped them evolve quickly. Sure, they got a lot of press and backing.

Was that your first time working with Neil or had you done stuff for the acts that he'd been involved with before he started his label?
No, I had never met him before. I was working more with Aucoin. I got into this through Jules Fisher. Jules Fisher was the person that Bill Aucoin called to be the production supervisor for this. He's a Tony award-winning line designer. He dabbled a bit in producing things and got contacted by Bill Aucoin. I was one of Jules' students at NYU and I had already done some work for Jules once I graduated. He called me up. So, he called me earlier in that year to do KISS and then later in 1974 I got a call to do "Diamond Dogs" for David Bowie. That started me on my David Bowie stuff.

You've done a lot with David Bowie? I think you mentioned a couple of the other tours?
I did the three tours and "Saturday Night Live." I did "Diamond Dogs," special props for "Saturday Night Live" in 1979, "Serious Moonlight" in 1983, and "Glass Spider" in 1987. That was the last time I worked with him.

One last question about early KISS. You also designed their spider-web backdrop, didn't you?
Yeah, they had a private night at the last dregs of the Fillmore East. They had gone out of business, but we did a private night and that was a private press night. That was a big reveal with Casablanca and all.

It was. Did you attend that?
Yeah.

So, where does KISS fit into your professional résumé? You've obviously worked with Bowie who is about as big as they get. But you've done iconic staging for KISS. The "Destroyer" tour is kind of their measuring stick, both musically and in terms of the touring. You built their KISS logo, and that's so iconic in Americana.

I didn't design the logo, though. That's Ace. I was told by the group that Ace designed it. In high school we had loose-leaf notebooks where you would take your notes. They were usually in this loose-leaf book holder that had this light bluish-grayish fabric cover on it. The real "geniuses," if you will, quote/unquote, would use the cover and make markings on it or put their name on it. Whatever it was there's always somebody in the classroom that sits in the back and doesn't do anything but doodles or goes over one letter over and over. This was like Ace making the S-S, the S-S from the, I won't say from the Nazis or whatever, but I don't know what else had the S-S like that. The shape of that comes from Ace. And then the rhinestones, I'm not sure if they came from a different band member or if they came from Aucoin, because [he] was very involved with the whole rhinestone thing and the studs and all that kind of stuff. This is what I was given from KISS.

From that I brought that to life, and we made four plywood light boxes with regular incandescent bulbs inside and power cords coming out holes. So, I made a variation of that with a 3-inch Plexiglas disc and some kind of Plexiglas prism I found on Canal Street in Manhattan. I bought a lot of them! That was a variation on the rhinestone and would break up the light coming out from the box. That was the initial logo.

And that essentially stayed a mainstay on their stage all throughout their career, so that's quite incredible to have built the first one.
It was. The first one was only 4 feet high. Then when they went to "Destroyer" we scaled it up and I forgot how big it was. It was 10, 12, [or maybe] 15 feet high. They're in the drawing somewhere but I don't recall how big they are. Definitely scaled up and they've stayed scaled up since.

By the late '80s it was up to something like 30 feet and then they got a bit too big!
You're right.

That's quite amazing. Even in the early days, they sometimes couldn't hang that 4-foot one behind them onstage they had to put it to whichever side of the stage. It is quite a sight to see!
Yeah, depending on where they played.

Is there any reason why you didn't work with them after "Destroyer" until they came back to you in 1981? Was it just you didn't get the call or you were busy doing other things or ...

No, I just didn't get a call. They were happy and successful doing what they were doing. Then, five years of the same thing gets a little tired, so they were looking to just start changing it up.

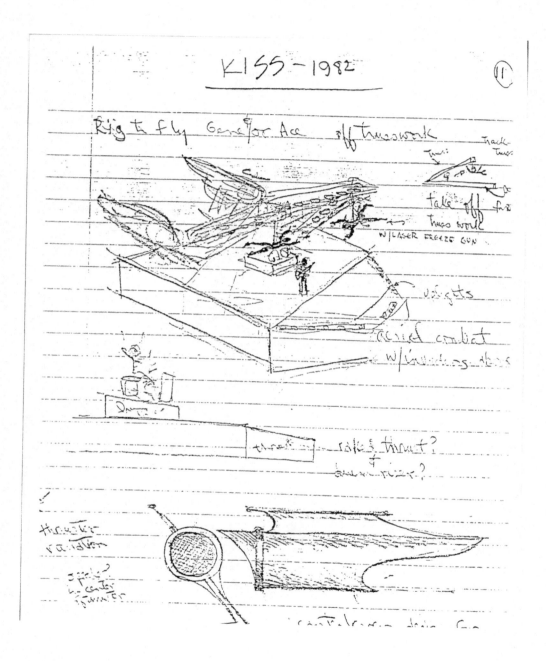

Kate Parker/Jennifer Parr

An exclusive conversation with Kate Parker and Jennifer Parr, daughters of the late Antony Parr, a versatile actor who read the Council of the Elder role for the album's spoken word dialog

In more ways than one, "Music from The Elder" is the most mysterious album in the KISS catalog. And a large part of that mystique lies in the things we don't know.

Case in point, the project's spoken word component, which was designed to thread the album's concept between songs. While we know that there was dialogue recorded, only a small portion actually made it onto the final album. The rest of the dialogue? The specific whereabouts are unknown, though it would seem to be tucked away somewhere on a lost shelf deep in the bowels of the KISS vault.

What we do know is that the services of Canadian-based actors Robert Christie, Chris Makepeace and Antony Parr were contracted. Though he is officially credited on the album's back cover, Makepeace is nowhere to be heard on the album. By process of elimination, that leaves Christie and Parr as the voices heard during the closing sequence.

Born April 30, 1925, in Nottingham, England (Robin Hood country), Parr was a versatile actor who impressively garnered roles across theater, film, television, and radio, as well as voice-over work. Born in 1913 in Toronto, Christie amassed a diverse career as well, acting in theater, TV and film, in addition to serving the Canadian Army during World War II. (A career coincidence, both Parr and Christie each landed guest roles on the Canadian TV comedy/drama "Seeing Things," which starred Louis Del Grande and aired between 1981–1987.)

Unfortunately, Christie and Parr passed away in 1996 and 2002, respectively. To our knowledge, neither actor ever went on record regarding their contributions on "Music from The Elder."

Parr's daughters, Kate Parker and Jennifer Parr, filled us in on their father's storied career and their recollections of his involvement on this mysterious KISS album, including a confirmation on which character he read.

Can you tell KISS fans a little bit about your father and his professional background?
Kate Parker/Jennifer Parr: Dad was a professional actor who worked in theater, film, TV, and radio. Originally from England, he trained at Sterndale Bennet's Canadian Theatre School in Toronto, and launched his career playing the leading role of the Governor General in the iconic smash hit Canadian musical "My Fur Lady" as it played in theatres around the country, including at the Royal Alexandra Theatre in Toronto. He continued to perform across Canada for many years in new and classic plays, including two seasons at the Stratford Festival [Ontario] as well as appearing on film and TV. Well-known for his deep rich voice, he was often asked specifically for voice-over work on TV and for radio.

What were your father's music tastes like? Who were some of his favorite artists?
He loved the Beatles and also enjoyed musical theater including the hard-hitting balladeer Tom Lehrer, Jacques Brel, Al Jolson, the English cabaret performers Flanders and Swann, and also classical Broadway musical fare such as Lerner and Loewe's "Camelot" and "My Fair Lady."

Do you recall anything about your father mentioning that he had been approached to work on a KISS album?
Yes, we remember clearly the excitement that this project engendered as it looked to be a larger-scale project that might lead to a film of the album.

Circa 1981, what other work was he undertaking?
A mix of theater, TV and radio. On TV he played the regular role of the Desk Sergeant on "Sidestreet," as well as guest starring on "The Great Detective" and "The New Avengers." His radio work included "The School for Scandal" on CBC. In film, he starred in "Agency," starring Lee Majors. Plays around that time included Emlyn Williams' "Night Must Fall," Peter Shaffer's "Equus" at Arbor Theatre, and Checkov's "The Seagull" at Manitoba Theatre Centre, which also starred a young Kathleen Turner and Tom Hulce.

Prior to his work on "The Elder," did your father have any spoken word experience?

As we answered above, yes, absolutely! A well-known actor and voice performer, "spoken word" was at the heart of his professional work.

Were you or any of your siblings KISS fans?
Our brother was!

Was your father aware of the band prior to working on the album?
He knew of them as they were big at the time.

Do you remember your father saying anything about how it was odd to have been contracted to work on a KISS concept album?
It was unexpected but he was pleased and excited to be part of the album.

Did your father have an agent at the time? How would the request to contract his services have come through to him?
Yes, his agent at the time was Gayle Abrams of Oscars and Abrams in Toronto.

Did your father know either of the other spoken word actors used for "The Elder," Chris Makepeace or Robert Christie, personally?
Yes, he already knew Robert Christie. We believe they had worked together. Not sure if he knew Chris Makepeace personally, but Chris was a busy working child actor in Canada at the time.

Sadly, the only piece of spoken word dialogue that made it to the album is the dialog that concludes the album. There are two voices. One is Morpheus, the story's caretaker, and the other is a member of the Council of the Elder, which is the voice that is heavily processed with studio effects. Can you verify which voice is your father's?
Dad's voice is the leader of the Council of the Elder. We remember him talking about being asked to be the voice of a "God-like" figure.

Did your father ever mention anything about his "Elder" spoken word recording session?
We remember that he enjoyed the process and was looking forward to more happening.

And did he ever mention anything about meeting the album's producer, Bob Ezrin?
Not that we remember.

Would you recall what your father would have been compensated for his "Elder" work?

No. He would have been paid his professional rate at the time. As a top "voice performer" at the time, he usually automatically received "triple scale."

Do you recall your father mentioning anything about a possible "Elder" film project, aside from his spoken word contribution to the album?

Yes, there was talk of future projects taking the concept further — even possibly a film, but nothing specific.

"A World Without Heroes," which was sung by Gene Simmons, was released as the album's first single. It charted decently (No. 56), but didn't maintain any traction, perhaps due it being such a left-turn from the usual type of KISS song. I'm curious, what is your first reaction to it? And given his musical tastes, what do you think your father would have said about this song?

It is a beautiful ballad, and [we] think he would have liked it.

Do you know if your father had any communication with the band? Did he receive anything from them?

We don't remember other than that he received a signed album from the band, which he was very proud of.

Did your father make any contribution to another music-related recording in his career? Or was "The Elder" his lone foray onto an album?

This was the one album he was involved with.

Though it failed to perform well, commercially speaking, "The Elder" has garnered a dedicated legion of fans some three decades later. Do you think that your father enjoyed being part of this project?

Our father did enjoy being a part of this project. We remember him talking about it a lot at the time and enjoying the concept and process. He loved being a part of something so "current," that was a part of his children's generation. He was philosophical although disappointed about it not going any further.

Chris Makepeace

For the first time in KISStory, Chris Makepeace shares his recollections regarding his spoken word role on "Music from The Elder"

Imagine "Music from The Elder," the album KISS fans are all too familiar with. Now imagine it complete with not only the 11 songs on the album, but with compelling spoken word dialog weaved between the songs, drawing you in further and helping to unravel the legend of "The Elder."

According to multiple sources interviewed for this book, the purpose of the spoken word dialogue was designed to do exactly that: to help thread the tale of "The Boy" and his epic odyssey. Producer Bob Ezrin contracted the services of Canadian-based actors Robert Christie, Chris Makepeace and Antony Parr, a recording session was scheduled on Sept. 16, 1981, and dialog was, in fact, recorded. Makepeace, a teenage actor who had garnered success in films such as "Meatballs" and "My Bodyguard," played the role of "The Boy." Veteran actors Christie and Parr read the roles of the caretaker "Morpheus" and "Council of the Elder" representative, respectively.

What happened next is not clear. In what could have been a last-minute decision, someone — perhaps an executive at PolyGram — made the call to discard the dialogue component; save for the lines during the album's final sequence. One has to wonder why Ezrin would go through the trouble of recording dialogue only to not ultimately use it?

Whether there is a "complete" version of "Music from The Elder" that exists with the dialog interspersed, or if there is simply a standalone recording of said dialog, is unknown. Adding even more confusion, the spoken word participants never went on record regarding their respective spoken word roles. As a result, this component has remained one of the biggest mysteries in KISStory.

Now, some 35 years later, the album's lone living spoken word participant, Chris Makepeace, shares his recollection of his "Elder" experience in the form of the following open letter:

Dear Tim,

I'll tell you what I remember about my "Elder" experience, but I'll have to confess that there isn't much to tell. I'll apologize in advance for any inaccuracies. Memories are funny things, and as time goes by and the stories get told and retold, I wonder if it's the memory that's being told, or the memory of the story versions. But here's what I remember:

I got a call from my agent telling me about the project, pretty easy stuff — a few pages of dialog and they'd pay me a nice salary for one day of work. Apparently, Bob Ezrin knew of me and my work, and requested me. There was also the possibility of a feature film version of the album, and I was the first choice to play the lead. I was in! We were both fairly amused that I, a little shy guy from Canada, had booked a bit on a KISS album.

On the day, I headed downtown to a recording studio in my hometown Toronto. Pretty exciting for me as a music fan to be in this place, with gold records and signed pictures of rock stars on the walls. Bob Ezrin introduced himself and gave me the nickel tour. Bob was very nice — I was a bit starstruck as I have always been a big Pink Floyd fan. He then introduced me to the other performers, Antony Parr and Robert Christie, both well-respected fellow Toronto actors. Here I found out that Robert's son David was at the same high school as me and in many of my classes — I didn't know David's dad was the Robert Christie!

At this point we had some time to discuss the movie. Bob, fresh off the success of Pink Floyd's "The Wall," said that the plan was, should the album do well (and why wouldn't it?), that KISS would unmask for the first time and tour while we made the movie. Bob gave me a copy of the treatment (a "short story" version of the eventual script), which I got to read in between recording sessions. I liked it and was hopeful it would all work out.

As for the dialog recording, we took some time beforehand to go over the lines, I think we tweaked a few to help the flow and make them sound more natural coming out of our mouths. Bob was very easy to work with. I do remember that it didn't take very long to record the dialog. These kind of things go pretty quick when you are working with very talented people. I felt like I was like an amateur tennis player playing with the top ranked guys, so I had to up my game!

We said our goodbyes and that was it.

A few weeks later I received a package with the "KISS" logo on the envelope. Gene Simmons had sent me a signed copy of the album (with all the guys' signatures on it), and a handwritten thank you letter to me on "KISS" stationery! Very cool. I still have that letter (and the album)! It was very kind and very well-written. You may be surprised that this struck me so, but that kind of generosity after a project is completed was pretty rare in my line of work. "Here's your paycheck, nice to have known ya."

As time went by, and as we never heard back about the feature film version, we assumed that things hadn't gone as planned. I was disappointed, not just at the loss of the film opportunity, but at missing the chance to again work with Bob, and perhaps the chance to actually meet Gene and the boys.

It only adds to my disappointment when I see IMDb's trivia note on me about actually making "The Elder" movie, as clearly we never did (or at least I wasn't invited!). Can't somebody change that note?!?!

But I must say that I am extremely proud of that album. I was lucky to have made some movies, and some TV shows, but being on a KISS album? How did that happen?!?!

All the best,

Chris Makepeace

Following his open letter, here is our conversation with the Boy who had "the light in his eyes and the look of a champion, a real champion":

Chris, for "The Elder" spoken word dialog, you read the role of the main character, "The Boy." Do you recall if your character had a name?
Chris Makepeace: Nope. I think the treatment said, "The Boy."

There is actually one sole tidbit of dialog that made it onto finished album — it actually concludes the album. There are two voices, one is "Morpheus" and the other is a member of the Council of the Elder. Robert Christie is Morpheus and Antony Parr is the Council of the Elder character.

Sounds right to me.

The antagonist in "The Elder" story is a character named "Mr. Blackwell." According to press materials, Mr. Blackwell was a Washington, D.C., power broker "who turns out to be the story's villain, and the worldly representative of the Powers of Darkness." Does Mr. Blackwell ring a bell? And did anyone read for this character?
Any memory of that is gone. It was just the three of us who recorded dialog the day I was in studio.

Is there anything that you remember about the treatment: approximate pages, general plot, time in which the story took place, a specific line, or approximately how many lines your read?
I'm afraid not. I do remember there being a "caretaker" who was posing as a janitor at a high school in order to meet "The Boy." Most of my dialog was with him [Morpheus, I assume], but I could be confusing that with one of the thousands of scripts I read over the years. It was present day, not futuristic.

Was the function of this spoken word dialog explained to you? From what we've been able to gather, the dialog was originally going to sit between the album's songs and help thread the album's concept.
Yes, that was my understanding. Very much like "The Wall," bridging songs and flushing out the story.

Unfortunately, someone made the call to discard "The Elder" spoken word dialog. I take it nothing was communicated to you as to why the spoken word dialog was ultimately left on the cutting-room floor?
Nope. Frankly I was surprised they even left my name on the album if they had cut all [of] my dialogue.

Some fans have guessed that you may be singing on some of the album's tracks, including "Only You," a song that features a heavily effect-processed voice that is hard to decipher. The verdict?
For the record [that's] really not me singing. Always wished I could sing, but if it was me, it would go a long way to explaining why the album didn't do so well.

Chris, prior to your involvement with "The Elder," were you a KISS fan at all?
Was never really into the heavier rock, and my tastes have mellowed over the years — although I'm a lifelong Springsteen fan. Saw him in nearby Hamilton where he only played a mere three-hour show — in August [2012] he played a 3 hour and 45-minute show here in Toronto! Come to think of it, I did go see a KISS show in Hamilton quite a few years ago, I remember the crowd being as entertaining as the show was [and] a lot of smokin' hot girls.

You mentioned you have a signed copy of the album and a note from Gene, which is very cool. I'm wondering if you listened to the album once it was finished?
I did take a listen but didn't really put it on my "playlist."

Looking at your acting work, you starred in the 1981 film "The Last Chase," with Lee Majors. Robert Christie also had a brief role in this film. This would have been a few months prior to "The Elder."
I had forgotten about that. It's one of those "I did know but had forgotten until you mentioned it" deals.

Chris, correct me if I am wrong, but I have never read an interview with you talking about "The Elder," even for a KISS publication. I've always wondered if you ever formally spoke about your involvement with this project, say circa 1981–1982? And do you recall ever subsequently talking about it with friends or family?
I honestly don't remember if I was ever asked about it during an interview — press tours were usually film specific and most questions were about that particular project, or my personal life, which I got good at deflecting.

Interviews, in my case anyway, were almost always arranged by a PR firm hired to promote the project — no one asked me to promote "The Elder."

I think a lot of people forget that an unsuccessful project was just as much work as a successful project. You care about it and carry pride for the finished product, and if it's not received the way you'd hoped, it doesn't mean you stop caring about it. Some of my fondest memories and greatest experiences working on films were projects that most people don't know about. The world moves on and forgets and dumps the work into insignificance, but all the folks who labored to make it don't feel that way. I think "The Elder" would be a good example of this, certainly for the band and the producers.

My involvement was pretty minimal, but I still get a kick out of having my name on a KISS album, and of course, have told lots of people about it!

THE ELDER   T.

-4-

ANTHONY:
WE WELCOME OUR BROTHER, MORPHEUS...

ROBERT:
MY LORD.

ANTHONY: CONVENE
...AND WE DO SO CONVENE THIS GATHERING OF THE ELDER IN THE SHADE OF
THE ROSE. (PAUSE) MORPHEUS... YOU HAVE BEEN SUMMONED HERE TO OFFER
YOUR JUDGMENT OF THE BOY. YOU HAVE HAD HIM IN YOUR CARE FOR HIS FIRST
CYCLE OF YEARS... HE APPROACHES MANHOOD NOW. DO YOU STILL DEEM HIM
WORTHY OF THE FELLOWSHIP AND OF THE TASK WE MUST SET HIM?

ROBERT:
I CERTAINLY DO, MY LORD...MATTER OF FACT, I THINK YOU'RE GONNA LIKE THIS
ONE. HE'S GOT THE LIGHT IN HIS EYES... AND THE LOOK OF A CHAMPION. A REAL
CHAMPION.

(Part of the 9 page "dialogue" script used on Sept. 16, 1981)

Tim Trombley

"Music from The Elder" production coordinator details his recollections of the album and recounts his role as Bob Ezrin's assistant

Let's rewind to 1981. How did you learn that Bob Ezrin was looking for an assistant?

Tim Trombley: Well, there were a lot of local promotion people in Detroit for the major labels that called up my mother [Rosalie Trombley] and there were a number that she kind of mentored that ended up going on to national jobs, whether it be in New York or in L.A. And this one particular person, Kenny Buttice, was at Elektra. He had actually moved from promotion into A&R and had been working with Bob on this band from Toronto called the Kings. And I guess it just somehow came up in conversation that Bob was looking for a personal assistant and Kenny put my name forward. Of course, Bob certainly knew of my mom and I think had probably met her a couple of times. [Editor's Note: Rosalie Trombley, a golden-eared DJ at Windsor, Ontario-based CKLW-AM, played a significant part in "Beth" getting radio airplay in 1976.] Basically, Bob said to Kenny, "Have Tim send me a résumé and reach out." So, I did that, and I recall going up on the train from Windsor, right after the first of the year in 1981. We had a good initial meeting. He said he wanted to think about things and then he asked me to come back up again, and that was literally the end of January, just after my 22nd birthday. He offered me the job and he said, "there's only one condition, you need to be here by the third week of February." So, I got on the train, went back home. I was working at [CKLW] in the production department and tendered my resignation. And it was actually February 23, if I'm recalling accurately, that I got in my car with all my clothing and whatever else I had and drove up to Ezrin Farms in King City.

What did your job entail?

It was a personal assistant — basically whatever Bob needed me to do to make his professional hours as focused as possible. If that meant going to the accountant's office with invoices, [I did it]. Because he had a production company at the time, Migration Productions. And there was a lady, Wendy Shore, who worked in the office, and she was more the office manager. Whatever Bob needed me to do, running to the accountant, going out and picking up a piece of equipment, picking up his kids from school. At the studio, if there were sundries that were needed — it was really whatever he needed me to do. In the case of KISS, once they were in Toronto and we're recording at Phase One, I was charged with going to the Four Seasons every morning and bringing Gene to the studio.

It sounds like you came into the picture right as Bob and KISS were getting back together. Is that your recollection, you're coming onboard, and KISS were first in the queue?
Well, they were. I think literally [two weeks] after I started, we literally flew to L.A. and he mixed this Murray McLauchlan record ["Storm Warning"] at Producer's Workshop on Hollywood Boulevard. I remember when he was mixing that record, Paul Stanley actually came to the studio for a meeting with Bob. That was probably early March. Once Bob got that record done, I think we jumped right into KISS.

KISS initially convened at SIR in late April/early May. Do you recall SIR Studio and the dynamic of Bob and the band getting together there to hash out material?
I wasn't here for that. I recall Bob flew to New York on his own but I'm sure, if it was like other rehearsals I witnessed Bob with other bands, I'm sure they were running through the songs with him and Bob was offering up his professional producer opinions, insights and suggestions.

Multiple parties have noted Bob has an uncanny ability to be able to see a big musical picture as well as focus down to a core riff, drum beat and pluck it out of thin air.
100 percent, yeah.

"The Elder" came to pass as a concept album but the signs point to KISS and Bob getting together initially to record a more traditional KISS album. Does that ring a bell?
Honestly, I wasn't aware of that.

What are your recollections in terms of the direction the album was taking?
By the time I started working for Bob, certainly my understanding [was] it was going to be this concept album and there was a lot of discussion because of the concept album. And with the concept really being the focal point, it was an opportunity for KISS to take the makeup off and really kind

of presents themselves. This is never something that was actually expressed to me by Bob or the band, but what I always sensed was that, while they were hugely successful on a global scale, there was always this feeling that it bothered the band — especially Gene and Paul — that in terms of the critical circle they weren't viewed with a lot of legitimacy. And I think that they went back to Bob because he had done this epic instant classic called "The Wall" and I think they were really looking, to some extent, for that kind of critical credibility.

This was certainly a different direction for KISS. Being on the inside, did you sense any reluctance from the band in terms of veering into concept album territory?
No. Honestly, I think they were all in. Again, I picked Gene up at the Four Seasons every morning. He was always very kind of animated. It was the polar opposite of when I picked up Lou Reed. Gene always was very personable; it wasn't like he just sat in the car waiting for the ride to be over. He was funny, he was witty, and I just never sensed that there was anything less than a total commitment and enthusiasm for the record they were making. I think they really believed at the time that they were actually making it that this was something they were very passionate about.

As you mentioned, Bob had just come off the Murray McLauchlan album. He was also undertaking an album with the Kings. All of this activity points to a busy 1981 calendar for Bob. Was the fact that he had just finished a record and was overlapping work with the Kings and KISS causing any additional stress?
I do recall that both bands were recording, not at the same time, although there may have been some crossover there at Phase One in Scarborough. I think the Kings record had been started before I started working for Bob. They had started on it and then I don't think they had got the full distance from the Murray McLauchlan project, because both the Kings record and the Murray McLauchlan record were being made for Elektra in L.A. I don't recall any challenges there. It's a long time ago but I do recall at one point we had both rooms rented out at Phase One, and Studio 1 was the tracking room. It had one of those extremely valuable old Neve [consoles]. I don't know if it was an 8056 or what series it was but it was the board that Bob always wanted to track on — especially for rock because it was such a punchy console with great EQ. At a higher level, there may have been some conversation between Bob's attorney in New York and Aucoin Management, but I'm not aware of there being any kind of issue there. All I can tell you is

that Bob was a workaholic and it was hard for some people to keep up — and I'm talking more about the engineering staff and the studio staff. We'd start some days with a 1 o'clock call, and then you'd work until 3 or 4 in the morning. Some days the call would be a little bit later and you'd literally work through the night and be going home as the sun was coming up.

There were also some album sessions at Ezrin Farms in King City. We have documented that there were a couple of rounds of sessions at Phase One, first in May and again in June through early July. Would the work at Ezrin Farms have taken place before the Phase One sessions, afterward or concurrently?
The timeline isn't entirely clear in my head but I tend to think it was afterwards because the only things that really could be done at the farm — just based on the studio space, I mean he literally just had one isolation room and then another area in the basement — [were] some good vocals and guitars. My recollection is that was more around overdubs because when I picked up Lou Reed at the airport, he was coming up to work on lyrics for the band. Lou actually stayed right at the farm because Bob's house was fairly sizable. It wasn't like what you would expect a mansion to be, but it was a fairly big country farm home, with probably five bedrooms and a big master suite. It was really, really nice. It was pretty property up there. Once you get outside of Toronto, in that area, you were into a little bit of rolling hills.

Bob also brought in the Record Plant truck for the work at the farm. So, the picture I'm getting is Bob is with the staff in the truck and the band are overdubbing vocals and/or guitars in the iso room.
That's my recollection.

It seems the band came up to also stay at the farm, though it appears they weren't all there at one time.
I don't recall all of the band staying there [at the same time]. I don't know that I ever drove Paul. If I did, it was only a couple times. But again, I was kind of charged with looking after Gene. I do recall bringing Gene up separately a couple times. Paul, I think, was always more kind of mobile on his own and would rent a car and stuff like that. I'm not clear when Lou Reed was in. I can't recall if Paul was actually there, if they were spending time together. I think there was time spent together, with them working on lyrics. Bob had known Lou previously through their work together and Lou being

the poet that he was, there was a feeling that he would really bring a lot to this conceptual record, [in terms of] imagery.

KISS and Lou Reed seem like such an unlikely pair.
[That's] true on one level. But if you think about KISS, they had such great commercial success compared to Lou, who was always more kind of underground. I think that KISS was very street and when they were starting out in New York, I think there may have been some level of mutual respect there that perhaps wouldn't have been obvious to the public.

Ace Frehley's home studio in Wilton, Ct., was also utilized for "The Elder." What do you remember about that facility?
That was a huge challenge for me because Bob's kind of approach was, "Hey kid, I've given you this shot and I'm just going to kind of throw you into the deep end." He basically charged me with getting his equipment from Toronto to Connecticut. And it was one 24-track machine — it possibly could have been two because Bob was way ahead of the curve back then, synching up two 24 tracks together to get more working space. It was a lot of equipment and I remember having to load up the truck. A couple of the engineers helped load the truck and secure all the equipment, of course. I remember crossing the border at Buffalo and just getting on the New York State Thruway. I think I drove through the night. Getting to Ace's place, it was kind of surreal. It was this beautiful place in the middle of lush Connecticut countryside.

As you were observing some of these recording sessions, did anything stand out in terms of challenges or issues? Or was it fairly status quo in terms of recording?
I don't really recall there being problems. I think that with Bob, at least with the KISS record, there was a lot of, "Let's try this." We're talking the analog world and I think even to this day it still happens where you'll do 10 takes of a vocal, you'll do 10 takes of a guitar solo, and then you comp it together. And I know that the band was in the studio — Paul, Gene and Ace, my recall is they were there virtually all the time.

And Eric Carr?
Yeah. My recall on that is Eric was very much in the band. Paul, Gene and Ace treated him very much as an equal.

The album's opening track, "*fanfare*," features a pair of very specialized medieval instruments, a crumhorn and a racket. Did you have anything to do with tracking these instruments down?

I think that's something Bob masterminded. I don't know this to be fact, but there was Michael Kamen who was obviously involved in the record. But there was another guy in Toronto that Bob worked with named Allan Macmillan. He was an orchestrator and it's possible that Bob may have sourced the instrumentalists for those two instruments through Allan. But I don't know that to be fact. When we worked at Nimbus 9 on a couple of other records, Allan Macmillan worked literally right down the street. I do recall Bob did a band from France called Téléphone [and] Allan being around Nimbus a couple of different times. Bob seemed to hold Allan in high regard, because Allan was a little bit older and classically trained. You know, he could write charts and all that kind of stuff. I certainly witnessed and knew that Bob would write charts himself. You know, Bob got Michael involved in the orchestration on the [KISS] record.

It's interesting that you're recalling that Ace Frehley was around for sessions. The dynamic that is frequently brought up by Gene Simmons is Ace never showed up.

He definitely was in Toronto. I can tell you that with absolute certainty because as long as I'm alive I will never forget one story. It was hilarious. They were doing some guitar solos. Ace had gone out to do a solo; I can't recall which track it was, but they'd done probably three or four different takes of this one solo and then Bob said, "Come on in, we're gonna have a listen." And he came in and Ace was drinking consistently at that time [during] the making of the record. He loved his champagne and when he came back into the control room, he had grabbed a flute of champagne and had gone to sit in one of the producer's chairs, one level up from the console. When he sat down, and he leaned back he went ass over tea kettle backwards. (Laughs) The chair went right over backwards, and he wasn't hurt, but somehow through falling backwards and landing on his ass he did not spill one drop of champagne and everybody in the control room just burst out laughing. (Laughs) There may have been several who pissed themselves slightly. It was just one of those things. You know, making records, being in that control room for hours upon hours, it gets stressful, it gets a little claustrophobic. Everybody was in hysterics and when he realized what had happened and that he hadn't spilled a drop Ace broke out in his quirky laugh as well. Of course, that just made everybody laugh that much harder. (Laughs)

(Laughs) That sounds unequivocally like Ace.
Yeah, as a guy that was still new at working with Bob and just being able to kind of sit there on the couch behind the console, it was just one of those things that I will remember for the rest of my life. It was just one of those classic moments.

With Michael Kamen, Bob had worked with him as recently as "The Wall." Michael conducted the American Symphony Orchestra for "The Elder" and signs point to those sessions taking place at A & R Recording in New York. Would you have helped to coordinate any of those logistics?
Michael came to Toronto a couple of times, to do some pre-work with Bob. I think it was a couple of times and I transported Michael from the airport to the house. I wasn't actually in New York for those orchestra sessions, although I would have loved to have been.

It seems that Bob and Michael were very much in sync with regard to the orchestral plans.
They were. They were very much simpatico in terms of the dynamics between the two of them. I could certainly see there was a tremendous amount of respect and love for each other and they joked with each other a lot, but it was all out of love and respect because I think that they both knew in their own humble ways that they were exceptionally intelligent people. Forget the music business. It's just that they were highly intellectual people that just happened to focus their gifts around music.

Do you have any recall of coordinating logistics for a St. Robert's Choir?
I don't recall that there was [a choir on "The Elder"]. That may have been just an inside joke kind of thing. I know on the McLauchlan record, for sure there was a school choir. I think it was the Upper Canada College [choir] on McLauchlan, because I remember they did that at Nimbus. There was actually quite a big room and I do recall that happening. I don't recall there being a children's choir on the KISS record although Bob certainly would have had access to it.

One of the important elements of "The Elder" was spoken word dialogue. It seems that dialogue was going to thread in between the songs and help underline the concept.
Yeah. I think that that there was [a] discussion around that; about there needing to be a thread [to tie the songs together]. If you go back and look at a couple of conceptual records that Bob had done prior, with Alice Cooper's

"Welcome to My Nightmare" they used the legendary late Vincent Price. And while there was no dialogue I can recall on "The Wall," there was clearly a conceptual thread through everything. I think on "The Elder," now that you mention it, there were conversations about it becoming something much bigger, with a film and stuff. What I recall is that the spoken word dialogue part of it would perhaps be the thread that kind of pulled it all together and help with the actual screenplay.

Would you have been involved in finding the actors?
Bob had a couple of agency friends in Toronto. Sounds Interchange was more of a commercial jingle house. They still did record industry recording there, but it always was predominantly a jingle house. My recollection of Sounds Interchange is that there were at least five or six different rooms there.

Christopher Makepeace was a popular teenage actor at the time.
He was. He was a Canadian teenage actor that was starting to have some success in America. So somehow Bob knew him and thought that he would be ideal.

Would you have been at the dialogue recording session at Sounds Interchange?
Yeah. I was there for that and I remember Christopher being fairly nervous. As a kid, he probably was a fan of some of Bob's work. I do recall that it was really kind of cool to sit back and realize that this was going to be yet another unique element of this record and how Bob, with the band, had this vision. He had this vision for what the dialogue needed to be that would actually be the tapestry that weaved it all together.

The dialogue is recorded, and that's where things kind of get hazy. "The Elder" is released, but there is only one piece of dialogue tacked on at the end. So, the natural question is what happened to the dialogue? If the effort was made to record it, I tend to think that at some point it was weaved within the songs, as intended.
Yeah. But it may have been a little too grand and outside of the scopes of people being able to kind of understand it.

One other thing that happened with the album is that PolyGram apparently requested that the album be remixed to bring up the guitars.

I honestly don't recall that happening. If it's anything like the process I had at EMI, where once we were in mixing a record, I'd have mixes overnighted to me so that I could pass an opinion on while the record was still being mixed. One of the things I learned from Bob, when you were in a mix situation, you mix it where you think the vocals need to be. And then you create alternate mixes where the voices are up half a DB, a full DB, and perhaps even a DB and a half. So that if the label asks for a mix with more lead vocal you already had it and you didn't have to go back in and remix it. So, it's possible, although I don't recall, that we had to go back in and do some guitar-up mixes. But my expectation would be that Bob would've had himself covered on that when we were actually doing the mix the first time.

The track listing for the album was also changed from the intended sequence to an altered sequence.

That sounds like a label thing.

If we fast-forward to November 1981, "The Elder" is released and ultimately does not perform well. For all intents and purposes, the album is dead in the water by February 1982. Do you recall Bob being affected by the album's failure?

Well, Bob always moved on. But at the same time, I can tell one other vivid memory that I have of working for Bob as it relates to the KISS record is at his working office in his house in King City. And I had been there working a little later in the office on a weeknight and he got the call that they weren't going to be taking the makeup off. And I remember him coming down to the office and he was very, very upset. He said, "I just got this call." I said, "Bob, what's the matter?" He said, "They're not going to take the effin' makeup off. I can't believe it. Why did I do this record? That was part of the agreement with me." And I don't think he meant the band. I think it was PolyGram or Bill Aucoin, or a combination. I think there was a concern, and again I'm just surmising. Perhaps the label didn't understand the record and it scared them because they didn't know what they were going to do with it. So perhaps the label to some extent had already said, "Well, we just need to get past this and get the band back to what they are, which are four guys in full costume and full makeup that make very hooky rock."

KISS ended up unmasking two years later. In hindsight, it makes for interesting speculation in terms of what might have happened if they unmasked for "The Elder."

Yeah, it sure does. I remember that very clearly Bob was really upset. Bob had a couple of cool cars. And one of them was this really radical Citroen Maserati, which had pneumatic air suspension on it. It was a stick and he let me drive it a number of times. Anyhow, I recall going out for a drive just to let go of this devastating call that he had. Like any record that I saw Bob making while I worked for him, he poured himself into [this project].

Would this call have come before or after the album was released?
No, not after [it was released]. I think after it had been completed.

How long did you end up working for Bob in this capacity?
Just under a year and a half.

Can you bottle what you learned from working with Bob during that time and how it helped serve you in your career?
What I learned from Bob is the craft of making records — the whole sonic side, especially mixing. How records had to have air. And sometimes less was more. And not compressing things too much. Just all the things like that. I was able to sit back and observe and questions that I might have for him, we would discuss at the end of a night or the next day, whenever there was some time. This served me so well through my entire career. What I saw of Bob's genius working for him in that year and a half, for me it really kind of set the bar high in terms of producers that I would come to work with. When you had an initial producer meeting with an act, there were some questions that I would ask, like, "What is your recording technique? How do you like to track? How many takes do you believe you really have to have to get a great performance? How much comping do you do? I just learned so much about making records and what went into it. Beyond that, working for him at a very young age, I was around some real heavyweight people. There were some challenges. The days were long — perhaps longer for some of the support staff than for Bob because you had to go out and do a number of errands before you actually got to the studio. I know in that year and a half, a short day for me was 12 hours when we were actually in the studio. He really put a lot of trust in me. You know, this young guy coming up from Windsor to the big city of Toronto. He didn't have to take a shot on me. There were probably a thousand young people that he could've hired in Toronto that would've crawled over ground glass to work for him. Yet he took the shot on me.

He really gave me the confidence [to think] that I can create my own career [and] have my own identity, because truthfully, I wasn't a real confident kid. My parents split at a very pivotal age. I was like 9 when my dad left the family and didn't have a male figure throughout my teen years to any real consistent extent. When it looked like the production company wasn't going to grow in the way that [Bob] envisioned, I wanted to get more exposure on the engineering side and kind of ultimately go down that road. And that didn't look like it was going to materialize in any kind of a timely manner. This other opportunity came up for me to go to work for this big music attorney [Bernie Solomon] in Toronto who at that time was representing the ATV publishing catalog in Canada. And this attorney started a little label [Dalcourt Records]. And this musician that I met through Bob, Domenic Troiano, he and I became buddies, which led to me going to work for this attorney. And all of a sudden, I got to sign a couple of bands and I was doing radio promotions and traveling across Canada. But honestly Tim, if I hadn't work for Bob first, I don't know that those doors may have opened for me. And I've told Bob this. I will forever be indebted for the opportunity he gave me in terms of starting my own career.

John Picard

Professionally known as Mister Zero, Picard is the guitarist/co-songwriter for
the Kings, a Canadian band Bob Ezrin was concurrently producing while
working with KISS on "The Elder." He recalls working with Ezrin and the
challenges that faced his band during their sessions

**Let's start with when you first started recording what would become the
"Are Here" album at Nimbus 9 studio in Toronto.**
Mister Zero: It was a Cinderella story. It really was. We had worked long and
hard to be ready when opportunity came knocking. And opportunity came
at Nimbus [9 studios] in Toronto doing our first album by ourselves and Bob
came in after finishing the Pink Floyd album, "The Wall." Our managers kind
of wooed him. We had original songs and he took home the tapes and his
kids liked them — there was something there. So, he agreed to mix some of
our songs. Then as he got into it, he realized that we had some good songs
and some good hooks, but we just didn't have the expertise in the studio
that he had. He was the No. 1 guy in the world, so he went to L.A. and
played the stuff for a guy at Elektra and we had a U.S. major label deal.

What happened when it came time to record the second album?
We worked long and hard to be ready when opportunity came knocking and
then he taught us so much on our first album — we absorbed a lot of the
techniques or just how to organize songs and all that kind of thing. We
traveled, doing a lot of gigs back then, working on songs on the road.
Sending in the tapes to Elektra, people there were excited about the
material for the second album and then once we started recording it, it was
a different story because whereas Bob was able to mold us and help more
on the first album, where it needed it, I think that we were a little better
prepared [for the second album] and the songs didn't need as much
[rework]. We felt that he was putting [in] stuff [and making] input for the
sake of doing it, as opposed to whether it was [really] serving the songs. So,
when we delivered the rough mixes our label started freaking out. "What
did you do to the songs!?" And it was like, "Well, Bob, you know..."

What was the label's response to the material?
They wanted us to can the album or disassociate [ourselves from] Bob. We
said, "Well, you know, he's the guy that got us here." We stuck with him and

the people at the label buried the album. It was a flop. Many of the songs from that album that were changed from Bob's input we, in subsequent years, have returned them to their original arrangements and played them the way that we [originally] wanted them. That was a really bad, bitter taste.

Where were you recording for "Amazon Beach"?
We did our first album at Nimbus 9 down in Yorkville, which is a very nice part of Toronto, and then the second at Phase One. [It's] a studio out in Scarborough in an industrial area and [was] not very nice — you know, the next-door business was a stone cutting place with dust everywhere. Bob set up shop there and took over. He had all his million gold records on the walls, and it was going to be home base for him. He had a farm up in King City just north of Toronto and had a mobile studio there that we did some recording at as well. When KISS came in, we got to hang around with them here and there.

They spent quite a bit a time at Ezrin Farms at various times.
It wasn't a big place, maybe 10 acres I think, and had a nice little house. Nothing grandiose but it was OK. The mobile studio wasn't the greatest, but it did its job. We did have dinner up there with them and Sonny [Keyes, the Kings' keyboard player] remembers we didn't say much because we were in awe of those guys. They could dominate the conversation, but they're very smart, witty guys anyway. They were staying at the Inn on The Park. We hung out with them a little bit.

I've got to ask you straight up, having heard rumors because Bob was working with both bands at the same time, did you contribute any work for the KISS sessions?
Yeah. Dave and I were in L.A. and Bob was working on mixing at Producer's Workshop. They wanted to do background vocals with a gang of people. We did do that. I don't have a copy of the album, "The Elder," but we did do it. What song it was I can't tell you or whether we got a credit on it. I haven't seen the album cover in so long.

You certainly did not get a credit on it. It seems that the credited St. Robert's Choir, I had thought that that was a bit of a play on words, Robert = Bob, but he actually got permission from a school in Ontario to use their choir's name. I'd always thought that it alluded to a gang of Gene, Paul, Eric and whoever else was around doing the background vocals.

Well, we were there! We definitely did it, you know. I don't remember which KISS members were in there with us, but I just talked to Dave [Diamond, bass/lead vocalist] an hour ago just to get the final thoughts in our head about your phone call, and yeah, we did do that.

That leads nicely into my question about ghost guitar players on the KISS record. There seems to be some material that might have been played by someone other than a band member?
I never played guitar on their album, that's for sure. I did play on a track on Murray's [McLauchlan - "Storm Warning"] album. I'm not a shit guitar player, but I'm not in KISS' league. I remember up at Bob's farm, they were not there at the time, and they were doing some of recording in the basement. There was one of their '58 or '59 [Les Paul] sunburst guitars.

That might have been one of Ace's.
Yeah, but I think Paul had one [too]. Anyway, I remember picking it up and strumming it. I have one, but mine is not 100 percent original so it's not worth 300 grand, but it's [still] a great thing. I remember picking his up and it had this really fat neck. The '58s and early into '59 they call it the "baseball bat neck" because it's just thicker. In '59 they thinned it down and that was the best year, then in 1960 they slimmed it down even more. Some people don't like them that much, and I remember thinking boy, I don't really like the neck on this guitar you know. It's so weird, but it was the real deal, and being one of theirs, worth a fortune.

It sounds like being around KISS during this time was a pretty positive experience for you.
Hanging out with them a bit, you know, they were always nice guys. They weren't into drugs, I mean Ace was the boozer I guess, but Gene and Paul were just into the money and success. Very straight and nice to us.

Did they seem stressed at the time? They were really stressing out about this album. Did they just seem just business like or were there any undercurrents of stress?
Not that we would have seen or that was apparent to us, because I know that they were piecing their album together and trying to make something. Our experience was more with Bob as opposed to with those guys and he was definitely stressed out! I guess he had committed to do all this stuff and it was just so much on his plate that it was very stressful for him and everything suffered. So that was unfortunate for all concerned. We were

trying to make a good album, and in our minds, it would've been a good album if not for this pervasive negativity that was the result of [Bob] being stressed out and overworked.

One thing that struck me about "Amazon Beach" was that you had Charlie Kipps [who later worked on Peter Criss' "One for All" album] involved. KISS had a similar sort of situation that turns out to be a little bit more rumor than truth. At one point they were saying that Bob simply wasn't around but was leaving "Post-It" notes for his engineers on what to do. It sounded very much like a parallel with your band, and Charlie Kipps doing the recording work and then Bob coming in and not liking any of it.
None of it! Like not one thing that he did passed muster with Bob, and so were just all throwing up our hands, "Well, what the fuck are we doing?" You know you got this guy in here who we could tell was not in the [same] league as Bob, yet, "OK, let's try to get this down." Then Bob would hear it and go, "Well, no, that's just not any good!" We had a word for it right because his name was Charles Harrison Kipps. We would say that it wasn't a keeper — it was a "kipper." (Laughs)

That must've been very depressing — you're doing the work and you're making the effort and it's then getting rejected — it sounds like you're chasing your tail in some ways.
Well it really was! I remember Bob was late a lot. We were always on time because we were excited and all that. Of course, when he's late that's OK, and then one time he got there before us, I don't know whether it's traffic or whatever, but we got there a little late and he blew out the whole day! He said, "If you guys don't have enough respect to be here on time..." And it's like, "Well, you're late every fucking day, buddy!" But what are you going to do? He's the star. We were just young people learning how to make records you know.

I'm curious about the contrast between the two Ezrin Kings' albums. How far along were you with your debut album at Nimbus 9 before Bob came in? Was it pretty much completely done?
We had most of the bed tracks and some of the over dubs done — enough for him to go in and analyze some of the tracks and then mix them. He did mix a couple. Our hit that we had ["This Beat Goes On / Switchin' To Glide"], and that's what he took down [to L.A.]. I guess three or four songs maybe, but we redid the whole thing. He said, "You're good, but you haven't got a clue and I've got the budget to do this." We actually went and rehearsed for

like a month at a rehearsal studio in Toronto and drilled every part. He had a real problem with our drummer.

Drummers are the bane [of a] band's existence really because a lot of the time the guys that you come up with from obscurity, you know you're a high school band or whatever it may be. The drummers are not professional guys and if you don't have a good drummer you can't make good records. It's just basic fact, and he had told us that he'd had a lot of trouble working with the drummers in Pink Floyd and KISS, and he wanted to kick out our drummer. He says, "You know he's not good enough. You know there's better." And it's like, well once again we're the loyal guys, and so we made it work. I think that it just added more work for Bob, to tighten up the unit and so most of the rehearsals that we did at that point were basically was getting the rhythm section tight, working at the parts and getting the bass and drums tight. That's the thing Bob knows – how to make real records. That's the key. I think most people don't understand about a real producer is that when you come out it's a real record. It sounds like a record! Nowadays I hear a lot of stuff that just sounds like demos...

Well that's because we can plug into our Pro Tools and record at home now; and do it ourselves without having an ounce of Bob Ezrin's, or any proficient producer's technical knowledge or understanding the science behind real recording — capturing sound, or perhaps more importantly capturing the performance. It's a little bit different than back in the day where you needed a proper studio, and you know there is a vast difference in quality isn't there, let alone the argument between analogue and digital?

I think there is, and as somebody said I think that just because everybody can make a record doesn't mean everybody should make a record! Of course, the digital revolution and Pro Tools and everything else has made it possible for everybody to make records, or call them records, I guess. But I certainly don't think that, because you can't compare going into a real studio with real guys who know what they're doing! You know, Abbey Road, and so on down the list. I also think that the Neumann microphone is the key to making records that sound like records.

I think some of the engineers would agree with you on that. We've gone into quite a bit of depth about microphones and those Neumann units are regularly mentioned, as are Shures, right down to the specific model engineers wanted for specific tasks.

Well, there's no doubt, the Shure 57 is a great snare mike, but the Neumanns, if you look at any picture of Frank Sinatra or you look at Abbey Road, they're all singing into the Neumann microphone. I've been in studios with our singer, Dave, and the engineer just got this new mike. "It's just great, you know!" So, I agree to try it, and it's "OK, but do you have a Neumann?" "Well, yeah, we got one of those." The other thing sounds like shit and then he plugs in the Neumann and there's Dave's voice again. It's just unbelievable. But once you got one, just use it. Nat King Cole, all those guys, they all sang into the Neumann mike and that's why the real ones cost $15,000. I think that that is a component of making quality sounding recordings and of course you probably know that, back in the day of Abbey Road, they all wore lab coats and walked around with clipboards.

They were audio scientists. It was a more of a vocation than just a profession. The studio was almost like a church in some ways. They would look at the sound waves on oscilloscopes! They don't just understand everything that went into making it as well as just capturing it. They understood the science of sound, which Bob did, as well as being a trained musician.

You're right. Bob knows all that and he learned at Nimbus with Jack Richardson. When we were in Nimbus, actually before Bob [came] onboard, Jack was there. I guess somebody called and he came in. He said, "You guys are pretty good, but your drummer is shit." He'd fall out of time all the time. This was before drum machines and all that kind of stuff. We used to make a loop back then. You'd get a tape loop and run it through a tape machine in a loop to keep the time straight on the headphones for the drummer. But old Jack came out; he said the control [room] was going nuts. He says "OK, I'm going to come out on the floor and conduct you guys." So then Jack Richardson, who had produced the Guess Who, and all these people, is trying to conduct our drummer. It fell apart in about 10 seconds. He just threw up his hands and left. And that was the end of that. It's [was] the same thing with Charles Harrison Kipps. We didn't have faith in him, in his ideas. We didn't like the things we were doing. Once bitten twice shy. It was just a futile exercise.

It sounds like a waste of tape and time and effort.
Yeah. Did you talk to Rick Hart? He was the engineer on that.

Not yet. He's still on "the list."
He did a lot of film work doing movie soundtracks. He was a good guy.

The big mystery is Ringo Hrycyna.
Ringo was Bob's boy and totally loyal. [He was] on a lot of records [and] projects. He was the tape operator, the gopher, the guy that did everything for Bob. Ringo was the guy, and Ringo was a great guy. He was very relaxed. Amidst all the clutter and the clamor and the furor, Ringo was just like a cork on the ocean. He just rode it out and put up with Bob's tempest storms and everything else. I'm sure he knows where all the bodies are buried, you know.

From the sounds of it, for "Are Here" you went through the famous Bob Ezrin "boot camp" if you spent weeks just rehearsing and working on your drummer. Again, there are parallels with KISS — he had to do a lot of work with Peter Criss to get him up to standard because Peter was totally self-taught, didn't understand things like when Bob would ask, "Play this in 7/8 time." He simply didn't understand terminology or theory. Bob would have to show him and took him to school on the "Destroyer" album. To this day it is the definitive KISS "studio" album. It's also the one where we celebrate Peter's effort because he suffered for those sessions and worked really hard. As you rightly said, without drums and bass, you don't really have a backbeat for anything else to be layered on top of.
That's right, and you're not making a real record then. Ringo [Starr] or Charlie Watts, they're great and they're kind of invisible too, a lot of the time. If you listen, you can listen to the parts and the other things, but the focus is always where it should be, which is on the singer and the song. That's sort of in the overall vibe. You can listen closely and pick out the bass and the guitar and all this other stuff, but the real thing about records is the overall picture that you get in your head. KISS had great singers. Gene and Paul are very different, but both [are] really good and [it was the] same with Floyd or any of the other bands that he did. Bob has had a checkered career, [but still] a stellar career. For all of the hits, there are a lot of records that he'd get paid, but they're not hits, and that's just the nature of the business. To this day we respect Bob. It kind of got messed up. But I think that we've mended some fences and you know, he at least talks to me now, which is good!

When you get into "Amazon Beach," how much of that material had you demoed before you go into the studio?
Most of it... We we're going to have two cover songs on [the album]. We were going to do the old Animals track "When I Was Young," which is a great song. We covered it live a lot, and it's actually on our live album, "Party Live

In '85." Then we were going to do "California Girls" by the Beach Boys. We had a killer rocking version of that, which is also on that same live album. We had the bed [tracks] done and we were working on it, [but] the stress factor and the timing [of the] thing just got so behind and out of control that those two tunes got dropped. This is before David Lee Roth put out his version of "California Girls" and I think our version is way better than his, rockier to be sure. If we had recorded it properly, it would've helped [the album]. Look at the bands that have great songs in their own right, but also help their careers by releasing covers. "You Really Got Me" from Van Halen, for example. That song could've helped us in a lot of ways too, but I guess it was not to be. So those songs fell by the wayside and it turned out to be an eight instead of ten-song album. Then the arrangements on the songs got all messed up, a lot of them. "All the Way," the first song is just horrible. It was a surprise; it was horrible you know! There's a few of them that we were just shaking our heads [about]. Bob would say, "Well, I know what I'm doing, you know. You guys don't know what you're doing." It's like, "OK..."

"All the Way" was the only single from the album, wasn't it?
Yeah, and Bob had this idea I guess, I don't think it was our idea, to put a little sound at the beginning of the album. On the album there's a "playlet," is what he called it, which is an aural sound/Pink Floyd-ian-type thing, with a guy getting up and having a cup of coffee and going and getting on his motorcycle and blasting away. So, we used Tim Trombley, who was the guy drinking the cup of coffee, and it was Rick Hart driving his Kawasaki 900 down the alleyway beside the Phase One [studio]. We wanted a Harley and we got a Japanese bike! We wanted "vroom-vroom," you know. It's [more] like "woo-woo." So, that was another thing that was a mistake. And then that thing at the beginning of the song and then the chorus repeats... It's just a mess for us.

The first thing that struck me when I heard "All the Way" is that it's a copy of "Detroit Rock City" of KISS' "Destroyer" in some ways. It starts out with a girl doing dishes, a guy getting in a car, revving the engine, turning on the radio and driving off. And here is a motorcycle basically being used to paint the same sort of picture. Did Bob tell you they were doing that, or did you just go in one day and find that it had been added on?
We were there for part of it, and I was in the parking lot watching Rick go up and down on the bike taping the thing. What it leads to is the fact that the guy at the radio station has to put a piece of tape covering up that part, so you [can] drop the needle on when the song starts instead of all that

nonsense. But we just dismissed that album — we can't even listen to it without just going bonkers. It just gets us all riled up. From what could've been, because we worked hard on it. We had thought that we had an opportunity with our record company to put out a good second record. Marty Schwartz flew up from L.A. to talk to us and go, "What the fuck is going on with you guys, with these demos! Now, it [the album] doesn't sound like that." We're going, "Bob, you know..." And we were one-hit wonders. So, welcome to the music business.

In hindsight, what would be your recommendation to a new act nowadays that found themselves in a similar situation to yours in 1981? Look out for yourself or stick with the producer even if you feel he's taking you in the wrong direction?
I mean everybody says hindsight is 20/20, of course, and at the time we just felt that it was the right thing to do so that's why we did it. It [would] have salvaged our relationship with the label [to dump Bob]. But if we'd scrapped what we did and started it over, we'd still have to pay for it. We're already a hundred grand in debt from it. So, we just tried to keep going, but they had no confidence in it and neither did we. Like I said, Bob was the reason that we were in the big time in the first place. I think that's kind of a tough question to answer. It's easier to say yeah, "Go with the label," which I think is probably the right answer, but at the [same] time we felt beholden to Bob. I think that he's a pretty brilliant guy, but there are other guys that make great records too. It comes down to mostly the band and the material that you're trying to work with, and then try to make it as true to itself as it can be; and try to put out a good product. That was the heartbreaker for us. We thought we had a good idea, and so did the label and it didn't happen.

What did you learn from your experience with "Amazon Beach" failing to capitalize on the traction "Are Here" and the single had generated the previous year?
I saw this show called "The Captains." It's a documentary made by William Shatner where he goes around and talks to all the other people who've played captains on "Star Trek" movies and TV series. He interviewed Patrick Stewart who was Captain Picard on "Star Trek: The Next Generation." And he said, "Patrick, you've done Shakespeare and you've done movies; and you've had this great career and all this other stuff. What do you think about the power of Star Trek and the fact that your career might be bookended around that?" And Patrick Stewart said, "Well, you know, you're right. I have done all these Shakespearean things and I've had this great career, done all

358 | O d y s s e y

this other stuff and all that. But "Star Trek," it catapulted me to the incredible lifestyle I lead now. This worldwide fame that I have now is all because of "Star Trek." At the end of the day when I'm on my deathbed I'm not going to feel bad about it. I'm going to think it's pretty goddamned great!" Shatner just sat there in his chair with his mouth open, and he says, "You know, you've given me a great gift because you are right!"

When I look back on my career it's like how can you hate the thing that got you there? You owe it — it doesn't owe you. Shatner was gob smacked. It was like, "Thank you for explaining that to me." I was in a band good enough to come out of Canada and play on "American Bandstand" with Dick Clark. You can't let the bullshit of the music business dictate your life. You know, we're lucky that we did have a hit and it still sounds really fucking great on the radio. I mean Bob did an amazing job on it. The mix is fantastic, and like Captain Kirk, I mean if that's what we have to be known for, then we're happy that that's the way that it is. It's better to be a one-hit wonder than a no hit nothing and we had a bona fide legitimate hit in the United States, so we're pretty proud of that.

Tony Powers

Key "Music from The Elder" contributor goes on record for the first time about his "Odyssey" with KISS

Tony, before getting involved with KISS, were you aware of their music? What were your impressions?
Tony Powers: Of course, I was aware of KISS! Absolutely, I must say I'm not a fan really. I sort of had quit pop music by then. I was on to other things. I was a little more political at [that] moment [and] doing other things musically. So, I really wasn't a KISS fan, quite frankly. But I like Paul. I met Paul and I liked him. He's a cool guy, very nice.

How did you become involved on the "Music from The Elder" project?
There was a bar/restaurant in New York called the Cafe Central. It was on 74th and Amsterdam in Manhattan. A lot of showbiz people used to hang out there: writers, actors, producers, director — names you would know. And we met there. Paul [was] aware I had recorded "Odyssey." [I'm not sure if] I had done the video by then [but] he knew the song and he really liked it. And he asked me if they could use it on the album and of course I said yes. I was quite flattered. And then he wanted me to come to Toronto with him to help finish this other song. I did that and I played piano for them on "Odyssey."

Did Paul share with you the concept aspect of "The Elder"?
Oh yeah. Sure.

When he explained it to you, do you recall your initial reaction?
I just thought it was a nice departure for them. I thought it was really good for them to do, to stretch [out].

The thing is that over the years Paul Stanley and Gene Simmons have tried to distance themselves from the album.
I know. I've read that recently.

That said, there are many KISS fans who really enjoy the album.
When you sent me those links to listen to the songs again, I read a lot of those comments and I was very flattered that people thought some of those

songs ... actually they thought "Odyssey" was the best thing on the LP, and aside from that, they really love this album.

You went to Toronto, where KISS was working with producer Bob Ezrin. Did you know Bob prior to getting involved?
No, I met him up there.

What were your impressions of Mr. Ezrin?
He was a good producer. He did his job. He was very welcoming. We stayed at his house ... did we stay at his house? You know, it's been 30 years ... (laughs) I might have stayed at a hotel, but I was at his house an awful lot. That I recall. We wrote there. He was very nice to me.

Getting into KISS' recorded version of "Odyssey." While acknowledging he likes the song, Paul has criticized his vocal performance on "Odyssey." Do you remember any hesitation on his part, and do you recall any talk of Gene singing the song?
I'm sorry, that I don't remember. I do remember Paul, even then he struggled with the lead. But I thought he did a great job. No, I don't remember anything about Gene being considered to do the lead [vocal]. He quite well might have been.

The song is very sophisticated musically — there are interesting chord changes and musical twists. The lyrics also have a cinematic quality. Tony, what was your inspiration for writing this song?
I have always been fascinated by the concept of time. To me, physics and time are very interesting things, very interesting topics. I'm writing a script right now that's got a lot to do with that. As far as "Odyssey" is concerned, it was just the thought that there are many times that exist in the same time. And everything — past, present, future — happens at the same time. And what we consider to be time is an illusion. I guess I was just dwelling and thinking on that. I'm pretty sure it just started with the very first line of the song, "From a far-off galaxy I hear you calling me." It just came quickly after that. And the lyrics to the chorus always knock me out. I just loved it.

"Once upon not yet/Long ago someday." That's such a lovely play on words.
It is, I think. I will accept that. (Laughs) I'm usually not one to toot my horn about those things, but yeah, that's it. Past, present, future — all at once at the same time. Right now, it's an illusion that there's a past, present and

future. You know, scientists think there are 10 dimensions. We only live in three of them. There's a lot that we can't see that's happening so. ...

Personally, in listening to the song, I can see how it fits in with the concept of "The Elder." But independently, the references to "I" and "you" in the opening lyrics have also made me think it could be a personal message to someone special.
I'd like to say yes, but it wasn't. It was just my personal thought about the nature of life and time.

The song is beautiful and extremely odd at the same time.
I thank you very much for that. I remember playing it once for a Russian concert pianist who flipped at the chord changes. He couldn't get over how different they were.

The song is harmonically complex, especially for a KISS album. Do you have any formal musical training?
No, I have no formal musical training. I have it all in my head. I had always wished that my parents would have given me training. I remember sitting at a piano in my grandmother's house when I was maybe 3 or 4 and nobody thought to give me any lessons. But no, I have no formal training. I just have a lot of music in my head. My theory about music is I want to surprise people. I don't want to hear the same things all the time. That's why I'm madly in love with people like Frank Zappa or Randy Newman — you know, something that surprises you at every turn. That's my goal when I write a song. I want to change tempo or change key or do something different that will arrest the ears.

"The Elder" came out in 1981. Do you remember when you actually wrote "Odyssey"?
I think I wrote it in '79 or '80 and I wrote it in my apartment in Manhattan on Riverside Drive and 77th. I remember sitting at the piano and writing it. And I remember being knocked out by where it was going, where it was taking me.

So, this song flowed out of you pretty quickly?
I finished it pretty quickly. Actually, I just loved playing it too, because I loved the change from the verse to the chorus.

You played piano on "Odyssey." Did you happen to play anything else on the album?
No, because the truth is, I can only play my own songs. (Laughs) I can't play anybody else's songs. I can only play my own. It takes me quite a while to learn to play what I hear in my head.

One thing about the lyric, it is originally written as "There's a girl in a sundress." I can't recall [who] changed it for "The Elder."

That's a nice bit of trivia. Tony, do you remember hearing a first playback of KISS' version?
I was at the studio when we recorded it. Sure. I thought it was terrific!

Any recollections of that recording session?
Yeah, there was a big orchestra ... I can't remember the name. It was a symphony orchestra. It was huge. There must have been 30 people in that studio. The only recollection I have is that we didn't take long on the track and that there were a lot of string players in the studio.

The American Symphony Orchestra was the orchestra.
That's right. And there were lots of them! The track sounded great.

Paul has said, "Me singing it was just tragic."
He doesn't think the vocal suited him; I understand that. I feel for him. A person wants to feel like he did his best work and put his best effort into it. I thought he did terrific. I really did. I think he wasn't as loose as he wanted to be, maybe. I don't know what it was. I know that he didn't think it suited him upon hearing it later on.

That's why some fans have thought that maybe Gene might have been, in hindsight, a better choice to sing the song.
I'd love to hear it!

Fairly recently, Paul and Gene discussed "The Elder" in a piece in "The Guardian." Paul shared a story about when the album was done and how he got together with some friends to play it. I want to read it to you. He said, "I remember playing that album for people at my house and you weren't allowed to talk. 'Sshhh, this is so brilliant. This is my statement.' I was sitting there completely enamored at what we had done." So, it seems Paul was really into the album but ...

Of course he was.

You're asking me, I don't know. I'm sorry he feels that way. He should be proud of [the album]. I thought it was a really adventurous project. I think, in hindsight, it was something they needed to do. I mean you can only do the same three chords over and over and whatever. And this, I thought was courageous. And I was listening to some of the cuts you sent me, and I thought they were quite good.

I think they should be proud of [the album]. I really think they took a shot. They took a chance. They did something quite out of their comfort zone, and I think they succeeded. It's really too bad that they disavow it.

Getting into your other songwriting credit on the album, "The Oath." That's been cited as sounding more KISS-like.
Yes, because I wrote that with them. They had written a lot of that already. I came in and redid the lyric on that one.

So, you contributed lyrically?
Lyric on that one. I probably had some input on the music as well. I don't recall. I know a couple of the changes sound like things I would want.

The bridge in that song is a bit of an odd contrast to the rest of the song. I've always been curious as to who wrote the music. Maybe Bob?
I don't remember. But I have a feeling from listening to it that it's something I might have had input on.

What do you recall about working on the lyrics for "The Oath"?
I think they left me alone to work on the lyrics. I think I did that at Ezrin's house. They pretty much left me alone. They gave me what they had. I pretty much changed the whole lyric. I don't even know if they had much of a lyric, actually. They had a concept on that song. They had an idea of what they wanted to say or do on it.

This is the part of the story where the Boy is asserting himself.
Yes, he wants to go forth.

In terms of the album's concept, some have criticized that it's vague and not fully realized. Tony, what's your take?

Well, to be frank, I really haven't thought much about that. You know, Picasso painted the same picture for 20 years. Nothing's ever realized, let's put it that way. You can work on something forever. You can always change things. I think critics have to have something to say. That's too bad sometimes. They can't just say "I hate it," or "I love it." They have to give you reasons. And the reasons are often really stupid. That's the way I look at it. Like you walk in and play a song for someone and they say, "Well I really like it but why don't you make it that word?" For no reason, they feel they have to give you some kind of input whether it makes sense or not. So, critics to me (pauses), anybody who reads their reviews is crazy.

It seems you worked closer with Paul. "The Elder" was really Gene's project in some ways. Any impressions of him?
I didn't have much contact with Gene, quite frankly. From what I understand, he's a really nice man and a very bright man. I did work more closely with Paul since we used to hang out together. Paul is an angel. He's a real sweet man. He actually lives pretty close to me.

You're from New York and moved out to L.A. Do you miss New York?
I love New York and I'm there quite often. I'm there maybe four times a year. Of course, I miss it. I miss the street life and the action. But I like it here. The weather's nice.

I can still hear that New York accent, Tony. (Laughs)
Yeah, you can take the boy out of the Bronx ...

How long have you lived in L.A.?
This is the second time. This time since 1990. The first time I was here was during the '70s. I worked for A&M Records for A&M Publishing as a writer then. That was my last gasp at commercial music, I think. Well, actually, the KISS thing was.

Do you have any original demos of the songs on "The Elder"?
I wish I did. No, I don't.

How long do you recall being in Toronto?
I believe I spent about a week in Toronto.

So, after you wrapped these two songs, what happened?
Yes, Paul and I flew back [to New York] together. That's the only time I've ever been to Toronto. It was a pleasure. It was fun.

I read some of the other comments under the YouTube links you sent, and I wonder too how come the two songs ["The Oath" and "Odyssey"] haven't been used in movies, in fantasy-type movies. They're perfect.

I can see "Odyssey" working in one of those type of movies.
Yeah, but who knows? Life is long.

So "The Elder" was released in November 1981 and unfortunately failed to catch on with both fans and the public. Do you have any recollections of the album's release and reception?
I really don't. I just moved on ... I don't even recall Paul being unhappy about it. I thought he really liked the project.

When's the last time you spoke to Paul?
Well Paul, we haven't talked in a long while. Maybe 20 years. The last time we saw each other was in New York.

Your recording of "Odyssey" can be heard on YouTube. Your version is accompanied by an elaborate concept video for the time.
Right.

It features the lovely Lois Chiles.
Yes, what an angel.

This was filmed after "The Elder"?
(Pauses) I think it was filmed after "The Elder" came out. [My] album came out in '84; I think we filmed [the video] around '82. The song was written before "The Elder," obviously. I had recorded it before "The Elder" on my own four-song EP. But then I filmed it after "The Elder."

Where was the video filmed?
The Staten Island Ferry in New York. It was a one-night shoot and you'll notice there are lightning strikes in the air. We had a rainstorm that was unbelievable and we only had about four or five hours of shooting and I edited that whole thing down from maybe 20, 30 shots. And you know something, because of the nature of the song; it was quite easy to put it

together as a film edit because it doesn't matter if it's in sequence, out of time or whatever. That's what the songs about. (Laughs) It came out really nicely. I edited it at home in my house. I had a Steenbeck machine in there, which was the old-time video machine we used back then.

Lois Chiles was an absolute professional angel. She was just great. I wanted a beautiful woman and she was one of the people who hung out at the Cafe Central. That's how I met her. I asked her to do it and she said yes immediately. And she showed up and boy she was a trooper. She did the work, she didn't complain. She sat and waited while everything was down because of the rain. We laughed; we had a good time. You see the last shot is at dawn. We spent all night on the Staten Island Ferry, and she was just great.

There is some striking imagery at the end. And Lois Chiles is indeed beautiful. I remember first seeing her in the James Bond film "Moonraker."
Not only beautiful outside, but beautiful inside. She's a great lady.

You mentioned "Odyssey" was part of an EP. What can you tell us about that project?
The musical part of that project was a four-song EP. "Don't Nobody Move (This Is A Heist)" was on it, which is another video that's on YouTube. Actually, what happened was I went on to make a video album that Sony released: it was "Odyssey," "Don't Nobody Move (This Is A Heist)" and "Midnight Trampoline." The thing about that EP, it was selling quite nicely until [I had a problem with] somebody who was disgruntled because I had to fire him off the set. He was responsible for getting the releases and he didn't put his release in. And because I fired him, since he kept making trouble, he came back and sued Sony because I didn't have a release for him, which was his responsibility! And Sony being a corporation just completely freaked out and pulled the EP out of the stores. That's just a side story.

Anyway, I'm very proud of that video album. They're all on YouTube and people have side quite nice things about them. Actually, "Heist" won at the New York film and video festival.

Getting deeper into your career, you started out working as a songwriter for Leiber and Stoller in the famed Brill Building.

Yes, in New York. Tin Pan Alley. I wrote with Ellie Greenwich, Phil Spector and Jerry Leiber. I wrote with all the greats ... Al Cooper. I wrote a lot of hits, actually, in my brief seven-year career. They're listed in my discography; it's like over 100 records. "Today I Met the Boy I'm Going To Marry," "Why Do Lovers Break Each Other's Hearts?" "Remember Then" — things you might not know, but if you look them up, you would know them.

"Today I Met the Boy I'm Going To Marry" was recorded by Darlene Love.
Yes, I wrote that with Phil Spector and Ellie Greenwich. We were young and full of juice. We sat in Leiber and Stoller's office and just made some music. Then I wrote for Don Kirshner as a writer at EMI. So, I was in pretty good company and I found it pretty easy to do. And it was a pleasure — it beats working!

You mentioned that you became disenchanted with commercialism in the industry. Around what year was this?
I think I first "quit" in about '70, then I got back into it in L.A. at A&M Publishers with Jerry Moss and I got disenchanted again. I just got completely disenchanted with the whole idea of the rules of pop music. [It was,] "Why keep writing the same thing?" as far as I was concerned.

That's a sentiment you alluded to previously with regard to KISS. "The Elder" was a bid to do something different, something artistic, something that broke the rules for KISS.
That's right. Someone's always going to bash you. I mean, van Gogh never sold a painting in his entire lifetime. Why? Because he was a terrible artist, right? When Gershwin first played "Rhapsody in Blue," everybody said it was terrible. You can't listen to people. If Paul and Gene let people's opinions sway them, I'm sorry. Again, you can't [listen to] the critics. People should have kept them from reading anything about [that album].

They might have gone on to make another great album or two, in that vein. Something different, a departure — who knows where they could have gone instead of doing the same thing over and over?

And interestingly at some point there was talk about there being an "Elder" album sequel. Any future plans for the project were quickly aborted.
Yeah, you know (pauses). I guess a lot of their fans don't have the sophisticated musical ear to appreciate it, too.

I believe that's a valid point. In 1981 KISS' audience was predominantly made up of teenagers who grew up with them in '70s. Maybe "The Elder" was just too left field considering their audience?
Here's the thing. Fans feel fiercely protective of their heroes. Look at a man like Bob Dylan. When he put on an electric guitar, everybody booed him. No matter how great the music was that he was making, he got booed.

I think ["The Elder"] is the best thing they ever did, how about that?

We'll quote you on that. Tony, you've also done some acting in your career. What films and TV shows have you been featured in?
I've been on "NYPD Blue," "Everybody Loves Raymond." I was Jimmy Two Times in "Goodfellas." I worked with Robin Williams in "Cadillac Man." I did Spielberg's "Catch Me If You Can." Yeah, I've done a lot of acting.

You have quite the résumé. Do you enjoy acting more than music?
No, I like them both. You know why, I just don't want to sit behind a desk. I'll do anything. (Laughs) Music, acting — they are more my passions. Right now, I'm writing and that's my passion. My partner/collaborator and I have a great idea for a TV show. We've been writing a treatment and three scripts: a pilot and two episodes. That's been taking up my time.

You released your latest solo album, "Who Could Imagine," in 2007. What can you tell us about this album? And what do you hope listeners get out of your music?
Well, the message most of all that I want to get out is don't be in a box. Write or do whatever appeals to you and disregard what anybody else thinks. As long as you're having fun doing it, and as long as it's something you believe in, you're going to produce something good.

That album, every song is completely different, stylistically, vocally, lyrically. That's the concept. The concept is that it has no concept (laughs). It's, "Who could imagine? Here's another one, can you imagine this one? Here it is ... imagine this." And it's things I've written over a period of, I guess, 30 years. I just went into the studio and recorded all of it with some great musicians. I am just so proud of it. Maybe 20,000 people will ever hear it and that's the way it is with my stuff.

Bob Ezrin

Legendary producer speaks on "The Elder"

I've had mixed feelings about The Elder for decades now. When we began the project, it was a grand notion, full of what I thought were "important" ideas and music. And we pulled out all the stops. It truly was a BIG production with orchestras, actors, concepts, co-writers and tons of ear candy.

We came into the project with *Great Expectations* but instead we somehow ended up with the wreck at the end of *Detroit Rock City*.

When "The Elder" was done and released, it was a great disappointment — perhaps even something of an embarrassment — to the band, the record company and me too. Plus, it was a commercial failure; the band's first.

I've been quoted in the press expressing my regret at having prodded them into attempting something like this. Sometimes I've made jokes about it saying things like "we should have been shot" or comparing the label playback to "Springtime for Hitler." Sometimes I've tried to justify the intention and other times I just talked sadly about the failure. I've also stated that I had just come off "The Wall" and was in a concept album frame of mind at the time, which is probably true. In a way, the entire 70's were filled with concept driven projects for me from "Berlin" to "Schools Out" to Peter Gabriel and culminating with "The Wall." So I know that factored heavily into my tendencies at the time.

But the bottom line is that I was wrong in my intuition that they needed to do something that dramatically different from what they had been doing up till then. In hindsight, Ace was absolutely right in his feeling that all this concept and drama stuff was bullshit and that we should just get back to Rock 'n' Roll. For that band, at that time, making a superhero concept album was a bridge too far and the audience spoke with their feet as many of them ran away from it as fast as they could.

But viewed in a different context, decades later, I think it may not be the awful mess that I had come to believe it was. When it was played for me recently and I really sat and listened to it for the first time in forever, I was actually amazed at the textural and musical sophistication of it as well as its sense of humor and the absurd. Some of the performances too were really stellar and a few of the songs were much better than I remembered when viewed on their own merit. Some, of course, were still not up the standard the band needed then and I take responsibility for that. And it was unquestionably over the top and melodramatic.

But listening to it now, I began to understand what motivates the die-hard "Elder" fans who would occasionally stop me and wax almost religious about the album saying stuff like "it changed my life" or "it was genius!" I always just dismissed those people as strange, and would remind myself that even The Shaggs had a rabid fanbase.

But listening recently I found myself fascinated by it, like they were. I didn't really get the storyline anymore — or at least I wasn't distracted by it. I was too busy enjoying the soundscapes, the performances and the sheer bravery of the thing.

And that reminded me of the moments of sheer joy when we first finished some of those songs, or first read Lou's lyrics, or first heard Stanley nail some of the high notes, or first heard Gene's intimate vocal on "A World Without Heroes," or when we first heard the orchestra play Michael's majestic charts. Those were heady and beautiful moments during which we were all pretty sure we were making a masterpiece. But then it wasn't quite that, was it?

And I know that Paul went through a period of disappointment in and even anger with me for what he felt was my falling down on the job. He has sometimes said that I was often absent without leave and that my drug abuse affected the quality of the album. But in listening now, I marvel at the amount of detail and intention there is in the album and I see that my recollections of endless hours of crafting the final piece were also true. As I've said in the past, for me it was a time of personal upheaval and heavier drug use. Unquestionably that affected my performance. It certainly changed my diurnal rhythms and I was that vampire who stayed up all night poring over things and then leaving little post-it notes before dawn for the engineers — lists of things to do when they came in the next morning.
But, whatever time of day the work might have been done, there was clearly a shitload of it in this album, done by all of us.

When we began the project, I spent the most time with Gene and Paul. Ace was out in Connecticut and a bit removed from the conceptual process. He didn't believe in it anyway.

My sense is also that, in retrospect, Paul might have become disenchanted with some of his own performances on the record, like perhaps the vocals on "Just A Boy" or "Odyssey" both of which we uncharacteristic of him. This might have added to his anger with me because I encouraged him to do it. At the time, I thought both were important for the character and that he sounded amazing singing them. Unfortunately, he didn't sound like the Paul Stanley that most of the fans wanted to hear at that time. But then, years later that bravado, range and dramatic sense played out brilliantly on the stage when he transformed into *The Phantom* and pulled that voice back out to the delight of months of sold out houses. So there was a place for that part of him, though perhaps not at that point in the band's career.

Gene and I were like two kids working on a comic book — which was actually a large part of the motivation to do this story. Gene was a comic fanatic, as was I. And the band was even perceived by some to be "comic book superheroes," which I think sat just fine with him. So here we were at his house going over storylines and drawings, combining the fantasy world of heroic comic books with the power of rock and we believed we were on to something really cool. In fact, before we ever started recording, we told the story of "The Elder" to a bunch of people, not just band members but collaborators, designers, Bill Aucoin and a few other inner circle folks who all thought it was very exciting — or at least that's my recollection. Now in the fog of history, almost no one admits to having been a fan of the idea. But I remember that we had convinced a lot of folks that this was going to be amazing.

We never convinced Ace though. He did his best to do his part, but his heart was never really in the thing. It all felt too contrived to him — and he was right about that then. KISS perhaps could or should do something like "The Elder" now; something truly radical and apart from their normal stuff. I think people would sit up and take notice. But for that band, at that time, this was an unnecessary contrivance.

One of the things I learned in doing this project was how truly talented those guys were and how much they had grown as musicians from the days of "Destroyer." Most great musicians have a form of genius that is mostly expressed through their craft but that also bleeds out into other areas of their lives. And I have to say that both Paul and Gene are great musicians each in his way but also two of the brightest, most ingenious and accomplished artists I've ever had the privilege of working with. And all of that was brought to bear in the making of this album.

Bob Ezrin
June 8, 2016
Nashville, TN

It's decided, "We're doing a concept album." Does Bill Aucoin need to be in the loop or is it maybe you and the band making that decision?
Bob Ezrin: When it came to making the records then, the band led the decisions, because they were already really big by that time.

They had some political capital at that point?
They had capital, political and artistic, and I think that they were able to say "we want to do this."

You're not recalling any reluctance from Gene and/or Paul.
No.

It was, like, "Let's do it."
Yeah... We thought: "this is great. How interesting." We're doing all kinds of interesting, strange and wondrous things, you know. And we were playing around with other writers too which we hadn't done before.

Yeah, I can't wait to get into that.
Tony Powers, who is a friend of Paul's. Paul brought that song in.

Tony actually said that he met Paul at this place called Cafe Central in New York, a hangout for musicians and actors. And it was a fascinating conversation. So Paul and Gene embraced it.
Paul picked "Odyssey" because he wanted to sing that heroic song, you know, and he wasn't arguing about that. He loved it.

Interesting.

And "I'm Just a Boy" when we did that together in that little studio in Aurora.

It's like a little four-track studio, you said, like a demo?
It was a four track studio and we played everything ourselves. I played drums, which was stupid because I'm not a drummer. I just whacked the drums, you know, to do the things we needed and we sang all the parts on it. We thought we were really on to something. It felt like we were composing almost classical music. Stanley is a brilliant musician on so many levels and he's also inspiring to work with so I got totally carried away with the excitement of that writing session.

We started off making a different record and were in Phase One Studios near Toronto for a few weeks until the console caught on fire. We were having pizza, at the front of the studio and I don't even know why I went back to the control room. I went back to the control room to get something and I walked into the control room and I smelled smoke — it smelled kind of strange and then all of a sudden, I looked at the console and literally, the center core of the console just went...

Boom.
It just started going... in flames!

What kind of console? Do you remember?
It was an old Neve. And it erupted in flames and all of our tapes were on the floor and then it was like a mad scramble to get the tapes out before –

Before they burn.
Or before the sprinklers went off... Either one would not have been good. So that, you know, that was pre-Elder days.

The decision to move the project to Canada; was that strictly for you wanting to be close to home?
For sure. But this is sort of the equivalent of what we did during Destroyer, when I lived in New York. Each of the, the guys would come to my house... Sometimes together and sometimes separately. They'd come to my house with stuff they were working on; with their demo ideas, um, that we would flesh out at my house.

And then we'd take them into the studio. So this was the equivalent of that. First Stanley came up to Toronto and we did some stuff together, and then Gene came to Toronto, out to the farm.

Obviously there's a certain point where you're recording at your farm. Your farm was located exactly where?
King City, Ontario.

That's its own city? It's around Toronto?
It's north of Toronto.

Can we get a visual picture? A farm invokes a certain type of imagery. Are we talking acres of land and it's literally a farm? Or was that more of a nickname?
No, it was a horse farm. And it had a very small barn on the property. As you came in off of (the main road), you came down a 300 yard drive to the left of which was the neighbor's property, to the right of which were my fields. And then it ended just before the house where there was a small barn to the right. That's where our horses were. Past the barn, there was a front lawn and down the front lawn was a pond. And then the house was large, but modest, just a farmhouse. Behind the house was another field and a big hill. The farm was surrounded by 100 acres of conservation land. So I only owned 10 acres, but it was 110 acre expanse.

Do you still have the farm?
No, I sold it. Anyway, when Gene showed up in his limousine and came down the long mucky drive, he comes up to the front of the house in his alligator boots —

And leather pants probably?
And leather pants... and steps into the mud. We put him upstairs in the guestroom, like next door to the kids. We had four kids upstairs. And Gene.

That's great.
It was hilarious. One of the things that attracted us to that house was that, for whatever reason, they built a bomb shelter down in the basement. So there was this big stone room in the basement that was everything proof, including soundproof. So the idea I had was to use that as the record room and we'd drive the Record Plant truck up, because I loved that truck. And with some people that I knew, that I had worked with in other contexts. Like

Rick Hart who had worked with me on Roberta Flack and "The Wall" too. Having the truck downstairs was great on one hand. But on another hand, it was just too rural.

Well, that being said, Toronto has no shortage of studios...
Well, no. Toronto's got no shortage of recording studios, but I was living 40 miles north. So it wasn't trivial for me to get back and forth during the day.

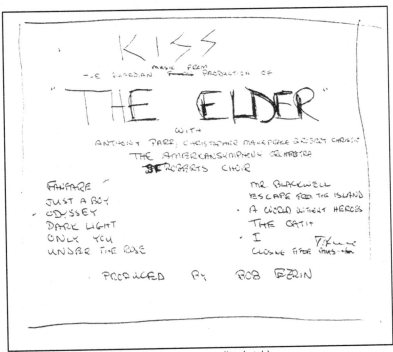

(Bob's rear cover credits sketch)

Whose idea was the dialogue? Was it your idea, like, "Hey, let's put dialogue in between the tracks"?
Well I think Gene and I probably came up with the idea of making it sound like the soundtrack to a movie that hadn't been made yet.

And it wouldn't have been taken out because, again, these were established actors, especially Robert Christie and Antony Parr. I think they're out of the Stratford School.
They were out of Stratford. Yeah, they were real actors. I remember hiring these people.

You personally found them?
Oh, yeah, for sure.

We uncovered a receipt. Robert Christie got paid $1,000 for his work. He and Parr have since passed away. I did find Christopher Makepeace. He recalled you giving him a brief tour of the studio. It's interesting to note Christopher Makepeace is nowhere to be found on the album — he's credited, but he's not actually on the album. So, again, the dialogue was recorded, and it was taken away at some point.
Isn't that strange?

Special Features

"The Elder" In The Press

The relationship between critics and KISS has always been one of interest. How did the critics respond to KISS's unexpected artistic urge? Here's a taste of some of the reviews the band received for their studio effort

KISS album smacks of rock sophistication

(Maureen Keenan, San José State University Spartan Daily, Dec. 9, 1981)
KISS — n., rock 'n' roll group consisting of four outrageously costumed men with painted faces; known for their appeal to 14–18-year olds; one member of the group spits blood occasionally. But the definition is changing. Kiss's album, "The Elder," is a transition for KISS. No haunted white faces appear on the album cover. Their music has changed, consisting now of smoother rock mixed with classical, in an interesting theme paralleling KISS's determination to forego the teeny-boppers and reach the older, mature audience.

The album tells the story of the Elders, the ideal. This group embodies the wisdom of the ages, the power of goodness and knowledge. It combats another eternal force, evil, the sole purpose of which is to destroy all that is good. The council of the Elder, which sits under the Rose, awaits word from Morpheus, the caretaker, to determine if a certain boy is deemed ready for the sacred rite of accession to the Order of the Rose.

"When the earth was young, they were already old... the Odyssey begins..." A high-pitched Paul Stanley sings like a young boy in "The Oath." He narrates in this rock tune the many times he pounded on the large wooden door, the one with the brass rose "a young boy goes in, then suddenly a man returns." In a softer tune, "I Am Just A Boy," the young lad searches for guidance but learns "something's wrong," being told to "wise up" and prepare for that "perversion in hate" evil.

One thing, though, that is right, is Ace Frehley's nimble-fingered, fast-paced guitar solo, giving a clue as to why he's named Ace. Next, Gene Simmons, known for his harsh, somewhat raspy voice sings softly in "Only You" while the boy, in his transition to manhood, demands answers; "Tell me the secrets... you are the mentor." In "Under the Rose" his questions are answered. He learns he's been "chosen to be king" and warned "Loneliness will haunt you." This particular song is rather eerie, evoking a picture of Satan-lovers holding a ritualistic sacrifice. But the sacrifice, the boy is told, is not a lamb but that of omitting evil from his life.

But without some sacrifice, life would be "A World Without Heroes," Simmons sadly sings, "a time without a place... devoid of grace." The tenderness is soon interrupted as a hard beat warns the listener that "Mr. Blackwell," an evil sinner, is trying to lure the boy into his ranks. "Mr. Blackwell" is a nasty little song with many uneasy sounds conjuring up images of indistinguishable forms milling and murmuring about in a dark pit. "I don't give a damn, I love to sin," Mr. Blackwell retches out as Frehley grates annoyingly on his guitar.

And in the far-off galaxy, the boy-turned man seeks his destiny. Stanley sang this dramatic song in a lower, deeper voice. In "I", a part -sprightly, part-hard rock song, the man confidently sings "I believe in me, I believe in something more than you can understand." At the end, one hears flutes and oboes in a ceremonial tune as someone walks up steps and knocks on a door. As the door creaks open, one can hear older voices of the "boy." The verdict is to "deem him worthy of the fellowship."

Whether KISS's success in foregoing the younger fans for a more sophisticated audience will [be determined by] who accedes to the Order of the Rose via maturation remains to be seen. But with this well produced album it seems KISS is definitely knocking on the right door.

Review of "Music From The Elder" album
(RS #363, Feb. 1982, JD Considine)
What could be less promising at this stage of the game than a concept album by KISS? After having written off Kiss as pure pap for eight-year-olds, who even wants to think about taking them seriously? Yet their twelve songs are catchy, the performances respectable, and, despite its concept, Music from "The Elder" is better than anything that the group has recorded in years.

Ah, yes, the concept. According to the liner notes, "The Elder are an ideal... They embody the wisdom of the ages and the power of goodness and knowledge." What, no part for Gene Simmons? "In every place, in every time, an evil is loosed whose sole purpose is to destroy all that is good." Oh, there it is. "It is the task of the Elder to find and train a warrior... a champion to conquer the evil." You can probably guess the rest.

For all its Marvel Comics predictability, however, Music from "The Elder" comes off quite well; thanks mostly to producer Bob Ezrin. By scaling down the band's bluster and adding orchestral sweetening, Ezrin makes KISS sound strangely like Jethro Tull. Throw in some honest-to-goodness melodies and you've got a KISS LP you can listen to without embarrassment.

Well almost.

What the Elder?

(Robin Smith, Record Mirror, UK)

It's the revival of that usually daunting prospect, THE CONCEPT ALBUM. Knuckles on the forehead and heads down poised in thought for six months at a time. This collective stream of consciousness has resulted in the story of a group of wise old codgers collectively known as The Elder, who select and train heroes to fight evil and injustice, maintaining the American way and fresh apple pie. In every age and each place, a hero is needed against the dark forces and in 1981 The Elder choose an orphan boy from the backstreets, to be guided by their powers of truth and justice.

Doubtless the album will spawn a film and a comic book as part of that great KISS corporate identity, but then I've always admired bands who can spin money. Whether you like KISS or not depends really on whether you have a comic book mentality. Simply, 'The Elder' is the best example of rock theatre since Queen's Flash Gordon soundtrack and Styx's 'Paradise Theatre' album. Masterful, believable fantasy and everywhere KISS have been totally involved in the project... So the haircuts and change in costumes have been worth it and KISS' feverish banishment to the recording studio has paid off. Regan's probably even playing this album up at the White House. +++++

KISS produces serious effort

(Dick Hogan, Cedar Rapids Gazette, 12/11/81)

Would you believe a serious album from KISS? Many of you may be laughing at the idea, but it's true. At least the band insists it is. KISS has come out with a concept album — their first — and it's sans suggestive, teeny-bopper lyrics. In fact, only one song on "Music from The Elder" almost fits into the old KISS category, and it *IS* consistent with the story the group is trying to tell.

The album also is the first with new drummer Eric Carr, who took the place of Peter Criss. Band members Gene Simmons, Ace Frehley, Paul Stanley and Carr all participated in writing the lyrics to the album, along with Bob Ezrin, Lou Reed, Anton Fig and Tony Powers. The basic concept of the album is the story of an orphan boy who, through a succession of events, comes to save the world. The album is a series of songs taken from a larger, more complete tale of The Elder, which, according to accompanying publicity, may be told someday on film, in a book, or as a legend from one generation to another.

The story is about an evil world and an order dedicated to doing good, called The Rose, which is to groom someone to save the world. The young orphan boy soon finds he's that someone.

The music in most of the outs still features KISS's heavy bass guitar line, with repetitive riffs. Overall, much of the music is more inventive — as are the lyrics — then those found on past KISS epics such as "I Was Made for Lovin' You" and "Shout It Out Loud."

But here's the killer: KISS uses the American Symphony Orchestra and St. Robert's Choir on some of the cuts. How's that for a turnabout?

When I began to read the publicity about this being a serious concept album, I thought, "Sure it is." But while listening to the album, it began to appear they are, indeed, serious. However, there were a couple of places where I began to wonder again because of the flippant way serious points of two songs were handled.

The better cuts, musically, include:

• "Under the Rose" which, with the addition of St. Robert's Choir, becomes very convincing. The song alternates between heavy bass runs, harpsichord, a heavy metal guitar lead and the chorus.

• "A World Without Heroes" is about the best cut on the album. It's a ballad, complete with strings, brass, violin, good lyrics — all something relatively new to KISS music.

• "Mr. Blackwell" is more in the old KISS school, with some of the band's former defiance, but it ties into the story. It opens with sinister sound effects, then breaks into a heavy rock beat. The background features many interesting tricks and occasionally sounds like some of the soundtrack from "The Exorcist."

The two instances where the album turns flippant include the third cut, "Dark Light" and the last track on the album, which apparently doesn't have a title. "Dark Light" is supposed to explain that there's something wrong with the world and tell us what it is. The song starts off convincingly with a menacing bass and slowly building drums, then bursts into rock guitars. But that impressive start is ruined by the flippant recitation of the last line of each verse. It sounds like a put-on.

The second semi-serious-sounding track features angelic background music and sound effects which give the impression someone is walking up to a high, secluded place. Then a voice asks the caretaker of The Order of The Rose if the boy is still deemed worthy of saving the world.

The response from the caretaker again sounds like a put-on, or like a fight promoter, or perhaps Mork talking to His Fatship on Ork. The caretaker's response goes, "I certainly do. As a matter of fact, I think you're going to like this one. He's got the light in his eyes and the look of a champion — a real champion."

Regardless, I still have to give the band credit for trying to change its image. But it's hard to take anything very seriously from four grown men with painted faces and weird costumes. And there's no indication in the album's publicity that they've changed that part of their act.

KISS takes risk with new album

(Michael Lawson, The Canadian Press)

It may turn out to be the most ambitious marriage of rock and cinema since The Who's Tommy was produced for the screen. Or, it might ultimately become nothing more than the biggest vinyl flop for the greasepaint rockers KISS. The fans will decide.

The Elder (Casablanca Records) is the first concept album by the heavy-duty quartet and their most daring venture to date. But its dramatic nature, built on a potentially viable supernatural storyline, might see the KISS "Army" of followers turning thumbs down on the generally uncharacteristic work.

By the same token, it contains enough interest and acceptable performance to make The Elder accessible to those who previously turned their noses up at the group. Gene Simmons, the bassist whose fire-breathing, blood-drooling bat character has become a rock legend, and guitarist Paul Stanley, KISS' "Starman," are deliberately vague as to where The Elder may lead.

The album has all the trappings of a film soundtrack: the notation "Music From" The Elder; the graphics which appear to be right off a Hollywood set, and a three man cast in the credits, one of whom is Christopher Makepeace, the young Toronto actor who charmed film audiences two years ago in My Bodyguard.

But Simmons and Stanley, while conceding that a full script for The Elder does indeed exist, say the band has not yet decided whether they will carry their project to the screen.

Furthermore, a second batch of Elder material, including dramatic dialogue by actors Makepeace, Antony Parr and Robert Christie, is in the can with possibilities of release still in the air.

Simmons says the original intent was to release The Elder as a two-record set — or at least one LP and one seven-inch single — but the group agreed it would be too much for one package.

What he and Stanley don't say — but undoubtedly is the case — is that further development of The Elder rests on what attention the record garners.

The music is rooted in the gritty, driving rock expected of KISS, but clearly the boys consider this secondary to their theme; the rock, in other words, is given an atmospheric quality and used more to carry the drama than to carry the band's formula. Prime examples are the cuts Mr. Blackwell, whose snappish vocals spell damnation for that nasty character; Escape from the Island, a galloping instrumental in the tradition of cinematic chase sequences, and a track simply entitled I, a shouter that has the story's young character proclaiming invincibility: "I can do anything I want. ... I believe in me."

The story concerns an ageless society of guardian angel-like beings who assume mortal trappings to carry their benevolence and help conquer the world's evil elements. But they need a young champion to help their cause — hence the tracks I, World Without Heroes and Just a Boy.

The album closes midway through the saga, with the elders approving a chosen fair-haired youth. Whether his mission is successful depends on the success of The Elder. The album, that is.

biography

(MUSIC FROM) THE ELDER heralds the entry of KISS into a whole new realm of rock music the band has never before approached. Making musical history as the first KISS concept album, this LP's overall significance outdistances the effect of the individual songs combining to tell a story as simple and age-old as time itself. The album is the powerful result of months of hard work and the combined intense efforts of KISS and producer Bob Ezrin. It also marks the first recorded KISS work with newest member Eric Carr, as well as reunites the band with Ezrin, who produced their 1976 album <u>Destroyer</u>.

While the basic story is that of an orphan boy who, through a succession of events comes to save the world, the greater principles behind the tale relate timelessly to everyone. **(MUSIC FROM) THE ELDER** is a series of songs excerpted from the larger, more complete tale of The Elder. The album weaves together .... more to tell a story of heroism and self-realization. The full

time, an evil is loosed whose sole purpose is ... in every time, and every place, it is the task ...rior...a champion to conquer the evil. ..., the council of the Elder sits at their ...ose. Once again they must combat the evil ...reading throughout the world. ...us, the caretaker, whether the boy be ...ssion to the Order of the Rose...and

...lack of a modern hero to emulate. ... the world. Something is afoot, but ... to ... of the darkness ... ...ucated for the

... he ascends to ... ... in himself ... one...the

... ...nd. No ... ultimate ...les to ...nd, ...albums

... want ... to ... ...ent ...ir ...ul

AUCOIN   PolyGram Records

(Part of the "Elder" press kit)

The Bloodline of The Concept Album

A brief journey through an ocean of fictitious bands, pinball wizards, isolation, suburbia, reflecting ponds, and more

While many music fans associate concept albums with the likes of the Beatles, the Who or Pink Floyd, the art form actually has deeper roots with artists such as Frank Sinatra, Nat "King" Cole and Johnny Cash. For instance, Ol' Blue Eyes' 1958 album "Come Fly with Me" was constructed around a playful travel theme. Though it's difficult to pinpoint music's very first concept album, Woody Guthrie's 1940 album "Dust Bowl Ballads," a collection of songs about the dust storms that ravaged the Great Plains in the '30s, is regarded as one of the earliest albums, if not the first album, tied around a thematic concept.

Of course, the concept album's rich legacy within the rock genre is undeniable. Albums such as the Beatles' "Sgt. Pepper's Lonely Hearts Club Band," the Who's "Tommy" and Pink Floyd's "The Wall" are not only shining examples of wondrous musical adventures, but proof that the decision to stray from the obligatory cycle of predictably formatted songs could reach a wider audience.

At its core, a concept album is part music, part theater and part fantasy — sort of aural comic book. All that's required to participate are headphones and an imagination. In that sense, an album such as "Music from The Elder" was the perfect idea for KISS, a band relying heavily on theatrics, visual elements and fantasy. Unfortunately for KISS and producer Bob Ezrin, listeners were ultimately not receptive.

Indeed, whether it's KISS, Yes or Iron Maiden, the concept album can be a risky proposition. There are simply no guarantees that listeners will become invested in the concept that is being presented. And there are also stereotypes associated with concept albums, with some critics labeling such works as overindulgent pursuits ripe with musical masturbation and lyrical gibberish.

Stereotypes aside, the concept album remains a powerful artistic statement. Even alongside today's digitally dominated and attention-challenged society, the art form is alive and well, evidenced by modern-day efforts by artists such as Mastodon, the Decemberists, Arcade Fire, and Rush.

Following is a brief selection of rock concept albums, offering a small taste of the complete concept album picture. Further examination is always recommended. And maybe, just maybe a concept album about some rotten to the core evil character, a wisdom-toting secret society and a boy's quest for self-discovery wasn't far-fetched after all?

Artist: The Mothers Of Invention
Album: "Freak Out!"
Year: 1966
Concept: Often cited as one of rock's first concept albums, "Freak Out!" is an overview of frontman Frank Zappa's satirical perception of American pop culture, cloaked in psychedelic guitars, brash political commentary and avant-garde musicality. "Freak Out!" is also notable for being one of rock's first double albums.
Peak Chart Position: No. 130
RIAA Certification: N/A

Artist: The Beatles
Album: "Sgt. Pepper's Lonely Hearts Club Band"
Year: 1967
Concept: The Beatles take on four "alter-egos" under the guise of a fictitious band in a bid to vent their musical freedom and creative impulses. The eponymous opening track introduces the band at a mock concert, with the following songs presented as if they were performed by the group. Billy Shears is the leader of the band. Score one for Ringo Starr.
Peak Chart Position: No. 1
RIAA Certification: 11x platinum

Artist: The Kinks
Album: "The Kinks Are The Village Green Preservation Society"
Year: 1968
Concept: This collection of songs laments the passing of old-fashioned English traditions. Changing times lead to nostalgia, resulting in a wide range of questions and thoughts about lost friends, dreamy escapes and mass

consumerism. All of this radiating from the mind of Ray Davies, who wrote all the songs on the album.

Peak Chart Position: N/A

RIAA Certification: N/A

Artist: The Who
Album: "Tommy"

Year: 1969

Concept: A full rock opera about a traumatized child, Tommy, who is blind, deaf and mute. After entering a semi-catatonic state, the boy finds a path to enlightenment through his subconscious. As years pass, he morphs into a young man who can interpret physical sensations as music. And he sure played a mean pinball.

Peak Chart Position: No. 4

RIAA Certification: 2x platinum

Artist: David Bowie
Album: "The Rise And Fall Of Ziggy Stardust And The Spiders From Mars"

Year: 1972

Concept: Ziggy Stardust is an alien attempting to present humanity with a message of peace and love in the last five years of existence. Ziggy Stardust is also the definitive rock star complete with a voracious appetite for sex and drugs. Despite his positive message, he ends up destroying himself through the fanaticism he creates.

Peak Chart Position: No. 75

RIAA Certification: Gold

Artist: Yes
Album: "Tales From Topographic Oceans"

Year: 1974

Concept: Clocking in at more than 80 minutes, this bombastic double LP features one marathon song per actual side. The concept is based upon Shastric scriptures, exploring the themes of truth, knowledge, culture, and freedom. It all proved to be too heady for "Rolling Stone," which labeled it as "psychedelic doodling."

Peak Chart Position: No. 6

RIAA Certification: Gold

Artist: Pink Floyd
Album: "The Wall"
Year: 1979
Concept: A double album encapsulating themes of abandonment and isolation. The main character, Pink, loses his father, and grapples with ridicule and abuse from schoolteachers, his mother, and the dissolution of his marriage. Eventually, he shields himself behind a metaphorical wall. Arguably, the most successful concept album ever, "The Wall" is the third best-selling album of all time in the United States.
Peak Chart Position: No. 1
RIAA Certification: 23x platinum

Artist: Iron Maiden
Album: "Seventh Son Of A Seventh Son"
Year: 1988
Concept: Loosely based on a fantasy novel by Orson Scott Card and European folklore, the storyline revolves around a boy who possesses special gifts such as telepathy and clairvoyance. "It's about good and evil, heaven and hell, but isn't every Iron Maiden record?" once quipped frontman Bruce Dickinson.
Peak Chart Position: No. 12
RIAA Certification: Gold

Artist: Queensrÿche
Album: "Operation: Mindcrime"
Year: 1988
Concept: The protagonist, Nikki, becomes a puppet under a secret revolutionary organization run by the nefarious Dr. X. While in a psychiatric hospital, Nikki watches TV reports of political assassinations that suddenly bring back floods of memories. Nikki is ultimately manipulated by Dr. X, but after he meets prostitute-turned-nun named Sister Mary, he begins to question his actions.
Peak Chart Position: No. 50
RIAA Certification: Platinum

Artist: W.A.S.P.
Album: "The Crimson Idol"
Year: 1993
Concept: "The Crimson Idol" revolves around Jonathan, a runaway teenager who steals a crimson guitar and dreams of rock stardom. In a case of "be careful for what you wish for," in accomplishing his goal Jonathan finds stardom isn't everything as advertised. After a pre-concert phone call to his parents turned bad, he proceeds to hang himself by the strings of his guitar.
Peak Chart Position: N/A
RIAA Certification: N/A

Artist: Green Day
Album: "American Idiot"
Year: 2004
Concept: Three lifelong friends, including the story's main character, Jesus of Suburbia, must choose between their dreams and the comfort of suburban lifestyle. Themes of disillusionment, heartbreak and sarcastic wit pervade this collection of songs that essentially outline a quest to find meaning in a post Sept. 11 world. "American Idiot" won a Grammy for Best Rock Album in 2005.
Peak Chart Position: No. 1
RIAA Certification: 6x platinum

Artist: Judas Priest
Album: Nostradamus
Year: 2008
Concept: Years in the making, Judas Priest's first (and probably final) attempt at constructing a concept album was created around the prophecies, and life and times, of 16th century writer/seer Michel de Nostredame (Nostradamus). Like the author the work represented, Priest's album — complete with orchestration and symphonic interludes — was misinterpreted and caused confusion to many listeners.
Peak Chart Position: No. 11
RIAA Certification: N/A

Artist: Arcade Fire
Album: "The Suburbs"
Year: 2010
Concept: Crafted by bandleader Win Butler, this song cycle reflects upon the suburban landscape in which he grew up, a place where he once dreamed of emancipation and rebellion. Upon returning home as an adult, he reexamines his upbringing and ideals. As such, is suburbia really a place to escape from or a path to enlightenment? "The Suburbs" won an Album Of The Year Grammy in 2011.
Peak Chart Position: No. 1
RIAA Certification: Gold

Artist: Steve Vai
Album: "The Story of Light"
Year: 2012
Concept: The second in a series of concept albums, Vai takes listeners down a spiritual path across 12 lush compositions. "The Story Of Light" is centered upon the idea of a "reflecting pond," a safe haven where people can examine different aspects of their personalities, leading to ultimate self-discovery. Not the plotline you'd expect from an album written by a guitar virtuoso, huh?
Peak Chart Position: No. 78
RIAA Certification: N/A

Artist: Dream Theater
Album: "The Astonishing"
Year: 2016
No strangers to concept albums, Dream Theater's progressive tale for "The Astonishing" is set in a dystopian future United States and follows the Ravenskill Rebel Militia in their efforts to defy the Great Northern Empire of the Americas through the magical power of ... you guessed it, music. According to the band, the concept was inspired by contemporary fantasy and science-fiction franchises such as "Game Of Thrones," as well as guitarist John Petrucci's observations on the prevalence of technological automation in modern-day society. Ever ambitious, Dream Theater performed the new album in its entirety during their 2016 worldwide tour, and even contracted the services of a production company to assist with the thematic presentation. With additional elements such as the band building a

stand-alone album website and incorporating promotional tools such as fan mailings lists and an animated album trailer, "The Astonishing" perhaps offers KISS fans a glimpse as to what could have been for "The Elder" in another time and place.

Peak Chart Position: No. 11
RIAA Certification: N/A

They Said What? "The Elder" Quote Book

Who said what about "Music From The Elder" and when...

What exactly is there to say about "Music from The Elder"? As it turns out, quite enough for a book! Alongside the fresh perspective offered within these pages, we thought it'd only be appropriate to look back at what has already been said about the album. Of course, the following quotes are but a tantalizing taste of what the band and other key individuals have said about the project over the past three decades.

Just how did "The Elder" evolve from a project that was originally slated to be a "life's work" in 1981 to something of a "nightmare"? We're not sure either but read on.

"'Music from The Elder' heralds the entry of KISS into a whole new realm of rock music the band has never before approached. Making musical history as the first KISS concept album, this LP's overall significance outdistances the effect of the individual songs combining to tell a story as simple and age-old as time itself. The album is the powerful result of months of hard work and the combined intense efforts of KISS and producer Bob Ezrin." — "Music from The Elder" biography (PolyGram Records, 1981)

"In our story, the boy laments the lack of a modern hero to emulate. He becomes aware of a dark light shining on the world. Something is afoot, but he doesn't know what it is. There is no one to guide us out of the darkness into the light. But unknown to him, he is being groomed and educated for the task. The first glimmer of truth begins to dawn on the boy as he ascends to the Order of the Rose. Our hero learns that he must first believe in himself so that he can live up to his destiny. He realizes that he is the one ... the only one. The odyssey begins." — "Music from The Elder" biography (PolyGram Records, 1981)

"They're scratching their heads over this record at PolyGram. They're not sure why we didn't just do another 'Dynasty.' And I can't say I blame them. I don't know if I'd be able to sit back and be objective about one of my biggest acts when there's a divergence from a tried and true formula. But the [KISS] formula is no longer true. It's tried — and it's trying — but it's not working anymore. If we'd just made a typical KISS album with a typical KISS cover, it wouldn't even have sustained a slumping level of interest; it would have really finished the whole career off." — Bob Ezrin ("Billboard," 1981)

"We all agreed that if we'd just stuck with the fans we have now, we would have kept going down. It's the law of diminishing returns. You have to broaden your approach so you can attract people of all ages. We want to satisfy buyers from 8 to 45. Maybe that's biting off a little much, but I don't think so. And the problem was that children who loved KISS five years ago are not children today and don't want to be handed kiddie stuff — and they assume that's what KISS still stands for." — Bob Ezrin ("Billboard," 1981)

"It's certainly a shock when you first put it on. It's kind of dreamy and a little softer than most people expect from KISS. The harmonies and different vocal sounds on this record are going to throw a lot of people for a loop." — Bob Ezrin ("Billboard," 1981)

"I like a style of construction where songs are strung together and there are special effects and sounds and dialog and certain things that just aren't part of a straight 10-song presentation." — Bob Ezrin ("Billboard," 1981)

"KISS has always been identified as a sinister force. There were occasional record burnings and a backlash in the South. The guys to a certain extent took that personally. They always felt they were no more negative than a Marvel comic. They felt they were vaudeville in rock 'n' roll form." — Bob Ezrin ("Billboard," 1981)

"I felt this move was important too because I have children of my own and I would like to do records that are anti-drug, anti-violence and not pushing nihilism and anarchy. I think they're hearing far too much of that as it is." — Bob Ezrin ("Billboard," 1981)

"We're going to make a life's work out of it ... if a film is made there might be a soundtrack, which would take it as far as three albums. But any further than that I think is too much." — Bob Ezrin ("Billboard," 1981)

"We sat around for six to eight hours a day, and we would talk and take notes before we even thought about picking up an instrument. Once we had the story written we mapped out the parts, and each person took a part. It was a whole different way of working. We were also looser as to who played what instruments. ... What happened in this LP, whoever fit the feel better, or whoever seemed more sympathetic to what the song was about, was the person who played it." — Paul Stanley ("Billboard," 1982)

"At this point we have thrown [everything] to the wind. '[A] World Without Heroes,' is not the kind of song you would expect Gene Simmons to sing. But why put restrictions on ourselves? That can only hurt us." — Paul Stanley ("Billboard," 1982)

"People are working on [the film] right now. Our idea was to do a musical concept — a big fantasy piece. We were just telling the story, and the characters in the film would sing the songs." — Paul Stanley (print interview, 1982)

"'The Elder' started as a story first. And then we decided to do another record with Bob Ezrin because we had already done one in 1976. Then everyone got very excited about the story and we decided to sit down and write a collection of songs that would basically outline the whole story. And thus, was born [mimics narrator style voice] the saga of 'The Elder.'" — Gene Simmons ("Flo And Eddie," 1982)

"The funny thing that's happening now is we're getting reviews on 'The Elder' about brilliance. You know all of the sudden, we've grown brains." — Paul Stanley ("Flo And Eddie," 1982)

"We never sat around and took orders from other people. So, it's a two-edged sword. So, you can't necessarily say that one person said that it was time to do it. I know that the original idea for 'The Elder' was Gene's, and maybe that wasn't the right thing to do. Who knows? It's hatched and then it's done and that's it. And I don't apologize for it." — Paul Stanley ("Hit Parader," 1982)

"It's not the entire project. The rest is yet to come. The project is being negotiated to be turned into a film of some sort, having nothing to do with the band. Our job in it would not be to act, the band is merely telling the story." — Paul Stanley ("Hit Parader," 1982)

"It is undoubtedly a mature step in the right direction for these cartoon princes of power-pop. I've got to admit on first hearing what did actually capture my ear sounded a little too twee, if not wimp-like, coming from the most basic barons of the banal. In fact, it was Ross [Halfin] who kicked off the interview when he announced that he thought the album sounded like a cross between Excalibur and a male version of the Wizard of Oz." — Pete Makowski (Sounds, 1982)

"Basically, I guess Gene came up with this idea, so I've got to give him the credit or the blame. We did the record and I guess we figured that, if there was time, we would probably do a film. I didn't really think that we would be involved with the film as much as the album was gonna kind of serve as a guideline. And we didn't have the time or the patience. Besides it's really hard to do a film from a Holiday Inn and that's usually where we are anyway." — Paul Stanley responding to a question about what happened to "The Elder" film ("The Metal Shop: KISS Special," 1984)

"Lou [Reed] was so into the project, when we called him and explained it over the phone to him, he said, 'I'll get back to you in an hour.' And he called back an hour later with good basic lyrics to 'Mr. Blackwell,' '[A] World Without Heroes' and a lot of stuff that hasn't been used yet." — Paul Stanley ("KISS Still on Fire," 1988, original source unknown)

"I personally wasn't happy with 'The Elder' — the drum sound, the producer, a lot of things. I have the original tracks that were cut and Ezrin left out half the guitar work in the mixing stages! I recorded the solos in my studio and half of them never made it. Also, a lot of the power chords on certain songs were missing, they had a really thick sound. I spent hours and hours getting it right, and he didn't even have the courtesy to call me! I think he got so involved with the concept that he lost sight of the music and I haven't spoken to him since." Ace Frehley ("KISS Still on Fire," 1988, original source unknown)

"'The Elder' wasn't a typical mainstream KISS album. It was a very cerebral piece of work, but I'm not apologizing for anything we've done. Everything has been valid and will continue to be so. I guess 'The Elder' arose from some of the ideas you get when you are young. There comes a time in your life when you feel a need to take up the sword and avenge wrongs. You feel very pure-hearted." — Gene Simmons ("KISS Still on Fire," 1988, original source unknown)

"I don't think ['The Elder'] is any more profound than 'Rock and Roll All Night,' it's common sense. We're not here to try and enlighten the world, we're still here very much basically on a street level. Only this time we've got an orchestra with us!" — Paul Stanley ("KISS Still on Fire," 1988, original source unknown)

"We really did this album for ourselves. After 15 or 16 albums you want to make an important album every time out, not just put one out for Christmas, that's not the point of what we're trying to do." — Gene Simmons ("KISS Still on Fire," 1988, original source unknown)

"He hypnotized us. We lost sight of what we really are. I'm just a heavy metal guitarist, that's my forte, and I don't think 'The Elder' is indicative of KISS. I don't hate the album, but I'm not crazy about it either." — Ace Frehley ("KISS Still on Fire," 1988, original source unknown)

"We didn't want to stay in New York all the time because it wasn't fair to Bob. So, we would go up to Canada for some tracks, back to New York to do some more, and towards the end we even separated and went into different studios and were simultaneously working. Ace would call me and say, 'Hey, listen to this solo,' and he would play me the solo over the phone. It was a very different way of working." — Paul Stanley ("KISS Still on Fire," 1988, original source unknown)

"['The Elder'] is actually a very, very good album. It's very, very different than anything else that KISS has ever done. I know a lot of people are shocked by it, so was I. But it's a great album. There's a lot of good material on it." — Eric Carr (radio interview with Eddie Trunk, 1988)

"'The Elder,' when it first came out and for a long time, was not a very popular album with the fans because it was such a different kind of thing for us. What's really weird is that in the last year or two all a sudden now there's been a lot of interest in the album again. I get a lot of fan mail, the fans come over and they're always talking about 'The Elder' now. It's like, 'Where did this come from?' So, I guess people are kind of rediscovering it. [Since] it's an older album [and] it's not what's happening now, you can put it on and listen to it and say, 'Whoa, this is really cool,' and not worry about what the direction of the band was going to be." — Eric Carr (radio interview, 1989)

Gene Simmons: "It was not made after a movie. The idea was based on a short ..."

Paul Stanley: "Hallucination." (Laughs)

Gene Simmons: "... a short treatment of a script and then we were all sort of in the Twilight Zone."

Paul Stanley: "And then we woke up. 'We did what??'"

Gene Simmons: "That's the only record out of all the records that has never gone gold. And it's the only record where we can truly look back and say, 'We did that one, not for ourselves, not for the fans, but for the critics,' which is why it's so warped."

Paul Stanley: "You never look worse than when you're trying to impress people with how smart you are. Then you really look like an ass. Actually, you're not the only person who thinks that's a great album. There's five other people with you."

Gene Simmons: "It's not that it's good or bad. Whatever problems there are of the record is really that it's just not KISS."

Paul Stanley: "It's not a bad album."

Gene Simmons: "It sounds like a bad Genesis record or something."

— Gene Simmons and Paul Stanley respond to a question regarding "The Elder" ("Rockline," 1992)

"I wasn't happy with 'The Elder.' The basic bottom line concept of 'The Elder' was a mistake. ... The story was [Gene's] idea. But the idea of doing a concept album was my idea — changing the makeup and doing all that stuff — I was wrong. We shouldn't have attempted to do that. I still think it was a great story. I uncovered our notes that he, Gene and I, did on the story of 'The Elder,' and it's like a 40-page mini film script. It would have worked great as a movie, but it wasn't as an album. It wasn't a great idea. We left Ace behind somewhere there. He wasn't happy about the whole idea." — Bob Ezrin ("KISSed," 1992)

"I don't think there was as much stuff [taken out] as [Ace] thinks. He may remember more solos than we actually did. But we tried to keep [what we could]. And it wasn't only Ace's stuff, all of us did more than we needed, and we took away that stuff." — Bob Ezrin ("KISS Fan Club Japan," 1992)

"It's not a 'KISS' album. It's a bunch of guys trying to deny who they are and create something else." — Paul Stanley (Miami Herald, 10/30/92)

"We started recording the album using the songs we had written before we called Bob, and in the middle of the whole thing Bob came to us and said,

'This isn't right — we have to do a concept album.' And our jaws dropped."
— Paul Stanley ("KISStory," 1995)

"We put all or eggs in Bob Ezrin's basket, but as we later found out, this Bob wasn't the Bob we knew — he was having a lot of personal problems at that point." — Gene Simmons ("KISStory," 1995)

"Gene came up with the concept he called 'The Elder,' and Bob and Bill Aucoin both thought it was great. I can remember Ace being completely thrown by the whole idea. He was very much against doing a concept album. The rest of us figured that Bob was gonna save us — that he would make it work." — Paul Stanley ("KISStory," 1995)

"We were convinced that this album was our masterpiece. We sat there and played the entire record from beginning to end, and the entire PolyGram staff was absolutely shocked." — Gene Simmons ("KISStory," 1995)

"We don't argue with anyone who says 'The Elder' is a really good album. Our only point of contention is that it's not a really good KISS album." — Paul Stanley ("KISStory," 1995)

"Eric was not happy with the record. He was clear from the beginning that it didn't sound like the KISS he knew. We thought it was just him being inexperienced and amateurish — like, 'What does he know?' That sort of thing." — Gene Simmons ("KISStory," 1995)

"That's my least-favorite album. I've tried to forget about that record. (Laughs) There was a lot of solos that I had performed that were edited out and there was nothing put in its place. They just decided it was too much solo work." — Ace Frehley (interview for Swedish media, 1995)

"I like the album. It's always interesting to me if somebody says, 'Here's a guitar and play these songs or you're dead.' I'd probably be dead. I can't remember any of that music; it was real foreign to us. It was us pushing ourselves to be difference. Once in a while we'd play some of that stuff and never make it four or five bars into it." — Paul Stanley ("Goldmine," Ken Sharp, 1996)

"I go on record saying it's not a great KISS record, but I think it's a really great record. It's a really good album but I don't think it's a really good KISS album." Paul Stanley ("Goldmine," Ken Sharp, 1996)

"Slowly, the story and the album's theme began to dribble out: It was to be a tale of a young boy who confronts good and evil, wanders through darkness and forests, and, in the end, finds his way through perseverance and self-reliance. There was a lot of mumbo jumbo in the Kahlil Gibran leitmotif about 'goodness and knowledge,' 'sacred duty,' and 'conquering evil' floating around in the original script. There were characters called Morpheus, the Boy, and a kind of secret society called the Order of the Rose. The deep secrecy was designed to imbue the album with a mystical quality; no one in KISS gave any interviews or even mentioned the project to the press during production." — C.K. Lendt ("KISS and Sell," 1997)

"We never intended to release 'The Elder' on CD, but the fans wanted it so we finally allowed [the record company] to release it." — Eric Carr ("Black Diamond," Dale Sherman, 1997)

"Paul may be pissed off that I said, this, but it's OK, it's a retrospective and it doesn't matter. I was so strongly against what we were going to do that I had a meeting with Bill Aucoin, Paul and Gene. I was in the band less than a year, and I'm feeling that strongly that we were making a mistake. I pointed out, 'We should not cut our hair, we shouldn't stop wearing the platforms, we shouldn't be doing this album. We've got to go out and rock.'" — Eric Carr ("Black Diamond," Dale Sherman, 1997)

"The recording of 'The Elder' ... the way the whole thing was done — it was not a pleasant experience. It's a great album. The problem was that I think it turned out exactly the way we wanted it to. That's the problem with it — it's too good and too different." — Eric Carr ("Black Diamond," Dale Sherman, 1997)

"When we started to think about doing another KISS album, no one was very much into it and we came up with an idea hopefully that would help us and would get us through this problem. And the idea was to do a concept album. That concept album turned out to be 'The Elder.' Now 'The Elder' was done helter-skelter, it was really a rough [album] to do. It was not easy in any respects, the songs were hard to write, no one was in the mood to do it. Bob was frustrated by it. Both Gene and Paul were [frustrated too]. Ace really didn't want to do it and he didn't want to work with Bob. He had had an argument over something that had happened on the 'Destroyer' album, so Bob was not his favorite producer at that point. We started off with the album and dragged ourselves through it and we finally finished it. And I must say that it's certainly a unique album, but most people don't consider it a KISS album. We delivered it to the record label and the record label hated it. In fact, when we first played it for them, they just said, 'Look it, why don't we can this album and do another album?' Well the thought of that was definitely not going to happen. It was hard enough just to get this album done. And that was really kind of the beginning of the end both with me and KISS and for a number of things." — Bill Aucoin ("13 Classic KISS Stories," 1999)

"[It's] a terrible KISS album. Stanley and I were in this dinky little studio — not even 8-track studio — some small town north of Ontario. We went in there and we started writing and we played everything. I played drums, he played guitar, and we came up with 'I am just a boy.' It was so emotional and big and stirring and melodramatic. And we should have been shot dead right there... before we went any further. I got this concept, sorry I was into concepts, and by then everybody had been touting all of my so-called concept work — I'd done all of these concept records — they really weren't in a story sense 'concept' records, they were just built around an idea that I wanted to put forward. Or a vision I had for where I though a band would go or a sense that I thought a show should have. Not really a beginning-to-end story concept. This was one where there was really a story. And of course, I caught these guys at a fairly vulnerable point in their career where they were searching for something and they needed a breakthrough. They wanted to get out of the make-up. Gene was toying with movies and Paul always had aspirations to something higher than rock. I guess we all just started drinking our own bathwater." — Bob Ezrin (KISS Online, 2000)

"We didn't sit down and say, 'Oh God, we have to do 'Destroyer.' We sat down and said the band wants to make a change and do something important and do something different. They didn't start out wanting to do a project like this. I talked them into it — I take full responsibility. But then of course, it wasn't like I was talking to a reluctant audience. They jumped in with both feet. Gene loved the idea of writing a story, and to this day I think the story of 'The Elder' is a great one. You don't really get it off the album, but we have a script that Gene and I wrote for this concept called 'The Elder' that I thought, and still do think, is a really cool weird kind of science-fiction movie. It would have been a better movie than it was a record. Much better..." — Bob Ezrin (KISS Online, 2000)

"They you had all these other guys coming in and people who were friends of the band. It was at a time when the band was in upheaval. It was certainly not at one of the better periods of my life. I was out of my mind and at that stage both personally and artistically sort of 'at sea.' We were really trying hard, and you can hear it. We were over-trying, and we just didn't have the material. We made a couple of valiant attempts, and there's one or two ideas in there that are worthwhile looking at, but for the most part it was really just a contrived album." — Bob Ezrin (KISS Online, 2000)

"I think the experience disheartened Ace. Ace was not into this, he thought it was bullshit. And he was right — he was totally right. But in the same way it wasn't a great time for me personally it wasn't a very good time for him either, and people weren't taking him very seriously. I think that upset him too... There was this magical confluence of creativity and talent, and all that stuff, on the making of 'Destroyer;' there was an absolute absence of that sort of confluence on the 'The Elder.' Everything was work. Everything was hard. It was really hard, and I just didn't do a very good job. Bottom line." — Bob Ezrin (KISS Online, 2000)

"The band actually liked it. We [had] talked ourselves into liking it. The band were lucky they weren't with me when I took it in for the playback. It was like the end Act 1, Scene 1 of 'Springtime for Hitler' in 'The Producers' where they pan the audience and everyone's sitting there with their mouths agape like, "Oooh!' It was unbelievable. People were trying to be polite, but they couldn't believe that this was actually a KISS album and I don't blame them." — Bob Ezrin (KISS Online, 2000)

"It was something that they had to go through." — Bob Ezrin (KISS Online, 2000)

"From those initial meetings in Hollywood, I came up with the idea for 'The Elder.' I wasn't sure whether it would be a record or a movie. All I knew, at first, was a line that stuck in my mind: 'When the earth was young, they were already old.' I conceived of a race of immortal beings, energy-based beings, a take-off of Marvel's Watcher. These beings were more observers than participants. They didn't interfere with human choice, and as a result people were ultimately responsible for their own deeds, good and bad. The

more I worked on it, the more I thought this would be a strong movie pitch."
— Gene Simmons ("KISS & Makeup," 2001)

"This was the first KISS project where someone — in this case, Bob Ezrin — talked the band members into the notion that credibility and respect from critics are as important as the love of the fans. As a result, it was a very serious record for us." — Gene Simmons ("KISS & Makeup," 2001)

"A number of other guitar players played because Ace just didn't show up." — Gene Simmons on "The Elder" ("KISS & Makeup," 2001)

"Unfortunately, all the work that went into 'The Elder' seemed to be for nothing. We had a record that, for the first time, bombed so badly it didn't even go gold. We truly were at a crossroads." — Gene Simmons ("KISS & Makeup," 2001)

"They were at a stage in their career, the lineup had changed of the band and Peter had left. And we got together, and we decided that we would come up with a new idea. At the time we were convinced that what KISS needed was a really 'classy' record... I thought this album was brilliant — I just thought this was a miraculous piece of work. I was abusing drugs and I was in bad shape, and I think my judgment was, to say the least, impaired. But we got through the damn thing, somehow, we got through it. I had the happy task of playing it for the record company. I took it in to PolyGram and at the end of the album playback you had just this array of guys standing there like [shows mouth agape, confused and bewildered expression]. And I'm going, 'Yeah! What do you think!? Great, huh!?' We should have been killed, right then and there. And that probably would have protected humankind from what we unleashed on them." — Bob Ezrin ("Beyond the Makeup," 2001)

"Though we did 'The Elder' at Ace's house he didn't play an active role in the creating the concept or the writing of the material. He didn't like the idea. He wanted the band to be more basic rock and get away from this airy-fairy crap, and he was totally right. Totally right!" — Bob Ezrin ("Beyond the Makeup," 2001)

"As far as 'I,' it is indeed Allan Schwartzberg on the drums. Allan was a well-known session player in NYC and Bob Ezrin our producer at the time felt Eric was not playing the sound with the feel that Bob felt it needed. One of the rules we have always tried to adhere to when we work with Bob is to give him final say. It avoids ongoing, endless and sometimes unresolved issues. Although sometimes someone may not like the outcome it's ultimately, I believe, for the best." — Paul Stanley ("Paul Speaks," KISS Online, 2002)

"This was a very awkward period for the band, and we weren't entirely sure how long we should keep doing the same look. Should we progress? Should we not? Somewhere along the line I have to take the blame. I had this brilliant idea, I thought, 'We should do a concept record. We should call it "The Elder."' And I sat down and wrote a story at the Beverly Hills Hotel — in the middle of Hollywood, of course — while I was seeing my new girlfriend at the time, who was also a singer, from sort of the disco world. And that wasn't making me more popular with the fans, it was making me less popular. But I was convinced that this would give us credibility and huge sales. The Who had 'Tommy'; we should have 'The Elder.' And Bob Ezrin became my co-conspirator.

He fell into the trap just as deeply as I did. And he actually believed this was the genius of all genius ideas and he would get ... Christopher Makepeace and Canadian actors and symphony orchestras. And we would actually get together at Ace's house and start planning this masterpiece. And that's what we actually thought. We thought, "Let's take a breather from the fans and let's do one for the critics. And let's prove to them that we were actually more than just makeup and rock and roll songs. And we fell right into that trap.

And I was responsible more than anybody in the band. I was convinced — and nobody can talk me out of it — that this was gonna be the huge, you know, sort of McCartney and 'Sgt. Pepper,' Gene and 'The Elder.'" — Gene Simmons, "KISSology Vol. 2" (2007)

"Lots of things happened. Along the way, Ace Frehley refused to show up in Toronto where it was being recorded. He insisted on having the 24 tracks mailed down to him so he could do his solos from home. [He] would not leave home. Eric Carr sometimes liked the material, sometimes not, but insisted on trying to push for a more rock and roll feel. At the end of the day, we had very few places to look to. And sometimes when Paul and I looked at each other, you just sort of shrug your shoulders, kind of going, 'It's the right thing to do, right?' And you're looking for somebody else to just agree with you to convince you that it was the right thing. 'The Elder,' I'll give it an A for effort. And that's about it." — Gene Simmons, "KISSology Vol. 2" (2007)

"The problem with the band around the time of 'The Elder' was that we were more concerned with how our peers viewed us than with how our fans viewed us. We had lost touch with the people who made us what we were and were more intent on making sure that the critics and other musicians saw the validity and the credibility of what we were doing. We were intent on showing them that we weren't just a gimmick; we were these brilliant deep-thinking musicians. The problem with doing something like that is that when people don't like you, they will continue not to like you. And the people who did like you will not like you. So, you wind up with nothing. We gave it our all. And honestly, the fact that Ace didn't want to be a part of it was partially because of his own personal problems. But he was actually right. It was the wrong thing to be doing." — Paul Stanley, "KISSology Vol. 2" (2007)

"We were way off course and unfortunately we found ourselves in Toronto working with Bob Ezrin and seeing him as the captain of the ship. And lo and behold, the captain was not capable of navigating the waters. We reached a point where he wasn't even coming to the studio so now, we were really in trouble. We're in a situation creating an album where we're not really clear on what it should be or how it's going to shape up. And the person who we're counting on to help us is not coming to the studio. It was a nightmare. We ultimately wound up with two studios going pretty much around the clock. While Gene might be in one, I might be in the other, getting tracks done to finish up this folly that ultimately when we played [it] for the record company, they were silent and not because they thought it was brilliant." — Paul Stanley, "KISSology Vol. 2" (2007)

"Nobody knew that we were on the Titanic until we actually had water come up to our nostrils. Till the very end, even on the day that it was being released, we thought this was the classic of all time. 'Paul's hand on the cover, knocking the door. When you open it, the band's pictures are not even on the album. Just seats. We're too big to have our photos in. We're big, we're icons. This is a concept record, it's about 'The Elder' ... it was all this sort of heir of importance. It certainly wasn't rock and roll. There may have been a moment or two, a good song here and there, but as an album it was misguided. And to this day — [it] shows you the love and affection the fans have — so help me God, we get emails that say, 'You guys should do an all 'Elder' show. Do a whole tour and just play 'The Elder' from beginning to end because it's such a classic.'" — Gene Simmons, "KISSology Vol. 2" (2007)

"It was sobering for us. You have to understand that people talk about preparing for the end. Sometimes you don't get any warning that the end is coming. So, you literally go from selling out arenas to not being able to sell out a theater. It's such a shock; it takes the wind right out of you. It's like nothing I've ever experienced, where you go from being, literally, on top of the world to being over. To be honest, I think part of the look change was not a result of anything except we wanted to cut our hair. We didn't want to be long-haired rock and roll musicians anymore. We lost the essence of what we were. We were now very wealthy, very comfortable, and were forsaking everything that put us where we were. And it wasn't, 'Let's have a new look.' It was, 'We're going to have to have a new look because we don't want to look like this anymore.'

One thing became clear to me around the time of 'The Elder' and that was how many vultures were circling to see us die. How many critics were waiting to finally see the death knell and celebrating it joyously. If I was lucky enough to get an interview, people had the audacity to ask me what it felt like to be on a sinking ship. There was a tremendous amount of joy and vindication of sorts, for these critics, that it was finally going to end. And it was then that, clearly for myself, I made the decision: Nobody is going to tell me when this is over. I will decide when it's over. And if it kills me, I am going to make sure this comes back full force because I'm going to rub it in the face of all these people because, once again, I'm going to show them they have no power over me and they have no power over real rock and roll." — Paul Stanley, "KISSology Vol. 2" (2007)

"The least favorite album, I can tell you right off the bat, was 'The Elder.' I told Paul and Gene at the beginning of that project, 'It's time to do a heavy record, not some concept album about some weirdo.' (Laughs) Who was that guy anyway? I remember seeing some kind of graphic of some guy with a hood on, some old guy, like some medieval kind of dude. ... They edited out a lot of the solos that I did but I probably went over the top with them." — Ace Frehley (interview with Eddie Trunk, 2009)

"Following the dismal reception of their 1981 concept album 'Music From The Elder,' KISS saw their already waning popularity plummet, and Glickman/Marks made enough of a case against Bill Aucoin that KISS finally edged him out of the picture in the spring of 1982, ending a very successful nine-year relationship." — Larry Harris ("And Party Every Day: The Inside Story of Casablanca Records," 2009)

"We all bought into Stonehenge and truly thought we were making a masterpiece, but we weren't — we were masturbating. A bloated, overblown, pompous piece of pap. Favorite track: 'I' — because that's the last one and the album's over." — Paul Stanley ("The Sun," 2010)

"Well, the boys came to me with a bunch of really heavy demos, initially. They wanted to make a very intense record to combat the criticism of the last couple of albums. I had just made 'The Wall,' and I convinced them to scrap those demos and do something different. So 'The Elder' was a victim of 'The Wall' and our mutual desire to do something "important," which really was antithetical to what KISS was about. KISS was never pretentious or precious and never took themselves seriously. They were always about fun, sex and power and were always, in effect, horror cartoon characters, so to suddenly do a concept album, something of "consequence," was an anti-KISS idea. It was a flawed concept from the beginning." — Bob Ezrin ("Fangoria," 2010)

"At the time, we were all looking for bigger, better things, and Gene — more so than Paul — jumped on the concept of doing 'The Elder.' I'm not really sure if he came in with it or we developed it together, but we both evolved a script for a little film to accompany it. We thought it would be the beginning of multiple projects to go under 'The Elder' banner. We were wrong, of course. But Paul and Gene were really into it, and they put their all into it. They both had to step out of their personas, and it was really bold of them to do that. They were attracted to the classic rock, almost Beatles-esque, complex structure of the album. They were seduced by that. We were all trying to be artistes. It was a huge mistake." — Bob Ezrin ("Fangoria," 2010)

"People dwell on that [Ace's relationship with Bob during the recording of *Destroyer*], but it's not entirely true. I loved Ace. It's just that *Destroyer* was a big project. It was ambitious and grandiose and had to be delivered on a finite budget in a very finite time frame. Gene and Paul were, as always, totally disciplined, but Ace was a free spirit and, like his persona suggests, a real space cadet. Sometimes we couldn't find him when we were in studio and had to record, so we had to proceed with Dick Wagner playing his parts.

But when he did play on the album, he was fantastic." — Bob Ezrin ("Fangoria," 2010)

"Here was this larger-than-life fantasy/rock record, filled with myth and violence and passion, and I believe some fans liked it. Some critics liked it too, which rarely happened with KISS. But most fans couldn't grasp it and they felt left behind, isolated." — Bob Ezrin ("Fangoria," 2010)

"There are some great moments in there, for sure, and some classics buried in the mix. But on the whole, it's way too self-indulgent and way too overproduced. It's also not fully realized. There's not enough material, and the story is not fleshed out. It's an interesting failure, I think." — Bob Ezrin ("Fangoria," 2010)

"I'm thinking about releasing some old jam sessions and songs that nobody's ever heard ... I haven't even heard in a long time. Like I said, I have over 100 reels of two-inch tape from my studio in Connecticut that I had in the late '70s and early '80s. ... There's unreleased solos that I did on [the album] ... what was my least-favorite album ... 'The Elder.' A lot of my stuff was edited out of that record, but I have a lot of the original solos. So that may be something interesting to KISS fans." — Ace Frehley ("Talking Metal," 2011)

"I thought it was great. I was so proud of it. All the sound effects, crazy production and big songs. And the great ballad, 'A World Without Heroes,' and the concept, the artwork, the recording of the voiceovers and all that stuff that we had done to put this thing together. When it came time to deliver it to the record company, I was elected to go play it for the record company, without the band. At the time, I thought it was an honor. I realized very soon afterwards ... they were hiding." — Bob Ezrin ("The Eric Carr Story," Greg Prato," 2011)

"Ezrin has willingly taken considerable heat for that album over the years and admitted he was doing a lot of drugs at the time, which clouded his judgment. Dammit! I was doing a lot of drugs, too, but I could still see that the project was going to be a flop. At one meeting after another, I went on record against it, but the other guys insisted on moving forward." — Ace Frehley ("No Regrets," 2011)

"I didn't understand the concept, and I didn't give a fuck about the central character [some old fart nobody knew anything about]. It was ludicrous. I kept trying to tell the guys that if we released an album of self-indulgent nonsense, complete with spoken dialogue and haunting wind instruments, we'd be slaughtered. Our core fans would get pissed, and serious rock critics would laugh at it. It was doomed from the beginning." — Ace Frehley ("No Regrets," 2011)

"After the project moved up to Canada, I decided to remain behind most of the time and continued to work on guitar solos and overdubs at home. To my dismay, a lot of the solos I recorded were missing from the final mix. Go figure." — Ace Frehley ("No Regrets," 2011)

"The thing is 'Music from The Elder' is not really a terrible album. It's just a terrible KISS album. The songs themselves aren't all that bad, but some of them simply aren't appropriate for a KISS album." — Ace Frehley ("No Regrets," 2011)

"We lost our focus. I found myself looking for the respect of people who were never gonna respect what I was doing. Critical acclaim? Who needs it? We built our career ongoing things our own way." — Paul Stanley ("Classic Rock AOR," 2012)

"That actually would be like taking a trip to a nightmare. I don't think it's a great memory for any of us. It was done with what seemed like the best of intentions at that time, but we were delusional. We were trying to please the critics, we were trying to please people who don't like us, and life's too short. We barely have time to be with the people who do like us, let alone try to make friends with people who want nothing to do with us. Ultimately, we said we want nothing to do with them." — Paul Stanley on the possibility of playing songs from "The Elder" ("Monster" book launch in Los Angeles, 2012)

"At the end of that record I decided to go back to Toronto. Because I said, 'This is so big that my career is made!' So, I moved back to Toronto, because I wanted to be with my wife and kids, and literally within 18 months it was, 'Bob who?' I swear! It took me about four years — not only was there not great work there was almost no work — and Randy Phillips, who now runs AEG, was a manager of a band called the Kings that I produced from Toronto said to me, 'Why are you here?' And I said, 'Well, I love this town and want to be here.' He said, 'You're going to die here. You have got to go to L.A!' So,

we moved to L.A. and six months later I was in the studio with Rod Stewart."
— Bob Ezrin (Music Matters 2012 Keynote Interview)

"They were making basic rock records. They were making 1-4-5 rock records and I went to see them play in Pontiac, Michigan, in front of 9,000 people. 9,000 fifteen-year-old pimple-faced boys. There wasn't a girl in the crowd, it was amazing. I met with them and I said, 'look, you guys look amazing.' And they actually played pretty well, and they sang great. I said, 'but, we've got to get you past that demographic group. We've gotta expand your market because I think girls need to see this and other people need to see it. But it's not going to happen if all you sing about is getting drunk and getting laid. So, we need to start developing material that shows a different side.' So, I told them about a famous movie, 'The Wild One,' starring Marlon Brando where Marlon Brando was a member of a motorcycle gang. In those days that was the most dangerous thing in America. They were total juvenile delinquents. They smoked marijuana, they stole things and they beat people up. He was the leader of a motorcycle gang. He was evil and horrible, but he had a soft and vulnerable side. And of course, the purest and most beautiful girl in the village decided she would tame that savage heart. So, I said, 'look, we gotta be 'Johnny' in the 'Wild One,' you guys can be cock and balls all you want. And you can be goofy and horrible but has to be another side. There has to be a more vulnerable more romantic side that we're almost ashamed to show, but we'll show every once in a while. And then every girl in America is going to decide that they need to fix you.' And so, we made the record which got slammed by KISS fans and critics at the outset but went on to be the biggest record they've ever made." — Bob Ezrin (Music Matters 2012 Keynote Interview)

"'The Elder' was the result of temporary insanity. We didn't know which way to go." — Gene Simmons ("Classic Rock AOR," 2012)

"We became enchanted with the idea of becoming the darlings of the critics and proving some sort of credibility. And for my money [we] put out this pompous piece of pap. We were totally drunk with this idea that we were suddenly brilliant. I remember playing that album for people at my house and you weren't allowed to talk: "Ssshhh! This is so brilliant! This is my statement!" Just sitting there being completely enamored of what we had done. We lost the script. ... It became calculated and contrived." — Paul Stanley ("The Guardian," 2012)

"We literally at [the time of 'The Elder'] had people opening doors for us. I don't mean figuratively. When we would go to the studio to record, there would be somebody opening the door for us. That's not what this should be about. It was sycophantic. We were surrounded by people who are paid to tell you how great you are. We snapped out of it, but it was a rude awakening." — Paul Stanley ("The Guardian," 2012)

"But we engineered our irrelevance. We really did. We lost the plot. We forgot why we did this. We forgot why we got into it. And I don't think we've ever forgotten that since. It was a wrong turn that took years and years to get back on the motorway from. It was not something where one album was going to rectify what we did. People abandoned us in droves, and rightfully so, because we betrayed them, and we betrayed ourselves." — Paul Stanley ("The Guardian," 2012)

"Bob's substance problems became so acute he didn't show up, either. I had always been aware that Bob had a drug problem, but he had managed it in the past. Now his 24/7 cocaine use had taken on epic proportions. The captain abandoned ship. He was supposed to serve as the visionary behind the concept, and all we were getting were notes sent to the studio by messenger after Bob listened to cassettes we sent to his home." — Paul Stanley ("Face the Music," 2014)

"Poor Eric — this wonderful guy who thought he had joined a hard rock band — was suddenly playing gibberish with a fox costume in his closet. He was completely thrown by this band that had lost its way and was stumbling along a ridiculous path. He wasn't comfortable making explicit objections at that point, but he did express bewilderment and discomfort. 'You know, this isn't what I was expecting,' he said." — Paul Stanley ("Face the Music," 2014)

"The songs we recorded had no teeth. We were gumming the music at that point. We had forsaken everything we loved and embraced. We were intoxicated with fame and success." — Paul Stanley ("Face the Music," 2014)

"If I played the tape for anyone at my apartment, I insisted on silence — as if I was exposing them to brilliance — and they had to sit through the entire thing straight through. We also had a listening party for the record company, with the same insistence that they listen to it in a manner befitting its artistic merit. The reaction at the end of the listening session was like the audience when they heard "Springtime for Hitler" from "The Producers." Mouths wide open. I already knew somehow that it wasn't because the sheer greatness of the album had taken their breath away." — Paul Stanley ("Face the Music," 2014)

"It got so far removed from a rock aspect. I put that all on Ezrin. Ezrin had just finished doing Pink Floyd's 'The Wall.' And if you listen to 'The Wall' and you listen to 'The Elder' you'll see a lot of similarities — not note for note, of course not. But the cadence of the album, the various instruments used, all of the instrumentation..." — "Big" John Harte (Decibel Geek Podcast, 2015)

"When the album came out, we were embarrassed. It bombed. There's just no other way to look at it. ... That was the one time I would say that KISS succumbed to the critics. We wanted a critical success. And we lost our minds." — Gene Simmons ("Classic Rock" magazine, 2016)

"The problem with 'The Elder' is it was the wrong album at the wrong time. If we would have done an album like 'Creatures of The Night' in place of where 'The Elder' was, things might have been different. I might have not left the band. But I was so turned off by doing a concept record at that point in our career — I really felt that it was so important to do a heavy hard rock album. I've always had that street sense, I've always been able to sense what I think people want and what they'd like, and I try and record that way. When I'm recording a song, or playing a solo, I try and imagine what my fans would want me to do, and I try and go down that road. From the beginning of 'The Elder' I knew that it was the wrong album. Nobody believed me. Nobody took notice. They were all going off the cliff and there was nothing I could do about it." — Ace Frehley ("Pods & Sods" podcast, 2016)

The Year In Rock: 1981

While KISS was busy experimenting with a conceptual departure, several competitors served up platters of straight-ahead rock and driving metal

"We sat around for six to eight hours a day, and we would talk and take notes before we even thought about picking up an instrument." — Paul Stanley, 1982

While KISS was lost in the mist of their attempt to create a grand conceptual statement in 1981, some fans have argued the band completely lost their footing within the rock genre. Of course, KISS had already strayed musically with 1979's "Dynasty" and 1980's "Unmasked," albums heavier on pop hooks and less reflective of KISS' traditional sonic blueprint.

In 1982 KISS would return to form with the metallic "Creatures of The Night." But despite its teeth, the album proved to be one year late and a dollar short in some respects. Looking back with the aid of hindsight, KISS proved to be the odd rock band out in 1981, toiling over a concept album that stalled upon arrival while a slew of others rock bands produced sharper-edged efforts, with many dashing to the upper echelon of the Billboard album chart.

Indeed, 1981 was a rockin' year. Here then is a brief overview of 12 of significant rock albums released that year, followed by a brief 1981 musical timeline.

Rush, "Moving Pictures"
Producers: Terry Brown and Rush
Released: Feb. 12, 1981
Peak Chart Position: No. 3
RIAA Certification: 4x platinum

KISS' former touring opening act hit their commercial peak with this magnum opus, which features Rush chestnuts "Tom Sawyer," "Red Barchetta," "YYZ," and "Limelight" right out of the box. And side two is just as compelling. (Check out the brilliantly haunting introduction to "Witch Hunt.") Sonically, "Moving Pictures" perfectly bottles a huge wall of Alex Lifeson's guitars, synthesizer textures, Neil Peart's thundering drums, and Geddy Lee's tasty bass playing and unique vocal stylings. The Canadian trio followed in October 1981 with the excellent live album "Exit... Stage Left." Proving the album's timeless quality, Rush played "Moving Pictures" in its entirety on their 2010–2011 Time Machine tour.

Judas Priest, "Point Of Entry"
Producer: Tom Allom
Released: Feb. 26, 1981
Peak Chart Position: No. 39
RIAA Certification: Gold

Judas Priest had opened for KISS on some dates during the Return of KISS tour in support of 1979's "Dynasty" album. At that time, they were an up-and-coming band, though by 1981 had experienced their mainstream breakthrough following the success of "British Steel." For "Point of Entry" the band returned to the studio without any real plan for the album they were going to record and instead tried a spontaneous approach, resulting in less aggressive and more melodic material. The album performed reasonably well on the Billboard 200, cracking the Top 40. Sandwiched in between "British Steel" (1980) and "Screaming for Vengeance" (1982), "Point Of Entry" has become somewhat lost in the band's catalog, even though it contains the popular "Heading Out To The Highway."

Van Halen, "Fair Warning"
Producer: Ted Templeman
Released: April 29, 1981
Peak Chart Position: No. 5
RIAA Certification: 2x platinum

Labeled Van Halen's "dark" album, "Fair Warning" may be the finest 31 minutes of Eddie Van Halen's career. The legendary guitar virtuoso's "brown" sound permeates the sonic tapestry throughout, evidenced by the six-string pyrotechnics in "Mean Street," the lush guitars in "Hear About It Later" and the drop-D riffery on "Unchained." (Check out "Push Come To Shove" and "Sinner's Swing" for two of Eddie Van Halen's more wicked solos.) Party maestro David Lee Roth commands the proceedings, per usual, even if he comes off cynical at times. Despite the album failing to spawn a major hit single, "Fair Warning" has remains a Van Halen fan favorite.

Iron Maiden, "Killers"
Producers: Martin Birch
Released: June 6, 1981
Peak Chart Position: No. 78
RIAA Certification: Gold

Iron Maiden had opened for KISS during their European "Unmasked" tour and returned in 1981 (the album was released in Europe in February) with their second, and final, studio album with vocalist Paul Di'Anno and first with guitarist Adrian Smith. While "Killers" peaked at No. 78 in the United States (No. 12, UK), it included Maiden catalog classics such as the title track, "Wrathchild," "Murders In The Rue Morgue," and "Purgatory."

Foreigner, "4"
Producers: Robert John "Mutt" Lange and Mick Jones
Released: July 2, 1981
Peak Chart Position: No. 1
RIAA Certification: 6x platinum

Foreigner's fourth studio album proved to be their sole long player to reach the top of the Billboard album chart. This melodic rock gem contains a trio of the band's bigger hits: "Juke Box Hero," "Urgent" and "Waiting For A Girl Like You," the latter two reaching the Top 5 on the Billboard Hot 100. The album was arguably Foreigner's musical peak and showcased the combination of the able talents of principal songwriter/guitarist Mick Jones and the soulful voice of lead singer Lou Gramm. The album also features two notable special guests: Motown alumnus Junior Walker plays the saxophone solo on "Urgent"; Thomas Dolby plays synthesizer on "Urgent" and "Waiting For A Girl Like You."

Def Leppard, "High 'N' Dry"
Producer: Robert John "Mutt" Lange
Released: July 11, 1981

Peak Chart Position: No. 38
RIAA Certification: 2x platinum

For their sophomore album, Def Leppard teamed with producer Robert John "Mutt" Lange, who was quite busy in 1981 having come off AC/DC's "Back In Black." The result was an AC/DC-inspired affair, heavy on Joe Elliott's screechy vocals, rugged guitars — courtesy of Steve Clark and Pete Willis — and big drums — provided by a teenaged Rick Allen. Straight off the bat, the album punches the listener in the gut with the trifecta of "Let It Go," "Another Hit And Run" and "High 'N' Dry (Saturday Night)." "High 'N' Dry" also contains the minor hit "Bringin' On The Heartbreak," a song offering a glimpse into the more melodic direction that would be explored on subsequent Leppard albums "Pyromania" and "Hysteria," and the atmospheric Clark-penned instrumental "Switch 625."

Journey, "Escape"
Producer: Kevin Elson
Released: July 31, 1981
Peak Chart Position: No. 1
RIAA Certification: 9x platinum

Coming off the platinum-plus double live album "Captured," this Bay Area quintet hit big with the chart-topping "Escape." Babys' keyboardist Jonathan Cain was added to the Journey lineup, replacing co-founder Gregg Rolie. Cain brought a new dimension of songwriting sensibility evidenced by songs such as "Who's Cryin' Now" and "Open Arms," which remain some of the more exquisitely crafted ballads from the era. Deep cuts such as "Stone In Love," "Keep On Runnin'" and "Escape" prove the band could also rock, driven by the instrumental prowess of drummer Steve Smith and masterful guitar work of Neal Schon. Scientists can't be sure, but it is possible the reverberations of Steve Perry's tenor will ring for eternity. Oh yes, some song named "Don't Stop Believin'" opens this album.

Rolling Stones, "Tattoo You"
Producers: The Glimmer Twins
Released: Aug. 24, 1981
Peak Chart Position: No. 1
RIAA Certification: 4x platinum

Though primarily comprised of prior studio outtakes, "Tattoo You" is the last Rolling Stones album to top the Billboard album chart. The album is well-balanced with traditional Stones rock flare — including the energetic "Hang Fire" and the Keith Richards-sung "Little T&A" — and dynamic ballads such as the dreamy "Heaven," the R&B/soul-inspired "No Use In Crying" and "Waiting On A Friend," which features a saxophone solo by Sonny Rollins. (One can almost imagine the latter being sung by inebriated patrons in a NYC dive bar.) The album's lead track, the anthemic "Start Me Up," reached No. 2 on the Billboard Hot 100, marking the Stones' biggest hit of the decade.

Black Sabbath, "Mob Rules"
Producer: Martin Birch
Released: Nov. 4, 1981
Peak Chart Position: No. 29
RIAA Certification: Gold

KISS had opened for a different version of Sabbath back in 1975, and this album was the second, and last, to feature the powerful singer Ronnie James Dio (contemporaneously, until his return in 1991 and later under the moniker "Heaven & Hell") and first with drummer Vinny Appice, who had replaced Bill Ward during the previous tour. Like KISS, Sabbath were attempting to adapt to a situation of losing original band members. "Mob Rules" was seen in many quarters as a continuation of 1980's "Heaven and Hell," and as a result the album has only attained gold certification by the RIAA. However, the number of classics the album contains can barely be argued: "Falling Off The Edge Of The World," "Voodoo," "Turn Up The Night," "The Sign Of The Southern Cross," and the title track.

Ozzy Osbourne, "Diary Of A Madman"
Producers: Max Norman, Ozzy Osbourne, Randy Rhoads
Released: Nov. 7, 1981
Peak Chart Position: No. 16
RIAA Certification: 3x platinum

Following 1980's impressive "Blizzard of Ozz," Ozzy Osbourne returned with this hard-hitting eight-song collection, which ultimately sealed his standing as a platinum-selling solo artist. With another potent musical showing,

Randy Rhoads cemented his guitar hero status, weaving big riffs and solos ripe with rock, neoclassical and blues elements throughout tracks such as "Over the Mountain," "Flying High Again," "S.A.T.O.," and the album's eerie title track. Bassist Bob Daisley proved a key contributor, co-writing all of the album's songs. Tragically, Rhoads died in a plane accident in 1982, cutting his blossoming career short. The guitarist remains an influential figure for metal guitarists to this day.

Mötley Crüe, "Too Fast For Love"
Producer: Mötley Crüe
Released: Nov. 10, 1981
Peak Chart Position: No. 77
RIAA Certification: Platinum

A limited number of copies of "Too Fast for Love," Mötley Crüe's debut album were initially pressed in 1981 via their own label, Leathür Records. A year later, Elektra Records signed the band and released a remixed version of the album. Bassist Nikki Sixx wrote all the album's songs with the exception of three tracks, which he co-wrote. Songs such as "Live Wire," "Piece of Your Action" and the title track perfectly captured the Crüe's inimitable mixture of Sixx's throbbing bass, Tommy Lee's spastic drumming, Mick Mars' buzz-saw guitars and Vince Neil's primal screams. Mötley Crüe opened select dates for KISS toward the end their tour in support of "Creatures of The Night." During the summer of 2012, the bands reunited for the highly successful The Tour.

AC/DC, "For Those About to Rock We Salute You"
Producer: Robert John "Mutt" Lange
Released: Nov. 23, 1981
Peak Chart Position: No. 1
RIAA Certification: 4x platinum

An album from another group who had opened for KISS. "For Those About to Rock" became AC/DC's first No. 1 album, a feat that its mammoth predecessor "Black in Black" surprisingly failed to manage. However, even though it sounds like a continuation of that album, it didn't match its success, selling only 4 million copies (yes, folks, that's tongue in cheek). The single "Let's Get It Up" did reach No. 44 on the Billboard Hot 100, while the title track has become a stalwart live performance for the band, complete with large stage cannons. AC/DC's label took the opportunity to cash in on the band's success in 1981, releasing "Dirty Deeds Done Dirt Cheap" for the first time in the United States.

(Some of the great albums released during 1981)

A Brief Musical Timeline: 1981

January
24 - Aerosmith's Steven Tyler is injured in a motorcycle accident, leaving the singer hospitalized for two months. Later in the year, Brad Whitford departs Aerosmith, and is replaced by Rick Dufay.

February
9 - Bill Haley dies. With is group Bill Haley & His Comets, Haley was an early pioneer of rock and roll music in the early 1950s. His iconic hits included "Rock Around the Clock" and "Shake, Rattle and Roll."

April
X - The RIAA adopts the digit #2 to denote CD audio media in the 10-digit Universal Product Code (UPC) system. Other common codes were -1 for 12" vinyl, -4 for audio cassettes, and -7 for 7" singles ("Billboard," April 3, 1982). The period 1978–1982 was one of a battle for the adoption of the UPC system within in the industry, with PolyGram being one of the major holdouts until late-1982. The UPC system was supposed to benefit product stock control and sales reporting.
11 - Eddie Van Halen marries actress Valerie Bertinelli of "One Day At A Time" fame.

May
11 - Reggae legend Bob Marley dies.
20 - Diana Ross signs with RCA Records, severing her ties with Motown Records. The deal, the most lucrative in music history at the time, is brokered by KISS' business management firm, Glickman/Marks Corp.

June
4 - U2 make their debut U.S. television appearance on the "Tomorrow" show with Tom Snyder.
5 - "Night Flight," a musical variety show featuring videos and interviews, debuts on USA Network.

July

17 - "Endless Love," a romantic drama starring Brooke Shields, debuts in theaters. The film's soundtrack features "Endless Love," a duet by Lionel Richie and Diana Ross, and KISS' "I Was Made For Lovin' You."

August

1 - MTV debuts. The channel airs music videos 24 hours a day.
7 - The film "Heavy Metal" debuts in U.S. theaters.

September

25 - The Rolling Stones kick off their U.S. tour in Philadelphia.

October

26 - Iron Maiden plays their first show with vocalist Bruce Dickinson in Bologna, Italy.
28 - Metallica are formed by James Hetfield and Lars Ulrich in Los Angeles, Calif.

November

X - Black 'N' Blue are formed by high school friends Tommy Thayer and Jaime St. James in Portland, Ore.
16 - "Music from The Elder" is released in the United States.

December

26 - REO Speedwagon's "Hi-Infidelity" is named the "Billboard" pop album of the year. "Billboard"'s top five singles of 1981 are Kim Carnes, "Bette Davis Eyes"; Diana Ross and Lionel Richie, "Endless Love"; Kenny Rogers, "Lady"; John Lennon, "(Just Like) Starting Over"; and Rick Springfield, "Jessie's Girl."
31 - Dick Clark's annual "New Year's Rockin' Eve" special airs on ABC, featuring Alabama, the Four Tops, Rick James, and Rick Springfield.

(X - exact date unknown)

Bruce Kulick Remembers An Unplugged Home Run

KISS's lead guitarist, 1984 – 96, recalls a special "Elder" performance during "MTV Unplugged," one of the more monumental events in KISStory

The select group of fans attending the performance on Aug. 9, 1995, witnessed not only a rarified acoustic set of KISS classics led by the "Revenge"-era lineup, but a reunion of the original lineup. Adding the icing on the cake, the one-off performance was taped for posterity, airing on MTV on Halloween night 1995, and received a formal release in March 1996.

As with any KISS-related topic, asking fans to identify their favorite "Unplugged" song yields a variety of answers. That said, arguably the biggest set-list stunner was the inclusion of "A World Without Heroes." The band had dusted off this "Elder" gem for the first time in more than 13 years in whipping it into shape during the preceding Konvention Tour. (During the Konvention run they'd also attempted "Under the Rose," "Mr. Blackwell," "Just A Boy," and "I" with varying levels of nonsuccess.) While it took two takes to nail, the memorable "Unplugged" performance of "A World Without Heroes" yielded a plaintive vocal from Gene Simmons, dynamic drumming from Eric Singer and sterling complementary guitar work courtesy of Paul Stanley and Bruce Kulick. It was as if justice had been finally served for "The Elder." (As for how the performance was received? Perhaps that's best answered by the thundering applause following Stanley's guitar solo and at the end of the song.)

Given his excellent commentaries on "Crazy Nights," "Hot in The Shade," "Revenge" and "Carnival Of Souls," who better to look back on this special "Elder" moment than Mr. Kulick himself?

"It's one of my favorite KISS songs. I was very excited when we decided early on to do this song for the Unplugged performances on the KISS Konvention Tour and then to have it immortalized for the MTV taping. It's extremely melodic, and easily performed on the acoustics. I felt this performance from Gene, who is not one to sing the 'sweet' songs from KISS, made the Demon more human. Gene's soft side, almost fragile sounding in his singing, was

quite a contrast for him. And that makes it very special. The intro solo was mine, but the main solo was taken by Paul Stanley, and I presume he did it for 'The Elder' recording. For me, the fact that we actually performed something from that infamous album made me smile. I knew that the more we pushed the envelope in our acoustic presentations, the better the reaction would be. And we hit a home run performing this song. Big thumbs up from BK!"

"The Elder" Under The Covers

From death metal to DIY YouTube videos, check out this playlist of interpretations from the "Music from The Elder" songbook

It's no surprise that when KISS dust off songs from "Music from The Elder," fans go positively ape-shit. OK, maybe only just a little.

Unfortunately, KISS have not played much from "The Elder" album over the years. Aside from a trio of live performances on "Fridays" in 1982, core inclusion of "A World Without Heroes" during 1995's "Unplugged" tour and broadcast, it's pretty much been a verse here and a riff or chorus there. KISS tried their first attempt of "Only You" aboard the KISS Kruise II, though the band barely made it through more than a minute, allowing the audience to sing more of it than Gene Simmons could remember. And more recently, KISS performed "The Oath" on the KISS Kruise III in 2013 and "A World Without Heroes" (electrically) on the KISS Kruise V in 2015.

Despite KISS' reluctance to perform material from "The Elder," a balance of the album's songs have been given makeovers via interesting musical interpretations by a diverse cast of musicians. From glossy pop to Swedish death metal and one-man bands, we've rounded up six notable renditions that have kept the legend of "The Elder" alive over the years. Read the descriptions and head over to YouTube to listen to the songs.

Doro Pesch, "Only You"

Doro Pesch's melodic reworking of "Only You" appears on her 1990 album, "Doro." Pesch has mentioned in interviews that the song is one of her all-time favorite KISS recordings. Coincidentally, the album was executive produced by Gene Simmons with Tommy Thayer in a co-producer role (with Pat Regan). Tommy performed the bulk of the guitar work on the album. Gene also contributed "Something Wicked This Way Comes," a song written in 1988 and considered for use on KISS' "Hot in The Shade" album, and the album's closing track, "Mirage." He also had Doro cover "Rock On" from the final Black 'N' Blue album, 1988's "In Heat," a song that he wrote with Tommy and Jaime St. James. The German native Pesch was KISS' label mate at the time, with "Doro" released via the Mercury/PolyGram label.

Right off the bat, this version of "Only You" features thicker-sounding guitars, which set the stage for Pesch as she expresses her thirst for the object of her affection. (The intro unfortunately lacks the presence of Simmons' melodic bass line.) Indeed, the lyrics are given a complete makeover (being reverted back to the pre-Elder form), speaking more to themes of lust and longing rather than a quest for self-discovery:

> "Only you can possess me/I need your love day and night
> Only you can deliver me/I need your love, I can't deny
> Only you can deceive me/I love you more than I can say
> Only you can complete me/I need your love every day"

The song's arrangement is tweaked slightly, and keyboards add a shiny if dated texture. Though Pesch's vocals are formidable (check her metalicious scream @ 3:42), the dynamics are a bit flat compared to KISS' original recording. That said, Pesch enjoyed "Only You" so much that she performed the song live in concert and included it on her 1993 live album, "Doro Live."

Cher, "A World Without Heroes"

It seems fitting that Cher would sing a song co-written by her once-high-profile flame. Appearing on her 1991 album, "Love Hurts," Cher's version of "A World Without Heroes" predictably sounds more modern than the 1981 original. A bed of keyboards and chorused guitars courtesy of guitar ace Michael Landau form the harmonic framework. Cher sings the song in the key of G# minor to accommodate her range. (KISS' recording is in the key of E minor.) While the lyrics are intact, sung by Cher, somehow the song takes on a sultry light. One notable difference is the presence of answering background vocals that repeat chants of "You don't know."

Paul Stanley's guitar solo is a true high point on KISS' original recording. Though still melodic in its own right, the guitar solo played by Toto's Steve Lukather seems a cut below. (Lukather is notable in KISStory for having played guitar on Peter Criss' 1978 solo album.) Aside from Lukather and Landau, other artists featured here include Richard Marx and Richard Page on background vocals.

While this particular Cher album received a mixed response, a critic once remarked, "The only song worth listening to is 'A World Without Heroes,' on an otherwise uninspired album." Cher lip-synced the song on ABC's "In Concert" program in June 1991.

Daniel Iasbeck, "Under The Rose"

This cover of "The Elder"'s fifth track comes courtesy of the wonders of technology. Daniel Iasbeck, formerly of the Brazilian rock band Exxótica, turns in a spirited performance of "Under the Rose." In the video's notes, Iasbeck boasts that "all the instrument and voice recordings [are] done in one continuous take. No punch in overdubs."

Iasbeck certainly nails the song to a tee. He mixes six-string textures with an acoustic guitar, a Strat and a Les Paul. The drums are played on an electronic kit. The choir vocals sound as if they are aided by the use of a harmony-enhanced plug-in such as Auto-Tune's harmony engine. Iasbeck's voice is pleasant — his feel in the verses is very similar to Simmons' original vocal. And the guitar solo is essentially note-for-note, right down to the use of delay.

The performance video gives off an honest DIY feel, and it is impressive to see Iasbeck play all of the track's instruments. In a more than three years, he's racked up an impressive total of more than 30,000 views. The only logical question is: How about a go at "fanfare," Daniel?

Tony Powers, "Odyssey"

In an interesting twist of fate, Tony Powers, who composed "Odyssey," released a music video for the song after it was recorded for "Music from The Elder." So technically he's covering himself after KISS covered him with this version that is featured on his 1984 EP/video LP "Don't Nobody Move (This Is A Heist)."

Though lacking the support of the American Symphony Orchestra, the dreamy track's grandiose feel is intact. While Paul Stanley's vocal can be described as quasi-operatic, Powers' vocals are much more subdued, with a loose delivery reminiscent of Tom Waits or Leonard Cohen. As he did on KISS' track, Powers plays piano. The additions of a female voice and carnival-like instrumentation to the bridge add an eerie atmosphere that is resolved by a synth solo, played by Chris Palmaro. Though heavily inflected with pitch bends, the solo bears strong resemblance to the guitar solo played on "The Elder." Powers' version was recorded at SoundMixers in New York.

Directed by Powers, the music video for "Odyssey" was filmed at the Staten Island Ferry in New York, a shoot that lasted the balance of an evening and went into dawn. Lois Chiles, who played Dr. Holly Goodhead in the 1979 James Bond film "Moonraker," plays the female interest. Incidentally, Powers met Chiles at New York celebrity hotspot Cafe Central, the same place he "met along the way" Mr. Paul Stanley.

Hair Of The Dog, "I"

Los Angeles-based band, Hair of The Dog, turned in this faithful cover of "I" on their 2000 album "Rise." A loud four-piece band with thundering drums and crunchy guitars, it's not surprising that Hair of The Dog were heavily inspired by KISS. "If there's one common thread for this band ... it's KISS," once said vocalist Ryan Cook. "We frequently close our shows with big KISS songs, but those songs have been covered to death. So, we picked a bit of a rare one and made it a little heavier and more current."

Ably supplying the guitar work is John Sepetys, who left the group in 2001. (Sure enough Hair Of The Dog subsequently disbanded.) As if recording "I" wasn't enough, the band proves their KISS worth by adding snippets of some klassics in the breakdown — can you pick them all out?

Arch Enemy, "The Oath"

"The Oath" received this maddening metal makeover courtesy of Sweden's Arch Enemy. The song was released as a bonus track on 2007's "Rise of The Tyrant," which hit No. 84 on the Billboard 200.

Right away, the beefy guitars are tuned down to a menacing C and manipulated by heavy effects processing. The tempo is revved up a few beats on the metronome, lending a sense of urgency. It may be hard to fathom, but the brutal vocals come courtesy of female lead vocalist Angela Gossow. The song's arrangement essentially remains intact though an acoustic guitar takes the place of keyboards in the song's bridge. The double-kick patterns, played by drummer Daniel Erlandsson, are much more prominent compared to KISS' original recording. The brother guitar tandem of Christopher and Michael Arnott add a few complementary melodic lines in the song's outro. There's no falsetto to be heard here, kids.

Not enough "Elder" covers for you? If not, you can always try and seek out information on the Athens High School Choir, which dedicated an entire musical production to the album in 1996.

Collecting "The Elder"

A brief overview of some of the more interesting "Elder" collectibles

Collecting "The Elder" can often be a murky world that involves distractions of pirate releases versus legitimate rarities; and then delving through numerous varieties of the latter. That's not to say, within this discussion, that the "über" cool Turkish pirate pressing of the album on Dallas Records isn't worthy of mention (nor the more recent and more numerous "reprintings" — a pirated pirate issue, how imaginative)! One of the main complaints about "The Elder" has been the design of its packaging, which almost seems to have been designed to camouflage the product and thusly hide it from consumers deep within the shelves of record stores — remember those? One must wonder whether that was a subconscious decision to protect the music buying public from the awesomeness that is "The Elder."

With all things KISS collectible, "The Elder"-related items from Japan often stand out from the crowd with the quality of production and attention to detail. Straight down to the quality of materials used the Japanese releases are indicative of a care and respect given to the product. What might be considered a "problem," with the album's nondescript "brown" cover art, was rectified in Japan by that market utilizing an oversized full-cover obi that included the expected images of the band members to the side of a traditional vertical obi strip listing the usual information about the release. This made the album more colorful, and it certainly stands out more than a plain brown door close-up. Ace's pose also alludes to the Japanese title of the album which loosely translates as "Wars of The Underworld." It should be noted that there are two versions of the obi, the first of which lists the premiums included in initial shipments of the album; and a second that replaces that list with an extra KISS logo. Copies of the album, with just the overlay, are easily obtainable though collecting a complete copy with all premiums can become a major financial challenge.

The first 50,000 copies issued included a number of premiums that were common to Japanese releases (though some four months following the release of the album it still hadn't sold that number of copies). The first of these was the incredibly rare color poster that used a picture similar to that used for the "KISS Killers" album cover, mirrored vertically. This item is very difficult to find, as is the logo badge, which was likely handed out at point of purchase rather than being included in the album. It's a small pin, so many were likely lost over the decades. Slightly more common, but still very difficult to find, is the black-and-yellow "KISS" logo sticker. Finally, and perhaps not quite as exciting, is a promotional bag (also likely distributed at point of purchase). The yellow bag, featuring a red KISS logo and "Elder" title, reaches into the realm of the near impossible to obtain or stratospherically expensive. In fact, in the 21st century one has to be more concerned with counterfeits — with little way to determine the authenticity of the items due to their rarefied status. Both "printings" of the album also include the ubiquitous lyric insert sheet. There is also a white label promo for the initial release. The album was also reissued in 1987 as part of the "Crazy Collection."

Like most other markets, the Japanese version is a gatefold issue. It came with the usual plain translucent inner dust sleeve and lyric/biographical insert sheet. More importantly, it retained the original mix and track order, excluding the "Escape from The Island" instrumental. This mix wasn't issued internationally (in full) until it was used as the basis for the 1997 remaster though it does also turn up on the Portuguese pressing. Sonically, it is vastly superior to other issues with elements either buried or omitted from being audible (foghorns and chanting monks immediately come to mind). This mix was released on CD in 1986 on the initial P33C series and remains superior to later versions in not being sonically mutilated via brick walling. The 2014 digital remasters, while boosting the base volume slightly, do an excellent job of representing this album sonically at its very best — comparisons with the Japanese 1986 version indicate numerous general similarities versus the 1997 international remastering. The album was also issued in cassette format, which for Japanese issues carry a hefty premium due to their scarcity (only 6,000 copies made).

In Japan the album was supported by two single releases: "I" / "Just A Boy" (Polystar 7S-46) and "The Oath" / "Escape from The Island" (7S-54). Both come with the standard paper cover overlay sheets and are available with a promotional white label and standard Casablanca "Filmworks" label stock. Neither of these singles is particularly rare or difficult to obtain in either format. As a result of its B-side status, "Escape from The Island" was also included on the Japanese edition of "KISS Killers" released in May 1982. This same track-order was issued in Portugal. Like the Japanese version of "The

Elder," it should be noted that some error copies of the Canadian release can be found in a hybrid condition with the original mix on the B-side and the altered A-side (right down to the matrix numbers). This results in the exclusion of "Odyssey" and "Escape From The Island" from that album version and the repetition of "Dark Light" and "The Oath" on both sides with different mixes — Side A: "The Oath," "fanfare," "Just A Boy," "Dark Light," "Only You," "Under The Rose;" Side B: "Dark Light," "A World Without Heroes," "The Oath," "Mr. Blackwell," "I." The matrix numbers for this strange hybrid: NBLP-7261A (2) SAB230 // NBLP 7261 B 3. Correct mix and sequence albums are far more common.

(Japan single picture sleeve)

Historically, one of the most sought after "Elder" versions is the one released in Turkey via Dallas Records (9002). It has long been of dubious provenance and is now generally considered to be a pirate release (though those who have "invested" in copies may be loathed to accept that, understandably). In terms of semantics it is not a counterfeit since it doesn't attempt to replicate the official product, nor (obviously) is it a bootleg (an unsanctioned recording). For the cover, a color version of the standard "Elder" promo photo was used along with a purple German "KIZZ" logo. This issue has long been sought after among collectors, with the prices varying from less than $100 to more than $400 for a mint copy. It should also be noted that there is an obvious song-title error on the rear cover, "The Darth" (also "The Dath" on the center ring), that is indicative of the quality of the product and should have set off red flags for decades. This album now turns up as a picture disc and while being appealing visually is often not worth the asking price (in the opinion of the author).

In Britain, the only unique release from the album was a 7-inch picture disc for "A World Without Heroes," backed with "Mr. Blackwell." Also released as a regular vinyl single, with unique picture sleeve, both were released in late February 1982. Only 7,500 copies of the 7-inch picture sleeve were pressed according to order documentation, dated Jan. 11, 1982 (as shared in a 1980s fanzine). According to that same documentation, the picture disc is more common with some 10,000 copies having been ordered. While the regular single sells for approximately $25, the picture disc often changes hands for sums of money not justified by its actual availability, which really puts it in the same category as the regular single. Britain seems to be one of the few countries to have issued promotional copies of the album, with gold-stamped versions (on the cover only) commonly being available. A black and white "gatefold" version, which is actually an intended store display, is sometimes married with test-pressing vinyl. However, an inevitable question mark remains about that particular item with the ease with which British Phonogram test-pressings can be faked.

The chicken or the egg? It's not clear whether initial pressings of the album can be identified according to the use of paper versus polyvinyl dust sleeves. In both cases, each was printed, but with the variation between pressing plants it is impossible to definitively narrow down whether one came before the other, or if they were concurrently originating from differing plants and may depend upon regional distribution. However, copies that included the printed paper dust sleeve were printed with the song lyrics and album details. Copies of this, with seams not split, can be hard to find due to the very thin paper stock used. It should be noted that the lyric order on the printed paper dust sleeve matches the adjusted track sequence and includes the credit for "Escape from The Island." Some copies included a separate lyric sheet insert, in addition to the credits printed on a special translucent dust sleeve. These polyethylene/polyvinyl inner sleeves, which had generally previously been used for audiophile releases, had started to gain popularity within the industry as offering better protection of the vinyl. In terms of cost they were cheaper than printed inner sleeves, but nearly double the cost of plain white. From an economic perspective, paper costs were rising while poly costs were expected to drop drastically as adoption expanded. However, PolyGram was hesitant, according to PolyGram's VP of inventory management and production Ed Simek, because "There have been reports that loading records in polyvinyl sleeves slowed the production process in the plants... Of course, from the consumer standpoint, the sleeves make for a nicer package" (Record World, 12/12/81). The lyric insert sheet ignores the two instrumentals and production credits suggesting that it was intended to be married with the translucent dust sleeve copies. The U.S. and Canadian record also initially had a photo center ring with the hand from the album cover. (Take note which side of the hand is used on the A- and B-side.)

Test pressings are more difficult to obtain though they do pose some interesting questions. Several dating from early October 1981 feature the original running order (as released on the Japanese version). This seems to suggest that the instrumental "Escape from The Island" was originally considered a B-side or was perhaps a late inclusion to possibly boost the involvement of Ace Frehley or guitar-driven material. Later printings (circa 1982/3 or 1985) purportedly do not have the photo center ring — though these seem seldom seen (if even extant) and are highly sought after. The existence of an U.S. "Filmworks" style label "Elder" LP is essentially supposition with the album having been released at least on cassette in 1985 (admittedly at a time when popularity of that format was near its peak). Incidentally, it should be mentioned that mention of "Filmworks" was removed from the LP with the label logo reverting to "Casablanca Records" on the 1981 issue. As is the case with both the original cassette and LP issue, copies with both track orders on either the J-card or rear cover are available. Promotional copies are suggested to NOT exist with the ubiquitous gold-leaf "promo" stamp or any "promo" printing addition to the center ring (at least in the U.S.).

Several international versions of the album are also worth noting: Some copies of the Australian release, similar to the Japanese release, came with a special black bag at point of sale, with gold "Elder" lettering, a cover-sized poster insert (also included on the New Zealand edition), and several versions of stickers and small badges. A later UK release came in single jacket sleeve configuration that included an inner dust sleeve in the design of the original gatefold image. A Norwegian version is more interesting as a non-gatefold for its inclusion of a poster. Using the "KISS Killers" image as the poster two variants are available with one of the versions having a mirrored image of the band — hence Paul's "star" being on the wrong eye on some copies — this version has become highly desirable in recent years. The design of the inner dust sleeve uses the gatefold image. The Singapore

PolyGram (ASEAN/Malaysian) and Hong Kong versions, as illustrated earlier in this book, comes with a faux ancient scroll background for the track listing on the rear cover. Staying in Asia, the Korean version, which was actually the first "current" album officially released in that country offers "Dialogue" as the final track listed on the rear of the non-gatefold cover.

(Australian insert sheet)

The album was also issued in Greece and Portugal (which comes with a printed inner dust sleeve using the gatefold art) as a non-gatefold. German copies of the album, as is usually the case, featured the altered logo. The Colombian non-gatefold via Philips features a black and white rear cover design which is basically a repetition of the front with the song titles added. Some rarer versions include a printed German language lyric sheet, which was available via mail (which is why they should show evidence of having been folded) per and advertisement on the lower left of the back cover. Also worth noting are differences between the West German and Austrian logos on the rear cover with the Austrian having a black background between the letters (and no mail-in address for the lyrics insert sheet). Three versions of the Austrian issue are known to exist, a record club edition and two versions with different back cover credits. The adjusted track sequence is simply printed on a black background that fills in the door panels. Like everything KISS-related, photocopy versions turn up with the album. South Africa (Star-6001), Philippines (Dyna 6302-163) and Venezuela (120.052) revert to the classic pre-1977 Casbah (a.k.a. "Camel") center-ring.

The singles released for the album vary widely with the American "A World Without Heroes" release (both promotional and regular) being easily obtainable for around $10. There are also varieties as noted by the style of font used for the text on the labels that can provide a challenge to locate. Australian singles for "I" and "A World Without Heroes" were both released and the former single, apart from including an edited version of the song that replaced "balls to stand" with the "guts to stand" lyric. It was the first Australian KISS single to feature a picture sleeve — as bland as it is (plain brown background with yellow title text). Copies of the single sell for around $25 while the "A World Without Heroes" issue is far rarer since it was only available for a very short time. It usually sells for more than $50. Most European countries released singles for "I" or "A World Without Heroes," but the rarest of these is the Dutch picture release of the latter track which sells for more than $100. South American copies are also highly sought after, particularly in higher grades of condition. Most European singles sell in the $25 range each, the noticeable exception being the Italian "San Remo" release for "I" (6000-717) that regularly tops $100 in poor condition.

Italy provides several additional interesting collectible releases related to "The Elder," though the list does not include the standard album version — which like most other markets was issued in a gatefold cover, albeit with the album's center-rings having been stamped to show that tax had been paid. The regular album cover art picture sleeve of the regular "I" single (backed with "The Oath") is one of the more common European singles from the album. Promotionally, there are several issues that are of interest. "I" (5000-599) was also issued as the B-side of an Angelo Branduardi's "Il disgelo" white label juke-box single and included on the B-side of a promotional 12" (5001-613), along with five other non-KISS disco, rock, and R&B songs. "The Oath" (5000-606) followed, backed with Julie's "Cuore Bandito." And "Only You" (5000-611) was the final "Elder" related issue, backed with Barbara Boncompagni's "Cuore Matto."

Most markets saw the album released on cassette. As mentioned, Japan probably tops the list in terms of cost, though plenty of obscure international release versions can provide a challenge to obtain — as well as the assorted reissue versions. Like the LP, the U.S. original issue can be found with either track sequence listed on the J-card. The album was also reissued in 1985, as part of the catalog refresh, with a black spine J-card. It even retains the "Odyssey Begins" dialogue on the inside. Multiple white spine/red text issues from 1989 exist with variants on the tape stock (clear or white, large window/small window) and the inclusion (or not) of the song timings on the tape stock. There's also the 1997 remaster cassette. Copies of the French cassette retain the original track sequence on the tape's paper labels which the contents matches the adjusted order.

Finally, the album was reissued in digital and vinyl versions in 2014 to mark the band's 40th anniversary. The vinyl edition is not an exact facsimile of the 1981 edition. While the rear cover reverts to the original track sequence listing, "Escape from The Island" is inserted as the penultimate track while "Dark Light" is moved from the first song on side B to last song on side A. The U.S. edition features a heavy matte stock printed paper dust sleeve with the song lyrics and production details similar to the 1981 version, though Aucoin Management and PolyGram Records are replaced by McGhee & Universal Music credits. Oddly, the old fan club mail address details are left intact. The European version is on gloss stock paper. It also includes a digital download coupon. For both versions, the colors have been deepened on the cover art, and the top hinge for the doorknocker is missing — it's present on photographs of the model door, so it wasn't an addition on the original cover. The center-rings are reproduced but are blurry compared with the originals and the fonts and layout are changed.

(Korean rear cover credits noting "Dialogue")

And, of course, let's not forget transparent window hangers and other assorted contemporary promotional items such as posters!

Why "Music From The Elder" Was DOA

When "The Elder" was young, it was already doomed.
Here are 10 reasons why

There has been a litany of memorable one-liners regarding "Music For The Elder" over the years, hasn't there? You know, stuff like:

As a bad Genesis record, it might get two stars.

"Just A Boy" was a mistake.

"The Oath" is token KISS.

I spent hours and hours getting the thick power chord sounds right.

"The Elder" is a bloated, pompous piece of pap.

We were delusional.

And the obligatory favorite: It's a good album, it's just not a good KISS album.

Blah, blah, blah ...

Let's cut the pseudo-psychologist-inspired drivel.

Musically speaking, the truth is there has never been such a confluence of talent on a KISS studio album. In one corner, you have Bob Ezrin, an all-star producer/instrumentalist/songwriter. In another corner, you have KISS in their creative musical prime. And in the mix, you have a Brill Building alumnus (Tony Powers), a lyrical poet (Lou Reed), a renowned orchestra (American Symphony Orchestra), and a master orchestrator (Michael Kamen). "The Elder" was overflowing with talent. It would be nearly impossible to amalgamate this much musical star power and not yield something reflective of a high quality.

Which begs the questions: Is it really the music that is lacking here? Are the performances really that poor?

Of course, the answers to such questions are ultimately a matter of taste. But I personally believe KISS could have painted the audio equivalent of the Sistine Chapel with "The Elder" and it still would have left fans and critics dumbfounded.

Empty Michelangelo references aside, "Music from The Elder" is certainly not without its flaws. What KISS album isn't? But in listening attentively, "The Elder" seems to have aged like a proverbial fine wine. More than 30 years later, it stands as an adventurous musical ride, replete with bold production, haunting melodies, dynamic passages, meaningful lyrics, emotive guitar solos, and sharp riffs. There are loud choral refrains and delicate lead vocals. There are interesting twists and unexpected turns. There are peaks and there are valleys. And in the KISS tradition, there is a final uplifting message: "I believe in me."

"The Elder" stands as a unique collection of songs in the KISS catalog, one that is ripe for enjoyment (and hopefully a "resurrected" edition someday). So, if the album delivered the goods in spades, why was it a commercial disaster? Without further ado, here are 10 reasons why "Music from The Elder" was doomed from the get-go:

1. KISS Fans' Resistance To Change
Let's face it; KISS fans can be an odd bunch. Unless it's the set list or the stage show, we really don't want change. For example, take Paul Stanley's standard "giraffe boy" makeup retort — there are fans who have come to agree with this sentiment. (And perhaps KISS' healthy attendance figures today are a reflection of this.) Isn't it an interesting coincidence that "Carnival of Souls," "The Elder," and Gene Simmons and Peter Criss' 1978 solo albums typically rank low on KISS fans' favorite album listings? The most well-received track on "Sonic Boom"? Arguably, "Yes I Know (Nobody's Perfect)," a song straight from the Gene Simmons cock-and-balls songbook. It all boils down to this: KISS fans want KISS to be KISS. We want big riffs, we want references to rockets in pockets, we want the big show, we want the hype, we want the bombast. We want "Strutter," not "Odyssey."

2. Order Of The Track Listing

Note to KISS and Bob Ezrin: If you're going to go down the road of a musical departure, there's no use in staying in the shallow end. You might as well take the full plunge. As odd as "fanfare" is, it was designed to be the lead track for this conceptual collection of songs. In rearranging the track listing to put "The Oath" and "A World Without Heroes" as the lead tracks on each side, the entire project was compromised. As a result, an admittedly confusing album became even more confusing. Thankfully, this issue was rectified with the 1997 remastered edition, which did the album justice and afforded many fans the opportunity to finally hear "The Elder" as it was originally intended, albeit 16 years too late.

3. Speak Up

Why go to great lengths to plan a spoken word component, write a script, contract the services of actors, and actually record dialogue, if you're not going to use it? It's a fair question. Of course, all signs point to the removal of the spoken word dialogue as a request that would have come from the label, but one would think that KISS had amassed enough political capital by 1981 to override such a decision, particularly if they felt strongly about it. Another possible theory is that the dialog was deemed disastrous. However, this would seem unlikely as the three actors who read the dialog — Antony Parr, Christopher Makepeace and Robert Christie — were quite talented thespians. The bottom line is that the spoken word component was designed to thread the album's storyline between songs, and its absence is another example of this project being sold short. Inserting spoken word dialog that was actually recorded for a concept album — what a concept!

4. Ace Was AWOL

For a KISS album featuring Ace Frehley to ascend to classic KISS album status, the Spaceman needs to be an integral ingredient. While Ace does make some fine contributions to "The Elder," his musical presence is severely lacking, relegating the resident Jendellian to some sort of nondescript sideman. Sure, Paul Stanley played capably, but imagine an extended solo on "The Oath" or some superlative lead guitar in "Only You" or "I." While some blame for his lack of participation can likely be tossed in the direction of his fellow bandmates or Ezrin, some responsibility has to be assumed by Ace himself. Despite his misgivings about the project, there is something to be said for being a team player and carrying through with your obligations for the betterment of the band. Ace's decision to emotionally discharge himself from the project certainly was not a plus.

5. No Merchandise

Let's get this straight: This is a band that a couple of years earlier released action figures, board games, color-forms, makeup kits, trading cards, and the like. Then 1981 rolls around, there's a new KISS album, and the merchandise plug is pulled? At least play to one of your strengths. Where was "The Elder" merchandise plan? How about a line of "Elder" action figures for the album's main characters? (A Morpheus action figure could have been the Boba Fett of Christmas 1981.) How about KISS action figures in their "Elder" costumes? How about a "Music from The Elder" video game? (Atari, Intellivision anyone?) What about an "Elder" spoken word album with an accompanying picture book? Better yet, how about an "Elder" comic book outlining the story in graphic form? How about an official "Elder" table and chair setting, complete with collectible candle holder? OK, maybe the last item is a stretch, but you get the point.

6. Come Hell Or High Water, Hit The Road

The Hottest Band in the World thrives in a live setting. KISS had just come off their immensely successful 1980 tour of Australia, during which they were rejuvenated by the presence of new drummer Eric Carr. The fact that KISS did not attempt to mount a tour in support of "The Elder" signed the album's death warrant. While some in the KISS camp have gone on record with saying a tour was an impossibility, with a creative team headed by the innovative Bill Aucoin, one would think there was a workable solution. And if the States were out of the question, how about taking the party somewhere else? "The Elder" hit the Top 10 (or near it) in Australia, New Zealand, Norway, Sweden, and Italy. It was also No. 21 in Japan. Back in 1981 rock bands toured to promote a new album. With these KISS songs not making their way to the concert stage, this album didn't stand a fighting chance at establishing meaningful resonance with fans.

7. That Packaging ... Um, Is This A KISS Album?

A wise man once said, "KISS is a band that has to be seen to be heard." Granted, "The Elder" album packaging has a certain charm to it all these years later. We've grown attached to the image of Paul's hand reaching for a mysterious-looking door knocker, and the gatefold with the table, chairs and candle, and that alluring block of text. But the fact is "The Elder" remains the only KISS studio album not to contain a photo of the band anywhere on the album's packaging. And the KISS logo is practically hiding. Part of the appeal of record shopping back in the day was browsing through the album racks.

With its wood panel-esque color scheme, the album looked like a brown blob of nothing. Who was going to pick that up, let alone buy it?

8. No KISS Promo Push
An album as grand as "The Elder" deserved to be ushered in with appropriate grand spectacle. Between Bill Aucoin and Neil Bogart, the latter whom was probably still a phone call away, some sort of KISS-like promotional scheme should have been concocted. How about something big, something that's going to get attention and bring "The Elder" to the people? How about a series of record store signings? How about public listening parties at a string of theaters in major markets. How about a one-off performance with the American Symphony Orchestra on Broadway? What about a big "Elder" press junket, engaging a group of journalists? Remember the "Black Box" for the solo albums? How about a similar pre-recorded "Elder Box" containing a collection of interviews for radio stations? How about an "Elder" TV special with exclusive interviews with the band and Ezrin detailing the project? How about a little ingenuity and creativity?

9. KISS Did Not Unmask
Multiple project participants have recalled there was serious discussion about KISS unmasking for "The Elder." In hindsight, this could have been not only the calling card that could have saved the album, it could have been something that garnered publicity. Consider 1983 and KISS' decision to unmask for "Lick It Up." "Lick It Up" is a fantastic album, but perhaps it benefitted even more given the fact the band had officially unmasked. With such an added push, maybe, just maybe "Music from The Elder" would have been viewed in a completely different light. Imagine the headlines: "An Unmasked KISS Get Serious With New Concept Album."

10. The Stigma Of KISS
Not to be flippant, but "Music from The Elder" was essentially a failure because it was released by KISS. Think quickly about what this band is best known for and think about "Music from The Elder." The answer is right there. In other words, if this album was released by a band that possessed a more progressive, experimental pedigree, chances are it would have been hailed a prodigious work. But since the music contained within was released by KISS, there was a snowball's chance for "The Elder" to be evaluated by its own merit.

The Elder's Heroic Journey

By Stephen Lord

Thirty-five years after its release, "Music from The Elder" has the dubious honor of being perhaps the most controversial entry in the KISS catalogue. Its birth and gradual evolution from the "straight-on rock and roll that will knock your socks off" comeback Paul Stanley promised in late 1980 into the album we know today is as well documented as its makers will allow. Stanley, Gene Simmons, Ace Frehley and producer Bob Ezrin have been blisteringly candid about the record's making and perceived shortcomings, but no one has shed much light on its attempt at a narrative. We know it began with a short story Simmons "had written for the screen" but, in the wake of the project's spectacular failure, his reluctance to go into detail is as understandable as it is unfortunate.

In Chapter 22 of his Album Focus, KissFAQ's Julian Gill describes "Music from The Elder" as "an obscure album built on an obscure premise." The saga of a young boy who learns to overcome his doubts and gains the confidence he needs to fulfill his destiny might have broken new ground for a band who built their career on simple three-chord party anthems, but the central themes are as old as stories themselves. Similar ideas appear in myths, legends and religions from all over the world. Again and again we meet heroes who must perform pre-ordained tasks and face a series of character building challenges as they do so.

Mythology expert and academic Joseph Campbell calls this process "the hero's journey" and his 1949 book "The Hero With A Thousand Faces" has informed the work of everyone from Stanley Kubrick, George Lucas and JK Rowling to Bob Dylan, Jim Morrison and the Grateful Dead. Given Simmons' fondness for movies and comic books, it's reasonable for him to have drawn some inspiration from it as well.

For all his influence, Campbell is not always easy to read. When Hollywood executive Christopher Vogler worked for Disney, he distilled the book's essence into a seven-page memo, which he later used as the basis for his screenwriting manual, "The Writer's Journey: Mythic Structure For Writers." That structure breaks the journey down into 12 stages.

1. THE ORDINARY WORLD: An introduction to the hero through his or her everyday life.

2. THE CALL TO ADVENTURE: An external or internal challenge to the hero to step away from his or her comfort zone and play their part in the larger world.

3. REFUSAL OF THE CALL: The hero tries to turn away from the adventure, and often uses prior obligations as an excuse not to participate.

4. MEETING WITH THE MENTOR: The hero either meets someone who gives him or her training, equipment, or advice that will help on the journey, or reaches within to a source of courage and wisdom.

5. CROSSING THE THRESHOLD: The hero commits to leaving their ordinary world and entering a new region or condition with unfamiliar rules and values.

6. TESTS, ALLIES AND ENEMIES: A series of tests which enable the hero to learn who to trust on his or her journey.

7. APPROACH TO THE INMOST CAVE: The hero and newfound allies prepare to face their major challenge.

8. THE ORDEAL: The hero enters a central space and confronts death or faces his or her greatest fear. Out of the moment of death comes either a new life or a new appreciation for their present one.

9. THE REWARD: The hero takes possession of the treasure he or she has won by facing death. There may be celebration, but also danger of losing the treasure.

10. THE ROAD BACK: The hero is driven to complete the adventure and bring the treasure home. Often a chase scene signals the urgency and danger in this part of the journey.

11. THE RESURRECTION: The hero faces another, more severe test on the threshold of home. Another sacrifice, or moment of death and rebirth, purifies him or her on a higher level. The hero's actions resolve the polarities, internal and external, that were once in conflict.

12. RETURN WITH THE ELIXIR: The hero returns home or continues the journey, bearing some element of the treasure that can transform the world as the hero has been transformed.

Vogler goes on to identify the character archetypes the hero meets on his or her journey. These represent familiar patterns of human behavior, which the examples below represent.

1. HEROES: Central figures in stories. Everyone is the hero of his or her own myth.

2. SHADOWS: Villains, antagonists or enemies, perhaps the enemy within. The hero's repressed possibilities or his or her potential for evil. This category may also include other destructive forces such as repressed grief, anger, frustration or creativity that are dangerous if they do not have an outlet.

3. MENTORS: The hero's guide or guiding principles, such as an inspirational coach or teacher.

4. HERALD: One who brings the Call to Adventure, either a person or an event.

5. THRESHOLD GUARDIANS: Obstacles that block the hero's important turning points on their journey. These may be jealous enemies, professional gatekeepers, or the hero's own fears and doubts.

6. SHAPESHIFTERS: Vampires, werewolves or, in a less literal sense, double agents or defectors. These characters represent change or ambiguity, the way other people or our perceptions of them vary.

7. TRICKSTERS: Clowns and mischief-makers, who are often more perceptive than their public persona suggests (e.g., the Fool in "King Lear"). They reflect the hero's mischievous subconscious and urge them towards change for the better.

8. ALLIES: These characters help the hero to manage change. They may be sidekicks, buddies or romantic partners who support and guide the hero through the transitions of life.

Many creative writing teachers, some of whom I've studied under, claim this model provides a foundation for any story worth telling. Anyone familiar with "The Elder" will recognize a few of the stages and characters I've listed above but, when evaluating how well the storyline "ticks all the boxes," it's important to keep in mind that the album as released was the first volume of a trilogy that never saw the light of day. Had KISS completed parts two and three, the tale they attempted to spin might have reached a more satisfactory resolution, likely by following the dependable if predictable three act structure of most motion pictures. I could hypothesize forever on how the band might have gone about this.

Painted in very broad strokes, "Music from The Elder" demonstrates a working knowledge of the heroic journey's early stages. After a portentous opening with "fanfare," "Just A Boy" shows us the anonymous protagonist's ordinary world, once a comfortable and familiar place now under threat from persons unknown. He wants to help save and protect it yet has little or no confidence in his ability to do so ("I'm no hero/Though I wish I could be").

To my ears, the earlier placing of "Odyssey" is one of few mistakes on the 1997 remaster. It's a track by an outside writer with no prior connection either to KISS or Ezrin, and I can only suggest they chose it for theme rather than content. If "Odyssey" belongs anywhere, I would put it after "Mr. Blackwell" and before "I." It makes the most sense for the boy to have his moment of revelation after he returns from the mental and physical journey the song suggests he's undertaken.

"Only You" gets things back on track, offering both the call to adventure and its refusal. Our hero to be meets Morpheus, who explains his destiny in cryptic terms ("Only you have the answers / But the questions you have to find") and suggests the biggest challenge he will face on his quest comes from within.

The boy, of course, will have none of it. He denies the caretaker's claims ("I can't believe this is true / Why do I listen to you?") and wonders if they've chosen the right man for the job ("If I am all that you say / Why am I still so afraid?").

Morpheus is an appropriate choice of name for The Elder's herald figure. It's a nod to the Greek god of dreams and translates as "he who shapes," a process which can refer to destinies as much as unconscious imaginings. The Wachowskis picked up this idea and ran with it in their "Matrix" films, using Laurence Fishburne's same-named character to wake Neo from the sleep of his everyday world and guide him towards his ultimate purpose.

"Under the Rose" brings our hero in waiting before the Council. They remind him of the task their caretaker has hinted at ("But now before you lies a quest at hand/and from this boy you may become a man") and warn him of the consequences if he decides to accept it ("Loneliness will haunt you, will you sacrifice?").

Meeting the mentor(s) continues with a couple of long overdue and very welcome pieces of exposition. "Dark Light" is about the state the world will soon find itself in, leading to the rise of "Sodom and Gomorrah / The malevolent order." Although Frehley's vocal delivery makes it less than convincing at times, the message gets through to our protagonist and his subsequent declaration that "A world without heroes is nothing to be / It's no place for me" marks a significant turning point in his development. He understands now that if there is no one else to stand against evil, he must do it himself.

"The Oath" follows an epiphany with a crossing of the threshold. This shows the boy leaving behind his ordinary world to take on the role the Council have appointed him for. Upon pledging himself to the Order of the Rose, he attains a new sense of confidence and realizes everything Morpheus and the unnamed Council members have told him is true. ("I gave my heart and I set it free / There's no turning back from this odyssey / Because I feel so alive suddenly").

As powerful an album opener as "The Oath" was in 1981, the remaster restores its rightful place in the timeline. There is no way the boy could "go forth surrendering to history" without due preparation, knowledge or self-awareness.

"Mr. Blackwell" introduces the story's antagonist, the earthly representative of an evil force as timeless as "The Elder." Whether the 'Washington, D.C. power broker" mentioned in one of the album's early plot synopses has sought this role on purpose is a matter for debate. The contradictory lyrics suggest internal conflict ("I never said I was more than I am" vs. "You're a victim, a real disgrace") and the chorus's concern for his health ("You're not well, Mr. Blackwell, why don't you go to hell") indicates an adversary who is no more prepared for his role than the untrained hero we met in "Just A Boy."

Difficult as it is to incorporate an instrumental into the plot, the title "Escape from The Island" and the use of sirens on the track itself present a couple of options. Since the struggle between good and evil is eternal and cyclical, it's possible Mr. Blackwell's unseen employers have hatched their latest scheme while imprisoned, and used his kidnapping of a world leader as a cue to break out and lose their plans on the world. Pure speculation on my part but, considering how little we know, anything's possible.

"I" is a chest-beating slice of self-affirmation, which reminds us how far "The Elder"'s new champion has come since we first met him. The shared vocals and anthemic chorus recall "Shout It Out Loud" and perhaps it's there to remind the listener that, under the progressive rock veneer of this new and very different album, lies the KISS spirit they once knew and loved. It's a nice touch that comes too late to save the album and, by extension, the band.

The first part of the tale they worked so hard to tell ends on a positive, upbeat note and showcases a hero who is ready to overcome the obstacles he will face on the rest of his journey but, unfortunately or fortunately depending on your point of view, neither he nor the fans got a chance to learn what these would be.

Recorded under very difficult circumstances by a band in the midst of an identity crisis, "Music from The Elder" presents a promising, if somewhat cryptic, take on the heroic journey. We'll never know how it might have continued or resolved and, while that may be for the best in commercial terms, it will remain one of the biggest "what-ifs" in KISStory.

(Instrument rentals)

Who's Who: "The Elder"

You have been summoned to learn more about the book's participants and other key contributors to "Music from The Elder"

Waring Abbott
Order of the Rose: Photographer for various "Elder" video shoots

A renowned music industry photographer, Abbott has photographed several iconic artists, including Bob Dylan, the Rolling Stones, the Who, Led Zeppelin, Lou Reed, Elvis Presley, Madonna, Bruce Springsteen, and Annie Lennox, among many others. Abbott first teamed with KISS in 1974 and subsequently photographed several iconic early sessions, including the band's memorable trip to Cadillac, Mich., in 1975. He served as photographer at "The Elder" video sessions for "A World Without Heroes" and "I" (the latter video was never aired), as well as the band's trio performance at Studio 54 in early 1982. A collection of Abbott's KISS photographs can be seen in the 2002 book "KISS: The Early Years."

American Symphony Orchestra
Order of the Rose: Performer on select "Elder" tracks

The ASO was founded in 1962 by legendary British conductor Leopold Stokowski with the goal of showcasing the talents of American musicians through "concerts of great music within the means of everyone." The orchestra, under the direction of Michael Kamen and Bob Ezrin, can be heard on "fanfare," "Odyssey," "A World Without Heroes," and the album's concluding dialog sequence. Aside from "The Elder," the orchestra has been featured on a multitude of classical recordings, including works by Tchaikovsky, Boulanger, Ives, Debussy, Prokofiev, and Sibelius, among others. The orchestra has performed at benefits for various organizations such as the Jerusalem Foundation and PBS. ASO's award-winning music education program, Music Notes, integrates symphonic music into core humanities classes in high schools across the tri-state area. Leon Botstein has served as ASO music director and principal conductor since 1992.

Bill Aucoin
Order of the Rose: Manager

Having served as KISS' manager from 1973–1982, Aucoin's importance to the group's success cannot be overstated. Aucoin was instrumental in bringing Bob Ezrin back to the KISS fold in 1981, citing his "good track record" and the fact that "Polygram suggested Ezrin as producer." Aucoin once described "The Elder" as being a "rough" album to complete. In "KISS: Beyond the Makeup," he added, "'The Elder' is probably more a Bob Ezrin album, than it is a KISS album." As a result of its poor showing, "The Elder" proved to be the final KISS album Aucoin would steward. He and KISS severed ties in 1982. Aucoin died on June 28, 2010. He was 66 years old.

David Braun
Order of the Rose: Polygram President

Originally beginning his career as an agent, Braun went on to become one of the music industry's most powerful attorneys, representing artists such as Neil Diamond, Bob Dylan, George Harrison, and Michael Jackson. Braun notably negotiated a deal with CBS Records netting Jackson 42 percent of the wholesale price on albums sold in the United States, a substantial increase from the standard artist percentage of 10-20 percent. Abandoning his law practice, Braun was appointed president of PolyGram Records in 1981. He held the position for less than a year, returning to his law practice in 1983. Braun once noted that he left PolyGram as "the compact disc was coming in" the industry. Braun died Jan. 29, 2013. He was 81 years old.

Eric Carr
Order of the Rose: Drummer/contributing songwriter

Carr replaced original KISS drummer/co-founder Peter Criss in 1980, playing tour dates in support of "Unmasked." "The Elder" was Carr's first studio album with KISS. He co-wrote two songs, "Escape from The Island" and "Under the Rose," the latter for which he wrote the music. Carr played on all of the album's tracks except for "I" and "Odyssey," which featured noted session drummer Allan Schwartzberg. After more than a decade as KISS' drummer, Carr succumbed to cancer in 1991. He was 41 years old.

Melanie Chartoff
Order of the Rose: "Fridays" cast member

An actress and voice actress, Chartoff's first TV role came in 1976 for the TV series "Search for Tomorrow." She earned her career breakthrough as a cast member for ABC late-night comedy show "Fridays." The show, which ran from 1980 to 1982, featured recurring characters and sketches, short films, a parody news segment, and musical guests. Chartoff later played the character Ms. Musso on Fox's teen series "Parker Lewis Can't Lose" and created the voices Didi and Minka for Nickoloden's "Rugrats" franchise. Also, a veteran of the theater, Chartoff has played roles in productions such as "Via Galactica," "Scapino" and "The Vagina Monologues." In addition to her acting career, today Chartoff offers acting and voice coaching services.

Brian Christian
Order of the Rose: Associate producer/engineer

Born in Chicago, Christian served as a recording engineer under legendary Canadian producer Jack Richardson, who became a mentor to not only Christian, but Bob Ezrin. Prior to his work on "Music from The Elder," Christian engineered recordings for B.B. King, the Guess Who, Randy Bachman, the Babys, Bob Seger, and Moxy. He also collaborated with Ezrin on projects such as Peter Gabriel's 1977 debut solo album and Pink Floyd's mega-selling 1979 concept album, "The Wall." Christian currently resides in Los Angeles, where he works in the gaming industry.

Robert Christie
Order of the Rose: Spoken word contributor

Christie was contracted to contribute spoken word dialogue to "The Elder." He read the role of "Morpheus" that can be heard during the album's concluding sequence. A University of Toronto graduate, Christie relocated to England in the mid-'30s performing with companies such as the Old Vic Company. He also served the Canadian Army during World War II and taught acting at Ryerson Polytechnic University in Toronto. His film work includes roles in "The Bloody Brood" (1959) and "The Incredible Journey" (1963). He performed the role of Sir John A. Macdonald in the 1949 play "Riel." Christie appeared on Broadway, performing in such productions as "Tamburlaine" (1956) and "Love and Libel" (1960). Christie also did some television work, acting in series such as "For the Record", "Wojeck" and "Seeing Things." Christie died May 22, 1996. He was 82 years old.

Marty Cohen
Order of the Rose: Friend of Gene Klein and Stanley Eisen

Marty was a pre-Wicked Lester friend of both Simmons and Stanley and played with them, separately, in several bands. More importantly, he was present when the two future partners were first introduced to each other. He remained friends with them, and continued his musical endeavors, and may have provided an indirect motivation for the band to attempt "The Elder."

Eric Critchley
Order of the Rose: Glass artist

Eric was a British glass artist who had started out working with the BBC painting backdrops prior to moving to the U.S. Some of his most notable work can be seen in the Michael Jackson "Billie Jean" (most of that set is Eric's creation) and Fleetwood Mac's "Gypsy" videos. He was responsible for the creation of the background used in the unreleased "I" video.

Kevin Doyle
Order of the Rose: Engineer

 A graduate of Fanshawe College in London, Ontario, Doyle was a staff engineer at Sounds Interchange, one of the studios utilized for "The Elder." Doyle was also on hand for album sessions at Manta Sound and Ezrin Farms. He was the engineer on Glenn Gould's classic "Bach: The Goldberg Variations," which earned two Grammy Awards in 1982. Some of the other artists Doyle has worked with include Alannah Myles, Van Morrison, Andrea Bocelli, Sinéad O'Connor, Hall and Oates, and Demics. In 2004 Doyle became a professor at his *alma mater*, Fanshawe College. Doyle has won three Juno

Awards, including one for his engineering on Myles' 1990 self-titled album, which contained the No. 1 hit "Black Velvet."

Bob Ezrin
Order of the Rose: Producer, engineer, songwriter, arranger, instrumentalist

By 1981 Ezrin had become renowned for his seminal work with Alice Cooper, Pink Floyd, Peter Gabriel and Lou Reed, in addition to KISS' 1976 album "Destroyer." Two years prior to "The Elder," Ezrin co-produced "The Wall," Pink Floyd's mega-selling imaginative concept album comprising themes of abandonment and isolation. Aside from collaborating with Simmons on "The Elder" storyline, Ezrin co-wrote five songs on the album and played keyboards on "A World Without Heroes," "Only You" and "Just A Boy" as well bass on "Dark Light" and "Escape from The Island." He also collaborated with composer Michael Kamen for the album's symphonic arrangements, which were carried out by the American Symphony Orchestra. While recording "The Elder," Ezrin was also producing sessions for the Kings' second album, "Amazon Beach." Circa 1974, Ezrin formed Migration Records, a label imprint distributed by Atlantic Records that is listed next to his album credit. In 2004 Ezrin was inducted into the Canadian Music Hall of Fame. In 2005 Ezrin co-founded Music Rising, an initiative that assisted the hurricane-ravaged Gulf Coast region. Today, Ezrin resides in Nashville, where he is a board member for the Nashville Symphony. In 2012 he oversaw the remix of "Destroyer: Resurrected" and produced Deep Purple's 2013 studio album, "Now What?!" Ezrin was inducted into Canada's Walk of Fame in 2013.

Simon Fields
Order of the Rose: Video producer

Serving as the liaison with PolyGram Records, Fields was a co-producer of KISS' videos for "A World Without Heroes" and "I." Following his tenure with Gowers, Fields & Flattery, he started his own company, Limelight Productions, which specialized in not only music videos, but commercials and films. Their commercial accounts included Calvin Klein and Nike and the company produced videos for Michael Jackson, Madonna, Prince, David

Bowie, and A-ha, among others. Today, he is the CEO of Fields Entertainment, a feature film and television production company.

Anton Fig
Order of the Rose: Contributing songwriter

In 1981 Fig was the drummer for the five-piece pop/rock band Spider, which featured Holly Knight of "Hide Your Heart" fame. At that point, Fig had played drums on KISS' prior two studio albums, "Dynasty" and "Unmasked," as well as Ace Frehley's 1978 solo album. Fig is credited as the co-writer of "Dark Light" with Frehley, Gene Simmons and Lou Reed. The song evolved from the Frehley/Fig demo "Don't Run." Fig is credited with the main guitar riff. As a member of Frehley's Comet, Fig played on the group's debut album, "Live +1" and Frehley's 1989 album "Trouble Walkin'." He was the longtime drummer for the CBS Orchestra, the house band for "The Late Show with David Letterman." More recently, Fig has played drums on albums by guitarists Oz Noy, Joe Bonamassa, and Eric Johnson & Mike Stern. He also played on Frehley's 2009 album, "Anomaly."

Bill Finneran
Order of the Rose: Maker of "The Elder" door

Finneran is a partner of Manhattan Model Shop, a business he oversees with his wife, Kathleen. Founded in 1974, Manhattan Model Shop specializes in model making and building 3-D props for major TV commercials and print advertising. The company has made torches for the Olympics, giant pills for Tylenol and the original MTV "Moon Man" trophy. Receiving direction from art director Dennis Woloch, Finneran built "The Elder" door, including the knocker. "Music from The Elder" is the sole album cover for which the Manhattan Model Shop has built a prop. Finneran is a graduate of Philadelphia's William Penn Charter School.

Paul Flattery
Order of the Rose: Video producer

A partner in Gowers, Fields & Flattery, Flattery was the conceptual video producer for the videos for "A World Without Heroes" and "I." His primary responsibility was coming up with the treatments for both videos. Throughout his career, Flattery produced more than 100 music videos, including work with John Mellencamp, Blondie and Michael Jackson, among others. He has also helmed more than 100 TV specials, including "Live 8," "The Concert For New York City" and "VH1 Rock Honors" in 2006 honoring KISS.

Rob Freeman
Order of the Rose: Engineer

From an early age, Rob enjoyed tinkering with reel-to-reel tape recorders provided him by his father. Years of fascination and experimentation with tape recording led to his first semi-pro projects recording bands in his hometown of Allentown, Pennsylvania. While still in his early teens-not yet old enough to drive-he frequented local venues, lugging a bulky tape recorder and a bag stuffed with reels of magnetic tape, microphones, cables, and audio adapters. In 1972 Rob's band RMI-TMI, in which he played keyboard, recorded an album at New York's landmark Media Sound Studios. After completion of the album he stayed on to intern in the studio for six months. These experiences helped Rob land his first professional position at dB Studios in Chicago in 1973. There he honed his razorblade editing and mixing skills while recording innumerable jingles and radio and television spots and managing the studio's extensive sound effects library.

From 1974 until 1979, Rob was head engineer and part owner of Plaza Sound Studios in New York City, a classic recording facility situated high atop Radio City Music Hall. His years at Plaza Sound coincided with the advent and growth of the New York punk rock scene. Trolling downtown for new artists to record, Rob made contacts at CBGB's, the epicenter of that scene, and managed to position himself in the middle of it all. Rob was privileged to be the recording engineer on such seminal albums as the Ramones' debut album Ramones, Blondie's Blondie and Plastic Letters, and Richard Hell and the Voidoids' Blank Generation. Throughout his Plaza Sound years, Rob made records with a diverse array of artists including KISS, Ace Frehley, Rupert Holmes, Twisted Sister, Salsoul Orchestra, Robert Gordon, Link Wray, Martha Velez, Sunny Fortune, Genya Ravan, John Miles, The Laughing Dogs, and many more. In 1979 the Rockefeller Foundation sold Radio City to the Disney Corporation, and Plaza Sound Studios closed its doors. So began the free-lance chapter of Rob's career that continues to this day. Early free-lance projects had him recording albums with KISS, Julie Brown, and The Elektrics and mixing a Top 40 single for Agnetha Faltskog of Abba. In time, Rob made the jump from engineer to producer, and, over the decade that ensued, produced singles, EPs, and/or albums for Twisted Sister, Lawrence Gowan (currently of STYX), Tim Moore, Jailbait, Single Bullet Theory, Regina Richards, The Go, Surgin', and Queen City Kids, among others. Notably, Rob co-produced, engineered and mixed the debut album by the Go-Go's, Beauty and the Beat. That album went multi-platinum around the world, topped the US Billboard album charts at #1 for six weeks, spawned two hit singles, was the first #1 album by an all-girl group who wrote their own songs and played their own instruments, and, incredibly, was crowned the CMJ (College Music Journal) Top Album of the Decade (1980-1990).

Rob's efforts over those busy years have garnered him a variety of acclamations and awards such as Billboard's Top 15 Producer of the Year (1982), Pro Sound News' Engineer of the Year (1983), Pro Sound News' 2nd Runner-up Producer of the Year (1983), one RIAA (US) Gold Single, two RIAA (US) Gold Albums, and two RIAA (US) Platinum Albums, eight Ampex Golden Reels, two BPI (UK) Gold Albums, one CRIA (Canada) Gold Album, one CRIA (Canada) Platinum Album. Today Rob resides in Florida with his wife Teresa, Broker/Owner of Florida Realty Elite. Though still taking on occasional music projects, Rob has refocused his sound recording skills to include production sound for feature films, documentaries, commercials, and broadcast television.

Ace Frehley
Order of the Rose: Lead guitarist/contributing songwriter/lead vocalist

Frehley co-wrote two tracks on "The Elder": "Dark Light," a song that morphed from the demo "Don't Run" with assistance from Lou Reed, and "Escape from The Island," an instrumental notable for not featuring either Paul Stanley or Gene Simmons. Though he plays lead guitar on "Dark Light," "Escape from The Island" and (allegedly) "Mr. Blackwell," Frehley recorded several lead guitar tracks that were ultimately unused. Some of KISS' recording sessions in 1981 took place at Frehley's then-new recording complex, Ace in the Hole Studio, in Wilton, Conn.

Bruce Gowers
Order of the Rose: Director
Gowers served as the director for the "I" and "A World Without Heroes" video shoots in New York City. As a partner in Gowers, Fields & Flattery, Gowers directed music videos for artists such as Michael Jackson, the Bee Gees, Blondie, the Rolling Stones, and Prince, among others. Gowers is renowned for directing the iconic music video for Queen's "Bohemian Rhapsody." An Emmy winner, Gowers has directed a variety of television shows, specials and live concerts.

Rich Hart
Order of the Rose: Engineer

Hart's credits as an engineer include work with Pink Floyd on "The Wall," David Gilmour, Pat Benatar, Andy Williams, and Alice Cooper. Hart was also one of the engineers on the Kings' 1981 album, "Amazon Beach." Hart currently works as a rerecording mixer in the film industry.

Bas Hartong
Order of the Rose: Phonogram International A&R manager

Appointed an international A&R manager for Phonogram International in 1979, Hartong brings an insight into the business equation during the period Casablanca had fully come under the control of the European multinational corporation.

Jerry Jaffe
Order of the Rose: PolyGram head of rock radio promotion

As vice president of rock music for PolyGram records, one of Jaffe's primary challenges was getting the music properly promoted in the marketplace.

Promoting "The Elder" was a challenging task, particularly after being given the record after it had been released to muted response.

Robert "Ringo" Hyrcyna
Order of the Rose: Engineer.

Considered "Bob Ezrin's right-hand man" by those who worked on "The Elder," Hyrcyna has been described as a hard worker and someone who kept copious session notes. Prior to "The Elder," Hyrcyna engineered recordings for the Kings, Peter Gabriel, Moxy and Alice Cooper. He also worked with Kansas, Berlin, Hanoi Rocks, and Pink Floyd.

Michael Kamen
Order of the Rose: Symphony arrangements

A Grammy-winning composer, Kamen was best known for his work on movie soundtracks and his collaborations with artists such as Aerosmith, Metallica, Sting, Eric Clapton, and Pink Floyd. Kamen worked with Bob Ezrin to flesh out the orchestral arrangements featured on "The Elder." He previously teamed with Ezrin and Pink Floyd to work on the orchestral arrangements for "The Wall." Kamen received an Academy Award nomination for Bryan Adams' "(Everything I Do) I Do It For You," which was featured in "Robin Hood: Prince Of Thieves" (1991). As a film composer, Kamen's credits included "Die Hard" (1988), "License To Kill" (1989), "X-Men" (2000), and the "Lethal Weapon" franchise of films. In 1996 Kamen created the Mr. Holland's Opus Foundation, an organization dedicated to supporting music education via the donation of instruments to underserved schools and community programs in the United States. Ezrin currently serves as the foundation's vice chair. Kamen died Nov. 18, 2003. He was 55 years old.

Chuck Klosterman
Order of the Rose: Modern author and music writer

Chuck Klosterman is the New York Times bestselling author of books, such as "Sex, Drugs, And Cocoa Puffs;" "Eating the Dinosaur;" "Killing Yourself To

Live;" and "The Visible Man." His debut book, "Fargo Rock City," was the winner of the ASCAP Deems Taylor Award. He has written for publishers such as "GQ," "Esquire," "Spin," "The Washington Post," The Guardian, The Believer, and The Onion A.V. Club. He currently serves as "The Ethicist" for the New York Times Magazine and writes about sports and popular culture for ESPN. His most recent book is 2014's "I Wear The Black Hat."

Ida Langsam
Order of the Rose: Publicity

During "The Elder" era, Langsam handled all publicity for KISS. She had just joined Aucoin Management and created and supervised worldwide PR for all of the firm's artists. She later started her own company, Public I Publicity Services, with clients including Triumph and Meat Loaf. Later she formed a close working relationship with the Ramones, with whom she would work with until their retirement in 1996. Other artists Langsam did publicity for include Barry Manilow, Linda Rondstadt, the Grateful Dead, and Styx. Since 1995, she has run ISL PR, a publicity firm offering a long track record of industry experience.

Christopher K. Lendt
Order of the Rose: Business manager

Lendt was an employee for Glickman/Marks Management Corp. from 1976 – 1990, ultimately ascending to the level of vice president. He served as business manager for KISS, managing their concert tours and overseeing the band's growing business affairs. Lendt also was the business manager for legendary artist Diana Ross. Since 1992, Lendt has been an adjunct professor of marketing at New York University. He also currently acts as a consultant for artists and entertainment companies. In 1997 Lendt released "KISS and Sell," a riveting account of his years with KISS. A graduate of the University of Southern California, Lendt today resides in the New York area.

Barry Levine
Order of the Rose: Photographer

Levine photographed some of KISS' more iconic '70s images, including the band atop the Empire State Building, the Spirit of '76 photo shoot, the 1976 "sparkle" shots, the band's shots in front of Buckingham Palace, and the "Love Gun" mylar photo shoot. Levine has stated that his "toughest" assignment with KISS was the shoot for "Music from The Elder." For this shoot, Levine built geometrical sets to photograph the band against. Two backdrops were applied, one of which was stark white and the other featuring a bright pink color coupled with what almost looks like a yellow light saber. A shot with the latter background can be seen on the "Killers" album cover. This was Levine's last session with the band until he photographed them in 1996 prior to the Alive/Worldwide tour. Some of the nearly endless list of artists Levine has photographed include Elton John, Sweet and ABBA. Levine was one of the producers for KISS' 1999 feature film, "Detroit Rock City." That same year, Levine published "The KISS Years," a book featuring a collection of his KISS photographs. He is currently the president and chairman of Radical Studios.

Christopher Makepeace
Order of the Rose: Spoken word contributor

A Canadian actor, Makepeace was contracted to play the spoken word role of "The Boy." While dialog was recorded, Makepeace's contributions to "The Elder" have never seen the light of day. Makepeace starred in films such as "Meatballs" (1979), "My Bodyguard" (1980) and "They Mysterious Stranger" (1982). An interesting coincidence, Makepeace and fellow "Elder" spoken word contributor Robert Christie star in the 1981 film "The Last Chase," which also stars Lee Majors and Burgess Meredith. According to IMDB, the most recent film Makepeace appeared in was 2001's "Full Disclosure."

Jeffrey and Russell Marks
Order of the Rose: Scriptwriters

In the 2001 Butterfields KISS auction, the one known 130-page "script" from the project sold for $488.75 (plus buyer premiums). That script was attributed to Russell and Jeffrey Marks.

Michael McCarty
Order of the Rose: Uncredited engineer

A graduate of Fanshawe College, McCarty began his career as an engineer/producer under the wing of Jack Richardson. He was the engineer/associate producer on the Kings' 1981 album, "Amazon Beach," a project that was produced by Ezrin during the same time he was overseeing "The Elder." McCarty participated as an engineer for "The Elder"'s sessions at Phase One Studios in Toronto, though he is not credited on the album. He is a founding director of the Canadian Songwriters Hall of Fame. McCarty formerly served as president of ole, one of the world's largest independent music publishers.

Antony Parr
Order of the Rose: Spoken word contributor

Another Canadian actor, Parr was contracted to contribute spoken word dialogue to "The Elder." He read the role of the Council of the Elder member that can be heard during the album's concluding sequence. Born April 30, 1925, in Nottingham, England (Robin Hood country), Parr's long-standing entertainment career spanned theater, TV, radio, and spoken word. Parr trained at Sterndale Bennet's Canadian Theatre School in Toronto, and launched his career playing the leading role of the Governor General in the iconic smash hit Canadian musical "My Fur Lady." On TV he played the regular role of the Desk Sergeant on "Sidestreet" as well as guest starring on "The Great Detective" and "The New Avengers." Additional TV credits included work on "The Littlest Hobo," "Murder by Phone," and "Seeing Things." He also appeared in films such as "Alien Thunder" (1974), "Agency" (1980), "Mark of Cain" (1986), "Mindfield" (1989), and "M. Butterfly" (1993). Well-known for his deep rich voice, he was often asked specifically for voiceover work on TV and for radio programs such as "The School for Scandal" on CBC. Parr also starred in several plays including Emlyn Williams' "Night Must Fall," Peter Shaffer's "Equus" and Checkov's "The Seagull," as well as plays at the Stratford Festival (Ontario). Parr died Sept. 26, 2002, in Toronto.

466 | O d y s s e y

John Picard
Order of the Rose: Guitarist for the Kings

Professionally known as Mister Zero, Picard is the guitarist for '70s Canadian-based rock band the Kings. The group's first two albums were co-produced by Bob Ezrin, with 1981's "Amazon Beach" being recorded during the same time as KISS' "Music from The Elder" sessions.

Tony Powers
Order of the Rose: Contributing songwriter/instrumentalist

A New York native, Powers is an alumnus of the famed Brill Building songwriting scene of the 1960s. During that time, Powers collaborated with Phil Spector and Ellie Greenwich, among others, co-writing several songs, including the Sapphires' "Gotta Have Your Love," the Crystals' "Today I Met The Boy I'm Gonna Marry" and Darlene Love's "Why Do Lovers Break Each Other's Hearts?" Powers made Paul Stanley's acquaintance at Cafe Central, a then-popular NYC celebrity hangout, and subsequently came onboard as a collaborator for "The Elder." Powers would contribute his self-penned "Odyssey" and lyric ideas for "The Oath," a song co-written with Stanley and Bob Ezrin. Powers also played piano on "Odyssey," a track featuring the American Symphony Orchestra. In 1984 Powers released a video EP, "Don't Nobody Move (This Is A Heist)." The EP contained a rerecorded version of "Odyssey," sung by Powers, and a video featuring Powers and actress Lois Chiles. Powers is also an actor, appearing in films such as "Goodfellas" (1990) and TV shows such as "NYPD Blue." Powers released his latest album, "Who Could Imagine," in 2007.

Mark Ravitz
Order of the Rose: Stage designer

Ravitz had a long history with KISS, with his work having encompassed the creation of their iconic stage logo in time for the Academy of Music show on New Year's Eve 1973–74 and the spider-web backdrop seen in other early photographs. In 1981 he was engaged to develop staging concepts for an unnamed KISS tour.

Lou Reed
Order of the Rose: Contributing songwriter

Reed is best known as a solo artist and a member/principal songwriter of the American rock band Velvet Underground, who were inducted into the Rock and Roll Hall of Fame in 1996. Reed was brought in as a collaborator on "The Elder" through his association with Ezrin, who had produced Reed's 1973 classic album "Berlin." Reed contributed lyrics to the songs "Dark Light," "Mr. Blackwell" and "A World Without Heroes." Lore has it that the latter song was based on a title scribbled down by Reed. Reed also wrote the unused lyrical idea "Morpheus Descending." In 2011 Reed collaborated with Metallica on "Lulu," a concept project based on two plays written by German playwright Frank Wedekind. Reed died Oct. 27, 2013, from liver disease. He was 71 years old.

Allan Schwartzberg
Order of the Rose: Uncredited drummer

A studio drummer extraordinaire, Schwartzberg has played on albums for artists such as John Lennon, Roger Daltrey, Rod Stewart, Nils Lofgren, and Astrud Gilberto, among others. He also played drums on Gene Simmons' 1978 solo album. Schwartzberg was a "go-to guy" for Bob Ezrin, having drummed on Ezrin-produced albums for Peter Gabriel and Alice Cooper. Schwartzberg was brought in for "The Elder" sessions specifically to play on "I" because "Eric [Carr] was not playing with the feel that Bob felt it needed," according to Paul Stanley. Schwartzberg also plays drums on "Odyssey." He would later contribute select drum parts to KISS' 1984 album "Animalize."

Roseann Shellnut
Order of the Rose: Glickman/Marks Advertising

Shellnut was a driving force behind the advertising of KISS product during the "Elder" era. She died in 2012.

Gene Simmons
Order of the Rose: Bassist, principal songwriter, lead vocalist, and "Elder" concept creator

Simmons developed the storyline that served as the basis for "The Elder" concept and would later receive input from producer Bob Ezrin. Aside from playing bass on the album (save for "Escape from The Island" and "Dark Light"), he co-wrote six songs. In many ways Simmons can be described as the band's principal leader on "The Elder."

David M. Spindel
Order of the Rose: Album photographer

A renowned photographer, the Brooklyn-born Spindel has captured images of icons such as John Lennon, Joe DiMaggio, George Burns, and Willie Mays, to name a few. His work has been showcased in various media, including newspapers, magazines, TV, and album art. For "The Elder," Spindel shot the entire contents of the album package, including the door and the gatefold table setting. Spindel now resides in Arizona, where he stays active with various design projects. Some of his images of Lennon can be seen in the 2010 book "Starting Over: The Making of John Lennon And Yoko Ono's Double Fantasy," authored by Ken Sharp ("KISS: Behind The Mask"). TV personality Regis Philbin once quipped, "David Spindel is a little eccentric; however, you have to put up with him because he is a genius."

St. Robert's Choir
Order of the Rose: Choral contributors

St. Roberts Choir was literally comprised of young members of the St. Roberts Catholic High School in Gormley, ON, Canada. Bob Ezrin had served as executive producer on the school's production of "Jesus Christ Superstar," which was recorded at Manta Sound in April 1981. A very rare private pressing of this production was issued on LP and may be one of the catalysts that changed KISS' musical direction that year...

Paul Stanley

Order of the Rose: Rhythm guitarist, lead guitarist, principal songwriter, and lead vocalist

Stanley co-wrote four of the 11 songs on "The Elder." He sang lead vocals on three songs, shared lead vocals on a fourth ("I") and contributes "The Boy" lead vocal part on "Only You." In addition to his usual rhythm guitar duties, Stanley played lead guitar on some of the album's tracks. In recent years, Stanley has criticized the album, calling it "a bloated, overblown, pompous piece of pap" in 2010.

Corky Stasiak

Order of the Rose: Engineer

Stasiak was one of the house engineers at the Record Plant studios in New York City. His credits include work with Lou Reed, Aerosmith, Jim Croce, Bruce Springsteen, and Three Dog Night. A KISS "veteran," Stasiak is credited as an engineer on recordings produced by Ezrin and Eddie Kramer, such as "Destroyer," "Rock and Roll Over," "Love Gun," and "Alive II." He also engineered Ace Frehley's solo debut, 1987's "Frehley's Comet."

Ty Tabor

Order of the Rose: Musician influenced by "The Elder"

Tabor is a founding member of the progressive-rock trio King's X. The group has released 12 studio albums, including their most recent effort, 2008's "XV." King's X have the distinction of being among the artists who performed at Woodstock '94. An acclaimed guitarist, Tabor also is a member of Jelly Jam, a trio project with bassist John Myung and drummer Rod Morgenstein. As a solo artist, Tabor's most recent release is the 2013's "Nobody Wins When Nobody Plays." Tabor is also the founder of Alien Beans Studio, a facility specializing in recording, mixing and mastering.

Chip Taylor

Order of the Rose: PolyGram head of A&R

A Songwriters Hall of Fame inductee, Taylor has written iconic songs such as "Angel of the Morning" and "Wild Thing." In addition to his songwriting career, Taylor has released three decades' worth of solo albums and launched the independent label Train Wreck Records. At the urging of David Braun, Taylor took a sabbatical from his recording career to become PolyGram's head of A&R, a position he held during the release of KISS' "Music from The Elder." In KISS circles, Taylor is perhaps better known for co-writing Ace Frehley's "Rock Soldiers," the lead track from his first post-KISS solo album. Trivia: Taylor is the brother of Oscar-winning actor Jon Voight.

Tim Trombley
Order of the Rose: Production Coordinator

Trombley served as Bob Ezrin's personal assistant throughout the recording of "Music from The Elder." Trombley later was with EMI Music for more than 20 years, serving as vice president of talent acquisition and artist development. Today, he is the director of entertainment at Caesars Windsor in Ontario, Canada. Trombley's mother, Rosalie Trombley, was a prominent DJ for CKLW, a Top 40 radio station located in Windsor, Ontario, whose signal stretched into Detroit and as far east as New York and Connecticut. Interestingly, circa 1976, Rosalie Trombley's daughter owned a copy of the 45 featuring the song "Beth," and began nagging her mother about it. "Beth" wasn't being promoted as the "A" side, but Trombley soon added it to CKLW's playlist. The song later was issued as a proper single and became a smash, and KISS presented Trombley's daughter with a gold record.

Jerry Watson
Order of the Rose: Director of video photography

Watson served as the director of photography for a number of music videos, many filmed by Gowers, Fields & Flattery, including KISS' "A World Without Heroes" and "I." He has also worked as director of photography and lighting designer for shows such as "America's Got Talent" and "American Idol." More recently, he served as director of photography for a live AC/DC concert film at Wrigley Field in Chicago.

Dennis Woloch
Order of the Rose: Album art director

An employee of Glickman/Marks Management Corp., Woloch served as the art director for KISS from 1975–1987. Woloch oversaw art direction for several graphically iconic KISS albums, including "Alive!," "Destroyer," "Rock And Roll Over," the 1978 solo albums, and "Creatures Of The Night." For "The Elder," Woloch was charged with carrying out the album's esoteric graphic vision. He scouted several New York church doors, taking photograph samples. Woloch served as the liaison with Manhattan Prop Works, the company that built "The Elder" door, and David Spindel, who photographed the album package. Aside from KISS, Woloch has also designed albums for artists such as Diana Ross, Starz and Peter Gallway. Today, Woloch designs albums, logos, advertising campaigns, books, and more under the auspices of his own company, Dennis Woloch Design.

Misc. Album Credits:
Ken Anderson is credited as production coordinator. Additional production assistance is listed as being provided by George Sewitt, Tex Holmes, John Harte, Stephanie Tudor, Bernie Meehan, and Jayne Grodd. David Brown is credited as an engineer. Tom Laughlin is credited as chief technician. The album was mastered by Ted Jensen.

Appendices

"Music From The Elder:" Track Sequences

There were several notable track sequences proposed for "The Elder." Some work, some obviously don't. For those you may not be aware of, queue up your digital "Elder" tracks and give the album a listen in a new way

Sept. 16, 1981

The earliest currently known sequence, this comes from a memo that included Bob Ezrin's rough sketch idea for the rear cover of the album. It was also included on a layout sheet for the album cover elements.

Side 1	Side 2
Fanfare	Mr. Blackwell
Just A Boy	Escape From The Island
Odyssey	A World Without Heroes
Dark Light	The Oath
Only You	I
Under The Rose	Closing Theme

What is the "Closing Theme" noted in the very first of these track sequences? Is it the same as "The Summoning," the surviving dialogue section that was included on the album? What is known is that the song-writing splits changed throughout the project. Initially, both "fanfare" and "Closing Theme" were derived from elements in "Just A Boy" and "Odyssey." As late as the orchestration session, in mid-September, sweetening was recorded for both tracks, though the former was changed (or finalized) later in the month to remove an "Odyssey" derived material — as a result the credits on "fanfare" changed from Stanley/Ezrin/Powers to simply Stanley/Ezrin by Sept. 22. With "Odyssey" appearing early on the first side, bringing back elements of the song in a musical album ending piece would have unified the overall feel of the album (similar to the use of parts of "Psycho Circus" in "Journey Of 1,000 Years" in 1998).

Sept. 22, 1981

Just a week later, in a new memo, the B-side sequence is changed, with the caveat that further changes are expected. "The Oath" takes its place as the story's *denouement*, the declaration of the boy as he embarks on his quest. It certainly seems to make more sense to end the album with this song, rather than "I." If there are test pressings of either of these first two versions, then it would be on these that any additional dialogue or interludes would be expected.

Side 1	Side 2
Fanfare	Escape From The Island
Just A Boy	Mr. Blackwell
Odyssey	I
Dark Light	A World Without Heroes
Only You	The Oath
Under The Rose	Reprise/Ending

Oct. 1, 1981

For want of not knowing the date of this "original" version, also known as the Japanese version mix, it'll arbitrarily be assigned the Oct. 1 date. Aucoin received test pressings from Hauppauge Record Manufacturing, Ltd. (HRM) in Long Island, NY, by Oct. 7, so this version definitely dates earlier than that date in terms of when it was physically pressed. The test pressing exactly matches what was used for the Japanese and Portuguese versions and what turns up on the hybrid Canadian version of the album.

Side 1	Side 2
Fanfare	Dark Light
Just A Boy	A World Without Heroes
Odyssey	The Oath
Only You	Mr. Blackwell
Under The Rose	I

Oct. 8, 1981

The same track order as the HRM pressing, which may indicate the same mix. Pressed by PRC-West in Compton, CA other details are currently unknown.

Oct. 26, 1981

The version most fans became used to during the 1980s, an abomination of chopping and moving songs around so that they made no sense whatsoever within the context of the story (as much as the story made any sense).

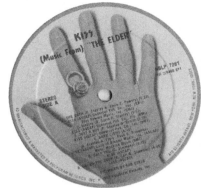

Side 1

The Oath

Fanfare

Just A Boy

Dark Light

Only You

Under The Rose

Side 2

A World Without Heroes

Mr. Blackwell

Escape From The Island

Odyssey

I

The Summoning

Oct. 7, 1997

The "Remaster," which while using the Japanese mix, inserted the missing song from that version of the album into an odd position. The sequence is taken from the cassette version.

Side 1

Fanfare

Just A Boy

Odyssey

Only You

Under The Rose

Side 2

Dark Light

A World Without Heroes

The Oath

Mr. Blackwell

Escape From The Island

I

June 29, 2014

The "KISS 40" vinyl edition made minor changes to the sequence.

Side 1

Fanfare

Just A Boy

Odyssey

Only You

Under The Rose

Dark Light

Side 2

A World Without Heroes

The Oath

Mr. Blackwell

Escape From The Island

I

Robert V. Conte Takes Fans inside "The Elder" Vault

KISS' 1990's catalogue consultant recalls his encounters with "The Elder" and working with the band on various projects.

Robert, we're going to talk about a focused part of your KISStory, so I don't want to rehash too much of the great information you provided on the Three Sides of the Coin podcast (episode #207). I do want to strongly recommend that folks check that episode out — it was certainly very engaging and entertaining. For the sake of introducing our past relationship, I believe we first crossed paths way back in 1997. I'd sent a fax to Mercury/Polygram in New York, while I was still living in Scotland. And you called me, since I'd used my father's fax, which had a "Dr." header, making it seem I was more important than I certainly was ...

Robert V. Conte: Yes, I tried to directly respond to KISS fans who attempted to reach me after the "KISS: The Remasters" project. I appreciate your remembering that!

What do you recall of that fax I sent? I think I criticized your liner notes, didn't I?

You certainly did, yes! You know, it's funny because when "KISS: The Remasters" were first released, the internet was still in its infancy. A lot of KISS fans chose to handwrite letters, as opposed to using email, so there was a time when a lot of mail was coming in and we received a mixed reaction. A lot of people commented, "Oh, my God — this is great!" There were others who thought they were "okay," but wanted more. And then, of course, there were those who said, "I don't really like this writing. I don't like these liner notes." You were initially in the latter group. I remember that! *(Laughs)*

I think I even sent you a copy of the atrocious U.K. "Double Platinum" remaster that was housed in a regular jewel case with gray print cover insert with black ink line art; rather than the beautiful, foil-embossed reproduction that made for the U.S. market... I always like to give people a 90,000-foot view of the person who I'm speaking with, in terms of their relationship with KISS. So, what was your "Ed Sullivan" moment within the

KISS construct; that moment that initially sparked your interest in the band?

It's funny; I'd have to say that it was three different instances combined into one — if that makes any sense. When I was around 7 or 8-years-old, I had seen the Marvel Super Special #5, the second KISS comic with the green-and-white logo cover. Around that same time — I think it was sometime near the first anniversary of Elvis' passing — Donruss had issued a series of Elvis trading cards. I was a big non-sport trading card collector at the time, so I'd go to the local smoke shop which also had a ton of trading cards. They had Star Wars, Close Encounters of the Third Kind, Superman the Movie, and then I saw the Elvis cards. Next to Elvis were KISS cards. I said, "Wait a minute!" So, that in conjunction with the Marvel Comic plus I remember seeing the TV ads on NBC for the "KISS Meets the Phantom of the Park" special. And then there were kids in my class — I think I was in third grade at the time — who brought some KISS albums to school. So that was probably when I was really first exposed to KISS — via the merchandising. But what got me into the music was around 1982. My now-deceased friend, Brian Aarons, had invited me over to his house for an overnight stay and he had a ton of heavy metal music. I was not as knowledgeable as Brian was at the time about this particular genre and he had some really obscure stuff. There was early Metallica, Saxon, Anvil, Twisted Sister — just a really eclectic collection. As I'm flipping through his enormous vinyl collection, I saw "KISS Alive!" We put it on and, honestly, from the second I heard that first explosion on "Deuce," I was hooked!

But what really got me into KISS was the night KISS unmasked on MTV [in September 1983]. Some may not be aware of this, but, before that special aired, David Lee Roth was featured on an exclusive half-hour long interview with MTV; so anyone that was a Van Halen fan ran home to watch it. It was also the very first time that MTV aired the "Pretty Woman" video; even though it was old it was the first time it had ever aired on MTV. And then afterwards was the KISS unmasking on MTV. The "Rock and Roll All Nite" live compilation that they aired beforehand, with primarily the Tokyo 1977 footage, just blew me away. I was fortunate enough that I videotaped it on my General Electric VHS recorder! I ran downstairs where I kept all my stuff in my house and dug up the Donruss trading cards, the KISS custom Chevy van model kit a kid had given me for Christmas, the KISS View-Master 3D reels, etc... All of a sudden, I was now a rabid KISS fan!

What was your first "new" KISS album?

I became a very devout listener immediately and my grandmother, who lived with us, would bring me home a new KISS album every week — as long as I did well in school. So, the very first KISS studio album that I owned for myself was "Dynasty." And then almost every week afterward I would get a new one.

What was the first album that you bought new? You're already into the band, what was the first album that comes out for you? Was it "Animalize," I guess? Or "Lick it Up" at that point?

It was actually "Lick It Up." I actually did not like the song "Lick It Up," but when MTV aired the "All Hell's Breakin' Loose" video I said, "Wow, this is great!" I went out and bought "Lick It Up." Then when "Animalize" came out I purchased that, and then subsequently every KISS album that came out, I bought on the first day of release.

Looking back at 35-plus years as a fan, what's your favorite KISS album at this point? If you have to pick just one album that you'd take with you to a desert island, which would it be?

I'm always torn with that because it's either the first KISS album or "Hotter than Hell." I love them both so much, so it's always hard for me to pick one. If I really had to pick one, I'd probably say the first album because there's just so much great material on that album. During the Alive/Worldwide reunion tour they played at least six songs off that record. Other KISS fans have said this too; it's like a greatest-hits album on its own in a sense. And that first album cover, it just blew me away! As I told you, my grandmother would get me a KISS album every week so the first one she got me was "Dynasty," the second one was "Hotter than Hell," which I thought had just a beautiful cover. But then the third LP she got me was the first KISS album. At the time I used to call it the horrific KISS album photo because they didn't look like superheroes yet. They looked like "pure evil." But that was just such a fantastic cover. I know a lot of people don't like it, but I love it! And "Black Diamond" on the album was just so cool. I just thought the fade out of the record was so brilliant at the time.

Before we get into the topic that we're actually going to discuss, I'm going to make you play favorites and choose your flavor of KISS Kool-Aid. Who is your KISS guy, the guy who kind of best sums up KISS for you?

I would have to say Gene Simmons because I got to know him personally more than any of the others. He was the one that picked me to be the first

KISS Catalog Consultant. So I'll go with Gene simply because of our personal relationship at the time.

It's kind of hard to fault a guy who opened that door for you!
Yes, basically I was being let into the KISS kingdom at the perfect time. I started working with them sporadically at the close of the "Alive III" era and then when the reunion tour happened. Just to be part of that experience in an official capacity and I was only 25 years old at the time! It was just such a wonderful opportunity and such an amazing gift from somebody I had idolized since I was 13 years old.

I know from some of the stories that you told in that excellent "Three Sides of the Coin" episode that I can totally understand why you're drinking "Demon" flavored Kool-Aid. Those were some great stories about your interactions with Gene and some of the calls that you received from him. However, we're going to focus on brown Kool-Aid, and I have no idea what flavor it would be... Let's talk about the remaster of "Music from 'The Elder'." I'm almost hearing the sound effects from that album in the back of my head as I speak (A door clanking open, the chains being dragged across the floor, footsteps shuffling). As a KISS fan, what was your first impression when you heard "The Elder" for the first time and where did it fall into you exploring the back-catalog when you became a fan?
The first time I heard "The Elder" was probably spring 1984. My school had taken us on a field trip during the time boom boxes were big and in-fashion to carry on your shoulder. A local record store had a special on certain cassettes and when I went to look for KISS, "The Elder" was on sale for $3.98. So, I bought it. I already had "Creatures of the Night" on cassette, so "The Elder" was completely new for me. I remember listening to it with some friends in a park during the field trip. Of course, it was the original American version that starts off with "The Oath." I liked that song, but then it got kind of interesting after "Just a Boy." I said, "Well, this certainly isn't 'War Machine' or 'I Love it Loud,'" or anything like that. It was also before I had owned "Unmasked" so it was kind of strange to me that the music wasn't as heavy as I had been used to already with "Creatures of the Night," "Lick It Up" and the first album. So, I won't say I hated it, but it wasn't one that I listened to every day like the other albums. Over time I appreciated it more.

I think any KISS fan has to be in a special sort of mood to say, "You know, I just want to listen to *Fanfare* today." When you were writing your critique

of the state of the KISS catalog in 1993, did you include "The Elder" in that analysis and what do you recall being the issues that you noted about that album specifically in terms of how it was being presented in the catalog at the time?

After PolyGram had purchased Casablanca Records in the United States, they started redoing everything with their logos and reissuing all the formats. This was also during the time that record albums started including bar codes, though initially PolyGram just took all the existing inventory of Casablanca's records and slapped stickers on them with the UPCs (Universal Product Codes). Soon afterwards they started reprinting the sleeves which included new bar codes and other current information. With "The Elder" I have to backtrack this a little bit. When I was about 20, in late-1990, I had gone into a record store in Manhattan, New York and they had a whole section of Japanese imports. They had a version of "The Elder" that had band photos on the cover overlay. I couldn't believe it, my heart dropped right away, and I said, "Oh my God, I gotta buy this!" Now to put this in perspective, to buy "The Elder" brand new American was probably $6.98 at the time. To buy the Japanese import version back then was $39.95. It was a big investment, but the plus side was that the Japanese track sequence was in a different order than the American sequence, in addition to the band photo on the front OBI overlay and other fascinating differences.

When I wrote the report for Gene, I noted, "Listen, if there's a way to put 'The Elder' back in its original track order that would be fantastic." Then during the remastering process, after I had written the essay and he reviewed it, I had put together a new track sequence. Another thing that some may not realize is that the Japanese version did not have "Escape from the Island" on it at the time. So what I pitched to Gene was, "Hey, let's do the ultimate 'Elder,'" meaning let's make sure everything that was on it, both the American and the Japanese versions would be melded together, and restore the album back to its original track sequence. He approved it and then we had to persuade Mercury/Island Def Jam to let us do it that way. Fortunately, "The Elder" remaster in '97 and its vinyl counterpart which was only available as an import has the full "The Elder."

Can you describe the approach that was made for you to take on the KISS Catalog Consultant role and how that role was defined? Were the parameters you'd operate under written down like a job description?

There was no official contract, if that's what you mean. Basically, I was hired as a freelancer. The title "KISS Catalog Consultant" wasn't mentioned to me until the Los Angeles KISS Convention (June 17, 1995). Gene announced that the band had hired me to be the official KISS Catalog Consultant! That was the very first time I ever heard the term! Of course, I was ecstatic because I'm finding out for the first time that I'm actually going to be in charge of the KISS Remasters project. You know, it's interesting, I think I'm the first of the three KISS Catalog Consultants. I believe Curt Gooch was in that role for the "KISSology" project and Tom Shannon consulted on the KISSteria vinyl reissues. I don't know if anybody else has had that position. To be the first one in that role, I tried to work with the record company, the band, the licensing agent (Sony Signatures) and McGee Entertainment, because they didn't really understand all the intricacies and all the minutia of the changes that occurred to the catalog over the years.

When I first went to Gene's guest house in 1994, I brought some of the KISS records and cassettes with me to show him what some of the differences were. He was just shocked that some of the catalog had been basically bastardized. There's a very limited run of "Alive!," "KISS Alive II," and "Double Platinum," where they basically shoved two records inside one sleeve. I showed all three of those versions to Gene and he just couldn't believe it. I remember distinctly he left me a voice mail the following day saying that he had called KISS's lawyers and the record company and things were going to be changed. To have been the "trigger man" to bring back KISS albums to their original intended form—and being invited to be part of that process— was just a wonderful experience!

You didn't really have any previous experience in the industry, did you, or is there anything in your background that you think set you up for being able to work with not just the artist, Gene in particular, but also the label folk as the KISS Remasters project kicked off?
My only experience in the music business beforehand was that I had written some rock and roll comic books and that most of my disposable income was used to build a massive record collection and my knowledge of the industry. There were a couple of Long Island local bands and another group in Los Angeles I had either managed briefly or tried to work with to get them record deals. But certainly nothing as significant as the KISS project.

Were the KISS Remasters on the table from day one or did the project evolve? Was there always a plan to remaster the whole catalog and was Robert V. Conte going to be heading up that to make sure it's done properly?

I was told one thing by the record company and another by KISS. The idea was because I had written the extensive report and included photographs of all the different variants and noted all of the changes (I used to call it the de-evolution of the catalog because it just fell into the wrong hands at some point), Gene wanted me involved to make sure that it was done right. Jesse Hilsen, who at the time was Paul's psychiatrist and also KISS's manager to some context, understood how fans were rabid for the toys, merchandise, tour books and everything. He couldn't, however, comprehend how or why I was buying multiple copies of the same records. At that time, I had 32 variants of "Alive!" He just could not understand why I or anyone else would care about that.

I remember him saying, "I wonder if you have Asperger's?" I didn't even know what that was! I'm like, "What do you mean by that?" He goes, "Well, do you have obsessive compulsive disorder?" I said, "I know I do!" (Laughs) But, no one in the KISS camp, up to that point, knew about and/or was willing to invest in 32 copies of "Alive!" to open and point out all the differences in each version; and then explain why one version differed from another. I think that got me in the door in that respect. I know that they had considered at least two other music journalists that I was acquainted with to write the liner notes. Ultimately, all parties involved decided that I was the best suited for the job. That was nice!

How early on in the process was it decided to release the albums in batches because obviously they came out on a staggered schedule in 1997 and 1998?
Originally, we were supposed to remaster "Alive!" and "KISS Alive II" and that was going to come out as a special box set, and then be followed up with the studio albums. At some point that had changed after we had already remastered the "Alive" albums. When that box set got canned, after we had already done the work, they decided to make "Alive!" and "KISS Alive II" part of the quarterly releases. I think it was every 3 months that they put out four records.

Were "The Elder," and the other non-original albums, such as "Creatures of the Night," "Lick It Up," "Animalize," "Asylum," and "Crazy Nights" always planned for inclusion in the project, or with the project being rooted in the reunion era, was there originally a focus just on the 1974–79 era?

No. From day one, after the "Alive/KISS Alive II" box set got nixed and they decided to do all the studio records, it was definite to do all the makeup albums. So, it was definitely from "KISS" through "Creatures of the Night," and then sales were good enough that it warranted doing "Lick It Up" through "Crazy Nights."

I'm curious about one thing in particular, especially as we're specifically talking about "The Elder." Was there any reticence from Gene and/or Paul about including that album in the KISS Remasters project? It had been such a commercial failure; they've never had too many good things to say about the album. It had also been omitted from previous reissues in the U.S. and ignored by the label for much of the 1980s. It did finally get properly reissued on CD in 1989, I believe, but was there any desire from the band to sweep it under the carpet?
No. When the KISS Remasters project was approved it was always with the idea from "KISS" through "Creatures of the Night." There was never any talk about taking the album out of the equation. As I said, once Gene and I had a discussion about making sure that the Japanese market got "Escape from the Island" on the same CD and we were able to put the tracks back in the original order, the band was very supportive of the idea. There was never talk about nixing it.

There was no talk either about making any other changes to it other than unify and original mix — which is what was released in Japan in 1981 — and putting "Escape from The Island" back in? They didn't want to make any other changes to the product in any way?
Actually, there was a time when we were going to do expanded Digipak versions of the KISS Remasters and there were plans to basically do them as limited editions that would only have been available through the KISS Army Depot and through the Mercury/PolyGram website. But the store editions did not sell enough for them to want to justify trying to do the limited editions. I begged and I pleaded, and we even designed the very first four of those, "KISS" through "Alive!" There are actually digital files that exist of the Digipak packaging designs and everything with extra tchotchkes [Ed. The premium goodies included in a release] and all the stuff. Sadly, we couldn't get Mercury to give us the green light, but it would have been something, you know! And, that leads to another project I'll tell you about a little later.

Hold that thought and don't forget! Was the whole catalog remastered in one shot or did they do it in batches? And what do you know about the

actual project to remaster the audio for "The Elder?" Where does that in terms of the timeline?

We did them all in order other than "Alive!" and "KISS Alive II" which were done first. But then when we started with "KISS" onward, we didn't stop. Certain records took longer to remaster than others, so it wasn't like every week I was doing a different record. Some records took maybe a week and a half to get right. The thing about "The Elder" though, was it had the most multi-track recordings in the warehouse than any other KISS album that was there. I mean there were just boxes and boxes of tapes, primarily from Ace Frehley's Ace in the Hole studio. Mercury/PolyGram had those tapes and they were just laying on shelves and we couldn't figure out [what it was]. Some of the tapes weren't logged into their computer system, so fortunately if the engineers had some time and we put some of that stuff on the reels... It was just amazing hearing that stuff for the first time! I had tried to pitch the idea of doing this remaster with a bonus disc with some of the alternates and outtakes, but because "The Elder" sales were amongst the lowest of all KISS records in the catalog, that idea was not looked upon very favorably.

You just touched on the New Jersey storage facility. Before we talk about "The Elder" in there, what was the first album — when you enter the doors of a hallowed facility (in terms of the KISS fans' desires for what they might find in there) — that you actually went to investigate in there?

"Alive!" and "KISS Alive II," and then any of the bonus live material that may have been in there on the multi-tracks because it was also around the time the compilation album "You Wanted the Best, You Got the Best" was being planned. The idea was to find any unused live material that they had in the vault for possible inclusion on that record.

I want to stay away from "You Wanted the Best..." because I'll start crying after hearing what you told us on Three Sides about the original conception versus what it became. I just don't want to relive that sorrow (laughs). Going back to "The Elder" cage, what sort of media are we talking about that was in there? Are we talking the full 2" multi-tracks or 1/4" mix-down reels, acetates, test pressings, cassettes, or any other sorts of stuff that kind of sticks out in your mind?

Regarding "The Elder," there were tons of reel-to-reels of various sizes. There were about 50 to 60 boxes of tapes in total of multi-track recordings. I'm not just talking about the mastered LPs, cassettes, reel-to-reel, and 8-tracks. The problem was that I wasn't permitted (sadly) to open up a lot of that stuff because when we were remastering, each album had a budget at Sterling Sound, the mastering studio. So, we really couldn't go over what that time was allotted for each album. We got "The Elder" remaster done in enough time that I was able to listen to some of those mystery tapes. But not the whole tape from beginning to end; we would put a reel onto the player and then run it for a few minutes to hear the basic gist of what was on that particular tape. And then we'd move on to something else. But once that budgeted time got allocated, we couldn't really do anymore with it than what we had.

So how do you identify which master source is going to be used as the basis for the remaster when it comes to "The Elder?" How do, how do you find that? Is it recorded accurately that a certain source is the actual mix? Because we know, from assorted studio documentation, that there were multiple mixes done of the album. There were mixes that were rejected and then remixes that were done. How do you find which one was the one that you needed to go off in order to keep it authentic to what was originally released?

We had each master that was used for replication to make albums, cassettes, and 8-tracks, so on and so forth. They would all be marked "Approved for Replication." We went back to the original master recording that was approved for the American version and then we also got the Japanese version sent to us. And then we worked on both those masters together to reconstruct the version that you ultimately hear on the '97 remaster.

What sort of condition were "The Elder" reels in? You have previously mentioned that some of the boxes that you went into, the materials were in pretty dire shape.

Almost pristine mint condition. The Japanese one was actually amazing. The way they store their tapes is just incredible. You would think like you were walking into a perfect vault.

With "The Elder" master reverting to what was the essentially the original mix, only released in Japan in 1981; would it be fair to say that it forms the primary foundation for the remaster and only "Escape From The Island" was taken from the U.S. version?

The Japanese master tape was used to duplicate the complete "*fanfare.*" Other than that, it was a reference guide for us to create a new EQ from its track listing. Then we took "Escape from the Island" from the original U.S. master and digitally "spliced" it in.

Going back to the track sequences again, and I don't want to make this sound too much like an inquisition, but there were numerous sequences that were discussed. How did you decide where to put "Escape from the Island" into the Japanese version when the original Japanese track listing obviously didn't have that song and the American track order was so different?

I had selected three possible spots to put it in and we made what were called remastered reference CDs. One set was burned for Gene, one set was burned for me, and a third set was burned for the record company. Basically, it came down to a voting process. It was like okay, "I think it should be here. What do you guys think?" Gene and I agreed on where it ultimately rested and I think the record company, to be honest, didn't care. When the record company wanted something, they made their position known, let me put it that way. You've got to remember that the record companies, they're looking at back catalog as, "Okay, we're investing money in old catalog to hopefully recoup." You've also got to remember that at this time Mercury/Island Def Jam was upset that the "Carnival of Souls" album had had to be shelved because of the reunion tour. Here's a company that's hesitant because they invested a ton of money into "Carnival of Souls," then had to shelve it because it wasn't the original four members who played on the album. They were also very disappointed at the sales of "You Wanted the Best, You Got the Best," and we know why. When it came to "The Elder" it was really more of, "Okay, this is a creative choice. Just keep it within budget"

Going back into the vaults, you took notes of what you were kind of finding in there and I know you're working on a project that we'll probably hear quite a bit more detail about it, but do you recall any like reels from Penny Lane Studios in particular? That's where they did a lot of their pre-"Elder" recordings before Bob Ezrin became involved in the album sessions. They were working out of Ace in the Hole and finishing up the vocal and overdub work at Penny Lane. Does that ring any bells?

Off the top of my head that doesn't ring a bell. Ace in the Hole does because the majority of those multi-tracks that were on the shelves did come from there. The other reason I remember that so well was because of the Federal Express packaging — a lot of those tapes were sent back and forth via Federal Express. I know this sounds corny but I'm a big fan of pop culture.

So, seeing the evolution of the Federal Express logo I remember noting because these early FedEx logos were actually pretty cool. However, when I go through my diaries on "The Elder" if I did see something that says Penny Lane it will be noted because I wrote everything down.

I guess the one key question about "The Elder," particularly to someone who has actually been in the presence of all these reels, is: Did you find any of the missing spoken word dialogue? Obviously you didn't have time or the budget to go listen to everything, but there's always been the assumption that there is a version of the album that does contain the snippets of dialogue that were recorded in September 1981 that were ultimately were cut out (with only the section at the end of the album remaining). Did you hear any of that dialogue?
No. The one thing I did hear that really sticks out was basically just Ace doing scat vocals and he would make comments like, "Oh, my God!" or "What time is lunch coming!?" and stuff like that. One thing that he did turn in, which I thought was really cool, was a really tight version of "Don't Run," which was an earlier version of "Dark Light" that was almost complete. I would say the way I could relate it to KISS fans is on Ace's album, "Anomaly." The first song, "Foxy & Free" compared to the demo for "Hard for Me" that's streaming right now. That's how I would compare it. The version of "Don't Run," that I heard in the vault, is actually pretty tight as far as his composition and his role in it. That was actually one of the songs I had fought hard for, to include on a bonus disk for "The Elder," because I just thought it was so cool. But it wasn't to be. There was definitely a version of that and the two engineers and I who heard it were just so excited about it.

That one has circulated in fan circles since the 1980s as have multiple takes and mixes of "Escape from the Island" and "Just a Boy," and various instrumentals. Many seem to be Eric Carr and Ace working together. The whole question about the spoken-word dialogue is kind of the albatross of the project. We know without doubt that the dialogue was recorded. We know the actors went into the studio, we have the script, we know what they planned to read, and we know there's just one line from that script that's left on the album. Everything else is missing and even Bob Ezrin couldn't recall whether they ever put a version together of the album that included it.

So, when we talk about the remasters, obviously there was quite a bit of work done on those to reproduce some of the original premiums in the

booklets, such as the booklets for "Alive!" and "KISS Alive II." Originally, "The Elder" came as a gate fold jacket primarily with a translucent printed inner dust sleeve because that had become popular in 1981. Was there any talk about how these were going to be packaged? You did mention the Digipak, but with the jewel case version was there any desire to do anything special with "The Elder" in terms of kind of bringing it back to the original packaging? You know in a way similar to how you handled the "Alive" albums?

It's interesting that you say that. I was a big advocate for trying to keep everything exactly the way it was on its very first release. However, the art department disagreed with me in the sense that they wanted — and I agreed with this ultimately — all the albums to be uniform looking. So that the albums lined up on a shelf all made sense visually. And I agreed with that. That was actually one of the problems I had with some of the other versions that preceded the remasters. They weren't concise in a lot of ways. As far as "The Elder," here's a little surprise I'll share with the world: A lot of people think there's only three versions of the U.S. vinyl of "The Elder." There's actually six. The project I'm working on for next year will show all six, amongst other things that some people aren't aware of. But the three that I believe most KISS fans are aware of are the one with the printed translucent inner dust sleeve, the one with the printed paper dust sleeve, which came later, and the one with the lyric sheet in either yellow (almost illegible) and subsequently black text.

Right, those are the three main variations of the original 1981 pressings, as far as I'm aware.

Okay. So, I was also a big advocate for including the lyrics in all the albums. I felt it was about time. I said, "Look, Japanese versions have them, other import versions have the lyrics in all these records. We should be really doing it as well." They nixed the idea again. You know, the sad thing is, the poor sales of "You Wanted the Best" had a domino effect into what we were really able to do with the remasters, because Mercury/Def Jam said, "Hey, if this brand new compilation isn't doing well then why would re-releasing these albums and making them look prettier do anywhere near what you're saying they're going to do?" That was a constant uphill battle. I had pitched a concept with one of the designers that worked on the remasters. I also did this with "Creatures of the Night" and "Lick It Up." But we had three initial designs where with "The Elder," you would open it up and then you would open it up again and you would see the photo from the Japanese version. And then you'd fold it open again and there would be the free poster than came with I believe the Norwegian version of the record. My idea initially was to take all the best elements from all the different countries and incorporate them into one remastered version, so you'd have a little bit of everything represented. We even created this compilation page where you would see the evolution of the first label, the blue-and-silver label to the blue-and-black label all the way to the Casablanca Records and Filmworks logo labels. Mercury, they just killed off all that stuff, which is so sad. But here's the good news: I kept all my copies of the Zip disks from that time. The thing that I found out after the KISSteria box set came out — I had thought that Mercury had kept or archived all the stuff that we did — when Mercury/PolyGram was sold to Seagrams, they downsized even more and threw a ton of that material away.

That's infuriating! And depressing...
You're not going to believe this, but the digital stuff that was created from the mid '90s until about two years after Seagrams took it over, they just got rid of most of that stuff. It's so heartbreaking because — I think I touched on this a little bit on the Three Sides of the Coin episode — "You Wanted the Best, You Got the Best" was originally supposed to be a gate fold cover. It was supposed to come with a poster, a bunch of tchotchkes. All those digital files, the copies that Mercury had, they're all gone according to what Universal stated to me. I believe McGhee Entertainment still has their set and I still have my set. So hopefully this stuff will ultimately see the light of day somehow. But, back to "The Elder," there was so much stuff I wanted to do with it and you know sadly when you've got the record company accountant saying, "sales don't justify the cost," it gets very frustrating.

You must have felt very impotent at times because you had pitched a very different idea for "You Wanted the Best," that from what you described would have been much better received by the fans. Obviously, I'm speaking for myself, but I don't think anyone's going to say, "Well, you know it's really missing a 17-minute interview with Jay Leno." Most fans would rather have had three more unreleased recordings or something that made sense. That interview just doesn't fit.
The record pitch I had turned in — all the audio that I had found and put in a sequence that I thought made sense — again this is one of those things that only three copies exist; I have a copy, Gene/McGhee has a copy, and the record company has a copy. What happened was, the multi-tracks for several of those songs were sent to the band — and you know the final product, as we all know, is very different sounding than what I believe it

should have been. But yeah, I had to learn a hard lesson very fast; which was even though you're a consultant, you're not the final say-so. There's a committee, there's a board, and then there's people who make decisions based on just hard numbers and nothing else. Again, in a sense there was a cloud over any KISS project, and it was very frustrating that the shelved "Carnival of Souls" was a used as a weapon. "We have to shelve this damn record because Peter Criss and Ace Frehley aren't on it?" You have no idea the stuff that some of the key people at Mercury would say to use as a reason not to spend money on the remasters. It was really unfortunate.

Having paid an advance to the band they weren't recouping with the completed product just sitting on a shelf, were they? And it had leaked. I understand the attitude they may have had of, "Now we have to spend more money on KISS?" I can understand the attitude from the label perspective. "Now you want _more_ money? We've got to do this for KISS? We've just, you know we've paid in advance!" I'll guess that it would have been 1995, or maybe even late-1994, that the band got the original advance when they started work on the "Carnival of Souls" album, so there would have been several years of real money coming in from that investment. "MTV Unplugged," as fabulous as fans believe the quality of the performance to be, didn't sell spectacularly in terms of album units moved. "You Wanted the Best," well I guess you know about that! I thought it was impressive that it even went gold, to be honest, in the form it took. It was disappointing.

Oh yeah. Do you remember H&H Distribution? They did the limited-edition vinyl versions of "Creatures of the Night," "Revenge" and "Alive III."

Yes. They did a good job with that product.
The original concept of "You Wanted the Best" was going to be an exclusive through them. It wasn't supposed to be a mainstream store item. It was supposed to be something that originally H&H was going to distribute, then it turned into, "Okay, we'll sell this exclusively through the KISS Army Depot," and then as it evolved it became, "Oh, no — we have to do this as a major release!" Okay, you have to understand something — by going in that direction you're trying to encompass a wider spectrum of listeners as opposed to the real diehards who really want to hear the rare and obscure stuff. You've just changed the whole dynamic of the album! When I started working on the record, it was with the idea that it was going to be the ultimate "bootleg album" for the KISS fan that's been waiting 15 years for the band to be back together. And here's some really rare stuff that they

probably won't do on the tour but hey, here's an ultimate package of really cool live stuff from the band, as a thank you to the KISS Army for supporting them all these years. That kind of thing... But when you're in a room full of a dozen people and everybody has their own opinion and ideas, instead of the soup coming out delicious like it's supposed to, it winds up being this mishmash of all these ingredients just thrown together. And it doesn't taste very good. For that being my very first contribution to the band on a record in an official capacity, when I got the promo copy of that record I was so upset. I couldn't even bear to look at the album designer. I didn't even want to talk to him I was so upset. It was just like, "This is not what we want." It was definitely not what I wanted.

How satisfied are you with the realization of "The Elder" specifically as a remaster, especially looking back 20 years? I mean this thing's still in stores — those that remain in business anyway! Did you expect the remasters that you worked on so long and hard to still be the standard CD versions available in that format some 20 years on?
Years ago, when "Sonic Boom" came out and Wal-Mart had the KISS kiosks in certain locations, I brought my kids to one just to show them. I had three young kids at the time, and I said, "Hey, your dad used to work on these records!" My daughter didn't believe me. So, I said, "Okay, I'm gonna buy one. You're gonna see!" I bought "Dressed to Kill," opened it up, and my name was in it. Just to see the excitement on my kids' face. "Daddy, you did this? Are you famous?" That just brought tears to my eyes. Here we are, I did this work 21 years ago — I mean there are babies that were born then that are now full grown adults — and it's just amazing to me, even the streaming versions, like on Spotify and stuff like that, are what we did. That's the stuff that most of the KISS fans are listening to now. It's so gratifying to have been a part of KISStory that, here we are a generation later, and that work is still out there. To this day, KISS fans reach out to me on social media who ask me for my address so they can send me their liner note inserts for me to sign and send back to them! And many of these fans weren't even born when these albums came out. So that is just so touching, and it makes me feel like, wow, here's a KISS fan, a diehard KISS fan whose dream came true and I was able to contribute to the next generation of KISS fans. It's just such a gratifying experience.

Per chance the band's current label decided, "It's 2017, and we did the K40 vinyl reissues last year for KISSteria. It's time to do the CD catalogue again, just like the Beatles did with theirs, we need someone to head up that

project." Would you be interested? Would you do it again? Would you go back and revisit all that knowing what you know now?

I would do it in a heartbeat. I would like to see the original concepts that we had happen now. And the good news is that a lot of those digital files still exist. I'll give you an example; when we did "Destroyer," Casablanca, back in 1976, had bought a bunch of Barry Levine images to use for promotional purposes and things like that. That stuff was in the art department at Mercury when I was working on the KISS Remasters. So, we came up with an idea to do a special photo loaded edition of "Destroyer." I would like to see that happen. We also, and a lot of people don't know this yet, but we designed an alternate version of the CD prints where each album used the original Casablanca label design. You know the very first "KISS" album used the original silver-and-blue Casablanca label [stock], etc. The versions fans have included the KISS logo and the song credits underneath on the actual disk with the Mercury logo on one side and Casablanca on the other.

Right, that would have been more visually appealing than just different colored "KISS" logos as were used. They did something similar to that with the CD version of the "Casablanca Singles, 1974–82" box set in 2012.

"Rock and Roll Over" was the first record with the tan label and "Love Gun" the first with the Filmworks label, but they decided not to go in that direction. We still have all those original files. So, to be able to do the ultimate remasters, I would be very interested in doing this on the level that would surpass any remaster that's been on the market to date from any band. I would want to do the ultimate remasters, if that makes sense.

That's the only thing that you can do with a band like KISS. If they do it now, it's got to be the "ultimate remaster remaster," for what would essentially be a final updating the catalog. To me, it's the only way: Go big or go home, so it probably has to be a premium product similar to the KISSteria box set if they're going to make any real money.

I was quite impressed with the AC/DC remasters when they came out and there was a set of Black Sabbath remasters I felt were brilliant. I don't remember if it was Castle or Warner Brothers that put them out, but those were beautiful. It's a matter of taking things to the next level, like what Metallica did with the boxed remasters for "Kill 'em All" and "Ride the Lightning."

And just look at the newly announced "Master of Puppets" box. It's got ten CDs, two DVDs, one cassette, a hardcover photo/story book and other premiums for $175. 10 CDs!

That stuff is phenomenal, and I would say, "Let's take it 10 steps further!" There's certainly enough material around. There's stuff that I'm working on in the project right now that I'd want to include because after 20-something years a lot of the stuff that I thought would eventually leak out has not. I was privy to a lot of information, a lot of documentation that a lot of KISS fans aren't aware of. The time has come to do something with them and to show fans, "Hey, this is what I learned decades ago, and you guys have a right to see this stuff." The fact that KISS is almost 45 years old is just so cool and, when you have a legacy like that, you know there's so much minutia that has yet to be revealed. You know, when you think you know everything, there's just something else that comes out of left field.

That's one of the important things, with KISS fans, is to remind us that we don't know it all, we never will, and there'll always be something else to discover or clarify. That's part of the magic for me — that we're always learning new stuff! And for those of us that do the archeology, we're constantly reminded that sometimes we're on the wrong track. And it's great to be wrong because you learn something new, or something unexpected, or correct something that was patently false.

It's funny because Universal sent me most of the vinyl releases from the KISSteria set — I didn't get the actual box, but I got most of the albums. I'm very happy that "The Elder" is the version that we created, but put on vinyl for the U.S. That's very cool to me. I wish I got the credit in it like I should have, and Universal knows it should make the revision. My name did show up in "Greatest KISS" and "You Wanted the Best," so I'm happy about that. Of course, with every re-released version of vinyl there's always something you're either going to appreciate or not be happy about. I'm disappointed that Bill Aucoin was basically removed from all of the albums. His credit on those new records is missing and it got replaced with McGhee Entertainment. I get that the new management should be on the current credits, but for the man who discovered KISS and what he had to do to get them a record deal, for him not to be on those records anymore is really disheartening.

It certainly wouldn't do any harm to have the Aucoin logo on there since it no longer exists as a business and of course Bill has passed on. Who knows what the kind of rationale is behind that sort of thing is?

It's not necessarily his logo that's got to be on there but just his credit as original manager. If your first exposure to KISS is the KISSteria box set or any of these vinyl records, you're not being educated about one of the original, most important people involved. That was very disappointing to see. I kept all my albums sealed, so I haven't listened to them, so I don't know if you feel the sound quality has surpassed the previous vinyl versions? Of course, these are more variants that we have to add to our collection because we're completists! (Laughs)

From my collector's point of view, you know I felt sonically they sounded just like the remasters, but on vinyl — to my ears, anyway or with whatever condition the stylus was in on my deck when I played them. Analyzing the new digital files that they made available through HD-tracks.com, again to me they appeared to be pretty much identical wave forms to the '97 remasters, albeit slightly louder as is all they seem to do these days. Like Spinal Tap, "Ooh, slightly louder, it went up to 11." Certainly, good though whatever they did.

The thing that's interesting is how do you go back to an analog medium using a digital master, you know? That's the one thing that I do not understand. You know these are vinyl upgraded sounds, but your base masters are probably the DAT tapes that we created back in 1996–1997. It doesn't sound likely that they went back to the original master recordings that were done in the '70s.

On the one hand it wouldn't make sense in terms of cost if you're going back to the original sources. One of the engineers did share pictures of the NBLP-7001 approved reel for Ampex from the storage library, so who knows. That would make a good interview too! I just don't see how the waves could really marry up as identically as they did to my eyes, so maybe that's an answer to discover. Certainly, we're in the realm of remaster rather than going back to the original 2" multi-tracks to remix and then remaster (or more accurately master anew), so there's probably not too much scope for change. A mix is a mix, and remastering, be it in 1997 or 2014, is in essence doing the same thing to the same source, just with a different engineer's skill set or taste.

I'm just curious for a fan perspective overall, but were a lot of people upset "Sonic Boom" was not a part of the KISSteria package or was that really not considered a big deal? For a guy like me that's a completist, if I'm going to spend $2,000.00 on a box set then I want everything. I don't want to have to hunt down one record!

Without a doubt it's something that was missing. It's a gap, and for me was tacky because I do like that album. But we don't know what the licensing arrangement with Wal-Mart was and how that might have impacted things. In my mind, or in a perfect world, it certainly could have been treated as a premium, just like "Greatest KISS" and the other five exclusives. So few were made originally, and they all ended up in a KISS associated store anyway, so it would have been nice to get that included, slightly different to not impact the collectability of the original pressing. How can you do a KISSteria 40th anniversary box set and exclude one of the band's studio albums? It doesn't make any sense to me logically and annoyed me, so I'd expect there's a business reason. Heck, that LP is pirated to death because it hasn't been re-pressed. Pennies add up eventually and then you've got a dollar...

You're certainly right. Thinking about some of the tchotchkes that came in there... There were a couple of cool things, but when you've been fortunate enough to see a lot of the assets that were in the archive, for me to know what exists, and for that stuff not to be utilized in some manner it's just so confusing. I guess part of it might be because Mercury/PolyGram has changed hands so many times and there's been so much turnover as far as employees go. Maybe the people that knew this stuff was around are gone and today's guys just don't know this stuff has been there in the vaults. It's just surprising to me that stuff that I helped uncover nearly 22 years ago, none of that stuff's been utilized in any other manner. It's very weird to be honest.

That must be disheartening, and for me ignorance is bliss from much of what you allude to. When you went into that project, bright eyed and bushy tailed and all these years on, there has been turnover at the labels. You know these bands are often seen as dinosaurs at best, and annoyances or worse in many cases. KISS' SoundScan figures tell one facet of the story without providing anything useful from the financial side — which is none of the fan's business anyway. The catalog has continued to sell decently (over 13 million copies in the U.S. since 1991), but it's certainly not selling impressively. I understand why the label wouldn't want to put the money in, because they're probably not going to recoup in the current market or using traditional release models. As much as my heart wants this or that, or to see things done in a certain way, you know the sales simply don't justify the effort in 2017 for mass-market versions. Which is why you end up with the sort of product that's going to be high dollar exclusive items that will piss off many fans but are what it takes financially to make things worthwhile doing.

While I've got you, I hope I can ask you a couple of questions about "Crazy Nights." That remaster was the final one released to date. When you were doing this project way back was that always considered the stopping point or were "Smashes, Thrashes & Hits" or "Hot in the Shade" considered as the non-makeup bookend?
When we decided to move forward with "Lick It Up" onward, the idea was to do "Lick It Up," "Animalize," and "Asylum in one shot; and then it was going to be "Crazy Nights," "Smashes, Thrashes & Hits," and "Hot in the Shade." We were going to repackage "Revenge" in an ultra-pack and re-release "Alive III," with one or two bonus tracks — the ones that were used in Japan and on the H&H vinyl release. But the initial sales figures were low for "Lick It Up" through "Asylum," and after that they just said, "You know what, we'll just do the first four non-makeup records and that's it." I had actually written liner notes for everything including the "Revenge" and "Alive III" ultra-packs.

That's interesting. Ending with "Crazy Nights" seemed odd in some ways, especially with how poor "Hot in The Shade" sounds, even if 1996 was closer to the recording technology used for those later albums.
The work was done; "Alive III" ultra-pack was frigging amazing. All that design stuff was fully conceptualized, and the images were selected and everything. The vinyl and CD for H.I.T.S. sound terrible; the cassette is much, much better. But Mercury said, "These aren't selling to our satisfaction so we're pulling the plug now." And that's it.

As a fan, what did you think about "Crazy Nights" when it came out? What was your reaction to the change in direction that the band had taken?
To be honest with you, as far as non-makeup records go, "Lick It Up," "Animalize," "Crazy Nights," and "Revenge" are my four favorite records. I love "Crazy Nights" and bought it the first day it came out. I thought it was superior to "Asylum." To this day I can only listen to one or two songs on "Asylum," but I thought the "Asylum" tour was amazing because of that super-duper large "KISS" logo with the multi-color changes. That was just out of this world for 1985–86, but I didn't really like the record very much. So, I'm a pro "Crazy Nights" fella!

My last question on "Crazy Nights..." In the "Crazy Nights" vault did you find anything of interest? That's one of those albums I'm very surprised they haven't knocked out a 30th Anniversary edition deluxe version for. It sold well internationally and could certainly benefit from a remix far more than "Destroyer" ever should have.

When I look at certain things that come out with KISS compilations and re-releases and deluxe editions, I'm really perplexed sometimes as to why they make the decisions that they do. "Destroyer: Resurrected," I thought was a great idea. The "Love Gun" deluxe edition was also a great idea, but I'm not too happy with the execution of it. That bonus disk could have had so much more on it and so much more varied material. I feel like they just said, "Hey Gene, you got any old demos in your garage?" "Yeah, sure, use this..." To give you an example, the whole sound board recordings from the Japan shows from 1977 were in the Mercury vaults. They were there, I heard them, and it was fantastic stuff. Why would you not put that out? They have a ton of stuff available but instead they do the "Love Gun" deluxe edition with a bunch of demos. But when you know what's available and you know what the fans know and you know the stuff that the fans don't know about, it's just like, "What?" "Rock and Roll Over," why wasn't there a deluxe edition of that? That certainly deserved a deluxe edition if anything did.

Indeed. There are few fans who would argue against you on that point. And marry it with the "Rock and Roll Party in Japan" unreleased live album! And they seem to have missed the boat for a 40th Anniversary edition of "KISS Alive II" — though there's time to prove me wrong!

I don't know why some of the decisions are made but I would be all for a 30th anniversary edition of "Crazy Nights." I think it's a great album.

A couple of years ago you contributed to a very well received book, "Star Wars: The Original Topps Trading Card Series, Volume 1." Congratulations on the reception that it received. It's got a lot of very positive feedback. Have you ever pitched a similar project to KISS on KISS' collector cards, particularly the Donruss stuff from late-1970s?

I would love to. I'm a big non-sports card collector so of course you know working on the Star Wars stuff it was natural that the KISS idea would come to mind. But, here's the thing; the problem is licensing fees and what they would want in royalties versus what's realistic as far as sales. What could you give the fans that would be awesome that they hadn't seen before? You know, stuff like that. The other thing is that I would want to get the original slides and rescan all that stuff. Can you imagine what those would look like today if done from the original materials instead of just scans of the cards? One of the sad things about the Star Wars cards books was that Topps had auctioned off their original negatives maybe about a decade or so ago. So that stuff was no longer available. I had to use all of my collection to create those books! While that part of it was fun, I was just thinking to myself, "Oh my God, if we had the original 35mm negatives how brilliant this stuff would look today!" I'll tell you something interesting, a little-known fact. Do you remember the Cornerstone cards I wrote in 1997/98?

Yes, those were great and were some of the few cards sets I actually collected at the time. There were two series.
We had actually written, created, and designed the cards for Series 3 and were all ready to be printed. KISS pulled the plug on them at the last minute because they were mostly non-makeup years. I still have my copies of those files so one of the things I'm excited to tell you about is — that I mentioned on Three Sides of the Coin also — I started working on my book, about what it was like being one of the KISS fans who was lucky enough to actually work with the band and contribute to KISStory. I'm shooting for a fall release for 2018 because Lynn Goldsmith's book and a few others are being released within the next few months. I don't want to have too many KISS related books out there at once as competition, so it would be better to wait until next year. But there's going to be a lot of minutia in there, a lot of stuff about working with Mercury, and working in the vault.

There's going to be 11 diaries worth of stuff. I'm going to be pulling a lot of notes to share with the fans. There's a lot of stuff that has been rumored, but I have the facts on a lot of things. A lot of the variations of the vinyl — everything up to 1997 — I have an exact accounting of everything that was made, where it was made, how many units, whatever changes they made to the labels. There were limited vinyl runs that were done only regionally. So, for instance, if you bought "The Elder" in California, your version differs than the one that I would have bought in New York at the same time. Not only with the manufacturing number on the actual disk, in some cases the label was totally different. All of that stuff will be seen for the first time next year.

That's the arcane side of the hobby. Knowing the difference between PRC West - Compton, CA, or Hauppauge Record Manufacturing in New York, or PRC in Richmond, IN, for pressing plants; or the various print facilities used for covers. And then label stock printers. Most sane people wouldn't care!

But also, the materials that were used were different, the inserts were different too. So, I'm also going clarify a lot of that sort of thing. There seems to be this belief that albums like "Rock and Roll Over," "Love Gun" and "KISS Alive II" were counterfeits done at the manufacturing plant at the same time that the authorized versions were being manufactured. That's incorrect. All of those versions are actually authentic and official but with the machinery back in the '70s you couldn't guarantee that the stickers or insert would be inserted in every single copy. That was just the limitations of the machinery and/or the employees that were doing hand insertions. There's this urban legend that's incorrect where they feel, "Hey, I didn't get my sticker for 'Rock and Roll Over.' It must have a counterfeit." No, you just have one that unfortunately the insertion machine or person just didn't insert the sticker. During my time on the remaster project I worked with some of the people who were working in marketing for Casablanca or for one of the distributors at the time. They filled me in on a lot of that stuff that had been made up beforehand. A lot of that stuff's going to be in my book which should hopefully be out in the fall next year. I've started going through boxes of stuff already and there's stuff I totally forgot I had.

Before we wrap up, a final question: You obviously will have seen some of the numbers — heck I've seen some numbers from PolyGram — but, do you believe "The Elder" has sold enough in the U.S. to be gold certified by the RIAA?
My personal belief is that all of the KISS records are probably Platinum at this point. Because if Platinum equals a million copies sold, from 1981 — when "The Elder" came out — to 2017, between all the formats, album, cassette, 8-track, etc.; if you combine all those units sold from 1981 to the present I'm pretty confident that the album has sold over a million copies. It must be Gold at the very least! I don't know what the record company's hesitation is in having all these things re-certified. The first three albums must be at least Platinum by now, too. I'm pretty confident in saying "The Elder" sold a 500,000 to one-million copies in a 36-year period. Do you agree?

"Creatures of the Night" didn't go gold until 1994. So, while it didn't sell initially over 12 years, and a couple of reissues — or with the new cover in 1985 — it did eventually get there. But it and "The Elder" had very poor initial U.S. sales and did better internationally. The word "abject" comes to mind, and while "The Elder" was reissued marginally along with the rest of the 1985 catalog updating, and then properly in 1989, I just don't see there

as having been enough product available in the intervening years. Or consumer interest if they even saw the product. The band was at or near their nadir at the time. Particularly while Phonogram contracted the distribution/manufacturing points in the U.S. and really streamlining things from the business side has an effect. But, as you know the numbers with KISS are so mired in fudge, shall we say, when "Alive!" is still only officially recognized by the RIAA as gold when internal Casablanca audits many times higher by 1979. But, that's Casablanca "math," and likely not the sort of thing you'd want in the same county as an audit with royalties and taxes involved! I don't know if I would push "The Elder" to a million in the U.S. alone, but I would certainly say it's been hovering around 499,999 for many, many years. Maybe the 10 copies the "Odyssey" project inspired people to purchase pushed it over the top and Tim and I will get RIAA awards for our efforts! It should certainly be Gold, just to keep the "All Time American Gold Record Champs" shtick going. The rest of the pre-SoundScan albums should be Platinum at minimum from what I've seen numbers on.

I agree with you. And think about all the kids that have listened to KISS for the first time by streaming them on Spotify or iTunes downloads and all this stuff. I mean adding those sales in, too. I mean it doesn't necessarily have to be a physical unit; it just has to be a paid for unit. So, if someone paid $0.99 to download "The Elder" on iTunes, I mean that's a sale. That should be counted as such though I don't know what the RIAA's rules are. It just seems unrealistic, when you think about all the millions of KISS fans worldwide, and you're talking about at least 2-1/2 generations worth of KISS fans that "The Elder" hasn't sold enough copies for Gold or Platinum certification? I just find that doubtful.

And that they'll certify product like the "Millennium Collection, Vol. 1," a 10-song compilation from 2003 and "The Very Best of KISS," and not bother going back to a studio record that breaks their consecutive track record of success. It totally doesn't matter to us KISS fans; we're going to love the stuff and the material no matter what. I appreciate your time, Robert; it's been a fantastic conversation that's gone far outside the scope of just talking about "The Elder!" Where can people find you?

The best way to reach me is at www.robertvconte.com, or you can email me at info[at]robertvconte.com. I'm working on my book; the title right now is called "My KISS Story" and it's due for release in the fall 2018. It's basically going to be a memoir mixed with minutia about all things KISS, and some really cool surprises. Hopefully it'll be a unique book that everybody will get something out of!

Brian Brewer: Inside "The Elder" Script

KISS fan Brian Brewer was the winner of "The Elder" script in the 2000 "KISS: The Auction" hosted by Butterfields/Greg Manning Auctions. As owner of the sole copy, Brewer reveals never-before-revealed insights into the "Elder" film that never was, plus an overview of the script's characters

Brian, back in June 2000 you were the lucky winner of the unique "Elder" movie script/treatment in the KISS auction. How did you first hear about the auction?
Brian Brewer: It probably was listed somewhere on the old KISS Asylum website and if it wasn't listed there it was probably listed on KISS Online.

There were several preview dates, including one May 12–14 in Chicago. Did you attend?
Yes. I believe that was either during or just before the Farewell Tour and my friends and I actually were interested in seeing some of these things. We heard about the auction and thought: "Well, why don't we take a look at what we can find here." And of course, the only thing we saw was a bland general description of the auction. It wasn't until later, when they started doing a traveling show with some of the stuff that we really started to take notice of it.

When did you first see the auction list? Were there any items in the initial one that drew your attention?
The first time I saw the list was the preview date that was in Chicago. That was when I got a hold of a copy of the auction catalog — basically that was the listing of all the lots. Thumbing through that, one of the first things I saw actually was "The Elder" script and being that my whole thing, about KISS and "The Elder" — I've been a fan since I was 2 years old and the opening of "Radioactive" scared the living daylights out of me. I told Gene that one time and he kind of chuckled. He thought it was funny. But it was great, since then I've been infected with the disease as they say. So, the first time I saw the lot list was when I got a hold of the book. And the book itself was actually quite the collectible. It's got all the pictures of everything in it, which is great. When I opened it and saw "The Elder," I thought, "OK, this is something that I might like to get." But I really didn't make the decision to go after it until the day of the auction.

What sort of stuff did they have at the Chicago preview? Did they have everything else available for people to see?

My understanding was they only had certain items at certain stops on this little tour that they had for the preview dates, and one of the main things that I recall was they had the original "Love Gun" painting [on display]. The first time I saw that was actually at the first KISS convention in 1995 and it was behind Plexiglas. We walked into Butterfield's in Chicago and here is the one-of-a-kind oil painting, Ken Kelly's "Love Gun" album cover right there for you to put your hands on and touch. Another thing I recall that was really cool to see was they had the Peter Criss "Alive!" mirror drum kit. That was the kit that he used after the "Dressed to Kill" tour on the "Alive!" tour. It had the mirrors on the drum shells.

There were all sorts of guitars and everything sitting around and the guys that were there actually encouraged you to pick up, touch, look, [and] play — basically do whatever with the guitars! So, I took them a step further. I don't think that they actually thought that I would do it, but I sat down at the drum kit without drumsticks, doing my best John Bonham or Tommy Aldridge imitation with my bare hands, and I played the opening riff to "Strutter"! And then they asked me to stop playing the drums! But, you know, I did get the opening riff of "Strutter" out so that was pretty cool.

Were there any "Elder" items available for you to see that day?

I don't remember whether or not the script was in Chicago, but I do want to say that I think one of the treatments — one of the handwritten treatments that Gene did — may have been there and that's the best of my recollection. Other than that, there were a lot of [guitars]. One of the guitars that I saw that was really great was one of Paul's flying Vs that had the tiger stripes [Editor's Note: From the "Creatures" / "Lick It Up" era] on it, which was really cool to see. They had a couple of odds and ends of like one of Eric Carr's electronic drum pads. They didn't have a whole lot else that really stands out to me 15 years later.

All right, so lot #1446 is described on page 84 of the catalog as "the original Gene Simmons personally owned script of the Elder."

Yep.

The screenplay treatment was noted as being written by Russell and Jeffrey Marks. What made you decide to go for that item rather than any of the other treatments or anything else "Elder"-related?

Well, as we all know the movie was never made. And at that point my consideration was — I don't really want to compare the two works — it's KISS' version of "The Wall," and there was a movie for that. We've probably all seen it. It's pretty avant-garde, pretty out there, but sticks with the story of "The Wall." I was interested in trying to figure out what they'd come up with as far as the story of "The Elder" went.

I was in college when they were doing the "KISS Nation" magazine that never really took off, and the Internet was new, and everybody didn't know what an email address was. I [had] tried my hand at writing a short story based on "The Elder." I got about three pages into it and stopped. Other things just got in the way and it just wasn't one of the things that I thought was a good use of my time, but I wanted to know what the official item was going to be like. As the day of the auction crept up, I was interested in getting this item and my interest peaked in it. Once the auction came up, I decided, "I might be a struggling law student right now, but I do have the money." I figured I would see if I could spend about $400 on it. And that's what I did. I registered for the auction, got a hold of it and tried to go from there.

There were several other "Elder" related items in the auction. Was it going to be that script or nothing?
Yes.

Did you bid on just the one item?
That was the only item that I wanted to get my hands on and that was the only item that I bid on.

Some of the other lots that went in that auction sold within the range of the listed estimates, which I thought was highly unusual. This "Elder" lot was estimated in the $300–500 range, and I think it went for $488.75, according to my documentation.
I do believe it went for a little bit more than that. I actually got into a bidding war with somebody over it. I thought at first, I would spend $400, but then once somebody else kept outbidding me I think that we pushed it up to at least $525–550, something like that. When the hammer dropped that's where it was.
And one thing about the auction that wasn't 100 percent clear until after I won it was there was the buyer's premium on top of it and then there was shipping. So yeah, I had to fight for it though, because somebody else really

wanted it as bad as me, then I outbid them and ended up winning it. I think that the final amount was probably somewhere in the neighborhood of $650, as I recall.

You probably also had tax on top of the shipping and the premium!
Yes. Then there was also the problem with the shipping that also wasn't really made clear to anybody. At least not to me! I was in contact with Butterfield's after the auction was over to figure out where to send the money. I sent them the money and then I said, "Well, how are we going to ship this?" And they said, "Call FedEx, call UPS. We don't have a shipping department." Now this was, I think, the L.A. office of Butterfield's. I'd spoken to people in the San Francisco office who were actually quite nice. They were not, as I'd say, as curt as the L.A. office was and that's the nicest way, I'm going put it. Eventually, they were absolutely refusing to help me in L.A. FedEx said, "You know, we can't do it." UPS said that they wouldn't do it and one of the other shipping options that they [Butterfields] recommended was actually for larger items like guitars, drums, or whatever.

The recommended shippers laughed. They thought it was funny that somebody wanted to ship this little book for what they were going to charge me. They kept saying, "Just use the mail." So eventually what I did was I convinced one of the guys there, I said, "Look, I'm going to send you packaging from UPS. UPS will pick it up. You don't have to do anything other than put the script in the package and send it off to me." This was some like two months after the auction because they absolutely refused to ship the thing to me! I eventually devised that plan and it got to me and it's been in my possession since.

That's an absolutely wild story. I don't recall having to jump through any of those hoops. I believe I had my stuff within I think three weeks.
Really?

That seems nuts for what was a major auction house. I think you would expect to be able to receive it less painfully!
Yes. I was extremely upset with Butterfields over this turn of events actually!

All right, so you didn't have much of a battle until the end and then someone tried to snipe you, right?
Yes. And as a sign of the times, my internet access at that time was dial-up AOL at 56K! And I still got it!

After a bit of a battle at the end of the auction you win it. What were your expectations of the script because there was not much to go by with that generic auction description? You can read some of the treatments in the auction catalog, which I don't think have much to do with the actual script's story and plot?

I was expecting as much as anybody could from it, you know. We already know, "When the earth was young, they were already old," and that whole spiel and that's about all I was going on. You know, "Morpheus we've summoned you here to offer your judgment of the boy," from the record. When I found that passage in the script, I was like a school kid! "Hey, look at that, that's actually in here!" It was really cool to see that. They actually used that dialog on "The Elder," but that's all I had. So, when I got it and read it, I thought that the thing was like watching paint dry! I think that assessment had a lot more to do with the medium of a screenplay as opposed to the actual story because later on, just a few weeks ago, I read through the script again, and I'd only done that once before.

I actually like the story a lot better than I thought I would. But at the same time, it's still got its pitfalls. But as far as what to expect I didn't have any idea what I was getting other than it was the script for a movie that was never made. And to me it just seemed like the cornerstone of my entire collection because there's only one of these things out there. I was very happy to have at least one little piece of the puzzle that nobody else can lay claim to. Now in the spirit of full disclosure: The minute I got the script I made a copy of it at a professional printer shop so, that I could read it without damaging the script. I do have an additional copy in my possession but that's only for me to read without damaging the original script.

That's a good idea. Let's get into some of the details on the script. How long is it? How many pages?

Including the title page, you're talking 130 pages and it's broken down in scenes obviously. If you've read Shakespeare or screenplays before, it's pretty standard as far as I can tell.

There are several prospective settings of the story during its creation, from the modern to the medieval/fantasy. How would you describe the "age" in which the script is set?

If you're going describe this particular story, it's kind of on the same level as "Through the Looking Glass" [by Lewis Carroll, "Alice's Adventures in Wonderland"]. It starts off in one era of time and you've got Blackwell, who's the king and chief bad guy, and his henchman Xyte, who was actually a sorcerer for the Elders before he picked up with Blackwell. Blackwell is under attack when the script opens. The story starts with Blackwell under attack in his day, which is apparently 600 years in the past. There are allusions to a varying number of years in the script — one says 600, one says 800, one says 500 — they jump around, but on an average, it seems to have been set about 600 years in the past. Xyte created another world inside Blackwell's mirror chamber with the rose, which was a ring that the Elders created with magical powers and Xyte got a hold of it. It had a diamond in it and, of course, if you've seen the cover of the album or the record's label with Paul's hand, it's the one that has a ring on it. That's the ring they're talking about. It looks like the rose. It looks like the door handle that they're knocking on, on the album cover. And there's a diamond in there.

As they're going through the portal, Blackwell gets stabbed with a dagger and drops the ring. The ring bounces on the floor and away from Blackwell, but the diamond bounces back into the mirror and as that happens, the portal shuts. So, the key to the portal is the ring. When they get inside this new realm, it's inferred that time stands still. The script then flashes to what appears to be a modern-day college campus — and this is one of the multiple montages in the script and in this movie that would make you think that it's like watching paint dry. Whatever modern day is, I'm suspecting 1981–82, you've got the hero named Eric. Eric is an aspiring Olympian, an aspiring gymnast [who] wants to make the Olympic team and you "see" him doing his thing during the montage. It jumps from the past to the present day.

So how often does the script jump between these timeframes and is it possible to even follow it in the script, or does it become distracting? We're 600 years in the past or 500, "Oh wait, now we're in the modern times." Does the focus stay in any one of these time spaces?
Once Eric passes through the portal, the timeframe is set in the new realm for the rest of the story. The first thing you notice is Eric keeps looking at his watch when he falls through [the portal] and it's always 11 o'clock. Eric wanted to be involved with a fraternity and he asks one of his friends about what he thought the best fraternities on the campus were and his friend made a recommendation. Then we get another montage. You know, two montages in the first 10 minutes can't be that great — probably the first 10 minutes of film time! Eric finally interviews with one of the head guys for the fraternity who tells him that the initiation for joining the fraternity is to

spend the night in a castle that's down the street from campus. It turns out this castle was the same castle that Blackwell had been in when he and Xyte created the alternate universe and crossed over.

When Blackwell and Xyte went through the portal and were locked out and the ring was left there, one of the Elders actually makes their first appearance, picking up the ring; looking at it and putting it back down. [The Elder] went back to the council and said the odyssey is beginning. So, you can see where that goes. There's a lot of tie-ins with the record — "The odyssey is beginning" — if you catch that one.

And time and space seem to be another?
Yes. Eric decides to sneak into the castle on a tour. As far as I can tell it's now a museum of sorts. He decides to stay behind from the tour, and he falls down a staircase. Basically, he's walking around the staircase and he falls into this chamber, which was the mirror chamber. He walks over and looks into a mirror and he sees the brass ring on the floor. He picks it up and puts it on his hand and it fits, obviously, or else he wouldn't have picked it up and put it on! By trying to avoid more rubble falling on him he actually falls into the mirror and falls into the first realm, the alternate universe that was created by Xyte. That's the "Forest World." So, while he's trying to figure out what happened and where he is, the script cuts back to Xyte and to Blackwell.

Xyte can probably be described as similar to the Wicked Witch of the West (in "The Wizard of Oz"). He has these flying animals — I'm not quite exactly sure what they are. I think they're kind of a cross between a dragon and a pterodactyl. They can see what's going on and when they fly back to Xyte, he puts his hands on their heads and he can see what they've seen. So, he sees Eric and knows Eric is there. He tells Blackwell that Eric is there. Blackwell never comes across any more harmful than say a Dr. Evil-type character (from "Austin Powers"). He's really not that blood-thirsty; although it's alluded to that he's kind of ruthless. He doesn't really have a lot of screen time either. It's more Xyte, and then what's going on with Eric.

But if Blackwell's supposed to be the bad guy or the main bad guy, with a song about him on the album, do you feel that he's just not well-defined?
Yeah, that's probably the case. And, you know, there are cues for the music in the script, music from the album. So that gives you the music from part of "The Elder." There is one part where Blackwell is taking a tour of his

dungeon and it's a cue for "Mr. Blackwell." The imagery in the script isn't necessarily what a director might put in a film. There could be something that's pretty horrific down there. You just don't get that from the script.

Who are the standout characters from your point of view? A lot of them seem very plastic, unfinished. When we look at the scripts for "Detroit Rock City" or "KISS Meets the Phantom of The Park," there's a lot of additional work that went in. Did any of these characters really jump out as being interesting, characters that you could actually enjoy?
Jest is one that strikes me as one that would. He plays a bigger role than you'd expect. Jest was Blackwell's jester and was banished to the forest world after overhearing Xyte and Blackwell plan to conquer the new world once they got hold of the ring. Jest seems to be comic relief and moral support thrown into one. He comes out at times when you don't expect him. You almost forget he's there during the script, and then, all of a sudden, he appears and pretty much saves the day in one of the battles that they encounter. I would say Jest is probably one of the better-defined characters in the script. I would also say Eric. When you have the name Eric it immediately gives you the vision of Eric Carr, and I wonder if that may have been on purpose, insofar as there are so many cues to the actual album in here, and then you've got Eric as a character. I don't know, we can always speculate on that, but it does strike me as maybe they were making a conscious effort to tie it into something concrete with Eric Carr. That's just my speculation on it. But he definitely comes across as the underdog.

[Eric] doesn't believe he's the hero. Everybody tells him he's the hero, because he wears the ring. Morpheus, who's the caretaker in the album, at least he's called the caretaker, does something else in the movie. He makes weapons. He actually does train or is supposed to train Eric, who's now the champion to conquer the evil which is Blackwell and set everybody free. Eric comes across as a little bit undefined at first, but he gains a lot more confidence along the way and then in the final battle he does strike down Blackwell. It comes full circle for him where his character is kind of building through the whole story. And then there's Tyler. Tyler is kind of along the lines of, if you want a comparison, a Han Solo to the story. He would rather save his own skin than put his neck out for somebody else, unless of course you're his friend. One of the other tie-ins to the script with the movie and the record, he has a gang and his two henchmen, or loyal muscle, are [named] Simon and Gamora. That just reminds me of [some of] the lyrics in "Dark Light." You've got Ace singing about Sodom and Gomorrah, so.

Yeah, the malevolent order.

Yes. Morpheus comes across Tyler previously. There's a back-story where Morpheus and Tyler's men actually tried to overthrow Blackwell in the past and failed. Morpheus was actually imprisoned by Blackwell but escaped and Tyler got away. You also have a Princess Myra, who is Blackwell's daughter, and who caused all this strife for Blackwell to begin with. She's the one who organized the other kingdoms to rise against Blackwell. In reaction to that, Blackwell had Xyte create this new world. Going back to the tie-ins with the record, Myra lives on a mountain where "stand the stallion and the mare." So, you have another tie-in to "Odyssey." To leave the forest world they have to build a boat and "steer the ship through the stormy sea." You know, "Just A Boy." Along the way Eric and Myra become a love interest. It has a lot of these elements that you would find in almost any coming of age story. It's a lot like "Star Wars," "The NeverEnding Story" and "The Princess Bride." It's got all of these elements to it and it's like a hodgepodge of everything.

Does it feel like they gave the writers the lyrics to the songs and said, "Here! Write a story and use these..."?

I believe they did. One could reach that conclusion. You know, when you get to the next realm of the universe it's the "Space Roads," where there's nothing but roads and space. By this time the party has picked up an Elder to walk with them. That's another thing: Myra and Morpheus are able to see the Elders. The Elders can make themselves appear to them, but the rest of the party doesn't have any idea what's going on with the Elder. This Elder's name is Keiser, who helps them get through the "Space Roads" when Myra loses the maps. She's the only one who has the maps. She stole them from Xyte. In this realm of the "Space Roads" they come across an orb. Just an orb sitting there. It almost reminded me of a scene in "Heavy Metal" [Editor's Note: a 1981 movie that included the Loc-Nar orb with magical properties] in some fashion. One of the henchmen, I believe it was Simon, went up to it and touched it and all of a sudden, this orb turns into a clone of him and attacks him. Of course, the party doesn't know which one is which, so they're fighting it out and one gets decapitated and [the other] falls off the road, with the decapitated body.

They make their way through the "Space Roads" with the Elder Keiser [who] helps them through without the maps. They get to the point where they have to go through Hell's Flames, or something to that effect as I recall, and they're avoiding this monster that lives there. It's called the Soul Keeper and literally it is what it sounds like. It would literally suck the soul out of somebody as its way of killing them or punishing them. This was all created by Xyte [who] knows and believes that the Soul Keeper is the strongest of the creations in his universe. He doesn't think anybody's going to get past that, and the Soul Keeper will bring the brass ring to them and they will then be able to rule in their new timeframe with all the technology that they didn't have 600 years ago. So eventually they fight the Soul Keeper and defeat it.

The portal to the next realm smashes before Keiser can get over. He then reveals himself as an Elder to the Soul Keeper who bows to him and knows that he can do nothing to this Elder and also knows that the Elder can really do nothing to him. So, they reach an uneasy truce. Keiser rejoins the party with another portal. I should mention too, these portals are mirrors — they're in all sorts of different places and can lead to all sorts of different realms, but the exact portals that they found take them to where they need to be. The next realm that they find themselves in is a snow world. And to me it reminded me of the snow world, Hoth, in "The Empire Strikes Back."

OK, so we've now gone from the "Forest World," which sounds similar to where the Ewoks lived, "Endor," and now we're on a facsimile of "Hoth"!
Yes.

From the sounds of it, the "Space Roads" and those descriptions of the pathways sound like some of the scenes at the end of "2001: A Space Odyssey," when Dave Bowman enters the monolith.
Yes, you do have a lot of that as well. I would agree with that immensely. They wind up freezing in this snow world and decide that they need to keep moving forward or they're just going to die. They eventually come across somebody who inhabits the area. His name is Nicholas and he gives them shelter. He gives them food, which consists of dead rats. After a while I guess rat can be like steak when you're hungry — at least that's the impression that I get from Nicholas! He starts telling them that he's a sorcerer. The only thing he's learned how to do is to make multiples of things. They have very few weapons with them, so Nicholas takes all of these weapons and makes multiples of them so that they have a full arsenal of daggers and swords, and bows and arrows, and all these medieval-type weapons that they carry with them.

While he's doing that, Tyler notices a staff on Nicholas' wall, and it brings Tyler to a flashback with Xyte. [It] turns out that the staff belonged to Xyte and immediately Tyler, after he gets out of that flashback with the conflict with Xyte, accuses Nicholas of being one of Xyte's henchmen. Nicholas says, "You know, actually I was studying under Xyte. I'm no longer studying under him. In fact, I was banished from the kingdom too, for heresy." I can't figure out why in the world the screenplay and the writers would banish somebody for heresy in a script that has almost nothing at all to do with any religion whatsoever. But that's why he ended up where he is, and he wants to take revenge against Blackwell and Xyte. So, he offers to get them through this ice world into the next realm, which is actually "The Kingdom."

They're on their way and while they're on their way, like [in] "The Wizard of Oz," here comes Xyte's little pets and they actually grab Morpheus and Keiser and take them back to the kingdom. So now you've got Morpheus and Keiser sitting in prison in the other realm. By the time [the rest] get to the portal it's very late, they're very tired and they decide to rest. When they wake up, they find Nicholas has frozen to death. Then they make their way into the next realm, which is where the kingdom is. You might remember I mentioned previously that there was a gang that was led by Tyler, and that Tyler and Morpheus knew each other, and it was these men who attacked Blackwell. There was one of this group that was presumed to be dead after that. Well they actually run in to him here in this realm. He's been hanging out there for 600 years. Solomon was his name. So, you had Simon, Gamora and Solomon.

So, Solomon has a bit more going on upstairs than Simon and Gamora did. We ended up losing both of those characters in the "Space Roads." One thing that struck me was when they were sailing the sea, in the "Just A Boy" phase, I thought "How many different characters did we have here?" We had Eric. We had Jest. We had Morpheus, Myra, Tyler, Simon and Gamora. There were seven characters in this party. Damned if you can keep them straight! If you're watching the movie, it's like, "And who are you again? And why are you here? And what are you doing here?" So eventually the characters get weeded out. That brings it down to the core characters at the end of the story.

Eventually they find the castle. They storm the castle. When they did [the] flashback into Blackwell and Xyte, the method of execution was described as putting a prisoner [into something like an] old stocks. You put their head in and then their arms in the wood blocks and they would lower this person down into this dungeon and some creature down there would basically eat [the victim] alive. And it was a very fast death. The only thing that was left was the arms.

Wonderful.

Yeah. So, you can get the feeling of, "You're not well Blackwell, go to hell." They put Keiser in these stocks and they're getting ready to send him down but for some reason they don't right away. [The script] jumps back [and] now we have Tyler, who's been gravely injured in a previous battle, overpowering one of the guards and now wearing that guard's uniform so he can move about in the dungeon. Eric's waiting to attack as soon as Tyler gives him the OK. Solomon and Myra are also waiting in the wings to help take care of business and Morpheus is just hanging around in the dungeon because they're not doing anything with him right away. Morpheus is sitting there, and then they take Keiser and put him in the stocks and that's when Tyler notices Keiser is there. Tyler makes his presence known and starts a chain of events that begins the final battle.

The final battle is pretty much what you would expect: Lots of bows and arrows, lots of swords, lots of daggers. Eric gets captured and when they let Keiser down [into the execution pit] and brought him back up there were no arms left. Nobody puts two and two together here, other than Eric who realized that Keiser was an Elder, one of the Elders that Morpheus had been telling him about. Nobody else could have survived. The scene then cuts away to them putting Eric into the stocks. And then [it] cuts away to Keiser, who has now confronted Xyte in another room. Remember Keiser and the Soul Keeper came [to] an uneasy truce? Well at this point the Soul Keeper decided that he was going bite the hand that feeds him. He attacks and kills Xyte at the behest of Keiser. So now we no longer have Xyte in the picture and we cut back to Eric. Eric [is] still in the stocks — Eric was a gymnast and his specialty was the parallel bars — so what you're supposed to hear now is — it's not clear as I can't recall whether it was Morpheus or Keiser's voice — that basically told Eric to "use the Force," kind of along those lines. "Eric, use your talents! Don't forget your talents!"

So, Eric remembers that he has this ability to swing himself around as a gymnast and escape the stocks. He then defeats Blackwell and finds the diamond in Blackwell's crown. He picks up the diamond after he kills Blackwell and puts it on the rose. Now the story cuts back to present day: The members of the fraternity are coming into the castle to see where Eric is, and they find the mirror chamber amongst the staircase rubble. They look at their watches and its 11 o'clock. "He's got to be done with this by now let's, let's take him home." They look in the mirror and they see all of this happening and Eric can look out the mirror and see them and it's almost like two worlds are colliding here and the script automatically says boom, cue "I," and end credits. It leaves open a huge gate for a sequel. It wouldn't surprise me because as I recall there was talk of an "Elder: Part 2." If you ask me, I think that the "Elder 2" would've probably consisted of Eric coming back in and bringing some of his buddies over to try to right the rest of the wrongs over there. That's just speculation on my part. But I think that ending was actually the cleverest thing even though it was kind of clichéd.

Does it feel like a standalone film? And does it work in terms of the story told and the conclusion reached?
It could. But then again, you know, you could end up finding something along the lines of a trilogy out of this if somebody were creative enough. I think that the first one is too weak for a trilogy to be based upon. It's possible we could've had a sequel, but we don't have the ability of knowing what these people were going to do after the fact. We never even got this. I would say that they were probably looking to find a way to create at least a sequel out of it.

Right, so an open ending gives them that.
Yeah.

You resolved this first part. You don't know if he's made it back, you know, if they're looking at each other in the mirror.
You notice they cut to "I" in the end credits. That was expected, just one more tie-in to the album if you ask me. There it is, boom, "I believe in me," because I just did this, you know. But we don't know if Eric returned to the present day, or if anyone else joined Eric through the portal.

That's going to be something else I come back to as well. When you open the gatefold of the album you've got that "When the earth was young" introduction. Does that appear in the script in any sense, in any way?
You know, the very first thing that you see before you get any action is an [introduction] scroll and it reminds me of the scroll before "Star Wars." It starts scrolling and right in there is where you get this idea that the Elder are the alien race that's watching over a virgin world and keeping them safe from evil. That's where you get something like that. But in honesty, I don't think that you get the exact verbiage that you got in the album. In fact,

what's there [is] a little bit of back-story before the action begins. But that's all you really get. You don't get too much more of the Elder at their council. Now there is one spot in the script where Morpheus actually speaks with the Elders. It's kind of inferred that he takes a portal with Keiser back to where you would find this table and the council, although it doesn't give a whole lot of description there. But it's kind of inferred that he's addressing the entire council as well as Keiser when the album's ending dialogue appears: "Do you still deem him worthy of the apprenticeship?" and then, "I certainly do my lord. In fact, I think you're going like this one. He's got the light in his eyes and the look of a champion."

So yeah, you do get a little bit of that but it's not as much as you would think. The Elder are kind of in the background here. I mean, it's called "The Elder" and you would have almost expected that the Elder have a bigger role, but they really don't. I mean the role comes when Keiser and the Soul Keeper have made their little pact and the Soul Keeper attacks Xyte. It's like you get done in by your own creation. There's a little bit of "KISS Meet the Phantom of The Park" in that.

Right and of course "Phantom" had the animatronics and the band fighting evil versions of themselves, right?
Yeah.

And you've got the doubles in this movie.
Yeah.

I've wondered if the writers were big fans of "The Lord Of The Rings" and "Star Wars," because with the swamp planet I immediately think of Dagobah in "The Empire Strikes Back" and "Return Of The Jedi."
That would be where Yoda is right?

That's right.
You know, the Antarctic area that they were in is also like what you find in Hoth in "The Empire Strikes Back" and the Space Roads, you find that in "Star Wars" or you find that maybe even "The Lord Of The Rings" in the middle earth or something like that. So yeah, you've got a whole lot of [these similarities] going on.

We talked a little bit about the dialogue. The only dialogue that we know of that was used is the dialogue that's tagged onto the end of the album,

which also appears in the script. You've also noted a few instances where songs are specifically cued in the script: "I," "Just A Boy" and "Mr. Blackwell." What about pieces like "The Oath" or "Escape from The Island" or "The Chase" as it was known at one point?

I don't recall "Escape from The Island" being in the script as a cue. "The Oath," I believe, was used somewhere along when Eric finally figured out what he was doing and why he was doing it. I think that that was in the kingdom world, which was kind of swampy too. They fell into a swamp — it's kind of like the forest and the swamp put together but that's where the kingdom was located. "Just A Boy" was used when they were crossing the Great Sea. "Odyssey" was cued very early on. I believe "Odyssey" was cued even before Morpheus mentions that Myra lives on the mountain that bears the stallion and the mare. "Dark Light" was cued when they first entered the Space Roads. "Mr. Blackwell" was cued when we learn of Blackwell's dungeon. You have all sorts of cues to the record. "Only You" plays in the background during one of the montages. I honestly don't remember whether "Under the Rose" made it in or not, but it wouldn't surprise me that it's somewhere in there and I just didn't make a note of it.

I guess the last song there is "A World Without Heroes."

"A World Without Heroes" is the opening credits.

So that becomes a very different kind of sequence than any of the album track sequences, even the original intended album track sequence?

Yeah, it is all over the place. And you don't find things in the places that you would've thought in the sequence that you're accustomed to. To me, the remastered CD is still foreign. The very first CD I ever purchased, even before I owned a CD player, was "The Elder." And that original track listing from 1981 is still what I'm accustomed to even after having the remastered version for as many years as we have. So looking at the script and finding all of these different places where these songs show up in an even different order, is just mind-boggling because again, not to compare it to "The Wall," but if you watch "The Wall" you can almost listen to the album with the movie. There's very little deviation from the record's sequence. Here we have Bob Ezrin making his sequencing decisions and it just doesn't sound like the writers put a whole lot of thought into where songs were going when they wrote the script.

Right, it would be interesting to re-sequence the album to fit in with how it actually comes across in the linear format of the script.

Yeah.

What about "fanfare"?
I don't recall whether the "fanfare" was even used in the script. It would almost seem to me that it would have played a bigger role somewhere because it's a pretty dramatic part of the album, but I don't recall that it did.

That's the only other part that I was going ask you about because the "fanfare" has the monks, or whomever, chanting, fog horns, wind chimes. Do any of those elements appear in any scene where there would be chanting or some arcane gathering?
The only time that that would actually happen is when the first Elder finds the ring that was lying outside of the mirror. He then lays it back down and goes back to the council and says the odyssey has begun. And it might be somewhere in there, but I don't believe that the "fanfare" was a cue for that.

Would you say that you have a favorite part of the script? Is there any particular scene that you think, "That's cool, I would love to see that on the screen!"?
You know, the Space Roads seem like it would be an interesting thing to see — it could be great with the right director and the right special effects. You've got to remember, too, this being in the early 1980s; I don't know that they would have had the same special effects that we would have now to make this pop like it could. Another reason why I think giving it a fresh look helped me along with the story, as opposed to the actual format, which I think was the whole reason why it was like watching paint dry, is because I'm reading a screenplay. I think that with the proper special effects and the right director that the Space Roads section could be outstanding. It could be really unique, it could almost take on an air of say "Tron," when they're riding the light-cycles, or they were riding around in the tanks. I don't want to give it a computer-generated feel, but kind of like they're floating around, and they've got no real aiming point. They're just trying to move from point A to point B, whatever that might be. And all the roads are floating and there's nothing but space underneath. I mean it could be monumental. It could really be very good if done properly.

Conversely, is there any like area of the script that just leaves you shaking your head?

Too many montages, far too many montages! I mean there is a montage every 10–15 minutes in this film. If you're not going tell the story with anything but a montage and music, you're failing as a screenwriter. There's got to be more dialogue than that! I might be spoiled because I'm a big fan of Quentin Tarantino — so his movies are all dialogue driven. "Reservoir Dogs" could be put up on a stage. I think that what they really needed to do was put forth a little bit more dialogue. Also, a little bit more feeling as to how and why Eric and Myra became a love interest, because really all you get to see is them smooching a little bit during one of the montages and that's it. I think those are the biggest drawbacks from the script.

If you think of KISS' demographic and the change that the band had gone through in the late '70s into the early '80s, with the age really dropping, is this script age appropriate? How is the violence portrayed? Is it cartoonish or more graphic? Is it going for a younger audience or are they trying to be a more serious?

This probably would've gotten a PG rating if it was done right. It reminds me, again I'm not trying to draw too many comparisons, but it reminds me of "The NeverEnding Story." It reminds me of "The Princess Bride." It reminds me of "Star Wars" and "The Lord of The Rings." I think I mentioned before, Blackwell, even for being the chief bad guy, does not come across any more evil than Dr. Evil himself. I mean you have this caricature of a guy who's supposed to be so bad and yet he comes across pretty much like "sort of." It's all off-screen. You don't always see his actual "badness," is the best way I can put it. It's inferred that he's done all these evil things and you don't necessarily see him do them. You hear him plotting with Xyte and you can almost hear him doing a Simpson's "Mr. Burns" voice and saying "Excellent"... Or like Dr. Evil wants "One. Million. Dollars!" I think as far as age appropriateness, in 1981 I would have been 6 years old, so this may not have been totally appropriate for me. It might have been appropriate for somebody 10 or 12 years old.

So, it's pretty safe, pretty comic-bookish?
Yeah.

As comics were back in the early '80s?
There are a few choice words. There are no "F" words but there's a "shit" or two in there. There's a few "hells" and a few "damns," but there's nothing really that's going get you a R rating as far as the dialogue; or even a PG-13 rating these days as far as the dialogue goes. Depending on the director's

vision and how graphic he wants to get with the battle scenes you could push into some PG-13 territory these days, but there wasn't a PG-13 at that time. So, you probably would've wound up with a PG rating.

Brian, you spoke with Seb Hunter a few years ago when he was working on his now-abandoned "Elder" movie. What do you think of his project?
I think he tried very hard to conceive something and I really saw only a couple of trailers. I think he was getting on a path that is kind of evident in some aspects of the script, but it's a totally different story. I really didn't know exactly what his story was about. The only things that I really saw were a couple of the trailers he put up and it had a medieval feel to it. It had kind of a swashbuckling feel to it. Almost like when they're wandering through the forest world is what it really reminded me of when I was reading the script. So that's about the only real comparison I can draw. It could've been decent. I really don't know what would've happened with it. I think that if it were done right, he probably could've had a nice attempt at it.

I think he was doing kind of English-countryside, post-apocalyptic, guns and monks movie. Some of it looked interesting, some of the scenes he did.
Yeah. It looked promising, but who knows — and we don't know the full story on that. I haven't read his script either.

Let's talk about the album quickly. What did you think the first time you heard "The Elder?"
Well, you got to remember that "The Elder" was an accidental find because, up until that point, I had been trying for probably five years to get a copy of the album. I believe it was 1989 when I finally got hold of the CD and one of my goals prior to that was to search every secondhand shop, every garage sale, rummage sale, flea market, and store and try to find "The Elder" and it was nowhere. You couldn't walk into a store and buy it and that left me with the impression it was deleted from the catalog ... you couldn't find it anywhere. When I first got it and popped it in and "The Oath" blasted me I said, "Now this is pretty cool!" You know, a lot of falsetto here Paul, but that's not bad. I kind of like it. And as the story, as the songs went on I got hold of the story I'd been reading the CD booklet for months because I didn't have a CD player yet, so I was already absorbed into the whole, you know, mystical thing and "when the earth was young they were already old." So, it really did live up to my expectations that I thought it would. And I can't say that for many other things. It was one of those items, it's the era of "The

Elder," and because it took me so long to finally track down a copy of it, that's why I'm fascinated with what went on during what I think of as the lost period of KISS.

Absolutely, it was a very strange time for the band in 1980–1981 when Eric Carr first came in. Do you have any favorite songs on the album?
"The Oath" is one that stands out always. The only thing about "The Oath" that I could always have done without is Paul's falsetto. I think he could've sung that in a full voice, instead of falsetto, and been OK. I like "Mr. Blackwell." I've always thought that was an interesting exercise in songwriting for Gene. The music is just so different than anything they've ever done. It's got a real funky feel to it. You know, you don't get funk out of KISS and there's some funk in "Mr. Blackwell." I like "Dark Light" a lot because of Ace's solo. One of the things that always struck me, when I first heard the "Strutter" demo from 1973 with Eddie Kramer, one of Ace's licks that he used in "Dark Light" he was using as far back as 1973.

When you put something like that together you realize these guys have a bag of tricks that they reach into and that's what they go to when something is needed. It's that one lightning fast lick that's at the end of "Dark Light" that is also in the end solo on the "Strutter" demo. I put that together, and it's like, "OK, now I'm kind of understanding a musician's point of view a lot better than before." And of course, this was when I'm 12 years old at the time so it's like light-bulb revelation. I also really do like, it's corny, but I like "Odyssey." I do like "Odyssey," it has a certain feel to it. It's got an otherworldly feel. It's also one of the few times you find KISS covering somebody else.

I don't care what Paul says. I don't think his vocal performance is "tragic" in any way. I think it's actually very good and an unusual style for him to sing in, so it's successful.
Yes.
The last thing I do have to mention is "Escape from The Island" is just a blistering instrumental. Another thing that you didn't get from KISS for a long time was an instrumental. You know, you had "Love Theme From KISS" and then there's a long stretch there without any instrumentals. And there's just something about the placement in both versions of "The Elder," where "Escape From The Island" just is a perfect intermission, where you have the story and then it kind of stops for a minute and you get this little kick-ass

instrumental and then it starts up again. So that was what I always liked about "Escape from The Island."

Yeah, it's a cool instrumental. Did the script change your mind about the album? I mean do you hear the album any differently now when you listen to it?

Well, I did listen to the album today to psych myself up for this interview and I have to say, "No." I don't think that I got anything out of the script that wasn't already there on the album in my own mind's eye. I think the reason for that is because this wasn't made into a movie. I've only read it on paper and only looked at the screenplay. And I get the story, but it didn't change what I view as "The Elder" to be. Now if this had been made into a movie, I might have a different answer to that question. But at this point it doesn't seem to me that it's done that or made any change to what I feel the story is or made any type of impact to what I have in my own head about the story of "The Elder."

I do appreciate you taking the time to talk about the script, and it sounds like an incredible collectible to have and to savor. You had the script autographed — how did that come about?

Yes. You've seen the photos of the script, so you know it's been autographed by Gene and Paul. There are interesting stories behind obtaining those signatures.

For Gene, it was 2001, and Gene was appearing at the Wizard Convention, kind of a Comic-Con in Chicago. He was appearing to hype the Dark Horse series of KISS comics that were just about to be released. I was studying for the bar exam at the time, and I did not plan to go to this event at all, I was not really concerned about it. The day came along, and I was certain I'd kick myself if I didn't at least try to get Gene to sign this script. At the time, I only lived about a five to 10 minutes by car from Rosemont, Illinois, where the convention was being held. I drove over, parked and paid the admission, only to find there had a lottery to get a ticket to meet Gene, and they'd already handed out all of them. I waited around the Dark Horse booth until Gene was escorted by security to the booth. Security actually put up a human wall, of sorts, and I stood in front of the shortest guard and yelled, "Gene! Look at this! I have 'The Elder' script!" Gene looked up and replied, "Wow, there's only one of those! Would you like me to sign it? Wait around and when I'm done here, I'll sign it." I told Gene that I needed to find a camera. He said he would still be there, but to hurry back. I then took off looking for a souvenir shop to find a disposable camera, in the days before cell phone cameras and digital cameras. Half an hour later, I made my way back, camera in hand, and Gene was finishing up. As he was leaving, the security detail swarmed around him and hassled me for approaching Gene. Gene wouldn't have it, told them he said it was OK and he was meeting with a "real" fan — he emphasized "real" in his statement. He signed the script in gold ink, and then posed for a couple photos with me and the script. The photos I have since lost, unfortunately.

Fast-forward to Paul Stanley and his period of selling paintings. I bought one, a print of his "Purple Haze," hand-numbered 59/100 and signed by the Starchild himself. The purchase was an automatic invitation to a gallery event with Paul, where he would personalize your painting and talk with you for five to 10 minutes about it, since you just dropped an ungodly sum of money on his painting. Wentworth Gallery was adamant this was not a memorabilia signing, but if I didn't try, I would again have reason to kick myself! I brought the script with me to the event.

I told Paul that I understood this was not an average meet and greet, but the true cornerstone of my KISS collection was the script. When I pulled it out of my bag, Paul lit up like a Christmas tree. He looked at it, said it was probably one of the rarest pieces he'd ever seen and was more than happy to sign it in silver Sharpie, to give it a "gold and platinum" look! He even showed it to his son, Evan, who was with him for the show. Even as a kid, he was probably 14 or 15 at the time; Evan was quite the cool cat, a good kid with what appeared to be a good head on his shoulders.

So that's how the script was signed!

Is there anything you'd like to add?

When "The Elder" came out I was 6 years old and at that point the only albums that I had were "Destroyer" and "Rock and Roll Over." So all I know is, I'm seeing this TV commercial with this British guy talking about the new KISS record and seeing no mention of KISS, and just hearing "A World Without Heroes" playing in the background and this tight shot on this candle burning and it just blew me away. From that point on I always wanted to get "The Elder" and I could never get it. And I think the other thing was that I could never figure out the name of the record. I didn't know the name of the album for the longest time when I was younger. So it took me that long to figure it out, but I knew it by video or by visual, you know, it had the picture of the hand reaching up to grab the door, you know, the door knocker and bang on the door. And that's what stuck with me.

So when all of that came about and I finally got a hold of it — and then when I got older and I was able to get all the video footage that I could get my hands on, you know — it just became this quest to figure out what the hell happened in that six-month period when they were recording "The Elder" and when they were putting all this together. I think nowadays that I've got a pretty good handle and idea as to what went on. I do appreciate the record more. I do appreciate the story more and having the script has helped me even have a little bit more appreciation for it. But the story as I knew it and wanted it is still there and I can differentiate between the two and the script is what it is and it's not bad. You know, [not] as bad as I used to think it was, but it's still [a bit] like watching paint dry.

So, it probably would've ranked right up there with "KISS Meets the Phantom of The Park"?
Yeah, but that's a whole different story!

"The Elder" Script: Characters, Significant Objects and Realms

By Brian Brewer

The following list compiles the characters, in sequential order in which they appear in the script, with some plot elements that help explain their context within the screenplay. Not all of the plot elements or adventures have been revealed, but just enough to give a feel for the characters. Without giving too much away, the Soul-Keeper makes another, rather unexpected, appearance before the end of the story...

Blackwell

King and chief bad guy, Blackwell devises a plan to avoid being overthrown, resulting from betrayal by his daughter, by escaping to a newly created universe located inside a mirror. Supposed to be quite the tyrant, but the script does not bring that out so much detail. He's more of a cross between Dr. Evil and Richard III, every bit as scheming but not quite as comedic or barbarous.

Xyte

Formerly the sorcerer for The Elders, Xyte now serves Blackwell. At Blackwell's request, he created the new universe in which the majority of the story takes place. A bit like the Wicked Witch of the West, he has creatures that can spy upon anyone in the realms and report back to him.

The Rose

A brass ring with a diamond that serves as the key between the Real World and the newly created world inside Blackwell's mirror. The Elders gave Xyte the Rose ring, but Xyte misused the ring for his and Blackwell's gain. Blackwell was to be the final person to enter the portal and, with the Rose, lock the portal. It is presumed, though not fully resolved, that the Rose will allow passage between the Real World and the new. As Blackwell entered the portal, he was hit by a dagger from an opposing army, dropping the ring on the floor as he was halfway between realms. The ring bounced on the floor, the diamond separated and bounced back into the portal, but the brass ring did not, effectively trapping the kingdom in a realm where, by design, time does not move.

The Elder
It is inferred there are many Elders. We know of at least two, and possibly three, that play a direct part in the story line. The first Elder appears after the ring is dropped by Blackwell. He examines it and returns to the Elder chambers to announce the beginning of the prophecy, the chosen one having arrived after 600 years.

Eric
The hero. A college student, Olympic gymnastics hopeful, and candidate for the Alpha-Beta fraternity. Eric winds up in the castle once occupied by Blackwell, which is now a museum of sorts, as initiation for the Alpha-Betas. Required to spend the night there, Eric falls through a staircase and ends up in the mirror chamber. He finds the Rose on the floor and puts it on his finger, noticing it fits perfectly, and in avoiding additional rubble from the stairs, falls into the mirror and into the new realm. Predictably, when told he was the hero fulfilling the prophecy to save the universe from all evil, he is unsure he is the right person. He nevertheless moves forward on the quest to find Blackwell and the diamond in the hope he will be able to return to his time, not wanting to kill anyone. The entire time Eric is in the mirror realm, his watch says 11:00 p.m.

Jest
Blackwell's court jester, banished to the Forest World by Xyte when he overheard Blackwell and Xyte discuss their plans for world domination in the new technologically gifted world, once they obtained the Rose from Eric. Jest is comic relief and moral support in one character, as through the adventure he gains self-confidence, which serves to show Eric can overcome if Jest can overcome.

Morpheus
Despite the description of Morpheus as the caretaker, Morpheus is a weapons maker and jack-of-all-trades. He is older than most, but not ancient. He has had run-ins with Blackwell in the past and is keen on seeing his destruction. The Elders utilize Morpheus to find and train the warrior that is to be Eric. Possessing the Rose is enough to fulfill the prophecy. The Elders can also reveal themselves to Morpheus, which is evident on the record as well as in the script, with the familiar passage of Eric having "the light in his eyes and look of real champion."

Monster
Attacks Morpheus, Eric and Jest in Morpheus' hut. After defeating the monster, Eric gains more confidence in his abilities, but still questions his role in this prophecy.

Tyler
The Han Solo of the ensemble. A sketchy, swashbuckling figure who would prefer saving his own hide over anyone else's, unless you happen to be his friend. Tyler has history with Morpheus and Blackwell, he and his three men having teamed with Morpheus to rob Blackwell at one point. While Tyler and his men were able to escape, Morpheus did not, and was once imprisoned by Blackwell. Tyler's initial impetus in joining with Morpheus and Eric is solely to bring down Blackwell.

Simon
One of Tyler's gang. Loyal muscle.

Gamora
Another member of Tyler's gang and loyal muscle. Simon and Gamora are quite skilled fighters and join the group to help take down Blackwell.

Solomon
The missing piece of the puzzle from the prior heist. One of Tyler's men that attacked Blackwell with Morpheus. Believed to be dead for 600 years. Helps the remaining members of the group reach the castle to free Morpheus; Keiser has been "executed."

Princess Myra
Blackwell's daughter. It was she who brought him down. It is never explained how Princess Myra wound up in the new dimension, but it is explained that her betrayal of Blackwell stemmed from Blackwell killing her mother. Nevertheless, Morpheus seeks her out as Myra has maps of the remaining realms that will lead them to Blackwell. Myra lives on the mountain that bears the stallion and the mare. Myra is also privy to the Elders. On their travels, Myra and Eric become a romantic item.

Keiser
An Elder who accompanies the group on their odyssey. He is brought into the fold by Morpheus under the guise of being a retired sorcerer. Myra also knows Keiser is an Elder, but none of the others do.

Forest World
From the time Eric falls into the mirror and meets with Jest, the action takes place in the Forest World, which is like it sounds. The portal to the next realm, the Space Roads, lies across the great ocean.

Sea Monster
Creature in the Forest World that lives in a giant ocean. Attacks the ship the party is using to reach the portal to the next realm.

Space Roads
As it sounds, the roads simply float through space. This is the realm of the Soul Keeper. The maps show the party must travel a specific route and get through Hell's Flames before reaching the next portal. The Soul Keeper can appear at any time. The fall on to the Space Roads from the Forest World causes Myra to lose the maps, but Keiser knows the way.

Sphere
A sphere the party comes across. Simon touches it, and it turns into a clone of him. Simon's clone attacks Simon, but not knowing, which is which, no one can step in. The clone eventually decapitates Simon, but both fall into the abyss, off the Space Road.

Soul Keeper
A demon-like creature that, as its name implies, will literally suck its victim's soul from him. In doing so, the Soul Keeper throws an object at the victim, which starts out round but becomes a spiked object en route to the victim, sticking in the victim and causing the victim to become a zombie servant of the Soul Keeper. Xyte believes the Soul Keeper to be his greatest creation, as it is next to impossible to defeat. The Soul-Keeper claims Gamora on the travels through the Space Roads.

Warning In The Road
A warning written in a language the party does not know. Rather than decipher it, they press forward, not knowing it is a warning the path leads to Hell's Flames, which ultimately means they are on the right path. The Soul-Keeper attacks the party, again, in the Hell's Flames. Eric is able to temporarily diffuse the foe with a special sword Morpheus made for him, allowing the party to move through the Hell's Flames to the portal. Eric and Myra diffuse the Soul Keeper multiple times with the sword before the party reaches the portal.

Zombie Simon and Zombie Gamora

Simon and Gamora return as the Soul Keeper's lap dogs. While Tyler mistakes them for his friends, Simon picks Tyler up by the throat, while Gamora reaches for one of Tyler's own daggers to stab him with it. Jest foils Gamora's act, stabbing him with a dagger and kicking him over the edge of the Space Road. Simon tells Tyler to kill him, or the remainder of the party will perish. Tyler struggles with this ultimatum before eventually killing Zombie Simon. Soul Keeper again appears while the party goes through the portal to the next realm, but the portal shatters. All but Keiser were able to go through. Keiser confronts the Soul Keeper as an Elder — and the foes reach accord, since neither can harm the other. Keiser produces a mirror portal of his own and enters it.

Snow World

From the Hell's Flames to the Snow World, the party arrives in what appears to be a realm similar to the planet Hoth from "The Empire Strikes Back." Keiser falls into the realm a few minutes after everyone else.

Nicholas

Nicholas saves the party from freezing to death. A would-be sorcerer who wishes to learn his craft though, at present, all he can do is multiply objects, which comes in handy since they party is nearly out of weapons. He was once a pupil of Xyte, and he came to hate Blackwell. Nicholas was eventually excommunicated on the grounds of heresy but took Xyte's staff with him. Tyler noted Nicholas possessed Xyte's staff and initially believed Nicholas to be one of Xyte's henchmen. In reality, Nicholas seeks vengeance for being excommunicated and agrees to travel with the party to the next portal. Nicholas freezes to death before reaching the portal, but successfully guided the party to the mirror.

Snow-Squid

Yet another monster that attacks the party on their way to the next portal. It nearly kills Tyler, but the monster is defeated by a team effort.

Flying Dragons

Quite similar to the winged monkeys in "The Wizard Of Oz," four winged dragons accost our heroes, who fight back. Eventually, one picks up Morpheus and Keiser and carries them away to Blackwell's castle, and the dragons retreat.

Swamp Realm
The realm where Blackwell's castle is located.

"Music From The Elder": The Studios

Take a brief historical tour of the various studios
KISS utilized for their recording sessions in 1981

Befitting its grand design, KISS' "Music from The Elder" was completed as a result of work at no less than nine recording studios. Nine recording locales for one album project — including pre-production, recording, mixing, and mastering — constitutes a high-water mark for the KISS discography. ("The Elder" shares this distinction with 1992's "Revenge," which also utilized nine facilities.) As was standard procedure to that point in their career, KISS' recording home base was the East Coast. However, the band's odyssey to finish "The Elder" ultimately found them hop-scotching from Ace Frehley's home studio in Connecticut to facilities in New York and north of the border in Canada. Interestingly, "The Elder" marks the first and only time the band ventured to the Great White North for album recording sessions.

From Ace in The Hole and Ezrin Farm Studios to world-class facilities such as Record Plant, Manta and Phase One, learn more about the technological laboratories that helped give birth to KISS' lone concept album.

A & R Recording

Founded on 48th Street in New York by Jack Arnold (A) and Phil Ramone (R) in 1958, A & R Recording emerged as a premiere East Coast facility. The studio later expanded to include facilities on 7th Avenue (formerly Columbia's Studio A) and at 322 West 48th Street (today, the location of American Federation of Musicians Local 802). A variety of notable acts recorded at A & R's studios, including Bob Dylan, Aretha Franklin, Billy Joel, Elton John, Madonna, Paul McCartney, and Carly Simon, among others. Prior to sessions for "The Elder," A & R was used previously by KISS and Bob Ezrin to record orchestral and choral overdubs for "Beth" and "Great Expectations" on 1976's "Destroyer." Some of those sessions were documented via a press-attended photo session on Jan. 13, 1976. According to engineer Rob Freeman, the PolyGram Records listening party for "Music from The Elder" was hosted at A & R. Ezrin had also used A & R for sessions for Alice Cooper's 1975 classic album "Welcome to My Nightmare." The facility closed in 1989.

Ace In The Hole Studios

Housed in the basement of his Wilton, Conn. residence, Ace Frehley's custom-built studio was tapped for the bulk of KISS' early 1981 recording sessions. Ace in The Hole Studios was designed by noted Electric Lady Studios designer John Storyk, who described the studio, and its equipment, as "state of the art" for its time. Ace continued to work out of his studio after he refused to join the band when sessions for what would ultimately materialize as "Music from The Elder" segued to Canada with Bob Ezrin. The studio was shuttered when Ace sold his home in the mid-'80s. In October 2015, Frehley's former Wilton residence was put on the market by Sotheby's International Realty for $1.15 million.

Ezrin Farm Studios

Located in King City, Canada, north of Toronto, Bob Ezrin's 10-acre farm was surrounded by 100 acres of conservation land, making for a comfortable recording location not too far from civilization — and still offering the convenience of avoiding a daily commute. The modest farmhouse included a bomb-shelter basement that was converted into a studio with an API console. For professional grade recording, Bob brought in the Record Plant White truck (his favorite), which would be used for the tape equipment and as a control room, with the cables running through a window to the basement. For "The Elder," both pre-production work and actual recording sessions were conducted here, and Ace Frehley most certainly made the trip and stayed with Bob to work on material.

Manta Sound Studios

Originally built for $1.5 million, Toronto-based Manta Sound Studios opened its doors on Nov. 4, 1971. The facility was utilized for mixing sessions for "The Elder." Manta's Studio 2 was known to be able to accommodate up to 70-piece orchestras, making it an ideal studio for wide-scope projects such as "The Elder." According to "Elder" co-engineer Kevin Doyle, some of the orchestral sessions and production effects may have been finalized at Manta. Aside from projects by artists such as KISS, Neil Young and Oscar Peterson, among others, Manta was home to sessions for "Tears Are Not Enough," a 1985 charity single to benefit Ethiopia famine relief that was recorded by Northern Lights, an all-star collective featuring Bryan Adams, Gordon Lightfoot, Joni Mitchell, and Platinum Blonde, among others. Manta was ultimately acquired by Command and Post Transfer. The studio was demolished in the early 2000s.

Penny Lane Studios

This New York-based facility was owned by Harley Flaum, the late founder of Radio Band of America, a Clio-winning company specializing in producing commercials and jingles. The primary function of the studio was to record commercials and ad spots for Radio Band, but it also served artist clients given its two fully functional studios with 24-track capability, which were designed by acoustician Al Fierstein and architect Maurice Wasserman. With engineer Rob Freeman, KISS used the facility for overdubs and vocals on their pre-"Elder" demos, including "Nowhere to Run" and "Love's A Deadly Weapon." The first artist to utilize Penny Lane Studios was Aretha Franklin, who recorded her 1979 album "La Diva" there. Other artists who recorded at Penny Lane include the Brecker Brothers, Donald Fagen of Steely Dan, the Go-Go's, and Hilly Michaels. The latter is notable to KISS fans for being one of the band members photographed alongside one Vinnie Cusano on the sleeve inside Dan Hartman's 1978 album "Instant Replay."

Phase One Studios

Located in outer Toronto suburb of Scarborough, Phase One Studios was the vision of Torontonians Paul Gross and Doug Hill. Designed by architect George Augspurger, the facility was initially equipped with two studios: Studio A, with a large live floor and Vintage Neve console; and Studio B, which was generally used for overdubs. Phase One was known for having a direct Neumann lathe hook-up that afforded recording artists direct disc facilities. (The facility had an in-house label, Labyrinth Records, which was renamed Kiras in 1979.) During the period KISS recorded there with Bob Ezrin, Robert "Ringo" Hrycyna served as his engineer. According to uncredited "Elder" engineer Michael McCarty, considerable work was done at Phase One to get the facility studio-ready for KISS, including "tearing out rooms" and reviewing the technology on the premises. This work included installing a Stephens' 24-track machine, which was a personal favorite of Ezrin's at the time. McCarty recalled that bed tracks were accomplished at Phase One, including bass, rhythm guitars and keyboards. Aside from KISS, Phase One's artist clients include Alice Cooper, Bono, Pink, Keith Richards, and the Tragically Hip, among others, as well as fellow KISS producer/engineer Eddie Kramer. Still in operation today, Phase One celebrated its 40th anniversary in 2014.

The Record Plant

Renowned within the studio community, The Record Plant was founded in New York in 1968 by engineer Gary Kellgren and music industry professional Chris Stone. The studio ultimately expanded to include additional locations in Los Angeles in 1969, and Sausalito, Calif., in 1972. Notably, the New York facility's Studio A became the first studio equipped to mix quadraphonic sound. Artists who recorded at Record Plant New York include Alice Cooper, Aerosmith, Cheap Trick, Eric Clapton, Jimi Hendrix Experience, and John Lennon, among others. KISS' final recording sessions for "The Elder" took place at the Record Plant in New York following work in Canada. In addition to "The Elder," KISS' history at Record Plant New York includes sessions for "Destroyer," "Love Gun," "Dynasty," "Unmasked," and "Lick It Up." Corky Stasiak, who worked on the former two KISS albums and "The Elder," was one of the house engineers at Record Plant New York. In 1987 the New York location was sold to legendary Beatles producer Sir George Martin and closed shortly thereafter.

Sounds Interchange

Opened by Jeff Smith in 1972 under the moniker Jeff Smith Interchange, Canadian brewing company LaBatt's later purchased the facility and rechristened it Sounds Interchange. Under LaBatt's leadership, Sounds Interchange ultimately grew to five studios, serving music clients while branching out into advertising, broadcast and film post-production. For "The Elder," the studio — which was equipped with a vintage Neve console — was used primarily for vocals, notably the St. Robert's Choir and Gene Simmons' lead vocal on "A World Without Heroes," according to "Elder" co-engineer and Sounds Interchange staff engineer Kevin Doyle. Additionally, at Sounds Interchange on Sept. 16, 1981, Robert Christie, Christopher Makepeace and Antony Parr participated in a session with producer Bob Ezrin to record the album's spoken word dialogue. Aside from KISS, Sounds Interchange's music clients included Canadian acts such as Alannah Myles and Rush as well as Black Sabbath, who recorded their 1978 album "Never Say Die" there. Belgian brewer Interbrew acquired LaBatt's in the '90s and subsequently renamed the studio facility Dome. As of 1999, the facility was known as Dome Audio Video & Effects (DAVE), specializing in film post-work. Today known as Technicolor Toronto, under the Technicolor umbrella, the facility boasts to be "one of the most advanced audio-production facilities in North America."

Sterling Sound

Located in New York City, Sterling Sound was home to the mastering sessions for "Music from The Elder," overseen by mastering engineer Ted Jensen. The facility occupies the top floor of the Chelsea Market in the Meatpacking District. There are three surround-sound-equipped studios at Sterling, including one overseen by Jensen, with the studio being designed by Fran Manzella. The studio has served as home to literally thousands of mastering sessions. Jensen's mastering credits include Norah Jones, Eagles, Green Day, Bon Jovi, Megadeth, and Soundgarden, among others. Jensen is currently Sterling Sound's chief mastering engineer. Jensen would later master 1987's "Crazy Nights."

Acknowledgements

Tim McPhate:

The title of this book is fitting in so many ways, particularly in the sense that it has been quite the odyssey to see it come to fruition. Special thanks to all of the talented individuals who welcomed our interview inquires: Waring Abbott, Melanie Chartoff, Brian Christian, Marty Cohen, Kevin Doyle, Bill Finneran, Paul Flattery, Rob Freeman, Bruce Gowers, Bas Hartong, Seb Hunter, Jerry Jaffe, Chuck Klosterman, Bruce Kulick, Ida Langsam, Christopher K. Lendt, Christopher Makepeace, Michael McCarty, Charles McCracken, Kate Parker, Jennifer Parr, John Picard, Tony Powers, Mark Ravitz, David Spindel, Corky Stasiak, John Storyk, Ty Tabor, Chip Taylor, Tim Trombley, Jerry Watson, and Dennis Woloch. Additional thanks to Derrick Anderson, Dinah Christie, Fiona Christie, Michael Delahoyde, Dave Ferri, Quirine Hartong, Richard Hess, Dr. Stefan Klöckner, Tony Makepeace, Doug McClement, Kim Markovchick, Lynne Meloccaro, Pascal Nadon, Father Anthony Ruff, Kelley Wright, and Paul Zollo. Thank you to Brian Brewer and Stephen Lord, who are worthy of the fellowship! With appreciation to York University and Suzanne Dubeau, and the powers of Google. Special thanks to Paul Stanley, Gene Simmons, Ace Frehley, the late Eric Carr, the late Bill Aucoin, Bob Ezrin, and the entire cast who worked on "Music from The Elder." I would like to extend a special heartfelt thanks to Julian Gill for his invaluable contributions and for all of his efforts to publish this work. I wish to thank my father, Jim McPhate, for his support. I dedicate my efforts on this project to my beloved late mother, Janice McPhate, who always encouraged and supported my musical interests and my love for KISS. And finally, endless love to my dearrrrrest sweetheart, Daiga Buretsa.

Julian Gill:

I would like to thank Tim McPhate for the dedication and passion that he brought to the KissFAQ during his tenure as co-admin of the site, not least represented by the vast majority of this work (and the "Gene, Ace, Peter & Paul" book)! I also want to thank all of those interviewed for this effort, for so kindly sharing their memories of the album, the band (and those around them) and those who worked hard in creating the album. Thanks to Alain Bellicha, Alex Bergdahl and Roney Lundell for their contributions to this work. Also, an enormous "Thank You" to **YOU** for **YOUR** support of this and so many other KissFAQ projects. And my family who continue to tolerate this affliction I suffer!

Both Tim and Julian would like to thank Nils Brekke Svensson for the creation of the incredible artwork for this book and Stephen Lord and Brian Brewer for their contributions!

(Japanese "Elder" ad)

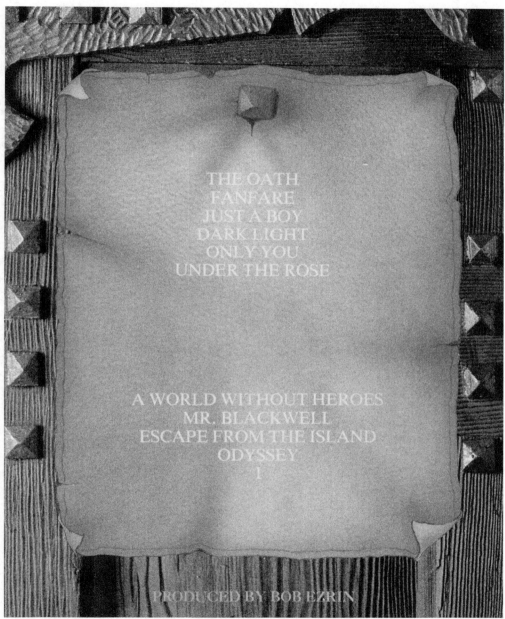

(Singapore Pressed PolyGram issue — an interesting way to deal with the change in the rear cover credits)